RIS A' BHRUTHAICH

Criticism and Prose Writings

Somhairle Mac Gill-eain

Edited by William Gillies

The publisher acknowledges subsidy from the Scottish Arts Council towards the publication of this volume.

Published in Scotland in 1985 by Acair Limited, Unit 8A, 7 James Street, Stornoway, Isle of Lewis.

ISBN 0 86152 041 6

Designed by Acair Ltd and John G Eccles.
Printed by John G Eccles Printers Ltd, Inverness.
Cover design by Jim Thomson Graphic Design.
Cover Photograph by Peadar Slattery, Dublin.

Acknowledgements

The writings in this book were first published as follows:

TRANSACTIONS OF THE GAELIC SOCIETY OF INVERNESS:
Realism in Gaelic Poetry (Vol XXXVII 1934-36)
The Poetry of the Clearances (Vol XXXVIII 1937-41)
The Poetry of William Livingston (Vol XXXIX/XL 1942-50)
Alasdair MacMhurchaidh (Vol XLI 1951-52)
Mairearad Nighean Lachlainn (Vol XLII 1953-59)
Domhnall Donn of Bohuntin (Vol XLII 1953-59)
Notes on Sea Imagery in Seventeenth Century Gaelic Poetry (Vol XLIII 1960-63)
Silis of Keppoch (Vol XLV 1967-68)
Some Raasay Traditions (Vol XLIX 1974-76)
Some Thoughts about Gaelic Poetry (Vol LII 1980-82)

SCOTTISH ART AND LETTERS:
Aspects of Gaelic Poetry (No 3, 1947)

GAIRM:
Am Misgear agus an Cluaran (Aireamh 6, An Geamhradh 1953)
A' Bhaidhearn (Aireamh 12, An Samhradh 1955)
Cha do sheas an Cuil-lodair (Aireamh 31, An t-Earrach 1960)
Dh'fhuirich Clann Dòmhnaill (Aireamh 40, An Samhradh 1962)

OSSIAN (Glasgow University):
An t-Ollamh Aonghas MacMhathain (1957)

MEMOIRS OF A MODERN SCOTLAND (ed. Karl Miller, London 1970):
Old Songs and New Poetry

STUDENT (Edinburgh University):
A bheil dòchas ann airson na Gàidhlig? / Is there a hope for Gaelic?
(January 1974)

CALGACUS:
Màiri Mhór nan Oran (No 1, 1975)

CHAPMAN:
My Relationship with the Muse (No 17, 1976)

Beul na h-Oidhche, An Tìr bu Mhiann Leam and Uilleam Mac Dhùn-Léibhe are printed here by kind permission of the BBC.
Lament for the Makar is printed here by kind permission of Times Newspapers Ltd.
Ceit NicLeòid is printed here for the first time.

Do Mhurchadh
agus
do Aonghas

Contents

Editor's Foreword

The idea of publishing a collection of Sorley MacLean's prose writings was an exciting and attractive one from the moment it was first mooted, in 1981. It seemed desirable both because of the general dearth of accessible and readable critical writing on Gaelic literature, and in view of the unique qualifications of the author, as a tradition-bearer, scholar and practitioner of Gaelic poetry.

The project took root and grew. Dr. MacLean's support, readily given, led to several additions to the 'corpus', including originally broadcast material in his possession. The Scottish Arts Council's equally positive response included the suggestion that English translations should be provided for the extensive Gaelic quotations in the critical essays, in view of their wide potential readership. Dr. MacLean himself kindly undertook to supply these, despite many other commitments. While this labour was in hand it proved possible to fit in two further items, as it were 'hot from the press'. It is proper to acknowledge here the goodwill of the various copyright holders, especially the Gaelic Society of Inverness, whose cooperation enabled the enterprise to get off the ground.

Forty years separate the earliest and the most recent essays contained in this collection. As Dr. MacLean remarks in the Introduction, his own perceptions have changed in various ways over the years, and changing emphases in criticism and developments in Gaelic scholarship have brought with them the possibility of fresh insights and interpretations. While substantial revision was a theoretical option, it would necessarily have involved sacrificing the flavour of the times at which the essays were written, together with what must surely count as a valuable *entrée* into the mind of the creator of *Dàin do Eimhir*. Moreover, it is undeniable that what Dr. MacLean has had to say over the years retains its vitality and relevance to a high degree. The texts in this collection, then, are in the form in which they originally appeared, subject to the following qualifications:

(1) As stated, English translations have been supplied to quotations of Gaelic poetry in those critical essays which originally gave only the Gaelic. Further, an English version of the Gaelic essay on

1

Mairearad nighean Lachlainn has been added, to bring it into line with the other studies of individual Gaelic poets.

(2) Dr. MacLean has added occasional annotation, printed as end-notes to the essays in which it occurs, indicating where he would now wish to modify the views expressed (e.g. as a result of subsequent scholarship), or where additional clarification seemed desirable.

(3) The opportunity has been taken to correct printers' errors detected in the original published texts. Further, given the diversity of sources drawn on, a modicum of standardisation in editorial practice has been found expedient; but beyond that the editorial touch has deliberately been kept as light as possible, and has in any case been confined to questions of form and presentation.

William Gillies
June 1985

Introduction

This book contains pieces of prose written as long ago as 1938. Already in 1933 I had read a paper to Céilidh nan Gàidheal in Glasgow on the traditions in song and story on the drowning of Iain Garbh Mac Gille Chaluim of Raasay. That paper was prompted, as a great deal of my writing in Gaelic and English prose was, by my fascination with the vast body of 'folk' and 'sub-literary' song poetry composed in Gaelic during the 16th, 17th and most of the 18th centuries. This song poetry went underground with the impact of the great Evangelical movement on the Protestant parts of Gaelic Scotland, and a vast amount of it was lost in the Clearances. 'Realism in Gaelic Poetry' was an immature protest against the dominance even as late as 1938 of the 'Celtic Twilight', which was manifest in the fashionable opinion that Mrs Kennedy-Fraser's work was the authentic culmination and treasury of Gaelic poetry and an invaluable presentation of it to the world, even in the English versions of the words of the songs.

In 1938 the continuing existence of Gaelic as a spoken language seemed a forlorn hope and Europe itself appeared about to be delivered into the hands of Teutonic racist fascism, a most horrible and seductive form of Romanticism. I believe the paper was useful in its day, though nowadays I consider the terms 'Romantic' and 'Realist' question-begging, and believe that most great poetry is Romantic in one way or other. It is, of course, largely a question of language.

The Celtic Twilight was among other things a haze over the realities of the Clearances. Its implied moral was at best a vague quietism; but to me and to most of my generation the late Thirties was no time for quietism of any kind, for in 1938 Munich had made it all but certain that Teutonic, Italian and Spanish fascism was going to rule Europe in the interests of capitalists and landlords. My next two papers to the Gaelic Society of Inverness, 'The poetry of the Clearances' in February 1939, and 'The poetry of William Livingston' in March 1940, arose out of much the same pre-occupation. When I read the strongly Socialist and Scottish Nationalist 'An Tìr bu mhiann leam' for the BBC in March 1946, it seemed to me that the government of Attlee, the best government Britain had before or has had since, would fulfil the Scottish Labour Party's commitment to Home Rule for Scotland, which I have always considered a hope for the preservation of Gaelic. I was greatly cheered when the Labour Corporation of Glasgow began the teaching of Gaelic in two Glasgow Secondary Schools, and that to pupils who did not know Gaelic already. Glasgow was, of course, only following the invaluable example of Argyll, and especially the great work of Donald Thomson in Oban.

Among my earliest memories were those of my Matheson grand-mother singing the songs of Mary MacLeod. These memories, and the enthusiasm of James Carmichael Watson, had induced in me frequent thoughts on the rare and indefinable graces of certain 17th century and early 18th century Gaelic poets — as, for example, in Mairearad Ni Lachlainn's 'Gaoir nam Ban Muileach', Sile Ni Ragh-naill's lament for Lachlan Mackinnon and many more. This led me into the labyrinths of research about dates, persons, places, motives, the very spade-work of academic scholarship, and into conjectures which cannot be proved one way or another. I acknowledge the basic necessity for academic spade-work and I am glad that it is being carried on by others. Naturally, certain of my conclusions have to be modified in the light of new evidence and I have indicated some such occurrences by footnotes.

Both my circumstances and the state of Gaelic literary criticism at the time dictated the sort of criticism I attempted. Perhaps, I was trying what was impossible for me; certainly my ideal of poetic criticism was too high altogether, for it involved the putting into words of intuitions about the obscure territory between the explicit and the implicit. Even more difficult is finding words for the quintess-ence of Gaelic popular song poems or William Ross's 'Oran Eile' or Roderick Morrison's 'Oran Mór MhicLeòid', in which the poetry and the 'music' are integral.

The chronology of most of the pieces is established by their appearance in periodicals or by their reading on the BBC. For example, I was able to date the short story 'Beul na h-Oidhche' from a letter written to me by Hector MacIver on the night it was broadcast in February 1952. The piece on the great singer Kitty MacLeod has never been published; I know, however, that it was written in the early Fifties.

During the Sixties and up to 1972 the inordinate amount of work I undertook in Plockton School, and the fierce campaign I was fighting for the provision of a Learners' Paper in Higher Gaelic inhibited my literary work; but the success of that campaign was a first necessity for

4

any substantial advance in the teaching of Gaelic in Secondary Schools.

As well as literary criticism and writings on the Gaelic language and tradition the book contains some creative writing, including three short stories, the earliest of which Hector MacIver called 'a first-rate short story (and in a new Gaelic mould)'. I have reason to think that my literary criticism has stimulated other Gaels to similar efforts, and I hope its publication in collected form will continue to encourage others to go up that steep and slippery brae.

Somhairle Mac Gill-eain
Peinachorrain March 1982

My relationship with the Muse

I have been asked to keep in mind three questions: what started me writing; what keeps me writing; and what I see as my relationship with poetry or the Muse.

In my early teens, that is from about 1924, I realised that I was a traditional Gaelic singer manqué, for I was born into a family of traditional singers and pipers on all sides, and that in a Free Presbyterian community, of all the most inimical to such 'vanities'. My Matheson grandmother, my father's mother, lived with us until she died, when I was between 11 and 12. Her Matheson great-grandfather had come to Staffin in Skye in the 18th century, after his family had been 'rascally deprived' of their land in Glas na Muclaich in Lochalsh by the Earl of Seaforth. She lived in Staffin, then near Portree and latterly in that dumping ground of the cleared, the Braes of Trotternish. Although in her seventies when I first remember her, she had still a very fine voice, and early collectors of traditional songs, especially my maternal uncle Alexander Nicolson used to come to her for old songs and for the Gaelic names of all animate and inanimate things. Her family must have brought to Skye and preserved many fine old songs of Lochalsh and Kintail, and she had in her head a great deal of the folk-lore of the large range of Trotternish. When she married my grandfather, Malcolm MacLean, she brought those with her to Raasay. Malcolm MacLean had died when my father, the youngest of three sons and two daughters, was only about nine, but he, my MacLean grandfather, was reputed to have been a very good singer and a bit of a bard. From certain things that my elder paternal aunt Peggie had and which her mother did not appear to have, I deduce that my paternal grandfather must have had songs current in Raasay that his wife had not learned. My MacLean grandfather was a fairly close relative of the great Mackay pipers, through the MacLean mother of Angus Mackay, but that does not mean that the MacLean blood added to the Mackay genius. My father, however, turned out to be one of the very fine pipers who never competed, and he was a great devotee of John MacDonald of Inverness, whom he used to hear at the Portree Games. The eldest of the three brothers, John by name, had died in his twenties and of course I do not remember him, but my father's older brother, Alasdair, was a piper too, but as he lived in Glasgow I seldom saw him when I was young.

I think that the first great 'artistic' impact on me was my father's mother singing some of the very greatest of Gaelic songs, and all in her own traditional versions. Among those I especially remember from her are the greatest of the four extant laments for Iain Garbh, two of the great songs of Mary MacLeod, and the Crò of Kintail, but, as far as I can remember, my father was better at the Crò of Kintail than his mother was. My father's voice was good, and in some songs his timing and weight was such that I now find it difficult to listen to those songs from anyone else. He was especially striking with the Crò of Kintail, the lament for William Chisholm, and with William Ross. My father too had a great interest in language for its own sake. He was keenly and sympathetically aware of phonological and semantic variations in Gaelic dialects and remembered very well the usages of the innumerable ministers and 'men' whom he had heard expounding at the Raasay communions. The South Argyll man, Alexander MacFarlane, who had been a schoolmaster in Clachan in Raasay for all the years of my father's schooling in Raasay had spoken as much Gaelic as English to his pupils even in the eighties and nineties of the last century. His influence on my father's sense of language was immense, and he had taken his best pupils to something like the modern level of fourth year Secondary. My father's interest in all kinds of Gaelic poetry was very great. Among my earliest memories was arguments between him and Alexander Nicolson, the eldest of my mother's seven brothers, on the relative merits of Duncan MacIntyre, William Ross and Alexander MacDonald. Unfortunately, in anti-Catholic Free Presbyterian Raasay not even my father knew much about Alexander MacDonald, but he knew a lot about Rob Donn and a surprising amount about Iain Lom.

Both my father's sisters were unusually good singers. The younger, Flora, was living in Glasgow but I remember from her a cradle-rocking refrain for the 'Braes of Uig' that I have never heard from anyone else. The elder, Peggie, ten years older than my father, used to stay with us for a whole month every year. She had a mania for fishing, sea fishing of course, and I had then a mania for boats, that is from my earliest memories until I was about 20, when the Cuillins seduced me from the sea. Peggie could depend on me to take her out thrice a day. Most of the fishing was the very leisurely deep-line fishing for haddock, whiting etc. That left enough time for Peggie's singing, my listening, and many political arguments, for the First World War had made Peggie a Tory although she had been before that a Socialist, a Scottish Nationalist and a militant suffragette. I became rather a good rower for my physique, and until fairly recently I could not forget the words of any Gaelic song I liked even if I heard it only once. My ear's defect in pitch seems to me now to have been compensated for by a painful sensitivity to what I felt faults of rhythm and time.

My elder brother John was always a good singer. I remember him in his last year in Portree School being picked out by the notable Ethel Bassin as one of the three or four best male singers in the school. Later, in his early twenties, he took to Ceòl Mór and very soon had as colossal a memory for pibroch as he had for Greek poetry. Thus he was able to transmit accurately the tunes, as I the words, of the many great versions of old songs preserved by our family. In our later days in Portree School one of our greatest friends was John Mathieson from Kilmuir. He frequently stayed with us in Raasay, learned many of our songs well, and gave us wonderful versions of others such as Beathag Mhór's song for Martin Martin and the song about the MacDonalds at Auldearn. His singing of the Lament for Gregor of Glenstrae was beyond words and his 'feel' for most kinds of Gaelic poetry was to my mind always 'right'. His version of the song for Martin Martin (he came from the Martin country) was even better than the version sung by my uncle, Angus Nicolson.

Of my mother's seven brothers and two sisters, two brothers were pipers, two others were singers, one a bard, and one sister a very good singer. They had learned many old songs from their MacLeod mother, who had died before I was born, and who had a fine voice, and many old songs even though she was a pious 'adherent' of the Free Presbyterian Church. My brother John and I went to Braes for about a fortnight every year and heard many songs from our Aunt Katie and our Uncle Calum, who specialised in Màiri Mhór, but Katie also had added to her songs some learned from her great friend, a sister of the late Dr Allan MacDonald. Our Uncle Angus Nicolson was in those days very seldom in Skye, and more seldom in Raasay, but on the rare occasions when he was at home in Braes or visiting us in Raasay we heard some of his great store of songs learned from his mother, from the incomparable Mary Macintosh, a near neighbour of theirs in Braes, from the Buchanan sisters, and from many others on the mainland. Much later his recorded voice earned very high praise from a great friend of Gaelic songs and Ceòl Mór, the late Professor Sidney Newman. In spite of difference in religion and physique, Angus was strangely like Calum Johnstone, both rare human beings even without their remarkable sensibility. He frequently talked of his Stewart grandmother, of her intelligence and lovable nature. She was the wife of my great-great-grandfather, John Stewart, in whose house I now live. It was said that the Stewarts had brought 'brains' into our family. Two of them were among the three joint-tenants of Peinnachorrain in the rent-roll of 1733 and were relatives of the exiled poet Norman Nicolson of Scorrybreck. It is said that the celebrated vagrant Gilleasbuig Aotrom used to come to John Stewart to make epigrams for him. If it was John Stewart who made that on the minister and factor Souter, mentioning Neil MacLeod of Gesto, John Stewart must have had a turn of witty language.

Even to this day, I sometimes think that if I had been a singer I would have written no verse, but perhaps, if I had been a singer, I would have tried to create original melodies. I know 'original' is a relative word and I think I have always been enough of a scholar to be troubled by the question of 'originality'. It is important, very important. One of the reasons, perhaps the chief reason, why I think it extremely unlikely that there is a poet equal to MacDiarmid living in Europe today is the complete originality of MacDiarmid's lyrics, their out-of-this-world quality, which rings true and hugely significant, moving in the extreme to whatever I have of sensibility. That, and because the lyrics of the 'Drunk Man' are mostly not so original is why I would still put the book 'Sangschaw' above the 'Drunk Man'. But that is a digression. What I am trying to say is that very early in life I came to be obsessed with the lyric, first of all because of my unusually rich Gaelic background; with the lyric in the Greek sense of a marriage of poetry and music, and then, because I was not a musician, with the lyric in the Shelleyan and Blakeian sense of a short or shortish poem suggesting song even if it could never be sung, a concentration running or flying away from anything that could in any way be called *sermo pedestris*. Before I came to Edinburgh University at the age of 17, I had come to be entranced by the peaks of Wordsworth's 'Prelude', the expressions of a sensitivity to certain impressions from external nature that I found original, subtle and true, emanating from the discursive sermo pedestris of nine tenths of the very long poem. I admire Wordsworth's poetry still although by the age of 18 I had come to acknowledge the half-truth of Arnold's dictum that he 'averted half his ken from human fate'. He did not always.

From the age of 16 or so onwards I had been writing a fair amount of verse in Gaelic and English, and reading all the poetry I could lay hands on in Gaelic and in English, but from the age of 12 onwards I was primarily an idealist democratic revolutionary and I fancied my future role in life as a politician helping to change the world, rather than as a scholar or a poet. 'Negative Capability' I understood but it was not for me. In the Thirties I used to be very sceptical of the Scottish writers who seemed to attribute most of Scotland's ills to Calvinism. What did they know of Calvinism? Not one of them had been brought up in a small island where nine out of ten of the people were adherents of the Free Presbyterian and the rest of the Free Church, which was in Raasay at any rate very liberal by comparison. Both sects believed doctrinally that not only were the secular arts dangerous vanities but also that the great bulk of humanity, and the great bulk of Free Presbyterians as well, were to spend an eternity of physical and mental torture. Although my father and mother were only lax Free Presbyterians, I supposed they too believed that at the level at which human beings can believe it and continue sane. One always believed that somehow in the long run one could 'make one's calling and election sure', but the odds for eternal damnation were terribly high against a very high percentage of the lovable people one knew. The obvious fewness of the Elect made me anti-elitist in most ways. My mother's Braes was almost totally Free Presbyterian, but rather anti-clerical. Gladstone's Irish Home Rule bills had made the clerical Elect Tories, and no matter how lovable as individuals a great number of those Elect were, they were politically discounted. This scepticism about the Church's politics inevitably loosened doctrinal holds or, if they did not, it led to questions about the individual minister's doctrinal orthodoxy. The *lacrimae rerum* seeped through the protective walls of the individual very early and made for pessimism and I believe toleration and a sympathy for the underdog. I do not think it made for self-righteousness at all, for was not human righteousness filthy rags, by-products but necessary by-products of Saving Grace? The 'Confessions of a Justified Sinner' are, of course, a travesty of the Calvinism of the Scottish Highlands, and I believe of the Lowlands too. At the age of 12 I took to the gospel of Socialism, and I believe that in my later teens a dichotomy took me psychologically: my 'pure' aesthetic idols of old Gaelic songs, and my humano-aesthetic idols of Blake and Shelley.

I had read no modern English poetry before I came to Edinburgh University at the age of 17. Although I was still a devotee of Blake and Shelley, my English verse then became more influenced by Donne, Eliot and Pound. I had taken English because it seemed economically disastrous to take Celtic, and I believe it was for the best. My English verse could try to follow Donne, Eliot and Pound because I could not follow Blake and Shelley. It was not that the great Grierson himself was half as pro-Donne as his undergraduate admirers or rather the undergraduate admirers of Eliot. Among them it would have been blatant heresy to suggest that Milton was as great a poet as Donne or Yeats as great a poet as Eliot. The first undergraduate I ever heard voicing that heresy was James Caird and that when I first met him, in 1933, my last years in the University. Caird was two years younger than I. I did not listen to him on Yeats enough to get past the early Yeats, but I did listen to him on MacDiarmid, to whose poetry from *Sangschaw* to *Scots Unbound* Caird and Davie soon introduced me. The intellectual stimulus of Davie and the literary stimulus of Caird was very great, but the lyrics of Hugh MacDiarmid might very well have destroyed any chances I ever had of writing poetry had my reading of them not been immediately followed by my reading of *The Drunk Man*, *Cencrastus* and *Scots Unbound*. To me, the best of them were, and still are, the unattainable summit of the lyric and the lyric is the summit of all poetry, but they could not be followed even 'afar off' by me or anyone else. In them I saw a timeless and 'modern' sensibility and an almost implicit 'high seriousness' and an unself-conscious perfection of rhythm that could not be an exemplar because it was so rare. *The Drunk Man*, the greatest long poem of the century that I have read, is more accessible because, along with the subtlest and most daringly imaginative, the most organic and marvellously sustained use of symbolism, it has the variety that has something for most natures. It converted me to the belief that the long medley with lyric peaks was the great form for our age. I know I did not have the *vis comica* at all, but it made me want to write a long medley with as many lyric peaks as might grow out of it. Hitler had come into power in 1933 and with the prescience of the pessimist, I saw that the political task of our generation, or of the Thirties decade, was to save what could be saved of a bad state to prevent an infinitely worse one of long duration. By 1932, before I met Caird, Davie or MacDiarmid, I had written a Gaelic poem about a heron, and I thought it worth preserving, it and some other Gaelic poems which I thought much more true to myself than anything I had done in English. Later a translation of the poem earned very great praise from Edwin Muir. So I was committed to Gaelic poetry before I had read a single poem by MacDiarmid; but the Spanish Civil War, the increasing likelihood that the Fascists would conquer Europe, my private family circumstances, the facing of questions that I long after came to be familiar with in the writings of French Existentialists, changed the directions indicated by 'The Heron', increasing urgent tensions, and from 1936 to 1939 I became, if a poet, a very different one from what my pre-1936 writings indicated. It was significant that the English poem produced by the

Spanish war that impressed me most was Cornford's 'Heart of this Heartless World'. Compared with it, Auden's 'Spain' seemed superficial, and still does. From 1939, almost till I went away to Egypt and Libya late in 1941, I was faced with a terrible personal dilemma, and from August 1941 to 1944 I could not decide whether the situation was really tragical or a farce.

Only in very rare moments, and never at all during the years 1936 to 1945, did I think of the poet primarily or secondarily as a virtuoso or craftsman, nor has my practice implied that he should be a 'committed' propagandist even in the very best sense. If 'committed' the poetry must be in some way confessional if it is to be true to the perpetual dilemma of the 'Existentialist' choice. Iain Lom's famous words to Alastair MacDonald 'You do the fighting and I'll do the praising' I consider disgusting, however expedient they might have been to the exigencies of the situation, and however wise they might have been in the long run. I could not have been an Iain Lom at Inverlochy or an Auden in America in 1939.

My mother's long illness in 1936, its recurrence in 1938, the outbreak of the Spanish Civil War in 1936, the progressive decline of my father's business in the Thirties, my meeting with an Irish girl in 1937, my rash leaving of Skye for Mull late in 1937, and Munich in 1938, and always the steady unbearable decline of Gaelic, made those years for me years of difficult choice, and the tensions of those years confirmed self-expression in poetry not in action. I have to admit with shame that it was not until the early Fifties that I realised the great significance for Gaelic of what Donald Thomson and other school teachers were doing in Argyll, that is teaching it to those who did not know it already. Munich and the unparalleled heroism and self-sacrifice of Communists in the Spanish Civil War almost made me a Communist in 1938. I think Mull had much to do with my poetry: its physical beauty, so different from Skye's, with the terrible imprint of the clearances everywhere on it, made it almost intolerable for a Gael, especially for one with the proud name of MacLean. Just after Munich, indirect approaches were made to me to accept a Territorial commission in the Eighth Argylls. I was tempted, but replied: 'Not while this government (Chamberlain's) is in power.'

It was in Mull in 1938 that I conceived the idea of writing a very long poem, 10,000 words or so, on the human condition, radiating from the history of Skye and the West Highlands to Europe and what I knew of the rest of the world. Its symbolism was to be, mostly, native symbolism. I started it in Edinburgh in the summer of 1939. The idea came from *The Drunk Man*. It suffered interruption after interruption, especially the beginning of the war in September 1939. The final interruption stopped it abruptly in December 1939. Events in Poland in 1944 made me question its 'commitment' and at any rate much of its symbolism is not in proportion with its theme.

The long poem was always to me a *faute de mieux* as compared with the lyric but I have come to regard it as a necessity if poetry is to deal adequately with much of the human condition. By 'lyric' I mean something far removed from the sermo-pedestrian short poems that now pass for lyrics; rather, short poems like many Gaelic songs and the lyrics of Blake, Shelley or MacDiarmid. I think two of the reasons for my long silences and burning of unpublished poems have been my long years of grinding school-teaching and my addiction to an impossible lyric ideal. During my 16 years at Plockton the burden of school teaching was aggravated for myself by my starting of the teaching of Gaelic there, and that to pupils who did not know it already.

I think I have indicated my 'relationship with poetry or the Muse'; whether I am a first or a 42nd cousin I leave to others who are not of the Gaelic city establishments cherishing comfortable ultra-Minch ideals.

What keeps me writing nowadays is a question I cannot easily answer, nor could anyone else in my position. I have always had long silences, periods of no writing, but these have generally been accompanied by frequent burnings and long delays in publication because I could not get round to type things or write letters, or because an English translation was required by all publishers, except Caithness Books, who would publish my work. Besides, it was difficult for me to abandon my lyrical ideal, even when I came to believe that non-lyrical poetry could be the product of long and deep thought 'carried alive into the heart by passion', and could recognise some such poetry as subtle, delicate and true. I had for long been fascinated by Yeats's and Màiri Mhór's power of expressing common 'thoughts' barely and as if a common truth had come home to them for the first time. In spite of MacDiarmid, the 'full-time' professional poet is not for me and never has been. If I have time to do it, I brood over something until a rhythm comes as a more or less tight rope to cross the abyss of silence. I go on it, as far as I can see, unconsciously. Nowadays I shun 'free verse' because so very little of it in others satisfies me and because its rope is so often so slack as to be loose bits of Chopped Prose, even if courtesy gives them the name of rhythm. I could not be primarily a Gael without a very deep-seated conviction that the auditory is the primary sensousness of poetry. The invention of convincing new rhythms that are not primarily prose 'rhythms' is so rare that I can think of no-one who has done it convincingly in Gaelic this century except Campbell Hay and two others in a few poems. There may be more but, if there are, their rhythms have not impinged on me, or I have not read them. By saying that they have not impinged on me means that I felt their wheels were poor for their loads. Gaelic poetry that is published with English translations cannot be assessed on its translation alone even by the most honest and perceptive of critics who do not know Gaelic.

Some say that the habit of writing grows on one and that, once it is formed, it is not easy to eradicate. That may be true of most writers, but I think its truth depends on the chances of life. The chances are very much against the 20th Century Gael, who has always had to make a living in other ways, and too often he has to do it by what must be one of the most exhausting of all ways, school teaching.

Realism in Gaelic poetry

Poetic realism differs from prose realism in its greater concentration, which sometimes involves a greater intensity than the intensity of prose, and sometimes a greater capacity for comprehensive generalisation than the capacity of prose. Thus, generally, the word realism, as applied to prose, has come to be used where 'naturalism' or 'naturalistic realism' would be more correct terms. 'Naturalism' is always expansive, always detailed; it works in a smaller compass with greater fullness of detail, whereas poetry works, for the most part, in a large compass with greater concentration, and consequently greater economy of detail. As compared with prose, poetry says much in little. Hence naturalism is the complete and most developed expression of prose realism, and the realism of poetry is usually, but by no means always, very different from the naturalistic realism of prose. The use of verse form, which is an 'artificial' thing, makes poetic realism, of necessity, very different from prose realism.

I confess I use the word 'realism' of poetry with some misgiving, but that misgiving is due to the fact that the word 'realism' tends to an unjustifiably limited connotation. I know the word 'realism' is now chiefly applied to prose literature, and that its special modern connotation is naturalism as manifested in much of the European novel since Zola's time. But there is no necessity to limit the word thus. I see no reason why it cannot yet be applied to poetry to denote the opposite of romance, escapism, fantasy, and their concomitants, affectation, fancifulness, far-fetchedness, and falseness.

It is a dangerous thing to make strong distinctions between the form and the content of poetry, but realism in poetry is clearly enough a quality of content rather than of form, and therefore poetic realism may be best examined by examining the matter and the object of the poetry. As its matter, poetry has the life of man or external nature, and thus poetry may embrace all knowledge. The matter of science can be the matter of poetry, *vide* Lucretius, but poetry contemplates with emotion whereas science may at least appear wholly emotionless. The dynamic of poetry is never intellectual contemplation alone, and intellectuality or merely sense impression must be suffused with

15

emotion, and the emotion has as much to do with the suggestion of the form of the verse as the intellect has, if the poem has any degree of spontaneity, and if verse form is not wholly an artifice. As a result of this fusion of intellectuality and emotion in varying degrees, a feeling of totality, which is simply emotional and intellectual satisfaction, is imparted by great poetry to a degree that philosophy or science cannot impart, and in this satisfaction the relatively greater sensuousness of poetry is all important. Milton put the whole thing admirably: 'Poetry is simple, sensuous and passionate.' He meant that it was more sensuous and more impassioned than prose. By its relative simplicity he probably meant both its clarified concentration and its greater concreteness.

The matter of a poem must therefore be contemplated emotionally. The object contemplated may be hopeless love, a ship in the sea, the destiny of mankind, a deer on the mountain, the death of a hero or the ugliness of a reptile, a lost cause or a base success. The emotion may be love, reverence, awe, world-weariness, hatred, anger or disgust, and it may be apparent or latent; for instance, there is more emotion in the dryness of Dugald Buchanan or A E Housman than in the gush of Tennyson or Swinburne. Now the emotion with which the object is contemplated, allied with the rhythm and tone which that emotion does much to suggest, has a completely transfiguring effect on the matter contemplated, but this transfiguration is not necessarily un-realistic, and in fact the greater the poem the greater is its realism in spite of this emotional and formal transfiguration. The greater the emotion the more realistic does the poem tend to be, at least in certain ways, for the strength of emotion checks the wandering imagination, and it is from the straying of the imagination that lack of realism comes. Emotion tends to romance only when it discards the evidence of the senses or the intellect. It will be asserted that emotion very often does disregard the evidence of the senses or the intellect, that the 'bleeding heart' does often 'run away with the bloody head'. I agree, and therefore poetry, which depends so much on emotion, cannot be realistic in the same way as science is realistic or matter of fact. But, after all, emotion itself is a reality, a human characteristic, and natural laws determine the length to which it goes before it is called craziness. Poetic realism is thus a strictly relative term. My business tonight is to try to show that Gaelic poetry is not less but more realistic than most European poetry. It will be asserted that Gaelic poetry is intensely emotional. I agree, but I can say that its emotionalism is less fantastic than the emotionalism of most European poetry. The point surely is that it is not emotion itself that makes a poem unrealistic. Lack of realism usually comes not from emotion but rather from a lack of emotion, whose place is taken by mere fancifulness, day-dreaming, wish-fulfilment, or weak sentimentality. In a person of any brain power at all, intensity of emotion conduces rather to an intense realisation of reality. The great poem is thus always in some way realistic in that, however transfigured it is by passion, emotion, or fusion of emotion and intellectuality, it has its roots in reality, not in a dream world. A few weeks ago a prominent Lowland journalist, Mr Power, asserted that the Celt lived in a dream world. Gaelic poetry makes such a statement appear utter nonsense. Mr Power was thinking not of the Celt but of the Celtic Twilight, a very different matter. Living in a dream world is the result not of emotion but of weakness or stupidity; that is as true of poetry as it is of actual life. Great poetry may cry in despair for something that exists or that it would like to exist, but it never assumes the existence of something which it knows perfectly well doesn't exist, whereas one of the typical features of unrealistic romance is the use of outworn myths. For example, compare William Ross's great lines:

B'fheàrr nach mothaichinn fhéin
Do mhaise, do chéill 's do chliù,
No suairceas milis do bhéil
As binne na séis gach ciùil.

Better that I myself did not perceive
your beauty, good sense and good name,
or the sweet courtesy of your mouth,
which is more melodious than the tune of any music.

with the Rev. Kenneth MacLeod's lines:

Iubhrach bhàn, na fàg mi am thruaghan
   Taobh nan cuantan mór,
Doimhne cràidh is gràidh 'gam dhuanadh
   Gu Tìr nan Og.

White galley, do not leave me forlorn and piteous
beside the great oceans,
depth of pain and love spell-binding me
to the Land of the (Ever) Young.

Now the object of Ross's emotion was real, but the Rev. Kenneth MacLeod knew perfectly well that if he sailed out into the Atlantic he would see the Woolworth Building before he saw 'an t-Eilean Uaine'.

A comparison of the two verses clearly shows the difference between realist and false or romantic emotion. Ross's poem is greater not only because he was a greater poetic technician than the Rev. Kenneth MacLeod, but also because the very matter of his poem has the intrinsic superiority of having its roots in reality.

It is undeniable that a halo of strong emotion constitutes what is often called 'romance', but romance is not always the antithesis of realism. When the matter is transfigured by strong emotion alone such a transfiguration may be called romantic, but it is not of necessity unrealistic; but romantic poetry is unrealistic when the transfiguration is wrought not by passion or strong emotion but by fancifulness, or daydreaming, or by the introduction of extraneous decoration — that is decoration not induced by the passion or emotion. That is what the English poet Wordsworth had in mind when, affirming the essential realism of his own poetry, he declared that he had always 'striven to look steadily at his subject', and that he had not allowed any 'foreign splendour' to be interwoven with the matter suggested by his emotion. This extraneous decoration or 'foreign splendour' is the chief stock in trade of most romantic poets, and anyone who knows Gaelic poetry knows that Gaelic poetry is exceptionally free from it, that real Gaelic poetry seeks extraneous decoration neither from fairy love, foreign countries, Gothic castles, superstition nor religiosity, Greek myth or Celtic Twilight.

The very greatest poetry tends in its greatest passages to a realism that eschews extraneous decoration, and also its object never is something to which the human mind denies existence. If it be an idea or emotion with only subjective existence, that idea or emotion must not be based on the fanciful, fantastic or conjectural. Day-dreaming produces poetry that is cheaply transfigured by unreality, whereas great poetry achieves transfiguration by intensity of sensitivity, emotion or wisdom. The great poet may move like William Ross tensely in a real world, or like Alexander MacDonald with unfailing power and boisterous *joie-de-vivre*, or like Duncan Macintyre with abnormally acute sensitivity to the impressions of external nature, but never like our latter day Twilightist does he move vaguely in a half-light however remote, meretricious, or wish-fulfilled. Twilight or half-light as applied to Celtic poetry is an optimistic euphemism for the darkness of pretentious, dishonest stupidity.

To those whose chief poetic diet has been the poetry of 19th century England, the words romance and poetry are sometimes synonymous. I confess that for some years I myself was foolish enough to prefer Wordsworth to Duncan Macintyre and Keats to William Ross, and I am quite sure that it was the greater realism of the Gaelic poets I disliked after the romanticism of the English. But modern English criticism finds the poetry of the English Romantic period not grown up, and therefore most attractive to adolescence. In all Europe, at least in France and Germany as well as England, the 19th century saw a wave of romantic poetry that was largely a pure escape from reality and mature masculine intellectuality. What was the reason for this 19th century escapism? Why did Walter Scott flee to the Jacobite Highlands or the Middle Ages? Why in England did Coleridge, Keats, Tennyson and the Pre-Raphaelites do the same? Why did Wordsworth bury his head in an illusory intuition into the message of hills or hedge-rows? Why did Tennyson, good bourgeois as he was, celebrate King Arthur instead of Sir Robert Peel? Why did Browning flee to Renaissance Italy? Why did those who acutely recognised reality flee, like Shelley, to unreal terrestrial paradises or, like Byron, shroud themselves in a halo of proud, romantic egoism? Why was there the same escapism in France in the poetry of de Vigny, de Musset, Gautier, etc, and why did even Goethe flee to ancient Greece? There is little doubt that perhaps the chief reason for this romantic escapism in the poets of England, France and Germany was the fact that the 19th century poetry, a product of the bourgeoisie, found the industrial capitalism erected by that class so sordid that poets had to eschew contemporaneity by an escape to the past or the exotic. In the 20th century escapist romanticism is at a discount, its place having been taken by the deliberate romanticising of racism, brutality and irrationality fostered by fascist propaganda. That is the new and most terrible opium for the people ever devised. Its high priests, however, are politicians not poets. There is a limit to the depth to which a poet can sink.

It is a very different type of romanticism that has been predicated of the Gael and his poetry. The special brand of romanticism attributed to the Gael and his poetry is a romanticism of the escapist, other-worldly type, a cloudy mysticism, the type suggested by the famous phrase, 'Celtic Twilight'. This Celtic Twilight never bore any earthly relation to anything in Gaelic life or literature. It was merely one of the latest births of the English literary bourgeoisie, and its births are to Gaelic eyes exceedingly strange, whether they be Mr John Duncan's St Bride or the late Mrs Kennedy-Fraser's 'Mairead òg with her sea-blue eyes of witchery'. In Ireland the Celtic Twilight had a more respectable manifestation in the early poetry of Yeats, but that poetry too is now utterly discredited in Ireland as being completely un-Irish and un-Celtic, and this is being amply proved even to non-Gaelic speakers by the remarkable verse translations of Irish poetry being produced by men like Frank O'Connor. Their verse has the hardness and clarity and firmness of outline, all realist qualities, common in all Celtic poetry.

I suppose that many with Celtic pretensions will be shocked at a declaration that Gaelic poetry has not less but more than common realism. They invoke the names of 'Ossian' MacPherson, 'Fiona MacLeod', Kenneth MacLeod and Marjorie Kennedy-Fraser, and hosts of lesser Twilightists, but they will have no competent native critic on their side. Of course, with the kind of people who call Mrs Kennedy-Fraser's travesties of Gaelic songs 'faithful reproductions of the spirit of the original', I have no dispute. They are harmless as long as ignorance and crassness are considered failings in criticism of poetry. They have had their hour in the drawing-rooms of Edinburgh and London; they have soothed the ears of old ladies of the Anglo-Saxon bourgeoisie: they have spoken after dinner, hiding with a halo the bracken that grew with the Clearances; they have cherished the Iubhrach Bhallach and forgotten the 'Annie Jane' that went down in the Kyle of Vatersay, and some of them have had their earthly reward.

A modern English critic, T.E. Hulme, pointing out that poetry did not require to be morbidly romantic and hazily mystical, declared that some refused to give the name poem to a piece of verse unless it were 'fozy with infinity'. The Celtic Twilight had very little else but a 'foziness with infinity', a vague, misty, cloudy romanticism. In fact the Celtic Twilightists achieved the remarkable feat of attributing to Gaelic poetry the very opposite of every quality which it actually has.

I am afraid I am wasting the time of the Gaelic Society of Inverness attacking a phenomenon whose absurdity was plain to any Gaelic speaker, and I shall first deal with the oldest existing popular Gaelic poetry. By the oldest existing popular poetry I mean the largely anonymous, orally preserved and tradition-modified poetry which is contained in the simpler songs of the 16th, 17th and 18th centuries, and which survived, but at a much lower poetic level, well into the 19th century. Much of it has been published in collections like the MacDonald Collection and Sinclair's *Oranaiche*, but a great deal is still unpublished. It is all song poetry, but many of the melodies are irretrievably lost. This poetry has a counterpart in the Lowland Scots ballads, but in bulk, range and quality the anonymous Gaelic poetry is immeasurably superior to the Lowland Ballads, which sometimes do contain splendid poetry. Suppose I quote an example of the kind of poetry I mean. In form this example is one of the very simplest:

20

Mo nighean donn á Còrnaig,
Gu robh thu buidhe bòidheach,
Mo nighean donn á Còrnaig.

Gur olc an sgeul a chuala mi
Di-luain an déidh Di-dòmhnaich:
An uair chàidh càch do'n t-searmon
Chàidh na sealgairean do'n mhòintich.

'S gu robh do chuailean slaodta riut,
'S do léine chaol 'na stròicean,
'S do chìochan mìne geala
Ag call na fala còmhla.

Mo nighean bhuidhe bhadanach,
'Na cadal air a' mhòintich;
Gur olc an obair maidne dhomh,
Bhith cur nam fear an òrdugh,

'S gur olc an obair feasgair dhomh
Bhith deasachadh do thòrraidh;
'S an leann a chaidh gu d'bhanais
Air t'fhalaire dh'òladh.

'S truagh nach robh mi 'n taice ris
Na balaich rinn an dòbheairt,
Is claidheamh fada rùisgt' agam:
Gu feuchainn lùths mo dhòrn orr'.

My brown-haired girl from Cornaig,
you were golden and beautiful,
my brown-haired girl from Cornaig.

It was an evil tale I heard
on Monday after Sunday:
when the rest went to the sermon
the hunters went to the moorland.

And your hair was trailing down your body,
and your finely woven shirt in shreds,
and your smooth white breasts
spouting blood together.

My girl of the heavy golden hair
sleeping on the moorland;
it is a bad morning's work for me
to be putting the men in order.

And it is a bad evening's work for me
to be preparing for your burial;
and the ale that went for your wedding
at your funeral was drunk.

I wish to God I was at grips
with the young men who did the evil,
with a long naked sword:
I would try the strength of my fists on them.

This song, imperfectly preserved as it is, is a good example. The subject is tragedy of crime and circumstance, the murder of a young girl by her brothers to prevent a marriage of which they disapproved. The poem is characteristic in its simple intensity, its sheer economy of word, the lack of any romantic appurtenances, the horror that makes little comment, letting the story speak for itself. It crystallises an attitude to tragedy strangely common in Lowland Scots poetry as well as in Gaelic poetry. It is life contemplated with intense emotion, an emotion that is all the greater because of its reticence; there is no haze or mysticism of any kind. Hence it is essentially a realistic poem if the realism is on the level of the realism of tragic poetry.

There are literally hundreds of examples of such poems, all records of passion or strong emotion uttered with reticence and a brave realism, though the range of emotion and verbal sensuousness is far greater than in the Lowland Scots ballad. I need only cite a few examples — for instance, the poignant poem containing the following verses:

Ann am bothan na h-àirigh
Ghlac am meàirleach mi air m'éiginn.

Ann am bothan a' ghlinne
Far nach cluinneadh iad m'éigheach.

Ann am bothan an t-sùgraidh
'S gun 'ga dhùnadh ach créitheach.

In the hut of the shieling
the robber took me by force.

In the hut of the glen
where they could not hear my screaming.

In the hut of the love-talk
with no door but brushwood.

Again a tragedy of passion as well as of circumstances. I now quote another poem, this time a record of heart-break rather than of crime and tragedy. This is a Skye poem never before published.[1] It is a *tàladh*:

Tha mo shealgair 'na shìneadh,
'Na shìneadh, 'na shìneadh,
Tha mo shealgair 'na shìneadh,
   'S e 'san fhrìth gun tighinn dachaidh.

Tha na féidh am bràigh Uige,
Am bràigh Uige, am bràigh Uige,
Tha na féidh am bràigh Uige,
   'S e mo dhiùbhail mar thachair.

Tha an crodh air na lóintean,
Na lóintean, na lóintean,
Tha an crodh air na lóintean,
   'S na laoigh òga 'nan casaibh.

Iad gun togail ri aonaich,
Ri aonaich, ri aonaich,
Iad gun togail ri aonaich,
   Fireach fraoich agus glacan.

Gura fuar Lag na h-àirigh,
Na h-àirigh, na h-àirigh,
Gura fuar Lag na h-àirigh,
   'S tha mo ghràdh fo na leacaibh.

My hunter is lying stretched,
lying stretched, lying stretched,
my hunter is lying stretched
   in the moor with no home-coming.

The deer are in Brae Uige,
in Brae Uige, in Brae Uige,
the deer are in Brae Uige,
   my loss is what happened.

The cows are on the brook-meadows,
the brook-meadows, the brook-meadows,
the cows are on the brook-meadows
   and the young calves by their sides.

Not driven up the hill-side,
up the hill-side, up the hill-side;
not driven up the hill-side,
   heathery mountain and hollows.

Cold the Hollow of the Shieling,
of the Shieling, of the Shieling.
Cold the Hollow of the Shieling,
   and my love is under the flag-stones.

What could be at the same time more intensely emotional, more realistic, and more lovely in sensuousness?

This is another, and probably earlier, poem than Domhnall Donn's, who made a song to the same tune, when *his own* death, at the hands of the laird of Grant's men, was imminent.

Consider Donald of Bohuntin's famous poem 'A Mhairearad òg, 's tu rinn mo leòn', with the terrible pitch of emotion realistically expressed in its climax:[2]

'S a thé rinn dhomhsa léine chaol,
Cha dèan thu, ghaoil, gin tuilleadh dhomh.
Ged théid mi suas do'n bhaile ud shuas,
Cha bhi mo chuairt ach diomain ann.
Air leabaidh làir chan fhaigh mi tàmh
'S air leabaidh àird cha chuir iad mi.

Mi an diugh 's an dé air cnoc leam fhéin
A' sileadh dheur 's mi turaman.
A Dhia nan gràs cum rium mo chiall,
Cha robh mi riamh 's a' chunnart so.
'S a Mhairead òg, 's tu rinn mo leòn,
'S tu dh'fhàg fo bhròn 's fo mhulad mi.

And girl who made the fine-woven shirt for me.
you will not, love, make me one ever again.
Though I go up to the town yonder,
my trip to it will be but brief;
on a bed on the ground I'll get no rest
and on a high bed they will not put me.

To-day and yesterday I am on a hill alone,
shedding tears and rocking.
O God of grace, keep my reason to me,
I was never before in this danger;
and young Margaret, it was you who wounded me,
it was you who brought me to grief and sorrow.

To give a few more examples, the two 'Ailein Duinn' poems have the same realism even although in one of them the emotion becomes frantic:

Dh'òlainn deoch ge b'oil le m'chàirdean,
Cha b'ann de fhìon dearg na Spàinne,
Ach de fhuil do chuim, 's i b'fheàrr leam.

I would drink a drink in spite of my kin
not of the red wine of Spain,
but of your body's blood, I would prefer it.

The frantic emotion is expressed in the same poem as the quiet realism of

> Ailein duinn, a laoigh mo chéille,
> Gura h-òg a thug mi spéis dut,
> 'S ann a nochd as bochd mo sgeula,
> Chan e bàs a' chruidh 'san fhéisidh
> Ach a fhliuichead 's tha do léine.

> *Brown-haired Allan, darling of my love and reason,*
> *very young I gave you affection.*
> *To-night the tale I heard is misery;*
> *not the death of the cows in the quagmire*
> *but how wet your shirt and shroud is.*

The other 'Ailein Duinn' poem has a tragic realism that dwells on the most mundane matters, the value of cows, sheep, or household goods in comparison with the dead man.

> Ailein duinn, a nì 's a nàire,
> 'S goirt 's is daor a phàigh mi màl dut,
> Cha chrodh laoigh no caoraich bhàna,
> Cha bholla, cha pheic 's cha mhàm e,
> Cha nì, chan innseiridh 's chan àirneis
> Ach an luchd a thaom am bàta.

> Bha m'athair oirre 's mo thriùir bhràithrean
> 'S laogh mo chuim a rinn mi àrach,
> Ach chan e sin a léir 's a chràidh mi
> Ach am fear a ghlac air làimh mi
> Leathanach a' bhroillich bhàn-ghil
> A thug o'n chlachan Di-màirt mi.

> *Brown-haired Allan, all I have and my honour,*
> *sore and dear I paid you rent:*
> *not cows-in-calf nor white sheep,*
> *not boll nor peck nor handful of grain,*
> *not property nor furniture nor gear,*
> *but the men whom the boat baled out.*

> *My father was on her and my three brothers*
> *and the darling of my body whom I reared;*
> *but that is not my searing torment*
> *but he who had taken my hand,*
> *MacLean of the fair-skinned chest*
> *who took me from the Clachan on Tuesday.*

There is a tense, unpretentious realism in those poems, from which strength of feeling has, as it were, burnt away the unessential. Technically they are simple, but this older Gaelic poetry has an imcomparable vocalic beauty and probably unselfconscious range and subtlety of rhythm.

Those five poems I have quoted are records of tragedy, mostly tragedy of pure circumstance. The emotional pitch is very high, but the range of emotion which has realist expression is not limited to highly pitched tragedy. Compare the quiet poem of the Skye Clearances:

C'àite an caidil mo nìonag a nochd?
C'àite an caidil mo nìonag?
Far an caidil luaidh mo chrìdh'
Is truagh nach robh mi fhìn ann.

Where will my girlie sleep to-night,
where will my girlie sleep?
Where the darling of my heart sleeps
I only wish I were there myself.

(By the way, note that it was Henry Whyte[3] who introduced the more ornate and romantic word "rìbhinn" for "nìonag". That is a little straw, but it shows how the would-be improvers of Gaelic poetry always tend to romanticise it, and usually end by substituting pretty-prettiness for intensity, the classic example of such improvement being Mrs Kennedy-Fraser's translations).

The expression of love in Gaelic poetry is like the expression of tragedy in that it is never fantastic nor far-fetched. Gaelic poetry has nothing at all anywhere like the frigidity of metaphysical conceit of, say 17th century poetry in Europe. Frigidity, of course, arrives when the fancy outstrips the emotion so much that it outrages psychology. It speaks greatly for the sanity and realism of Gaelic poetry that it is almost wholly free of the frigid conceit. That does not say that the imaginative effect of Gaelic poetry cannot be overwhelming as in the magnificent verse of 'O 's tu 's gura tu th' air m'aire':

Thug thu sear dhiom is thug thu siar dhiom,
Thug thu ghealach is thug thu ghrian dhiom,
Thug thu 'n cridhe a stigh 'nam chliabh dhiom,
Cha mhór, a ghaoil ghil, nach tug 's mo Dhia dhiom.

You took the east from me and you took the west from me,
you took the moon from me and you took the sun from me,
you took the heart from inside my breast from me,
and, fair love, you almost took my God from me.

26

The compelling imginative intensity of that verse is very different from the simple sorrow of:

> Moch 'sa' mhaduinn an ám dhomh dùsgadh,
> Shil mo shùilean 's gu robh mi brònach
> Mu sgeul a chualas air feadh an t-saoghail
> Thu bhith 'gad ghlaodhaich, a ghaoil, Di-dòmhnaich.

> *Early in the morning at the time when I woke,*
> *my eyes flowed and I was sorrowful*
> *because of the tale heard throughout the world,*
> *that you, my love, were being 'cried' on Sunday.*

The quiet realism of the latter is one of the key notes of Gaelic poetry. It is heard, for instance, in the fine lament by the wife of William Chisholm, who was killed at Culloden:

> Och, a Theàrlaich òig Stiùbhairt,
> 'S e do chùis rinn mo léireadh,
> Thug thu bhuam gach nì bh'agam
> Ann an cogadh 'nad aobhar.[4]
> Cha chrodh is cha chaoraich
> Tha mi ag caoidh ach mo cheud ghaol,
> Ged dh'fhàgte mi 'm aonar
> Gun sian 'san t-saoghal ach léine,
>   Mo rùn geal òg.

> *O, young Charles Stewart,*
> *it is your affair that has been my torment:*
> *you took from me everything I had*
> *in war for your cause.*
> *It is not cattle and it is not sheep*
> *that I mourn but my first love,*
> *even if I were left alone*
> *with nothing in the world but a shirt,*
>   *my white young love.*

But the expression of loss is frequently more piercing, while as matter-of-fact in expression, as in the lament of the wife of the executed Gregor MacGregor of Glenstrae, a poem older by two centuries, and one of the very greatest tragic lyrics in Gaelic:

> M'eudail de fhearaibh an domhain,
>   Dhoirt iad t'fhuil an dé;
> Chuir iad do cheann air stob daraich
>   Tacan beag bho d' chré.

Dhìrich mi do 'n t-seòmar mhullaich
    'S theirinn mi 'n tigh làir,
Is chan fhacas Griogar cridhe,
    'Na shuidhe mu 'n chlàr.

Dhìrich mi bheinn mhór gun anail
    Mun do ghlas an là,
Chuir mi gruag mo chinn ri talamh,
    Is craicionn mo dhà lamh.

'S truagh nach robh m'athair 's an teasaich,
    Is Cailean Liath am plàigh,
'S a h-uile Caimbeulach am Bealach,
    Ag giùlan nan glas-làmh.

My treasure of the men of the whole world,
    they spilt your blood yesterday,
They put your head on a stake of oak-wood
    a little away from your body.

I went up to the highest room
    and I came down to the lowest room,
and I did not see my heart's Gregor
    sitting about the board.

I went up the big mountain without stopping for breath
    before the day greyed,
I put the hair of my head to the ground
    and the skin of my two hands.

A pity that my father was not in fever
    and grey Colin in a plague,
and every Campbell in Bealach
    with fetters on their hands.

In the modern world it is a marvel how so much agony can find
verse form at all. In some older poems there is a more terrible passion,
as for example the frantic love of an old song heard by myself in Skye:

Mharbh thu m'athair is m'fhear pòsda,
Is toigh leam Ailean Dubh á Lòchaidh,
Mharbh thu mo thriùir bhràithrean òga,
Is toigh leam Ailean Dubh á Lòchaidh.
Ailein, Ailein, 's ait leam beò thu,
Is toigh leam Ailean Dubh á Lòchaidh.

You killed my father and my husband,
I like Black Allan from Lochy,
you killed my three young brothers,
I like Black Allan from Lochy.

28

Allan, Allan, I rejoice that you live,
I like Black Allan from Lochy.

But the note of old popular song is not always the realism of
tragedy. Sometimes one hears a tone of brave, scornful acceptance of
bitterness, as for instance in Beathag Mhór's song to Martin of
Bealach. She contemplates his marriage with resignation:

Ma théid thu dh'Uibhist an eòrna
Thoir bean bhòidheach dhachaidh leat.
Faigh bean laghach shocair chiallach
Riaraicheas na caipteanan.
Faigh bean laghach shocair chiùin
A dh'ionnsaicheas mo mhac-sa dhut.
Is ma bhuaileas i le feirg e
Gura mairg thug dhachaidh i.
Is ma bhuaileas i le fuath e
Guma luath do'n chlachan i.

    B'e sud e 'n cùl,
    So e 'n cùl bachalach,
    B'e sud e 'n cùl.

If you go to Uist of the barley
bring a fair wife home with you.
Get a kind, good-natured, sensible wife
who will entertain the captains.
Get a kind, good-natured, mild wife,
who will teach my son for you.
And if she strikes him in anger
a bad thing for him who took her home.
And if she strikes him in hatred
may she be soon in the churchyard.

    That was the head of hair,
    This was the curly head of hair,
    That was the head of hair.

Gaelic realism is not always one of tragedy or sorrow, but, whatever
the tone, there is a remarkable dislike for the romantic impossible.
Consider the wisdom of the fellow who went to woo the daughter of
the King of Ireland, and was asked the impossible:

Caisteal air gach cnocan gréine,
Muileann air gach sruth an Eirinn.

A castle on a sunny hillock,
a mill on every stream in Ireland.

He found solace in his shinty prowess, and concluded:

Mur bitheadh dhomh gur bean mo mhàthair,
Is té eile mo phiuthar ghràdhach,
Dh'innsinn sgeul do fhear nam mnathan,
Pàirt dhiubh tha gu beulach breugach,
Is cuid dhiubh tha gu modhail beusach.

Were it not for me that my mother is a woman,
and another my loved sister,
I would tell a tale to the ladies' man:
some of them are plausible and lying,
and some are virtuous and well-mannered.

And the step-mother's reply to the love-lorn girl in 'Mac Og an Iarla Ruaidh' has the same recognition of the probable reality. Pride and joy too are expressed soberly, as, for example, in the following:

Gura math a thig gùn dut
Air tighinn ùr as an fhasan,
Nighean oighre Shrath Shuardail
D'am bu dual a bhith beairteach.

Well does the gown become you
newly come in the fashion,
daughter of the heir of Strath Swordale
whose people were used to riches.

Chunnaic mi air féill Phort-rìgh thu,
Ailleagan am mìle pears' thu.

I saw you at the fair of Portree,
most handsome of a thousand persons.

Coisich a rùin, hu il ho ró,
Lùb nan geal lamh, o hì o bhó,
'S minic a bha, hu il ho ró,
Mi fo t'earradh, och hóireann ó,
Lagan uaigneach, hu il ho ró,
Chluain a' bharraich, o hì o bhó,
Do làmh fo m' cheann, hu il ho ró,
'S an téile tharam, och hóireann ó.

Come, my dear,
white handed one,

how often have I been
beneath your plaid
in a lonely hollow
of the birchwood meadow,
your hand under my head
and the other over me!

Doilleir dorcha air oidhche reòta
Chaidh do bhàta thar rudha Rònaidh,
Dol troimh na caoil a null a Bhròchaill,
A dh'amharc air maighdean an òr-fhuilt.

Dun and dark on a frosty night
your boat went past the headland of Rona,
going through the kyles over to Brochel
to visit the golden-haired girl.

Gheibhte sud an tigh an uasail
Bhith 'g òl fìon á pìosan fuara,
An tigh mór farsuing 's ùrlar sguaibte,
Ruighle dol sìos is suas air.[5]

That was to be found in the noble's house,
drinking of wine from cold silver cups,
in a big spacious house with swept floor,
a reel going up and down on it.

Those poems are certainly realistic in their complete lack of ex-
travagance of word or idea. The archness and realist wisdom of Burns'
Tam Glen has an exact counterpart in an old Kintail song:

Tha m'athair is mo mhàthair
A ghnàth 'ga mo sheòladh
Mi sheachnadh coinneimh anamoich
Ri sealgair na mòintich.

My father and my mother are
always giving me guidance
to avoid a late meeting
with the hunter of the moorland.

This popular song poetry achieves the realism of joy as well as of
tragedy. It is a realistic poetry because it is never far divorced from the
life of the people and, being such an expression of the joys or sorrows
of the ordinary man or woman, it constitutes a very important part of
perhaps the most remarkable peasant culture the world has ever seen.

31

Of course, the poems are sometimes aristocratic as, for example, the lament of the wife of Gregor MacGregor of Glenstrae, or the laments of the sister of Iain Garbh Mac Gille Chaluim, but those poems do not differ materially from clearly peasant productions like the second 'Ailein Duinn' poem I have quoted, or the song of the Sleat herdsman:

Mi ag cuallach na spréidhe
Aig a' bhaintighearn òig Shléitich.

As I tend the stock
for the young Lady of Sleat.

When the poetry is tragic the tragedy is usually the tragedy of pure circumstance so common in the life of the old Gael, especially on the sea, and the poetry is almost wholly pagan in tone. This paganism occasions the predominance of the tragedy of circumstance. It is Christianity that emphasises the tragedy of crime or passion; it mourns the loss of a soul; but to the paganism of old Gaelic poetry the lost life is a tragedy as great as is necessary. The poetry that enshrines the joys and sorrows of peasant life is necessarily realistic in content. The modern pseudo-Celticist may weave cloudy, elaborate regrets for outworn mythologies, but the authentic Gael is realist, recording simple human joy or sorrow. To the old Gaelic song realism is the *raison d'être*, the very breath of life. Those poems are great poems in their pregnant, sincere and realist expression of the central and simplest human themes. Besides, these old unknown composers were composing unconsciously in a great oral tradition of technique, and it is now a commonplace of poetic criticism that a minor poet working with sincerity in a great tradition may produce rare poetry. I think that one of the chief reasons for the inferiority of such Gaelic verse as is being produced at the present day is the fact that it follows the technique of 19th-century poetry, which is immeasurably inferior to the technique of the 17th and 18th centuries. The technical inferiority of 19th and 20th century Gaelic song is manifested in a flabbiness of rhythm, a lack of the clear, definite outline of the older song, and that is accompanied by an insignificance and worthlessness of matter and a lack of sincerity and realism unknown in the older poetry. For example, the 'pathetic fallacy' has found its way into modern Gaelic verse. To the modern Gaelic poet the sea gives spiritual messages; to the older poet the sea gives no message. It is either a power to be conquered or enjoyed by man or a ruthless force that destroys precious lives. Gaelic realism is inconsistent with the pathetic fallacy so overdone in the poetry of Europe.[6]

But to return to the popular song of the 16th, 17th and centuries, I may conclude my remarks about it by saying that ar who is doubtful whether I am talking of a characteristic body of p....., or merely talking of isolated examples has only to pick up the MacDonald Collection or Sinclair's *Oranaiche* and read page after page of the poetry I have been trying to describe, or in some of the isles he may still hear those songs among a few older people. I have dwelt on those poems for long because I believe they have never received anything like their due recognition as poetry, and I believe that their realism, sublimated or harrowed by emotion, is universally significant, that they have what Arnold calls 'high seriousness' or 'criticism of life' — that is the contemplation of life *sub specie aeternitatis*.

Having tried to examine the nature of the realism of the orally preserved popular song poetry of the 16th, 17th and 18th centuries, I now turn to the great poets of the 17th and 18th centuries, especially Mary MacLeod, Iain Lom, Roderick Morrison in the 17th century, and in the 18th century MacDonald, Macintyre, Buchanan, Ross, Am Pìobaire Dall, MacCodrum and Rob Donn. My first impression of such 18th century Gaelic poetry is the union of amazing brilliance of technique with great naturalistic realism. Macintyre's 'Beinn Dóbhrain' is the first poem that suggests itself. Exquisitely brilliant and subtle in technique, it is in content, I believe, the greatest example of naturalistic realism in the poetry of Europe. Naturalism is not generally the realism of poetry, but here it undoubtedly is. 'Beinn Dóbhrain' and MacDonald's 'Birlinn' are supreme examples of what I can only call a complete realisation and expression of dynamic nature. In English poetry, for instance, there is nothing at all that even faintly approximates to such a realisation and expression as it is manifest in these two poems. In 'Beinn Dóbhrain' the great sweep of the mountainside, the movement of a stag, a hind, a little bush, a spring of water, is realised with unequalled sensibility. That is the authentic natural magic that Arnold found in Celtic poetry. The very growth of vegetation is suggested by the sensuousness of the verse, a sensuousness that is comprehensive enough to be completely realist, not the limited, precious, decadent sensuousness, for example, of Keats or Tennyson or the English Pre-Raphaelites. The technical subtlety and brilliance is astounding. Now, briefly, which is the greater poetry, the poetry of Duncan Bàn, Gaelic Scotland's chief poet of external Nature, or the poetry of Wordsworth, the most celebrated of English Nature poets? In my opinion, Macintyre's objective naturalist realism is likely to be considered far more permanently significant than the mixture of sentimentalism, pure illusion and ruminating subjectivity,

lit up by great flashes, which constitutes Wordsworth's poetry.[7]
Between Beinn Dóbhrain and, say, Tintern Abbey no one who knows
both literatures will hesitate. Beinn Dóbhrain makes no pretension to
metaphysical content; actually its realisation of dynamic nature makes
its essential philosophic value as far superior to Wordsworth's poetry
as it is in pure technique. Beinn Dóbhrain is of a piece, and it has the
cumulative effect emphasised as essential to great poetry by all Greek
criticism, especially Aristotle.

To MacDonald's 'Birlinn' realism has been denied because of the
hyperbole of the description of the storm and the conventional
following of older models as in the Blessing of the Arms, but the total
effect of the poem is certainly realist; whole passages are triumphs of
dynamic realism unequalled except in 'Beinn Dóbhrain':

A' ghlas-fhairge sìor-chopadh
Steach mu dà ghualainn toisich,
Muir ag osnaich o shloistreadh a h-eàrlainn.

The grey surge ever foaming
in about her two fore shoulders,
sea sobbing from the swishing and pounding of low keel.

Generally the poem has the intense realisation of physical action
and movement. There is wild hyperbole in parts of the magnificent
description of the storm, but that hyperbole is merely the extension of
actuality to some degrees beyond actuality; it is not the consistent
projection of the dream world of romantic poetry. As for the incitement to rowing and the rowing song, they are splendid triumphs of
dynamic description, and it does not detract from their value that they
had been finely adumbrated in earlier poetry, notably by Iain Lom in
'Iorram Daraich' and by the obscure poet who even earlier composed
'Caismeachd Ailean nan Sop'. It is absurd to say that the 'Birlinn',
because of unimportant structural following of older models, is
merely an exercise in a traditional form of recuperaton. The point,
surely, is that the 'Birlinn' is a culmination of a great tradition and that
in itself it is unequalled in power, verve, *joie-de-vivre*, exactitude of
description of physical action and that, possessing such qualities, it is
essentially, a most original poem. To me it is realist as 'Beinn
Dóbhrain' is, the latter's realism being different only in degree,
having a greater acuteness and delicacy but not so much power and
abandon, and I think the difference in realist quality between the two
poems is largely conditioned by their very different subjects, Mac-
Donald expressing storm and struggle, Macintyre expressing the

34

nature of animals and their movements, and the aspects of landscape and vegetation.

Titanic struggle, MacDonald's subject, suggested and demanded power in description; Macintyre's subject demanded and suggested exactness and subtlety. Because exactness and subtlety are the very highest realist qualities, I consider 'Beinn Dóbhrain' the supreme example of Gaelic realism, in fact, Gaelic naturalism. The non-Gaelic speaker may think I am exaggerating, and I can only tell him that Macintyre's rhythms in 'Beinn Dóbhrain' are of all Gaelic rhythms the most hopeless of translation into any other language. I am prepared to say that no one who has not acquired Gaelic very early in life will ever be able to appreciate the rhythmic subtleties of 'Beinn Dóbhrain', 'Moladh Móraig', 'Iseabail Nic Aoidh', or any other Gaelic poem metrically based on ceòl mór. In the case of 'Beinn Dóbhrain' this is all important, as the poem is largely a description of movement, and in no poem is rhythm so all important as in a dynamically realist poem.

I suppose no Celtic Twilightist ever read 'Moladh Móraig'. Its abandon, its *joie-de-vivre*, its physical glow, its amazing virtuosity of technique makes it par excellence a Gaelic poem of the great period. Imagine Mórag swathed in a tenuous halo of the Twilight: Mórag is a creature of the real world that is full of self-confidence, a real world that jeers at papal asceticism in its exultation in the physical splendour of a woman. No wonder it carried the douce circumspect John Mackenzie off his feet. That is the nature of Alexander MacDonald's realism; he exaggerates qualities that are purely tangible. The result is a kind of physical apotheosis that differs from reality, not in nature but in degree. Romanticism differs from reality in very nature. C M Grieve's comment on MacDonald is very apt:

> O time eneuch for heaven and hell
>   Efter a man is deid;
> But while we're here it's life itsell
>   And muckle o' it we need;
> And, certes, coupin' up the earth
>   You found nae dearth.

Like 'Moladh Móraig' and 'Beinn Dóbhrain', there is at least one other great poem modelled on ceòl mór — Rob Donn's 'Iseabail Nic Aoidh'. Rob Donn, of course, does not have anything like the subtle sensitivity of Duncan Macintyre or the full-blooded power of Alexander MacDonald, but 'Iseabail Nic Aoidh' is a very notable poem in a peculiarly Gaelic way. It has great grace and virtuosity of technique imposed on matter very mundanely realist. Iseabail Nic Aoidh is not of the race of John Duncan's St Bride or Kennedy-Fraser's 'Mairead òg of witchery'. She is a creature of Rob Donn's very ordinary world, a pretty girl shamefully neglected by lovers because of her constant tending of cattle. Homely, and commonplace in theme, the poem is nevertheless delicately graceful. In the classical tradition of Europe, 'Iseabail Nic Aoidh' would be called an idyll. The Gael, in unconscious mockery of European tradition, makes his idyll realist and unsentimental. Any Gaelic speaker who wishes to examine a point of contact between Gaelic poetry and English has only to compare 'Iseabail Nic Aoidh' with one of Tennyson's idylls. A comparison will show that it is the Gaelic poem that is realist and unsentimental. Generally I have no very high regard for Rob Donn's poetry, but I would commend 'Marbhrann Triùir Fhleasgach Tigh Ruspuinn' as a study in futility recalling the brevity, restraint and realism of one of Horace's satires. 'Marbhrann Iain Mhic Eachuinn' has a noble truthfulness and restraint, while 'Briogais Mhic Ruairi', along with Archibald MacDonald's 'A' Bhanais a bha an Ceastal Odhar', would have delighted the heart of the early English realist, Chaucer. Rob Donn is a realist poet; his deficiency as a poet is not due to his realism but to the fact that, as John Mackenzie pointed out long ago, his realism is not lit up by great feeling or imagination.

That Rob Donn was in his own way a moralist is the only characteristic his poetry has in common with the poetry of Dugald Buchanan, a man poetically and temperamentally the very antithesis of Rob Donn. Buchanan is primarily an evangelical moralist, and didactic moralist poetry is necessarily realist because of its aim. Buchanan's themes are the world and death, the transience of all things earthly, the difference between youth and age. In 'Là a' Bhreitheanais', a part of 18th century Calvinism is expressed in a poem of terrible sublimity. Now, one may say that Buchanan's scheme of the universe is not likely the correct one, but the point is that his picture is not poetic fantasy. His description was literally true for himself, and still is literally true for many. Buchanan was not exercising his imagination. He was describing what was to him and those of his creed the very realism of eternity. He is a great poet because of the imaginative intensity of his poem. The intensity and sublimity is far superior to Milton's in English poetry, and in intention Buchanan's poem is wholly didactic and therefore realist. He does not disturb the homogeneity of his cosmic scheme by irrelevancies as Milton does in introducing the florid mythologies of the Renaissance. Buchanan would have been shocked if his poetry were regarded as anything else but strictly realist. 'An Claigeann' is the unrelieved realist picture of the stern democracy of death, the antithesis of the riot of sensuousness and *joie-de-vivre* that culminated in 'Moladh Móraig'.

I have refrained from dealing with satire, the type of poetry that in every language is realistic in aim, having as its chief theme the contrast between pretence and reality. Besides, the writing of satires involves the exploitation of a province of sensibility from which the romantic deliberately excludes himself. But satire is not one of the richest provinces in Gaelic poetry. Gaelic satire does vary from the torrential vituperation of MacDonald and Macintyre to the real wit of Rob Donn and MacCodrum, but I do not think that Gaelic satire had in the 18th century attained the degree of sophistication which appears necessary for the production of genuinely great satire. A great deal of Gaelic satire is mere 'flyting', pure vituperation, which fails not so much through lack of general realism as through lack of probable truth in the particular instance. Even when Gaelic satire is most telling, most restrained and realist in tone, even when it has the most convincing general truth, it may be false in the actual instance. Consider, for instance, the famous thrust of the Aireach Muileach at Alexander MacDonald:

> Cha b'e an creideamh ach sodal-cùirte
> Chuir thu a ghiùlan crois a' Phàpa.
>
> *It was not faith but court-fawning*
> *that drove you to bear the Pope's cross.*

Now that fine couplet is realist in that it could be applied perfectly to many modern neo-Catholics, but at least half of it is untrue in MacDonald's case. Alexander MacDonald was clearly as little troubled by religion as any poet who ever lived, but the Aireach was unfair to MacDonald's splendid political enthusiasm, for which the change of faith was an insignificant step in the achievement of a totality of Clanranald Jacobitism. But in spite of that the Aireach has left a fine piece of satiric realism. Whatever the general value of Gaelic satire, the great bulk of Gaelic poetry that is satirical or vituperative would alone damn all pseudo-Celtic Twilightism. This poetry shows that the Gael fully appreciated the aspect of realism that includes the ugly, strong and distasteful. While Gaelic poetry can be as coarse as any poetry, it appears to be completely lacking in romanticised sensualism.

As far as I can see the 18th century Gaelic poet did not dissociate his sensibility from any aspects of life. That is to the great credit of the realism of Gaelic poetry, as from the middle of the 17th century a very important feature of English poetry has been a deliberate cutting oneself off from aspects of life least amenable to romanticism. The catholicity of the Gaelic poet can be observed, for instance, by comparing the least realistic of Gaelic poets of the 18th century, William Ross, with any of the poets of the English romantic period. Imagine Wordsworth or Tennyson writing one of Ross's drinking songs. The fact that no Gaelic poet of the 18th century was confined to one province is a sure sign of the lack of romantic convention in the 18th century Gaelic poetry, and it is a sure sign of the realism of that poetry that even in the least realist of its poets there is never anything approaching an equation of poetry and romance. This lack of mealy-mouthedness is very striking in a poet like Ross, whose most common characteristic is a lofty passionate ardour, which in his greatest poem, 'Oran Eile air a' Mhodh Cheudna', becomes a cry of anguish express-ed in language almost as stately as a Greek sculpture or a MacCrim-mon pìobaireachd. This last song of Ross is to me almost unaccount-able in its blend of emotion and art. It is in essence one of the saddest poems ever conceived; it expresses not the sadness of disillusion with life; it is a more poignant sadness, the farewell to life and joy of a young man who is terribly in love with life. It is realist in its poignancy, in its complete lack of irrelevancies, but nevertheless it is a highly sophisticated poem in its musical elaboration and its chiselled perfection of line. The strange thing about it to me is that such a perfection of self-conscious technique should accompany such poig-nancy of emotion. Of such a poem it seems pointless to say that it is realist although it is clearly unromantic. To me it has the complete-ness of the largest utterance of Shakespeare and when I think of a parallel I think of Pàdruig Mór McCrimmon's 'Cumha na Cloinne'. I take Ross's greatest poems — 'Oran Eile' by far the greatest of all, 'Feasgar Luain', 'An Suaithneas Bàn', and the problematic 'Cuachag nan Craobh' — as the supreme examples of the transfiguration wrought by profound emotion, perhaps the greatest examples in 18th century Gaelic poetry of the union of emotion and art. They are romantic poems only if one clings to the equation of love and romance, which in literary criticism is very popular but wholly unscientific. Those poems are certainly not romantic in the strictest sense — that is the adduction of exotic ornamentation. Ross is acutely aware of mundane reality in spite of his infatuation:

Gach an-duine chluinneas mo chàs,
Tha 'g cur air mo nàdur fiamh,

Ag cantuinn nach 'eil mi am bhàrd
Is nach cinnich leam dàn as fhiach;
Mo sheanair ri pàigheadh a' mhàil,
Is m'athair ri màileid riamh,
Chuireadh iad gearran an crann
Ach ghearrainn-sa rann roimh chiad.

Every dolt who hears of my case,
which has left its mark on my nature,
says that I am not a poet
and that no worthwhile poem will grow from me;
my grandfather a payer of rent
and my father always a packman,
they would put geldings in a plough
but I would cut a verse better than a hundred.

Although the greatest Gaelic poetry, the poetry of the 18th century, is on the whole realist, there is much Gaelic poetry which is greatly lacking in realism. The eulogistic poetry of the 17th century, the natural successor of the old bardic poetry, is not realist. This poetry is sometimes the work of genuinely fine poets, Iain Lom, Màiri nighean Alasdair Ruaidh, Mairead ni' Lachainn, Sìleas na Ceapaich, An Clàrsair Dall, and Am Pìobaire Dall. About six weeks ago there was an article in one of the Scottish dailies, written by a Lowland journalist, who seemed to think that all Gaelic poetry consisted of this eulogy of chief and clan by flattering parasites. But the lack of realism of this type of poetry is not a sympton of general Celtic romanticism, and indeed, as I have already said of much Gaelic satire, this poetry is not so much unrealist as simply untrue. The qualities predicated of certain chiefs by poets like Iain Lom are not impossible qualities, and certainly in this eulogistic poetry one finds nothing of the fantastic extravagancies of eulogy which are to be found in English eulogy of the 17th and 18th centuries. For instance, the lies of Mary MacLeod are sober lies compared with the lies of Chapman about Queen Elizabeth, of Dryden about first Oliver Cromwell and then Charles II, of the stern realist Crabbe about some insignificant son of the Duke of Rutland. As far as I know, no Gaelic poet ever attained anything like the nonsensical indecency of John Donne writing of the death of Miss Elizabeth Drury.

Now, briefly, what is the value of this eulogistic poetry? Well, its only value is that, as the natural successor of the old bardic verse, it has great splendour of technique and often an evocative loveliness of phrase. I think first of Mary MacLeod:

Mo shàth-ghal bochd,
Mar a tha mi a nochd.

My miserable satiety of weeping
because of my state to-night.

Consider also the poem of Griogar Og Mac Griogair to Lachlan
Mackinnon of Strath:

Is cian 's gur fada tha mi 'm thàmh,
Gun triall air do dhàil,
A Lachlainn o 'n àirde tuath.

Nam biodh sneachda nan càrn,
'Na ruith leis gach allt,
'S gun cailleadh gach beann a gruaim;

Nan dubhadh an sliabh,
'S gun cromadh a' ghrian,
Leam bu mhithich bhith triall mun cuairt.

Cha b'e machair nan Gall
So bheirinn fo m' cheann,
Ach bràighe nan gleann so shuas;

Agus talla an fhir fhéil,
Ceann-uidhe nan ceud,
Cill ma Ruibhe fo sgéith a' chuain.

Far away and for long I am at rest
without going to meet you,
Lachlan from the land in the north.

If the snow of the cairns
were running down with every burn
and if every peak lost its gloom;

If the moorgrass grew dark
and the sun bent down,
it would be my time to be going on my round.

It would not be the plain of the Lowlander
I would set my face to,
but the braes of these glens up yonder.

And the hall of the generous one,
destination of hundreds,
Kilmaree under the wing of the bay.

Compare this verse of Am Pìobaire Dall:

A' gheug a thàinig 's an deagh uair
Dha 'm buadhach mùirn agus ceòl,

Ogha Choinnich nan rùn réidh
Is Bharain Shrath Spé nam bó.

The branch that came in the auspicious hour,
graced with courteous joy and music,
grand-daughter of Kenneth of the calm judgments
and of the Baron of Strathspey of the cows.

Mairead ni Lachainn has:

Mac Gill Eain nan lùireach
Bhith 'na laighe 's a' chrùisle
Ann an leabaidh na h-ùrach
An suain cadail gun dùsgadh.

That MacLean of the hauberks
is lying in the vault,
in the bed of the dust,
in a slumber of sleep not to waken.

And Iain Lom has:

A Dhòmhnuill an Dùin,
Mhic Ghilleasbuig nan Tùr,
Chaidh t'eineach 's do chliù thar chàich.

Tha seirc ann do ghruaidh,
Caol mhala gun ghruaim,
Beul meachair o'n suairce gràdh.

Donald of the Dun,
son of Archibald of the towers,
your generosity and fame went beyond that of others.

There is affection in your cheek,
thin brow without gloom,
tender mouth from which love is most endearing.

But by far the greatest of all those poems is surely the Clàrsair Dall's 'Oran Mór Mhic Leòid', which is realist in that it castigated a present which differed from a past that was splendid at least for the harper. But I am not making a general plea for this type of poetry. If any one is inclined to take its matter seriously he can study the Clàrsair Dall, who unblushingly reveals the real basis of this whole type of poetry, for the Clàrsair Dall admits his learning, through bitter experience, the wisdom of the children of this world. And, of course, the whole basis of the poetry is so apparent that it needs no Marxist analysis. The

Clàrsair Dall hit back savagely when the privileges of his own musician caste were curtailed, and he hit back with splendid realism to the extent of eight verses that proved too much for John Mackenzie, editor of *Sàr Obair*. The Clàrsair Dall's greatest poem probably did exaggerate the qualities of Iain Breac seen in retrospect and in contrast with the anglicised degeneracy of Roderick, Iain's son, but one has only to think of his description of the Pibroch to see that the genius of Gaelic poetry is essentially realist:

An uair a ghabhadh i làn
Is a chuireadh os n-àird na fhuair
Le meòir fhileanta bhinn,
Is iad gu ruith-leumnach dìonach luath.

When it (i.e. the bag of the pipe) took its fill
and what it got was raised up
with skilled melodious fingers,
running and leaping, swift and without a break.

That has the physical exactness which Macintyre brought to a great climax in 'Beinn Dóbhrain'.

I have spoken of Mary MacLeod's poetry as consisting of lovely trifles of eulogy, but there is something else. I have always been greatly affected by the beginning of two of Mary's songs. There is a haunting beauty in

'S mi am shuidhe air an tulaich,
   'S mi fo mhulad 's fo imcheist,
'S mi 'g coimhead air Ile,
   'S ann de m'ìongnadh 's an ám so;
Bha mise uair nach do shaoil mi,
   Mun do chaochail air m'aimsir,
Gun tiginn an taobh so
   Dh' amharc Dhiùraidh á Sgàrbaidh.

Beir mo shoraidh do'n dùthaich
   Tha fo dhubhar nan garbh-bheann. . .

As I sit on the hillock
in sorrow and perplexity,
looking at Islay,
it is my wonder at this time;
at one time I little thought,
before my world changed,
that I would come to this side
to look on Jura from Scarba.

42

Bear my greeting to the land
that is under the shadow of the rugged hills . . .

Quite as fine is

Ri fuaim an Taibh
Is uaigneach mo ghean,
Bha mis' uair nach b'e sud m'àbhaist.

Ach pìob nuallanach mhór
Bheireadh buaidh air gach ceòl,
'Nuair a ghluaist' i le meòir Phàdruig.

At the sound of the Western Ocean
how forlorn my mood!
I was once when that was not my wont;

but a great bellowing pipe
that would excel all music
when it was moved by the fingers of Patrick.

These two extracts are simply pieces of sober autobiography, tremendous with emotion, but not foggy with romantic haziness. It is only a pity that Mary MacLeod did not tell us more of herself and Patrick, and less of her interminable Rodericks and Normans.

Nevertheless, it is undeniable that the aim of this eulogistic poetry is to diffuse a false, romantic estimation of men and women who, in some cases, might have been as worthless as the bulk of their descendants. The fact that Mary MacLeod evidently believed what she said, and that Roderick Morrison evidently did too, does not greatly alter the ideological effect of their poems, but Roderick Morrison learned realism in suffering.

Iain Lom is different in temper. His purely eulogistic poetry has the same deliberately false romanticism; he praises the house of Sleat to annoy Glengarry, but his greatest poem, 'Inbhir Lòchaidh', is savagely realist:

Bhur sgrios mas truagh leam bhur càradh,
Ag éisdeachd anshocair bhur pàisdean,
Ag caoidh a' phannail bh'anns an àraich,
Donnalaich bhan Earra-Ghàidheal.

Damn you if I pity your state,
listening to the distress of your children,
lamenting the womanish band that was on the battle-field,
the howling of the women of Argyll.

That is not the cooing of the doves of the Celtic Twilight.

Before I leave this eulogistic poetry I have to notice one fact that is not at all consistent with ordinary romanticism: while this poetry is false in total effect, it is realist in sensuous detail. Its romanticism is one of ideology rather than of temperament, but, be that as it may, the verdict of history on the whole of this poetry is the bitter irony of the Clearances, when the most lauded houses proved among the very vilest.

The 17th century mercenary glorification of chief has as its antithesis the poetry of the 19th century Clearances, but for many reasons 19th century Gaelic poetry is not predominantly realist. Its most characteristic mood is a weak, half romantic nostalgia. It is a fact that the Clearances did not provoke a poetry of anger and realism like the post-Culloden poetry of Alexander MacDonald and John Roy Stewart describing the brutalities and depredations of the Hanoverians in Jacobite country. Of course, there is now and again realist anger, as in Livingston's 'Fios thun a' Bhàird':

> Tha Ile 'n diugh gun daoine,
>   Chuir a' chaora a bailtean fàs,
> Mar a fhuair 's a chunnaic mise,
>   Thoir am fios so thun a' bhàird.

> *Islay is today without people,*
>   *the sheep has laid waste in town-lands,*
> *as I found and as I saw,*
>   *take this message to the bard.*

Or the Mull song:

> Tha fearann ar gaoil fo fhraineach 's fo fhraoch,
>   'S gach machair is raon gun àiteach,
> 'S chan fhada bhios duine am Muile nan craobh
>   Ach Goill agus caoraich bhàna.

> Rinn peirceall chaorach fearann a dhaoradh,
>   Is dh'innis dhuinn daoine an fhàisneachd
> Gun cuireadh iad gaisgich nan gleanna air faondradh
>   Is duthaich nan laoch 'na fàsaich.

> Chan iongnadh mi idir bhith sileadh nan deur
>   'N ám cuimhneachadh gnìomh gach bàillidh,
> Mar chuir iad fo chaoraich gach aonach is sliabh,
>   'S na daoine chur cian thar sàile.

The land of our love in under bracken and heather
and every plain and field untilled,
and soon there will be no-one in Mull of the trees
but Lowlanders and white sheep.

The jaws of sheep have made land dear,
and men have told us the prophecy
that they would uproot the heroes of the glens
and make the land of the brave men a wilderness.

It is no wonder that I shed tears
remembering the deeds of each factor,
how they put every hill and moorland under sheep
and drove the people far over the ocean.

Or in Neil MacLeod:

Ach an diugh tha maor is lann
   Air gach alltan agus òb,
Chan 'eil saorsa sruth nam beanntan
   Anns a' ghleann 'san robh mi òg.

But to-day there is a ground-officer and a fence
on every little burn and creek,
there is no freedom of the stream from the mountains
in the glen where I was young.

And MacLachlan of Rahoy can be very realistic, but, in the main, 19th century Gaelic poetry is an expression of a somewhat romantic nostalgia for a hopelessly gone past rather than a realist examination of the change. There is no great dwelling on the actual details of the Clearances. Of course, people who lived in the 1930s can appreciate that reality is sometimes too touching for the sternest realist. I can well believe that many Highland poets could look on the Clearances only remotely; that they had to hold the Clearances somewhat away from them; there is a point in human misfortune when romance and realism appear equally pointless; and besides, for some reasons that I do not pretend to know, modern poetry cannot sustain the intensity of emotion which poetry could two or three centuries ago. The development of civilisation or sophistication brings a reticence in poetry as well as in actual life.

But the lack of political and social realism of the 19th century Gaelic poetry is accompanied by other symptoms of decline. Regret for the past sometimes suggests the unrealist pathetic fallacy hitherto unknown in Gaelic poetry. Neil MacLeod has it in 'Tha osag nam fuar bheann'.

Indeed, Neil MacLeod's poetry is symptomatic of the rapid decline in the backbone of Gaelic poetry. It is sentimental, pretty-pretty, weak and thin, only sometimes attaining splendour in its occasional realist moods, as in the magnificent impression of Skye in the opening of 'Fàilte do'n Eilean Sgitheanach':

Chì mi an Cuilithionn
Mar leóghann gun tioma
Le fheusaig de shneachd'
Air a pasgadh m'a cheann,
Le ghruaidhean a' srùladh
Le easanan smùideach
Tha tuiteam 'nan lùban
Gu ùrlar nan gleann.

I see the Cuillin
like a fearless lion
with his beard of snow
folded about his head,
with his cheeks streaming
with vaporous cascades
falling in loops
to the floor of the glens.

But that is not the usual strain of Neil MacLeod. Indeed, I think that his father, Domhnall nan Oran, and his brother, Iain Dubh, were far closer to the main realist current of Gaelic poetry than he was. To my mind Donald Mackechnie is not a poet of much consequence. He brought into Gaelic poetry a strain of insignificant reflectiveness, lacking the immediacy of impression, directness and sensuous vigour of the best Gaelic poetry; and William Livingston's poetry is vitiated by his dwelling far too much on the fighting of Gaels and Norsemen, MacDonalds and MacLeans, and the campaigns of Bruce, though in his treatment of contemporary themes he had power and realism, as in 'Fios thun a' bhàird' and 'Eirinn ag gul'.

It is not my business here to dwell on the great decline of Gaelic poetry in the 19th century, but on a decline in realism of content. 19th century poetry, as compared with 18th century poetry, has a weakness and flabbiness of rhythm due largely to the overdoing of artificial metrical stresses. That, of course, is a matter of technique, but with more space at my disposal, I think I could show the relation of this decline in form to the decline in matter.

Such Gaelic verse as is being now produced I consider very insignificant. I have already indicated my opinion that the fine talent of Kenneth MacLeod was dissipated in the fogs of Celtic Twilight, a purely foreign non-Celtic development. As far as I know the only poet of consequence in the 20th century was the late Donald Sinclair, whose talent again was outwith the main stream of Gaelic poetry. He expressed a Catholic mysticism in a beautiful but over-elaborate and artificial diction: 'Saoibhir sìth nan sian a nochd air Tìr an Aigh', but he is more poignant and poetically greater in his occasional simple flashes:

> Chan ìongnadh cill mo shluaigh an cois nan cuan bhith balbh,
> Chan iongnadh uchd nan tuam bhith 'n tòic le luach na dh'fhalbh.

> *No wonder my people's churchyard by the ocean shore is silent,*
> *No wonder the hillock of the tombs is replete with the value of the departed.*

To say that his verse in the main lacks realism is not, however, to deny that Sinclair was a very considerable and very shamefully neglected poet.

I am conscious that in this century a few have made a little reputation through the development of publicity, but I consider their work far too derivative to merit attention as original poetry. Far better than any of the known verse writers I consider an obscure Uistman, Donald MacDonald, and better still a Skyeman, almost as obscure, the late Charles Matheson, who had real and original brilliance of language and technique, but whose matter was mainly local and trivial; but Mr Ranald MacLeod has already brought his unusual quality of sparkling and witty language to the notice of the Society.

NOTES

1 There is a version in the *Gesto Collection*.
2 The first two lines as printed cannot be by Domhnall Donn.
3 I was misinformed about Henry Whyte's responsibility for this alteration. I apologise to his memory. But the point remains a valid one.
4 My father used to sing 'eubhar'.
5 This is how my grandmother sang the line. My aunt Peggy had 'Ruighleadh ubhal . . .'
6 The foregoing paragraph contains much that I would now express differently.
7 I do not now believe this to be a meaningful comparison.

The Poetry of the Clearances

I have decided to limit the title of this paper to 'The Poetry of the Clearances', and its scope to a consideration of poems dealing explicitly with the Clearances. The limitation is not easily justifiable, because very much emigration poetry that cannot explicitly be called Poetry of the Clearances was occasioned by emigration resulting indirectly from the Clearances. I have little doubt that four-fifths of the emigration from 1780 to 1880 was caused directly or indirectly by the Clearances, or by such close relations of the Clearances as rack-renting and appropriation, by landlords, of the best agricultural and pastoral land. Considerations of space, however, force me to the limitation because the general motif of emigration is so all-pervading in 19th century Gaelic poetry that, were I not thus to confine myself, I should have to survey a body of literature out of all proportion to the space at my disposal. All poetry reflects social phenomena, and in the Highlands of the 19th century emigration of one kind or another was the phenomenon of phenomena. I have, therefore, kept to the direct and explicit poetry of the Clearances and their aftermath, the people's struggle and partial resurgence in the eighties of last century. I regret the limitation because it involves the non-inclusion of poems like John MacLachlan's 'Gur moch rinn mi dùsgadh', 'Och nan och, 's na bheil air m' aire', 'Is fhada mi 'm ònaran', and 'Tha mi sgìth 'n fhògairt so'. I realise that very often my selection may appear arbitrary.

The Highland Clearances constitute one of the saddest tragedies that has ever come on a people, and one of the most astounding of all the successes of landlord capitalism in Western Europe, such a triumph over the workers and peasants of a country as has rarely been achieved with such ease, cruelty and cynicism. I have said 'cynicism', not forgetting the vast amount of pseudo-economic and pseudo-philanthropic unction that formed the ideological preparation, concomitant and justification. I have said 'ease', not forgetting the resistance in Coigach in 1792, in Glen Calvie in 1820, and at Sollas in Uist in 1829, because there was no concerted crofter resistance until after 1880, when the Battle of the Braes, the Lewis Deer Hunt and the Assynt Land Raid marked a new era, albeit a very short-lived one, the era of the crofters' counter-attack. The Leckmelm eviction in 1880 and the Battle of the Braes in 1882 mark respectively the end of the Clearance period proper and the beginning of the crofter resistance.

The landlords' triumph from 1760 to 1880 was a remarkably easy one, but there were many causes political, economic, social and religious to weaken the Highland people. This weakness is clearly reflected in the weakness, thinness and perplexity of most Gaelic poetry in the 19th century.

The failure of the '45 and the resulting legislation turned the Highland chiefs purely and simply into landlords. It is scarcely an exaggeration to say that, without the intervening feudal stage, the Highland people had to exchange a tribal economy for a landlord economy, and, as is inevitable in the telescoping of historical processes, the upheaval and suffering was immense. When the British Government took the captaincy of the clan and the power of 'pit and gallows' from the chief, it gave him a right to the many privileges of the laissez-faire capitalist. The Industrial Revolution and growth of big urban populations created a huge demand for wool and animal foodstuffs. Thus the Clearances were expedient and welcome in the eyes of the industrial capitalists of the South as well as to the landlord capitalists of the North. Hence the evicted Highland crofter could expect little support from the humanitarian feeling of the capitalist press of the cities, and he was geographically, politically, economically and linguistically isolated from the industrial workers of the South, who were engaged in their own struggle with capital. The failure of the '45 also gave the death blow to the Scottish Nationalist hopes, and put behind the capitalist the might of the British Empire.

The political and economic position of the landlords was secure, and certain ideological factors strengthened it further. The Highland chief could still take advantage of some at least of the old traditions of loyalty to the chief, for to an unsophisticated population tradition rendered more difficult the appreciation of economic fact. Even as late as the eighties of the last century the lingering traces of this tradition were manifesting themselves in the absurd tendency to blame the factor more than the landlord. But the religious factor was of far more consequence in the weakening of popular resistance, and it increased in importance as the Clearances progressed. Thus the fact that there were so many more examples of resistance to Clearances in the period between 1780 and 1820 than in the period between 1820 and 1870 is partly accounted for by the spreading and deepening of the religious revival after 1820. It may be that the clergy's silent acquiescence and even occasional open support for the landlord has been exaggerated, but it is probably true that not one in ten of the Highland clergymen supported the crofters in any tangible way. The ministers of the Established Church were economically attached to the landlord, and few of them attacked their patrons, while some of them actively supported the Clearances, preaching to the people that their sufferings were God's judgement on them for their sins, and that resistance to constituted authority was sacrilege. The connection of the landlords with the Established Church undoubtedly helped to drive great numbers of the people into the Free Church, but a church that considered the world a vale of tears, earthly affairs of little account, and original sin one of the two central things in human life,' could advise only submission and resignation and an escape to religion. The poverty that increased with every encroachment by the landlord on good land, and the resulting concentration of population on worthless plots, encouraged even among the more worldly the view that the world was indeed a vale of tears, and moreover, as Professor Tawney has proved, 19th century Calvinsim, however democratic in its church government, did not vitally dispute the theories of private property and laissez-faire that were the ideological props of capitalism. Ultimately, even for the Free Church minister, who had little cause to love the landlord, the dispensation was that the land was the landlord's and that he could do what he liked with it, his spiritual blood on his own head. He was of the powers that be, and, at any rate, such earthly matters were of little importance.

For all those reasons, the Highlanders' resistance, physical and moral, was bound to be very weak, and the poetry of the period reflects this impotence. There was one political factor which ought ideally to have helped the crofters, namely, the great services of Highland soldiers to the Empire. Alexander Mackenzie has called attention to factual comment on this: 'At the very hour that Nana Sahib was being crushed and Cawnpore taken by the 78th Regiment, the fathers, mothers and children of the 78th were being evicted within a few miles of Dunrobin Castle.' Contemplation of such ironies is one of the most perplexed and pathetic features of all the perplexed and pathetic Gaelic poetry of the 19th century. Most of the 19th century Gaelic poets gloried in the deeds of the Highland soldiers, and most of them asked why such things were, but, not having much of an insight into the ways of imperialism, they could give no answer. They could only utter the warning that depopulation of the Highlands would sooner or later end the supply of Highland soldiers.

Gaelic poetry in the 19th century is naturally depressing and even hopeless in tone, until the resurgent spirit in the eighties, especially in

Skye and Lewis, brought a new note of courage and hope. This resurgence had three main causes, mostly external in origin, the stirring of a working class Radicalism in the cities, the interest of the Liberal Party in the votes of the rural workers that they were to enfranchise in 1884 and, above all, the example of Ireland. In the words of an island crofter, 'We were hearing such good news from Ireland that we thought we would become rebels ourselves.' In the eighties exultation came again into Gaelic poetry with the songs of Màiri Mhór nan Oran — but it did not survive the first two decades of an active Land League.

There was a considerable number of Clearances before the end of the 18th century — the Drummond Clearance in 1762; the Glengarry in 1782; one in Strath Glass in 1788; and others in other parts of Ross-shire and Sutherland, but apparently they evoked little comment in verse, at any rate in verse that has survived. Of course, so much of the poetry of that period has been lost and much was undoubtedly kept out of collections dedicated to aristocratic patrons that one cannot know the reaction of poets between 1750 and 1880. For example, I know of no poetic mention of that grim foretaste of the Clearances, *Soitheach nan Daoine*, the experiment in slave-trafficking from Skye made in 1739 by MacDonald of Sleat and MacLeod of Dunvegan. There is, however, a traditional metrical reference to it in the simple and pathetic rhyme of place-names in Minginish and Bracadale, alleged to be the words of a girl who was kidnapped while pulling dulse on the Gesto shore:

Grùla 's Brunnal 's dà chnoc Scarrail,
Lag nam Bó, Airigh MhicLeòid,
Beinn Thota Gormshuil nam fear sgiamhach,
M'ionam 's mo chiall Beinn Dubhagraich.

Grula and Brunnal and the two Hills of Scarrail,
the Hollow of the Cows, the Shieling of MacLeod,
the Penny-land of Tota Gormuil of the handsome men,
my love and darling Ben Duagraich.

John MacCodrum commemorates the squeezing out by Sir Alexander MacDonald of the Uist tacksmen about 1770, and he sails as near the wind as a pensioner of Sir Alexander's could be expected to sail in deprecating the departure of the 'gentlemen' of the clan, and, not understanding the change in the status of chief, he foresees a danger to the chiefs themselves in the loss of their warriors. It is a strange poem. He talks of 'uachdarain ghòrach chuir fuaradh fo'r srònaibh', keeping discreetly to the plural, and says, 'Thug sud sgrìob air MacDhòmhnaill' — an ingenious and polite way of condoling on the results of a misdeed with the author of the misdeed. The going of the tacksmen was not, of course, a clearance in the ordinary sense, but it was gravely symptomatic, though MacCodrum hardly sees the symptom. What was going to happen to the commons if the gentlemen of the clan were not to be spared? The last part of the poem is surprisingly pointed and probably refers to clearances of commons, as well as to the liquidation of the tacksmen. The plural used of the landlords may be a discreet evasion to mark a particular reference to Sir Alexander MacDonald, but it is likely that MacCodrum was thinking of more than the going of the tacksmen. I do not think he would call the tacksmen 'truaghain'.

> Seallaibh m'an cuairt duibh
> Is faicibh na h-uaislean
> Gun iochd annt' ri truaghain,
>   Gun suairceas ri dàimhich;
> 'S ann tha iad am barail
> Nach buin sibh do'n talamh,
> 'S ged dh'fhàg iad sibh falamh
>   Chan fhaic iad mar chall e.
> Chaill iad an sealladh
> Air gach reachd agus gealladh
> Bha eadar na fearaibh
>   Thug am fearann so o'n nàmhaid.

> *Look around you*
> *and see the nobles*
> *with no pity for miserable ones,*
>   *with no kindness to kinsmen;*
> *They are of the opinion*
> *that you are not of the land,*
> *and though they have left you empty*
>   *they do not see it as a loss.*
> *They have lost their sight*
> *of every law and promise*
> *that was among the men*
>   *who took this land from their enemy.*

It is a very clear statement of the old view of the clan's right to the territory. Probably MacCodrum's being a pensioner of the chief most concerned has deprived posterity of some powerful satire.

Such powerful satire as MacCodrum could not, or would not, give on the theme exists in Ailean Dall's 'Oran nan Cìobairean Gallda', a poem entirely in the vigorous style of the 18th century, though probably composed in the early years of the following century. The first four lines are devastating.

Thàinig oirnn do dh'Albainn crois,
Tha daoine bochda nochdte ris,
Gun bhiadh, gun aodach, gun chluain,
Tha 'n àird a tuath air a sgrios.

There has come on us in Scotland a cross,
poor people are naked before it;
without food, without clothing, without pasture (?),
the Land of the North is utterly destroyed.

The poem goes on to describe the desolation of the Highlands and to express with great power an even physical contempt for the Lowland shepherds or shepherd farmers, their manners, their talk, their whole being, but not a disparaging word of the noble landlords whose pockets were being filled by the high rents paid by the shepherd farmers. I wonder if Ailean Dall's failure to indict the real authors of the villainy was due to stupidity, or to the intellectual confusion of the day, or to his intention of seeking patronage and subscriptions. Whatever he thought of the landlords — and we get an inkling of it from his laudatory mention of the 'Colonel of Glengarry' and Mackenzie as not being given to increasing the price of land — his whole soul hated the Lowland shepherds and shepherd farmers as a personification of all that was extinguishing the old Gaeldom of song, wine, bardic patronage and Gaels.

Neither MacCodrum nor MacDougall were rebels in temperament, and Duncan Bàn Macintyre was the least rebellious of men, but they were all three of peasant stock, and all three, and especially Macintyre, had a great zest for the joys of peasant life. In his piquant and spirited 'Oran nam Balgairean', Duncan Macintyre sees most of the implications of the coming of the sheep: untilled soil, no peasantry, no farms, no shielings, no houses, no vestige of any old Gaelic custom, no horse, cattle beast, farm servant, deer, no forester — only sheep and shepherds — and he sings success and long life to the foxes that destroyed the accursed animals that were desolating the Highlands; but Duncan had a great respect for the *uaislean*, and he omits the most important member of the trinity of sheep, shepherd and landlord. Ailean Dall's 'Oran nan Cìobairean' and Macintyre's 'Oran nam Balgairean', with their limited realism and their intellectual shuffling, are in every way different from that exotic poem which is the first piece in the second volume of the collection published by Alexander and Donald Stewart in 1804. This poem, 'Oran eadar Dòmhnall agus Dùghall, ann am bheil cor truagh nan Gàidheal d' an éigin an tìr fhéin fhàgail, air a leigeadh ris', is a direct imitation of the first Eclogue of Virgil, containing much unreal material borrowed from its original, but nevertheless clearly diagnosing the disease of Gaeldom.

A Dhòmhnaill, a ghràidh mo chrìdh,
'S e dh'fhàg mi trom, muladach, sgìth,
    Bhith smuainteach' an céin
    Air gach bochdainn tha 'm dhéidh,
'S mo chàirdean gu léir am dhìth.
    Chan àrdan no stoirm,
    Cha ghruamaich gharg bhorb,
Cha chogadh 's beag orm, no strì,
    Ach Ile bhith gann
    De'n òigridh a bh' ann:
    Chàidh am fuadach o làimh
    Do dh'America thall
'S gun neach ann am bheil dàimh no sìth.

Donald, loved one of my heart,
what has left me heavy, sorrowful and weary
(is) thinking in a distant land
of all the poverty left behind me,
and my lack of all my kinsfolk.
It is not pride nor storm,
nor bitter cruel gloom,
nor war that I hate, nor strife;
but that Islay has few
of the youth that were in it:
They have been driven far away
to America over the sea
with no one who is kin and no foe.

Then follows a most absurdly idyllic picture of the joys of America, patently indebted to the pretty extravagancies of the conventional pastoral of Virgil, but it contains also one of the most uncompromising attacks on landlords in all Gaelic poetry.

    Am fearann 's iad féin
    Gum bàsaich le chéil'
O na dh'fhàs iad 'nam béistean doirbh,
    Rag-mhuinealach, cruaidh,
    Gun iochd no ath-thruas,
    Iad puinnseanta, fuar

Ri 'n ìochdairean 's ri 'n tuath,
'Gan casgairt le uallach dhoirbh.

The land and themselves,
they will die together,
since they have become hard monsters,
stiff-necked, mean,
with no mercy or pity;
poisonous, cold
to their subjects and tenants,
killing them with hard burdens.

After that it bitterly describes their bloated parasitism, laments the Disarming Act in nationalist fashion, and ends with a wishful prophecy of vengeance. It is not a great or technically even a competent poem, but it contains the most clear-headed and uncompromising comment on the situation in the Highlands that survives from the Gaelic poetry of the 18th century.

Of a more homely strain is the satire on Riddell of Ardnamurchan, composed, according to the editors of *The MacDonald Collection*, by an unknown author about the middle of the 18th century. This is one of the few direct attacks on a named landlord. Very many were direct enough, but left the object nameless. The satire on Riddell is contemporary, the grasping laird having inflicted a threefold rent rise on the author. It is a vigorous and pointed poem. Riddell is the 'eucorach olc', who has not even the excuse of aristocracy. The author objects especially to being exploited by a laird without pedigree. If the author had lived to the mid 19th century, he would have seen the bluest of Highland blood devastating Sutherland, Ross, Lochaber, Perthshire, Argyll, Mull and Skye.

The satire on Riddell is as homely but not as fierce as the *aoir* on Sellar and Young, the agents of the Sutherland ducal family. This poem, which echoes in metre the simple, spirited rhythm of Mac Mhaighstir Alasdair's 'Hé an clò dubh', is a cry of such anger and hatred as had scarcely been heard in Gaelic poetry since the death of Iain Lom. Significantly, its tone is of the 18th century, though it must have been composed after 1809.

Nam faighinn-s' air an raon thu
Is daoine 'ga do cheangal,
Bheirinn le mo dhòrnaibh
Trì òirlich a mach de d' sgamhan.

If I had you on the open field
with men tying you up

> *with my fists I would take out*
> *three inches of your lungs.*

I know of only one poem like it in 19th century Gaelic poetry, that is Dr John MacLachlan's poem on an Ardnamurchan tacksman and factor, anonymous in *The MacDonald Collection*, but published under MacLachlan's name in *Mac Talla*. If it is MacLachlan's, it is very unlike his other work, for MacLachlan is in spirit and technique very much of the 19th century, but this poem has a grimness, directness and economy that is more of the 18th century. Of course, MacLachlan's known poetry is clearly an expression of only a few sides of his great personality. As a man, MacLachlan was evidently something much more than is implied in the phrase, 'the sweet singer of Rahoy', and he was sometimes capable of a surprising economy and force. This poem, however, has a forceful brevity with more than MacLachlan's occasional intensity.

> 'S nuair théid spaid de'n ùir ort
> Gum bi 'n dùthaich glan;
>
> Cha téid nì air t'uachdar-sa
> Ach buachar mhart;
>
> Cha bhi gal nam pàisdean
> No gàirich bhan;
>
> Cha bhi bantrach 's truaghan ann
> A bhualadh bhas.

> *And when a spade of earth goes on you*
> *the country will be clean;*
>
> *nothing will go on top of you*
> *but the dung of cattle;*
>
> *there will be no weeping of children*
> *nor wailing of women;*
>
> *there will be no widow or poor one*
> *striking their palms.*

As these poems I have mentioned speak with the voice of the 18th century, so does the famous poem by John Maclean, 'Am Bàrd an Canada'. John Maclean was in every sense but the chronological, a poet of the 18th century, though he was alive until 1848. In 'Am Bàrd an Canada' he dwells with an astonishing concentration of realistic detail on the hardships of settlers in Canada. Very strictly, the poem is not a poem of the Clearances, inasmuch as Maclean himself was not evicted, but its truth would have been even keener in the case of victims of the Clearances than in Maclean's own case. Its sombre but powerful note makes it a bitterly pointed retort to the idyllic picture of America in the 'Oran eadar Dòmhnall agus Dùghall' of the Stewarts' Collection.

The period 1820 to 1860 was above all the period of the Clearances. During those years huge masses of the Highland population were uprooted, poverty was terribly increased, and the economic and social revolution was completed. There was also in those years the great emotional and intellectual change occasioned by the evangelical movement, and there was, naturally enough, a big break in the continuity of Gaelic poetry, and a characteristic 19th century Gaelic poetry emerged. How much that poetry was inferior in inspiration and tradition to 18th century Gaelic poetry, it is not my business at present to consider, but, apart from the technical degeneration that resulted from the exaggeration of artificial metrical stresses, which as Rev. William Matheson declares, was greatly influenced by the importation of Lowland airs, there is a great decline in full bloodedness of matter. As compared with 18th century Gaelic poetry, 19th century poetry is flabby and anaemic; it lacks power, gusto, spontaneity, joie de vivre. Of course, form and content are so much inter-related in poetry that a failing in one cannot be distinguished from a failing in the other. I am inclined to think that only in a certain broadening and deepening of human sympathy has 19th century poetry advanced on 18th century poetry. 19th century Gaelic poets have, on the whole, a more tender and comprehensive sense of humanity than is common in the well-known 18th century poets other than Dugald Buchanan and William Ross. In some ways, 18th century Gaelic poetry is the poetry of a splendid, thoughtless, full blooded youthfulness. 19th century poetry has nothing like its sheer power, but it has a more persistent feeling for humanity. I think that this development of a humanitarian quality is due mainly to the Clearances and the great evangelical movement, but as the poet was most often rather an outsider to the religious movement, the first cause is undoubtedly the more important. The humanist and religious strains coalesce in the scanty but fine poetry of Dr John MacLachlan, who, born in 1804 and dead in 1874, lived through the Clearances in a country where they were exceedingly severe, Morven, Sunart and Mull. MacLachlan is not a great poet, though many reasons could be adduced for declaring him the best Gaelic poet of his century. I deal with him first for chronological reasons. He is pre-eminently a poet of the Clearance period, as he died in 1874, the very year when the men of Bernera in Lewis supplied the first glimmering of Highland resurgence, and eight years before the Battle of the Braes made it unmistakeable. From all accounts — and I heard a few during my year in Mull — MacLachlan was a splendid human being, greater as a man than as a poet, and possibly the only completely revealing part of his poetry is that part motivated by the Clearances. Here there is a union of anger and piercing sorrow which, though common in 19th century Gaelic poetry, is not elsewhere expressed with the same intensity and control that some of MacLachlan's poems have. Such a poem is that beginning 'Och nan och 's mi so am ònar', and ending

> Nuair a chì mi na lagain àlainn,
> A h-uile àirigh do fàs le cóinnich,
> Fo bhadain chaorach le'n uain 'gan àrach,
> Chan fhaod mi ràdhtainn nach b'fhàidhe Tómas.

> *When I see the beautiful hollows,*
> *every shieling a waste with moss,*
> *under clumps of sheep rearing their lambs,*
> *I cannot say that Thomas was not a prophet.*

Better still is that one so reminiscent of the splendidly simple technique of 17th century song:

> Dìreadh a mach ri Beinn Shianta,
> Gur cianail tha mo smuaintean;

> A' faicinn na beinne 'na fàsaich
> 'S i gun àiteach air a h-uachdar.

> Sealltainn sìos thar a' bhealaich
> 'S ann agamsa tha an sealladh fuaraidh.

> 'S lìonmhor bothan bochd gun àird air,
> Air gach taobh 'na làraich uaine;

> Agus fàrdach tha gun mhullach
> Is 'na tulach aig an fhuaran.

> Far an robh an teine 's na pàisdean
> 'S ann as àirde dh'fhàs an luachair.

> *As I go up the face of Ben Hiant*
> *my thoughts are very sad;*

> *seeing the mountain a wilderness*
> *with no tillage on its face.*

> *As I look down over the pass*
> *the view I have is very chill.*

58

there is many a poor hut levelled,
a green site on every side;

and many a roofless dwelling
a mound beside a spring of water.

Where the fire and children were
the rushes grow the highest.

I do not know of any other poem of the 19th century that has more of the intensity and economy of the old ballad. The sense of complete desolation and the equation of personal and general loss is a common motif in Clearance poetry, but I think its most taut expression is in MacLachlan. There is in Clearance poetry a tendency to a vague generalised regret without a definiteness even of indictment, a common failure to face the real cause, but MacLachlan is explicit:

Ach fhir shanntaich rinn an droch bheairt,
Liuthad teaghlach bochd a ghluais thu.

But greedy one who did the evil deed,
many a poor family you moved.

An uncritical idealisation of the pre-Clearance period, so common in 19th century Gaelic poetry, is not frequent in MacLachlan, though it does occur in the poem beginning, 'Trom tiamhaidh mo chridhe ag imeachd troimh 'n ghleann'. As in most Clearance poetry, a nationalist spirit is evident in much of MacLachlan, and there is the common execration of the Lowland shepherd and shepherd farmer. That weakness in confusing the cause and effect of the Clearances is one of the intellectual failings of 19th century poetry, but in MacLachlan it is probably explained by the fact that most of the Clearers in his district, with the exception of the Duke of Argyll and MacLaine of Lochbuie, were Lowlanders, but MacLachlan's own aristocratic strain no doubt tends to preclude the expression of class hatred in his poetry. It is only too common a feature of Gaelic poetry to blame Englishmen and Lowlanders for the crimes of Highland chiefs. This tendency gets an absurd expression in Màiri Mhór's wish to drive the Sasunnaich from Skye, where nearly all the principal Clearers had names at least as Gaelic as her own.

The nationalist feeling that has only a partial and inconclusive expression in the poetry of MacLachlan had a complete expression in William Livingston, who indeed wasted much of his splendid power on themes like the campaigns of Wallace and Bruce, wars between Gaels and Norsemen, and between different clans. He has, however, a few poems such as 'Fios thun a' Bhàird' and 'Eirinn ag gul' that are contemporaneous and perhaps the finest Gaelic poems of the century. Livingston does not equal MacLachlan in poignancy, but in the stately expression of a proud anger and sorrow those two poems are unrivalled. It is not that 'Fios thun a' Bhàird' contains emotionally or intellectually anything really original, but its peculiar emotional blend and classic form makes it unique in the 19th century. Professor W J Watson has rightly said of 19th century poetry that it is the 'wail of a harassed and dejected people', but Livingston is strong and proud in sadness:

> Ged a roinneas gathan gréine
> Tlus nan speur ri blàths nan lòn,
> 'S ged a chithear spréidh air àirigh
> Is buailtean làn de àlach bhó,
> Tha Ile an diugh gun daoine:
> Chuir a' chaora a bailtean fàs;
> Mar a fhuair 's a chunnaic mise,
> Thoir am fios so thun a' bhàird.

> *Though sunbeams impart*
> *the balm of the skies to the warmth of the meadows,*
> *and though stock are seen on a shieling*
> *and folds full of the young of cattle,*
> *Islay is to-day without people:*
> *the sheep has laid waste its townships;*
> *As I found and as I saw:*
> *bring this message to the poet.*

And again:

> Tha 'n nathair bhreac 'na lùban
> Air an ùrlar far an d' fhàs
> Na fir mhóra chunnaic mise:
> Thoir am fios so thun a' bhàird.

> *The speckled adder is coiled*
> *on the floor where grew*
> *the big men whom I saw:*
> *Bring this message to the poet.*

Livingston's Gaelic nationalism makes him see the tragedies of Ireland and Scotland as one. To him the accursed Anglo-Saxon imperialism was the one and only cause of the sufferings of both countries, and therefore his verse is devoid of the narrowness that makes other Gaelic poets of his time shut their eyes to the exploitation of their fellow Gaels in Ireland. To Livingston, Islay of Clan Donald and Ireland of O'Donnell, O'Neill and Maguire, were near in geography and nearer in blood, history and culture, and Ireland's tragedy was greater even than Scotland's. Strangely enough, I find this sympathy for Ireland only in one other poet of the time, Lady D'Oyly, one of the MacLeods of Raasay, one of the very few old Highland aristocratic families unstained by Clearances:

Tha a' Ghàidhealtachd is Eirinn
Fo dhóruinn 's fo éigin,
'S an Gall bho thìr gu tìr.

Gaeldom and Ireland are
under grief and dire need,
with the non-Gael (dominating) from land to land.

While a historical nationalism is perhaps the chief motif of Livingston's poetry, an unusual blend of Christian feeling and a sense of class exploitation is the chief motif of the poetry of John Smith, who is placed first among Lewis poets by Mr John N MacLeod. To me the poetry of Smith seems deficient in lyricism, but I think he has by far the most comprehensive reflective power of any Gaelic poet of the 19th century. Smith has a profound feeling for the suffering, folly and wickedness of man, and such an understanding of the causes of the Highland Clearances and their place in the development of capitalism that I should say he is an exception to all I have said of the intellectual weakness of 19th century Gaelic poetry. For instance, Smith correlates the Highland Clearances and the forcing of opium on China in a way that puts his political intelligence above any well-known English poet of his day except Morris. The radicalism of Smith's poetry is all the more remarkable because he died in 1881, and is thus chronologically in the period of the authentic Celtic Gloom. I use 'Celtic Gloom' in the sense in which it is used by Professor W J Watson in his introduction to *Bàrdachd Ghàidhlig*, not at all to indicate the largely bogus movement that arose from foreign imagination.

In tone, the bulk of 19th century Gaelic poetry belongs to the period of hopelessness, whether it belongs to it chronologically or not. Many of the poets who were writing before 1880 lived a considerable time after that date, as, for example, Dugald MacPhail, John Campbell, Donald Mackechnie, Neil MacLeod, Henry Whyte, Malcolm Mac-Farlane, and Màiri Mhór. Accordingly, their poetry is sometimes in

61

tone of the period before 1880 and sometimes of the period immediately after. Before dealing with them however, I shall say a little of the innumerable songs by obscure authors that reflect the Highland spirit at the depths of the Clearance period, the fifty years from 1820 to 1870.

Of the three poets with whom I have been dealing, MacLachlan is the most typical of the Clearance period, Livingston's strong national feeling and Smith's intellect making their poetry not so typical of the Clearance dejection as is much of the poetry of Neil MacLeod, Mackechnie and others, who were born late enough to experience the Land League resurgence while in their prime, but perhaps the most typical of all Clearance poetry is to be found in the mass of lyrics by unknown or obscure authors that bulks so big in a collection like Sinclair's *Oranaiche*, published in 1879. Very many of the songs deal exclusively with the Clearances, but many more consist of records of personal experience, the emotional problems of individuals involved in emigration resulting directly or indirectly from the Clearances. Of those songs which are only implicitly of the Clearances, one of the greatest and most famous is a very poignant and simple song by Donald MacCuithein, of Totascore in Skye, 'C'àit an caidil an nìghneag an nochd?' I am thinking of the proper version of it as published by *Mac Talla*, not of the uncritical 'improvement' of it, an 'improvement' which tinges it with romantic convention. It is a record of private sorrow arising ultimately from a Clearance. Another such song is the poem sometimes attributed to Donald Mackechnie, 'Och nan och 's na bheil air m'aire', perfect in a moving simplicity. Of course, in this song the motif is emigration in general, whether resulting from Clearances I do not know. Another very great song, 'Ged tha mi gun chrodh gun aighean', has an emigration motif, which is probably not of the Clearances. This song is addressed to a soldier, and is an example of the difficulty of differentiating between poetry of the Clearances and of emigration in general, for it is certain that a great number of the Highlanders who became soldiers in the first three-quarters of the 19th century, must have been driven to the Army by the economic stringency that was so greatly increased by the Clearances.

I need instance only these, but it is obvious that the Clearances and emigration resulting directly or indirectly are by far the most persistent single motif in 19th century poetry, love poems, patriotic poems, poems of nostalgia, and even nature poems reflecting the tragedy of the Highland people. I have included nature poems among the kinds deeply affected by the Clearances, and this at once suggests the great

62

difference between nature poetry in the 18th century and nature poetry in the 19th century. Nature poetry of the former century, which reaches its supreme expression in Duncan Macintyre and Alexander MacDonald, is a splendid thing, one of the three or four greatest manifestations of the Gaelic genius, but in a way it is rather unconcerned with humanity. Probably this relative unconcern with humanity was essential to its objectivity, but there is a startling difference between it and the very humanised nature poetry of the 19th century. One of the central themes of Clearance poetry is the contrast between unchanging, flourishing nature and human desolation. It is in MacLachlan, Livingston, Neil MacLeod, and almost all the 19th century poets. I take an example at random, 'Gleann Chill a' Mhàrtainn', by an obscure poet, Gillies. Of its twelve verses, only the first two are really nature poetry, the rest are occupied with the glen's human desolation:

> Ach bho'n thàinig caochladh air an taobh so,
> Dh'fhalbh na daoine, chan 'eil iad ann,
> 'S bho thàinig caoraich cho pailt air raointean
> 'S e dh'fhàg mi faondrach anns an àm.

> *But since a change has come over this district*
> *the people have gone, they are here no more,*
> *and since sheep have become so numerous on fields,*
> *I am rootless at this time.*

This is only one of hundreds of such poems. There is quite a common variation on the theme: in many poems the ravages wrought on man are aggravated by ravages even on the face of nature. Such a poem is the well-known song by Angus MacMhuirich, an expression of nostalgia and a contemplation of the physical and human desolation of Mull. It is to me a curiously affecting poem, ingenuous, even naive, commonplace in theme and rhythm, yet spontaneous and moving:

> Rinn peirceall chaorach fearann a dhaoradh,
> 'S dh'innis dhuinn daoine an fhàisneachd,
> Gun cuireadh iad gaisgich nan gleannaibh air faondradh,
> 'S dùthaich nan laoch 'na fàsaich.

> Tha fearann ar gaoil fo fhraineach 's fo fhraoch
> 'S gach machair is raon gun àiteach,
> 'S chan fhada bhios duine ann am Muile nan craobh,
> Ach Goill agus caoraich bhàna.

> *The jaws of sheep have made land dear*
> *and men have told us the prophecy,*

that they would uproot the heroes of the glens
and make the land of the brave men a wilderness.

The land of our love is under bracken and heather
and every plain and field untilled,
and soon there will be no-one in Mull of the trees
but Lowlanders and white sheep.

The artlessness of Angus MacMhuirich's song is very different from the highly conscious art of Donald MacIver's famous poem, 'An Ataireachd Ard'. MacMhuirich sees the visible and particular change in the face of Mull, but MacIver rises to a contemplation of universal change. It crystallises, by the skilful blending of the idea of human desolation and a mournful sound in nature, a mood of universal sadness, a sense of the transience of the world, which is outraged by the futile wickedness of the man who has wrought a cruel change in the life of man and on the face of external nature, which would, at any rate, change without human violence. The blending of open vowels, *ua*, *ò* and *à* is part of its wonderful effect.

Nostalgia is the most common sentiment in 19th century Gaelic poetry, and there is a huge body of verse that says nothing explicitly about the Clearances, but that an emigrant's sadness pervades. Indeed some poets specialise in a generalised nostalgia that neither explains nor attacks; hence arises a whole poetry of nostalgia, which is still common. Much of it is sincere and convincing, but it is a greatly overworked motif. Indeed much recent Gaelic verse would make one think that it is the only Gaelic motif, but in the 19th century it was still the dynamic of fine songs like 'An t-Eilean Muileach', which has a kind of typical glow. 'An t-Eilean Muileach' has no direct reference to the Clearances, but that other well-known poem by MacPhail, 'A Dhòmhnaill Bhig', has the passing reference that is so common:

Is iomadh cearn d'an d'rinn iad sgaoileadh,
Deas is tuath air feadh an t-saoghail:
'S iad na Goill 's na caoirich mhaola
Chuir mo dhaoine air allaban.

There is many a part to which they have scattered,
south and north throughout the world:
the Lowlanders and the hornless sheep
have made poor wanderers of my people.

Very often, as here, this passing reference has a poignancy that heightens an otherwise mediocre poem, but it is a reflection of the weakness of 19th century poetry that this passing reference is often the whole expressed reaction to the Clearances. It is only rarely, as with MacLachlan, Livingston, Smith, and later, Neil MacLeod and Mary MacPherson, that one finds a pre-occupation with the fate of the Gael that lasts the length of a whole poem. There are, of course, numerous exceptions to this limitation to the passing reference. Such an exception is 'Oran do bhochdaibh na rìoghachd', by Calum Campbell MacPhail, a remarkably vigorous attack on the evicting landlords, invoking Gaelic nationalist and strong class feeling, full of a virile contempt for the exploiters, and bitterly declamatory:

> Nuair thòisicheas an streupaid
>   Thig feum air a' bhochd,
> Bidh daoin' uaisle 'gan glaodhaich
>   Bhàrr aodann nan cnoc;
> Freagraidh mac-talla iad:
>   'Chan eagal duibh 'sa' chàs,
> Is pailteas chaoraich-mhaola
>   Ri aodann a' bhlàir.'

> *When the strife of war begins*
>   *the poor will come to be needed,*
> *gentry will be shouting for them*
>   *over the faces of the hills;*
> *Echo will answer them:*
>   *'There is no fear for you in this matter,*
> *when there is an abundance of hornless sheep*
>   *facing the field (of battle).'*

Another such is 'Oran na Bàirlinn', where there is the same anger at the injustice done to the Gael, and the more rare sense of shame for their subjection.

It is a remarkable characteristic of the poetry of the Clearances that it is mostly retrospective. Poetry has nothing like the contemporary prose accounts either written originally in English or translated from Gaelic. There is nothing like the detailed descriptions in verse that Alexander MacDonald and John Roy Stewart and others give of Hanoverian ravages after Culloden, but then 19th century Gaelic verse has not the stomach for strong realism that they had in the 18th century, and its greater subjectivity tends to make it describe a mood rather than a scene. Again Calum Campbell MacPhail is an exception, as in 'Oran na Bàirlinn', where he gives a contemporary comment on a Skye Clearance, and calls all Gaels to resist.

As a rule, the Gaelic poet of the Clearances is a Gael speaking to Gaels, but sometimes he addresses the rulers of the Empire with the question: Why this treatment of the Gael, who is of such great military value? Sometimes there is a pathetic confusion, as in John Campbell's 'Is toigh leam a' Ghàidhealtachd', in which he says:

Nis tha dùthaich ar gaoil fo chaoraich 's fo fhéidh,
Sinn 'gar fuadach thar sàile mar bhàrrlach gun fheum.

Now the land of our love is under sheep and deer,
ourselves being driven away like useless scum.

But he goes on to declare that, no matter what happens, the Gael will always be available for military duty as he was of yore, smashing Napoleon Czar Nicholas and giving freedom to India. Imperialist dope had badly muddled John Campbell, but it is a sad reflection on the political acumen of the Highlander that his song should be so much better known than that of a Lewisman, Malcolm MacKay, who very correctly assessed the role of the Highland soldier in the Boer War:

Tha àireamh nach gann
Anns a' chogadh á Leódhas,
A' cosanadh dhaimean
Is saoibhreas do chàch;
Bidh mise 'gan caoidh
'S mar is tric iad ri m'inntinn,
Am beatha 'ga call
Airson ghleanntaichean fàs.

There is no small number
from Lewis in the war,
earning diamonds and wealth for others;
I will be lamenting them
and they are most of the time on my mind,
their lives being lost
in return for desolate glens.

Of course, in the eighties Lewis put up a stronger fight than Argyll did, perhaps a stronger fight than even Skye did. I find a reflection of this in the uncompromising note in the verse of three Lewismen, John Smith, Malcolm MacKay and Donald MacDonald, the last of whom was one of those whom Màiri Mhór acclaims as 'ceatharnaich Bheàr-naraidh' with a pride and approbation she usually reserves for 'fir mhóra a' Bhràighe', but it must be added that John Campbell was already an old man in the eighties, and really belongs to the period of hopeless subjection, while MacKay is typical of the poets of the eighties, who express the crofter resurgence.

The change of temper that was brought into Gaelic poetry by the crofter struggles in the eighties is clearly manifested in the difference between nearly all the political poems of Sinclair's *Oranaiche*, published in 1879, and the new hope that is seen in the later poetry in *Modern Gaelic Bards*, published in 1908, and *Bàrdachd Leódhais*, published in 1916. Some of the poets of the second and third collections were dead or out of action by 1880, but the majority were in their prime about that year, and thus both collections contain poems that have not one ray of hope, and other poems that are even optimistic. Sometimes there is this difference between different poems by the same author; thus the later poems of Neil MacLeod are optimistic compared with his earlier.

The crofter resistance, which made Skye the cynosure of Britain in 1882 and developed into the Lewis Deer Hunt in 1887, is naturally most strongly reflected in the poetry of Skye and Lewis, but the two islands were linked in the person of a famous Argyll man, Donald MacCallum. The Rev. Donald MacCallum, who was imprisoned for the unministerial offence of 'inciting the lieges to class hatred', was not much of a poet, but his direct, forceful, unadorned verse expresses great courage and optimism. In 'Cumail suas an cliù gu bràth' he uses the metre of Neil MacLeod's despondent poem, 'An Gleann san robh mi òg', to sing of the manliness of the crofters of Bernera, Valtos, Crossbost, Siadar, Park and Aiginish in preventing the desolation of Lewis, and, as he was greater as a man than as a poet, it is no wonder that Màiri Mhór said of him:

Chunnaic sinn bristeadh na fàire
Is neòil na tràillealachd air chall
An là a sheas MacCaluim làmh ruinn
Aig Beul-Atha-Nan-Trì-Allt.

We saw the breaking of the horizon
and the clouds of slavery dispelled
on the day MacCallum stood with us
at the Confluence of the Three Burns.

MacCallum's poem, 'Cumail suas an cliù gu bràth', when compared with its technical model, 'An gleann san robh mi òg', shows the change of temper that the Land League brought into Gaelic poetry, for 'An Gleann san robh mi òg' is anterior to 1882, the crucial year. It is therefore a poem of the Clearance period, while MacCallum's poem is a poem of the resurgence. Thus the difference in tone is politically significant as well as indicative of the difference in temperament between the militant MacCallum and the gentle and retiring Neil MacLeod. Neil MacLeod is, however, a poet of both periods, but it is noteworthy that the best known and most characteristic of his poems are those of the earlier period. A hundred people know 'An gleann san robh mi òg' for every single person who knows 'Òran nan Croiteirean'. Indeed that has obscured the duality of MacLeod's verse: one tends to think of him as of the Clearance period and not of the Land League period. The truth is, however, that Neil MacLeod composed the majority of his poems after the crofter struggle had begun, and that there is expressed in nearly all those poems a new hope. MacLeod did not enter into the crofter struggle whole-heartedly; he had no deficiency in intellect, and his fine sensitive nature reacted keenly to the tragedy of his people, but he was incapable of expressing a militant ardour. It is not that he kept anything back; his whole poetry is permeated with sorrow for the dispersal of the Gaels, and it evinces as great a pre-occupation as that of any other 19th century poet, with the results of the Clearances and the possibilities of the Land League, but even his most hopeful poems seem pessimistic at the core. His hope does not ring as true as his sorrow. Indeed he appears to have had no great zest for life and to have had too keen a sense of the essential sadness of a transient existence to enter very strongly into any struggle. It would appear that the misfortune of his people had so struck him that, even when he was outwardly optimistic, there was a background of melancholy and dejection. He was incapable of bitterness and incapable of the adequate expression of strong indignation, and he saw human life as sad whether the sorrow was of a particular or universal nature. To me his typical utterance is:

Chaochail madainn ait ar n-òige
Mar an ceò air bhàrr nam beann;
Tha ar càirdean 's ar luchd eòlais
Air am fògradh bhos is thall;
Tha cuid eile dhiubh nach gluais,
Tha an cadal fuar fo'n fhòd,
Bha gun uaill, gun fhuath, gun anntlachd
Anns a' ghleann san robh iad òg.

The joyous morning of our youth has changed
like the mist on the top of the mountains;
our kinsmen and our acquaintances
are driven away in this country and over the sea;
there are others of them who will not move,
who are in a cold sleep under the turf,

people who were without pride, hatred or malice
in the glen in which they were young.

Or

Ach tha am fàrdaichean sguaibte
’S an seòmraichean uaine;
Iad fhéin is an gaisge
’Nan cadal fo’n fhòd;
’S tha osag nam fuar bheann
Le h-osnaidhean gruamach
’Gan caoidh mu na cruachan
’S a’ luaidh air an glòir.

But their dwellings are swept
and their rooms green;
they themselves and their heroism
asleep under the turf;
and the breeze of the cold mountains
with its gloomy sighs
laments them about the heights
and speaks of their glory.

It is typical of such a man that he sees happiness only in retrospect, as in the idyllic opening of 'Anns a' ghleann san robh mi òg'. For these reasons I find MacLeod's later and more militant verse, even a song like 'Oran nan croiteirean', which is in the metre of 'Agus hó Mhórag', unconvincing. The poem has brave, hopeful, even optimistic verses, but I cannot help feeling that it is more an echo of the unconquerable MacDonald than a profound expression of Neil MacLeod. Poetic sincerity is not the same thing as moral sincerity, and I think that 'Oran nan croiteirean', though the expression of a sincere man, is not poetically sincere. Neil MacLeod gave to the cause of the crofters as much as he was constitutionally capable of giving, but he could hardly be militant. As poetry, he is difficult to assess: it is exquisite in modulation and even in general technique, but too thin in texture of form and content to justify the claim that he is among the greatest Gaelic poets. Nevertheless, I think that its technical perfection, however limited a perfection it is, and its record of a finely sensitive nature, and its exquisite, if rather thin, lyrical note will ensure it a permanence co-extensive with the permanence of the Gaelic language.

What Neil MacLeod was by temperament incapable of giving to the cause of the crofter was supplied in full measure by a very different person, Mary MacDonald, variously known as Mrs MacPherson,

Màiri Nighean Iain Bhàin or Màiri Mhór nan Oran. In quantity she gave as much as almost all the other 19th century poets put together.

I have kept Màiri Mhór to the end though she was twenty years older than Neil MacLeod and though, in many ways, her verse has more kinship with older Gaelic poetry than the verse of MacLeod and most of the others I have mentioned, because she impressed herself on the Highland people as par excellence the poet of the Land League.

It is not easy to give a consistent account of Màiri Mhór's poetry, as she herself was the least logical of people. The only logic in her poetry is a logic of feeling and inconsistencies abound. She composed a flattering elegy on one of the worst landlords in Skye in her own time; she married a fine poem with trivial compliments on the marriage of the greater landlord who was the arch-enemy of the heroes, the men of Braes; she forbore to say anything against another enemy of her people because he had a good grandfather; and she attacked the English for their doings in Skye, although it was very plain that not one Clearance had been made in Skye by anyone who had not a name as Gaelic as her own. In spite of all that, she gave a great deal to the cause of the crofters, following every phase of the struggle closely and keenly, and when it came to a choice between the crofters and some of the people whom she had complimented, she was always uncompromisingly on the crofters' side. Mairi had a respect for *uaisle*, a respect that was absurd in the Skye of the 'Eighties, and it was difficult for her to attack anyone who bore a name that had been great in Skye tradition.

Màiri Mhór is so much a poet of the Land League that one is very apt to forget that most of her life was lived in the period before the Land League. Her sanguine, militant temperament is partly the cause of this misconception, but the chief cause is, of course, that she composed no poetry until the wrong she herself suffered in 1872 put an edge on her nature and liberated her expression.

Mairi has told again and again what gave birth to her poetry:

'S e na dh'fhuiling mi de thàmailt
A thug mo bhàrdachd beò.

*It is all the shame I suffered
that made my poetry live.*

Some think that her poetry might as well have stayed where it was, but I do not agree with those who consider her of little account. It is true that she is often garrulous even to absurdity; that she is often frequently and even amusingly prosaic; that she had apparently no kind of discrimination, but to me she has, not sometimes but often, a convincing lyrical cry, a strange evocative quality, and a simple, as it were unconscious, power that no other 19th century poet has. Of course, it is difficult for any Skyeman, who has a strong feeling for Skye and a certain conception of it, to speak coldly of Màiri Mhór, for her native land was in her blood, as it was in the blood of Duncan Macintyre and Domhnull MacFhionnlaigh nan Dàn. By her native land I mean not Scotland nor the Highlands but Skye and even then only that part of Skye bounded by Lochs Bracadale, Snizort, Sligachan, and the Sound of Raasay. It is not of her great roll-calls of Skye names that I am thinking; sometimes these have been compared to glorified tourist guides, though at other times they have their own evocative power. What I am thinking of is that glorious pride in her own people and her own soil, and that warmth for them that takes everything for granted, that neither invites nor expects questions. Màiri Mhór does not trail her coat to say, 'Skye is the best of all lands'. It would seem to her an obvious and unnecessary statement. For that reason, she is, above all others, poet of the people, and it was inevitable that the Clearances and crofter struggle would be an obsession to her, but the Skye of Skyes was in her youth, just before the Clearances, and it was in that Skye that her pride and joy was unqualified. Many Gaelic poets have idealised the pre-Clearance period, but no one else has idealised it with the same robust *joie de vivre* and the same lack of conventional romanticism of Màiri Mhór. I myself, who am left cold by the idyllic glen of Neil MacLeod, cannot resist Màiri's idealisation, which throws to the winds all romantic convention:

Nuair thigeadh an Fhéill Mhàrtainn
'S an spréidh 's am bàrr air dòigh,
Na fir a' dèanamh càinnteig;
'S na plàtaichean 'nan tòrr;
Ri taobh na brìg bhuntàta
Bhiodh baraille làn de dh'fheòil:
Sud mar chàidh ar n-àrach
Ann an Eilean àrd a' cheò.

When Martinmas came
and the livestock and crops put right,
the men making heather ropes
and the rush-made bags in a heap;
beside the built heap of potatoes
there would be a barrel full of meat:
that was how we were reared
in the high Island of the Mist.

I have purposely taken an extreme example to illustrate the point that Màiri's poetry is the most convincing expression of the joys of a peasant life that had gone that is to be found in the poetry of her time. This expression is undoubtedly heightened by nostalgic retrospect, but it has a splendid glow in a poem like 'Nuair bha mi òg', a song that has taken the hearts of Highlanders, and is showing a stubborn permanence that cannot be disregarded by the most fastidious.

I think Màiri Mhór had the qualities and defects that make a popular poet, a poet of the people, and I believe that her limitations have been exaggerated and her merits depreciated. I grant that it is not possible to take any one poem of hers, except 'Nuair bha mi òg', and say that it is truly a fine poem, but to me at least the cumulative effect of her poetry is very convincing. She was so near the people whose lives she sang; her poetry has such an immediate contact and such an utter lack of affection of any kind, of any self-consciousness, such a contagious *joie de vivre*, and at times such a poignancy of feeling, that I think it has not received anything like its due except in popular esteem.[1] I respect the popular feeling for Gaelic song that was. Before Mods, radio and gramophone records had created a taste for non-entities, Duncan Bàn was the most popular Gaelic poet.

The Crofters' Commission and the resulting Act did much. It stopped Clearances and the worst rack-renting, but it did not give back to the people the good land. Therefore it did not end the struggle, and Màiri Mhór was militant to the end. The popularity of 'Ged tha mo cheann air liathadh' and 'Soraidh leis an àit' has obscured the best part of her poetry, those militant poems in very competent 17th and 18th century verse forms, mingling reminiscence sometimes proud and joyous, and sometimes, as in 'Soraidh leis an nollaig ùr', wonderfully poignant, and following every phase of the struggle. Sometimes there is terrible anger as in 'Freagradh Màiri gu Gàidheil Ghrianaig'; sometimes there are surprising turns like the piquant comment on the clergy in 'Clach Ard Uige'.

Tha luchd teagaisg cho beag cùraim,
Faicinn càradh mo luchd dùthcha;
'S iad cho balbh air anns a' chùbaid,
'S ged bu bhrùidean bhiodh 'gan éisdeachd.

Preachers care so little
seeing the condition of my countrymen,
so dumb about it in the pulpit
as if their audience were brute beasts.

Sometimes there are most revealing touches, as that comment on the religious obsession:

> Tha 'n sluagh air fàs cho iongantach
> 'S gur cruithneachd leotha bròn.
>
> *The people have grown so strange*
> *that sorrow is wheat to them.*

And that comment on her own natural paganism:

> Ach bho'n is luibh an dìomhanas
> A riaraicheas an fheòil,
> Tha i leantuinn rium cho daingeann
> 'S tha am barr-iall ris a' bhròig.
>
> *But since vanity is a plant*
> *that satisfies the flesh,*
> *it clings to me as firmly*
> *as the shoe-lace to the shoe.*

At other times, however, she could express most exemplary orthodoxy. Pride and triumph, as in 'Ceatharnaich Bheàrnaraidh' and 'Oran Beinn Lì', alternate with a wistful sorrow for what is irretrievably gone, as in 'Ag ath-ùrachadh m'eòlais':

> Leagh mo chridhe stigh an Udairn,
> Sgoirebreac fo bheachd mo shùilean,
> Bha na laoich a dhèanadh tùbh rium
> Fad o'n dùthaich 's iad fo'n talamh.
>
> *My heart melted coming in by the Udairn,*
> *Sgoirebreac in the vision of my eyes,*
> *the good men who would remember their kinship to me*
> *far from their land and under the earth.*

Sometimes there is an amazing zest for life; often there is a mingling of many emotions. Sometimes there are such fearless attacks on people she does all but name that one feels it ungracious and ungrateful ever to accuse her of any failure in consistent courage. At other times she senses her own mistakes. For instance, in 'Duilleag gu Gàidheil Chanada', she recognises her own folly in attacking the English, and makes a most direct attack on the rack-renting, absentee landlords of Skye, who enjoyed in London the fruits of their exploitation of her people. Here there is no doubt whom she is attacking.

73

There is also optimism about the future which the subsequent history of the Highlands hardly justifies, and an acute and unusual shame for the subjection of the Clearance period. The last poem in her collected works, 'Fàistneachd agus Beannachd do na Gàidheil', has the splendid warmth and the brave optimism in full, and that remarkable sinking of her own personality in the sorrows, joys and hopes of her people:

'S nuair bhios mise 's na bòrdaibh
Bidh mo chòmhradh mar fhàistneachd,

'S pillidh gineal na tuatha
Rinneadh fhuadach thar sàile.

'S bidh na baigearan uasal
Air an ruaig mar bha iadsan;

Féidh is caoraich 'gan cuibhleadh
'S bidh na glinn air an àiteach;

Am cur is ám buana
'S ám duais do na meàirlich;

'S théid na tobhtachan fuara
Thogail suas le ar càirdean.

And when I am in the boards
my words will be as a prophecy,

and there will return the stock of the tenantry
who were driven over the sea.

And the 'beggars' of gentry
will be routed as they (the crofters) were;

deer and sheep will be wheeled away
and the glens will be tilled;

a time of sowing and of reaping
and a time of reward for the robbers;

and the cold ruined stances of houses
will be built up by our kinsmen.

That the prophecy has failed of fulfilment is not the fault of the big, brave heart of Màiri Mhór nan Oran.

NOTES
1   This was written before I had read Mr Murdo Murray's fine paper in Vol. XXXVII of the *Transactions*.

Aspects of Gaelic poetry

When I think of ancient and modern Gaelic poetry, there are few qualities which I fail to find in its varied manifestations except those ascribed to it by Ossianists and Twilightists and some later 'Celtologists'. We have heard of 'Celtic romance', 'Celtic sentiment', 'Celtic love of words', and so on, as if Gaelic poetry were all of a piece, as if there were any reason in the world why one Gaelic poet might not be as different from another as Shelley is from Chaucer. I am inclined to think Gaelic poetry is as varied in mood as English poetry, and in technique it is more varied. Hence it is no easier to talk about Gaelic poetry in general than it is to talk about any other poetry in general.

The only generalisation I would commit myself to is that, whatever else it may have, Gaelic poetry has style and is *de la musique avant toute chose*, and that is true whether it is at its 'simplest' or at its most self-conscious. The old song 'Mo Nighean Donn á Còrnaig' has music and style, just as 'Oran Mór Mhic Leòid' has them. This music and style is as surely heard in 'Uamh an Oir' as in Sinclair's 'Slighe nan Sean Seun'! The music may be the heady intoxicating music of MacDonald's 'Moladh Móraig' or 'Pìob Mhór Mhic Cruimein'; the 'echoing detonations' of William Ross's 'Suaithneas Bàn'; the great rises and falls and sweeps, the subtly varied and haunting cadences of 'Oran Mór Mhic Leòid'; the poignant simplicity of 'Na féidh am Bràigh Uige'; the hiss and clang of consonants that express Iain Lom's wrath, or the stately sweeps and swells of rhythm that express the line of Ben Dorain and the smaller eddies that express the welling of water on its side. There is no need to make any bones about it: Scottish Gaelic is, at any rate where auditory sensuousness is concerned, a superb language for poetry.

I see that Mr Bowra attributes much of the quality of Russian poetry to the intrinsic quality of the Russian language and not least to its beauty of sound, though he denies it the strength of ancient Greek. I am quite sure that Scottish Gaelic has as much beauty, variety, strength and magnificence of sound as ancient Greek or any Western European language. Metrically Gaelic can do anything English has done, but the metric of the great bulk of Gaelic poetry is impossible in

75

English. Hence Gaelic verse can never be even approximately rendered in English. Even in syntax the translator is faced with a hopeless task because Gaelic has a unique capacity for expressing varieties and shades and changes of emphasis, which English can never approximate. English translations from Gaelic which try to be accurate, will always have clumsy inversions to indicate changes of word order which in Gaelic are perfectly natural and very brief and neat.

I know that my preference for the musical overtones of Gaelic poetry to the musical overtones of any other poetry I know may be due to Gaelic's being my first language, but then I prefer the sound of Greek poetry to the sound of English, Lowland Scots, Latin or French poetry, and I certainly knew English and some Lowland Scots from the age of six onwards. A very learned professor whose learning is primarily in the Classical and Celtic languages once said to me: 'I know no poetry as musical as the old Bardic poetry.' He was referring to the pre-17th century court poetry of Ireland and Scotland. Another professor, of Classics this time, talked to me about the 'wonderful music' of some modern Gaelic poetry. Even in the 19th century, when in most cases the music and style of Gaelic poetry became relatively shoddy, there is a nobleness of both in the best poetry of Livingston and John MacLachlan, a grace, delicacy and polish in Neil MacLeod, and amid all her ramblings Mary MacPherson has a strong and poignant music. In the 20th century, Donald Sinclair has music which is at once ornate, unusual and evocative. But up to the end of the 18th century music and *loinn* or 'grace' are *omnipresent* in Gaelic poetry.

I often wonder whether any one making poetry in the Germanic dialects spoken in the British Isles has equalled in real poetic greatness the old Lowland Scots Ballads, and similarly I wonder whether any one making poetry in the Celtic dialects has equalled those anonymous or obscurely authored Gaelic songs of the 16th, 17th and 18th centuries. Whereas the Scots Ballads are primarily narrative with what Croce would call great 'lyric' peaks, the Gaelic songs are primarily lyrical with the story sometimes told fairly fully, sometimes only implied. All those poems are direct and immediate. Technically they are simple but adequate, their metrical basis being the old syllabic structure modified by speech stress (I think that is the most permanently satisfying basis for Gaelic metrics). They have their own astonishing music, apart from the glorious melodies to which most of them are sung, or were sung — melodies which seem to grow out of the words themselves. Generally they are passionate, but the emotional range is considerable; sometimes there is a mingling of emotions and frequently a detached comment on emotion. They have an exquisite visual as well as auditory sensuousness, for the sharp and exquisite expression of delight in nature is a very old thing in Gaelic poetry (compare, for example, Deirdre's Farewell to Scotland, or the ancient poem on Arran), and the images are from man's handiwork as well. One hears of 'gold candlesticks on white tables' as well as of the eye which is 'bluer than on a calm morning the blaeberry behind its leaves'. The vivid precise touches of description in those songs are very different from the bogus compound words which in the English versions of Mrs Kennedy-Fraser or Rev. Kenneth MacLeod have as an inevitable part the word 'dream'. Sometimes, however, there is a concentration in which the imagery takes short-cuts, as in this verse from the matchless Lament for Gregor of Glenstrae, executed at Taymouth in 1571:

> Though I am without apples,
> When all the rest have apples,
> My fragrant round apple has
> The back of his head to the ground.

This poem, which purports to be by the Campbell wife of Gregor, whom her Campbell kinsmen executed, is surely one of the greatest poems ever made in Britain. In it there is almost everything that there could be in such a poem: pride, remembrance of past happiness, desire for revenge but realisation of what that revenge would mean to other women, tenderness and anxiety for the infant son, fear that he will never avenge his father, and piercing lonely sorrow.

> When other men's wives are at home
> Lying and quietly sleeping,
> I shall be at the edge of your flag-stone
> Beating my two hands. . .

> I wish my father were in a sickness
> And Grey Colin in a plague
> Though Ruthven's daughter would be
> Rubbing her palms and hands. . .

> If I were in the lark's shape,
> Gregor's strength in my hand,
> The highest stone of the castle (would be)
> The stone nearest the ground.

But every single verse is almost equally breath-taking; musically it is beyond words.

The Lament for Gregor Roy is only one of the very many great Gaelic laments by obscure and unknown poets. In the expression of love, pride and sorrow those poems are unequalled. Just as the death of John Garve MacLeod of Raasay in 1671 occasioned one of the greatest of all the MacCrimmon pibrochs, it also occasioned a series of wonderful elegies by his sister, elegies in which pride and sorrow are heroic and tender:

> You without silk on your pillow
> On the cold flat stones of the sea,
> In an ebbless clachan
> My love is on his couch.

Or again:

> There was a time when I did not think,
> Though it is vain to protest it,
> That you would ever be drowned
> On a wide sea,
> While the rudder remained,
> And you behind her rigging,
> In spite of the violence of the elements
> And the uproar of the sea;
> While her planks and tackle
> Held fast
> And she could respond
> To your strong hand on the sea.

Again and again the notes of love, pride and desolation are heard, sometimes in an enumeration of 'prosaic' details very different from the conventional Twilight ideas. Take for instance the Lament for William Chisholm who was killed at Culloden:

> O young Charles Stewart,
> It is your cause that desolated me.
> You took from me all I had,
> In war for your sake.
> Not cows and not sheep
> I mourn, but my first love,
> Though I am left alone
> With nothing in the world but a shirt.

This matter-of-factness adds poignancy to many of those old poems, as in the far older poem 'Ailein Duinn, a nì 's a nàire':

Brown haired Allan, my treasure and shame,
Sore and dear I paid my rent to you:
Not cows in calf nor white sheep,
Not boll nor peck nor heap of grain,
Not goods nor gear nor furniture,
But the cargo that the boat spilt.
My father was on her and my three brothers
And the son of my body whom I reared;
But it is not they who pained and tortured me,
But he who had taken my hand . . .

Sometimes, as in the other 'Ailein Duinn' poem, there is the expression of complete love and sorrow:

My prayer, God on the throne,
That I go not in earth or linen,
In hole in the ground or hiding-place,
But in the spot where you went, Allan.

Such piercing grief is different from the equally complete expression of quiet heart-break of 'Na féidh am Bràigh Uige'.

It is true that some of the very greatest of the obscure Gaelic poems are tragedies purely of circumstances, poems of bereavement, but there is also the expression of a different passion:

You took the east from me and you took the west from me,
You took the moon and you took the sun from me,
And almost, white love, you took my God from me.

Or again:

You killed my father and my husband,
I love you, Black Allan of Lochy;
You killed my three young brothers,
I love you, Black Allan of Lochy;
Allan, Allan, I rejoice that you are alive.

I have harped only on one or two notes of this Gaelic poetry but not all of the greatest of them are laments or poems of terrible passion. There is the pain and love and uncertainty of 'Mas ann 'gam mhealladh', rhythmically and sensuously delicate and lovely:

I was late last night with you in a dream
Over in Jura of the cold mountains,

Your kisses were like green water-cress,
But the dream is gone and the pain has stayed.

And in Beathag Mhór's song to Martin Martin there are all in one
poem gaiety, bitterness, pride, generosity, and bravery. In the song to
the 'daughter of the heir of Strath Swordale' there is morning
freshness, and joy and wistful memories as well, while in the charming
expression of gentle wisdom and quiet joy 'Mac Og an Iarla Ruaidh' is
perfect. Indeed the subtle emotional blend of many of those songs is
very often even more wonderful than the unfailing beauty of style and
music, the immediate, the unaffected grace and the evocative phrases.
If Gaelic poetry consisted only of those anonymous song poems, I
should say that the Gaels were a people who had many rare poets, and
before the end of the 18th century a great tradition of folk-poetry in
which it is quite impossible to distinguish between the work of an
aristocrat and a peasant, between Beathag Mhór and the daughter of
Red Duncan of Glen Lyon, whose fame as a patron of poets was as
great in Ireland as in Scotland. In the 18th century the humble
Duncan MacIntyre is capable of a delicacy and virtuosity unexcelled
by the learned Ewen MacLachlan or the very 'well-educated' Alexander MacDonald ('Alasdair MacMhaighstir Alasdair') and William
Ross.

A comparison of the Gaelic anonyms of the 16th, 17th and 18th
centuries with the Lowland Ballads could be an important study
though the far greater range of the Gaelic songs would make it
difficult. In many of those Gaelic poems there is the same quality as
Edwin Muir, in his 'Note on Scottish Ballads' in *Latitudes*, finds in the
great Lowland Ballads 'pure passion seen through pure vision'.
(Indeed a great deal of what Mr Muir says in his admirable chapter is
startlingly true of those Gaelic songs as well as of the Lowland
Ballads). In the Gaelic anonyms, however, there is far more of the
variety of life realised on a high level, and though there is often in
them the same bare concentration, there is also very often a rich
texture of imagery, and always the Gaelic music and finish which
prevents them from being so unequal as the Ballads. The Gaelic
anonyms sometimes say great 'simple' things in an absolute and
inevitable way but at other times they can admirably express a
complexity of feeling and the compromises of life: they have 'Mac Og
an Iarla Ruaidh' as well as 'Mo Nighean Donn á Còrnaig' and 'A
Mhairead Og'.

The great pagan poetry has as its complement such religious poetry
of the people as is contained in the four volumes of *Carmina Gadelica*.

To contrast their acceptance of human life and the promised beyond with the pagan passion of the old songs shows the folly of generalising about a people's poetry. The gracious union of the material and spiritual everywhere in evidence in Carmina Gadelica is a product of the same people as in a later age and under the influence of Calvin and the Evangelicals produced the terrible and sublime poetry of Dugald Buchanan, whose power and economy and concentration express the horrors of Calvinism, but also a profound sense of the unsatisfactory nature of human life which is as moving to the sceptic as to the Calvinist. Buchanan can never appear a sectarian.

Buchanan's sense of the vanity of human life, his obsession with sin and misery, is very different from the joyous acceptance of life by the other two of the greatest of the 18th century Gaelic poets, Alexander MacDonald and Duncan Bàn Macintyre. MacDonald's poetry gathers many of the strands of previous Gaelic poetry, develops and transforms them. The clan-and-chief poetry of Mary MacLeod, Ian Lom and the other 17th century Gaelic poets had, in spite of the unfailing freshness and beauty and evocative power of its rhythm and phrase, a narrowness and lack of wide human significance, except occasionally, as in those great but brief moments when Mary Mac-Leod forgets her Normans and Rodericks of Dunvegan and we see herself in her loneliness, her memories of a great MacCrimmon and perhaps her love for Norman of Bernera, who was something more to her than all the rest of the MacLeods were. MacDonald makes the clan poetry truly national, and if he has less of a haunting beauty of phrase, he has far more fullness, verve and heroism. He is always the unconquerable MacDonald, a heroic and reckless man compared with whom a Byron appears a 'pansy'. In the 'Birlinn' he combines Titanic struggle with the naturalist realism in which 18th century Gaelic poetry excels. He realises dynamic Nature with a vigour, immediacy and exactness which would appear to me unrivalled if I could forget the delicacy which Macintyre adds and which makes the latter's poetry the very greatest of 18th century Gaelic Nature poetry. But Donald MacDonald, the author of the 16th century poem 'Creag Ghuanach', has this quality of Macintyre's union of extreme delicacy and subtlety with a richness and immediacy almost unique; though Roderick Morrison too had it in the 17th century, and that to a remarkable degree. William Ross, Macintyre's much younger contemporary, has it also, but his chief greatness is in the passionate echoing lyric, and in temperament he is poles apart from MacDonald and Macintyre. The troubled passion of Ross's greatest lyrics, always expressed in highly wrought sonorous language, gives an effect which is often curiously like Baudelaire though Ross's anguish is not of the Frenchman's morbid kind. His complete opposite in 18th century Gaelic poetry is Rob Donn, the most brilliant writer of *sermo pedestris* in Gaelic literature.

19th century Gaelic poetry is a poor aftermath to that of the 18th century, but the wrongs of the Clearances produced a widening of human sympathy on the social side, and the poetry of a century which saw William Livingston, John MacLachlan, Mary MacPherson and John Smith is not contemptible. They were all pre-occupied with the sufferings of the people, and Livingston at his best has a noble fire and eloquence, MacLachlan a great poignancy, and Smith a deep and wide humanity and thoughtfulness, while the Calvinist evangelical movement produced notable religious poetry by the saintly John Morrison and Patrick Grant, and the 20th century has seen the ornate and beautiful Catholic mystical poetry of Donald Sinclair. And, in spite of 'The Road to the Isles' and much of *Songs of the Hebrides*, everyone who knows Gaelic knows that, writing in his own language, the Rev. Dr. Kenneth MacLeod has expressed profoundly and delicately certain aspects of Hebridean life which are all but gone forever. Do not judge his Gaelic by 'The Road to the Isles'.

Notes on sea-imagery in seventeenth century Gaelic poetry

The imagery of a century's poetry is a vast subject in which generalisation is extremely difficult, or some would say impertinent. This is especially true of a century of the richness and variety of the 17th century in Gaelic poetry, and I therefore limited the title to 'sea imagery', though I am taking a glance now and then at imagery of other kinds. Also I have given the title 'Notes' in order to indicate that the treatment does not claim to be exhaustive or systematic.

I am using this vague and questionable word 'imagery' in the widest sense and in a double sense: first, in the very widest sense to connote the sensuous embodiment or setting of thought and feeling in language; and second, in the more restricted sense of those figures of speech like Metaphor and Simile, which are not primarily devices of style depending on the arrangement of the words.

It is on record that when one of the intelligent and accomplished daughters of Dr Hector MacLean, of the noted manuscript, translated some Gaelic poetry to Johnson and Boswell, they were not at all impressed by the 'images' (one of them used the word); but, of course, that proves nothing or, if it proves anything, it proves only that Miss MacLean's selections predominated in auditory images not susceptible of translation; and when one thinks of the relative poverty of imagery in their own admired 18th century English poetry, one would not accept Johnson and Boswell as reliable witnesses. I should hesitate to say which is the finer poem, the Blind Harper's 'Oran Mór MhicLeòid' or the anonymous popular song 'Ailein Duinn, a nì 's a nàire'. Quite obviously, it would be relatively easy to 'put across' in translation the vivid visual imagery of 'Ailein Duinn', but no translation would ever hope to give the slightest indication of the marvellous auditory images of 'Oran Mór MhicLeòid'; and very probably Miss MacLean chose to translate poems of the Oran Mór type, with their far greater literary prestige, rather than the more easily translatable popular or 'sub-literary' song. At any rate, Johnson's own treatment of the words and imagery of one of the most magnificent soliloquies of Shakespeare's *Macbeth* puts him pretty well out of court as a witness.

Nevertheless, there has long been a vague feeling that Gaelic poetry is richer in its appeal to the ear than to the eye; in other words, that while the sound of Gaelic poetry is astonishingly rich, varied and resonant in sensuous and emotional effect, the visual appeal is not normally so satisfying. This has led to the charge that the Gaelic poet frequently sacrifices many other things for the sake of the sound; that the Celt loves words for their own sake; but, oddly enough, the implications of Matthew Arnold's famous 'natural magic' are the very opposite. The most noted foreign doctors obviously agree.

A predominance of the sound effect would normally be expected as an overspill from the metrically over-elaborate virtuosity of medieval and 16th century poetry; and in 17th century and in post-17th century vernacular poetry it is obvious in many ways; and I think the generalisation can be made: that the more self-conscious and literary the poetry is in the 17th century, and in the 18th too, the more does the auditory effect dominate all the rest. Indeed, the long processions of adjectives so frequent in later 17th century and in all 18th century Gaelic poetry is substantially a reduction to the absurd of this sound-loving verbiage; but such processions are very rare in the popular song-poetry, which clearly indicates that they are a result of too much rather than too little 'art'. It must be admitted that a great deal of Alexander MacDonald's, Duncan Macintyre's and William Ross's verse suffers from this. Not that there are not hundreds of examples of the contrary. For instance, to take the big comprehensive and small particular images together, what big images could excel the simultaneous visual and auditory effect of

> Monadh fada réidh,
> Cuile 'm faighte féidh,
> Soilleireachd an t-sléibh
> Bha mi sònrachadh.
>
> *Long unbroken moorland,*
> *retreat where deer were to be found,*
> *the brightness of the moorland*
> *I marked most of all.*

Or what little image could excel the effect of the spring

> Tighinn 'na chuartaig o'n ghrinneal
> Air slinnein Beinn Dórain.

Coming eddying from the gravel
on the shoulder-blade of Ben Dórain.

To me the first equals the large visual and emotive effect of Byron's glimpse of the Alps:

I saw their thousand years of snow
On high; their wide long lake below,
And the blue Rhone in fullest flow.

And the second excels in exactness of visual impression, with accompanying rhythmic satisfaction, the most wonderful small image I can think of in Tennyson. When MacDonald talks of 'ràimh 'gan snìomh ann an achlaisean àrd thonn' there is such a powerful visual and physical effect that sensuousness can go no further: one can see and feel the oar almost breaking. But MacDonald too, like Macintyre, frequently makes the sound roll on further than the eye can follow, while Ross makes a curly golden head liquefy in glorious noise:

Gur bachlach dualach cas-bhuidh cuachach
Càradh suaineis gruaig do chinn.

Ringletted, wavy, yellow-wreathed, curly
the twisty set of the hair of your head.

Indeed, I feel that Ross, most of all, tends to achieve his effects almost completely through the sensuous medium of sound; but what effects they often are! Last year the young Lewis poet, Iain Crichton Smith, referred memorably to the 'infinite resonance that is in William Ross'; I think an admirable piece of criticism in a nutshell.

I am, however, dealing especially with sea imagery in 17th century poetry, too big a subject in itself. I think that two things mainly contribute to make the sea bulk even bigger than one would expect in Scottish Gaelic poetry. It is clear that for centuries the main focal point for the bards of Gaelic Scotland was the court of the Lord of the Isles, and after the decline of the Lordship of the Isles, the Campbells, MacKenzies, MacLeods, MacLeans could by no means be called inland powers. Then, because Gaelic has been preserved longer in the islands and on the west coast, more island and west coast poetry, especially of the more popular kind, has been preserved from oblivion. From the quality of the mainland poetry that has survived, it is quite obvious that it was in no way inferior to the island and coastland poetry, but the longer continuance of Gaelic in the islands and on the

85

west coast makes us have relatively more poetry in which the sea is prominent. Naturally the consciousness of the presence of the sea will vary, from a general feeling of its presence to a vivid detailed and intense sensuousness, but nearly always one is aware at least of the geographical setting. Sometimes it is only a passing glance at the geographical setting, as in the following examples:

Gun tiginn an taobh seo
Dh'amharc Dhiùraidh á Sgarbaidh.

That I should come to this place
to look on Jura from Scarba.

Cill Ma-Ruibhe fo sgéith a' chuain.

Kilmaree under the wing of the bay.

Beir mo shoraidh thar chaol
O nach cluinn iad mo ghlaodh.

Bear my greeting over kyles
since they will not hear my cry.

Sgeula leat, a ghaoth a deas,
Seirbhe do ghlòir na 'n domblas,
Gun fhuaim sìthe leat a steach
Air chuan Sgìthe, mo léir chreach.

You bring a tale, south wind,
more bitter your speech than gall,
no sound of peace (coming) in with you
over the sea of Skye, my loss of losses.

Tha do thalla gun smùid
Fo charraig nan sùgh.

Your hall is smokeless
under the wave-beaten rock.

Ri fuaim an taibh
'S uaigneach mo ghean.

At the sound of the (Western) sea
sad and lonely my mood.

Chì mi luingeas an Caol Ile
Tighinn an coinneamh Cairistìona.

I see ships in the Sound of Islay
coming to meet Cairistìona.

Doilleir dorcha air oidhche reòta
Chàidh do bhàt thar Rudha Rònaidh,
Dol troimh na caoil a null a Bhròchaill
A dh'amharc air maighdean an òr-fhuilt.

Dim and dark on a frosty night
your boat went past the head of Rona,
going through the kyles over to Brochel
to see the girl of the golden hair.

But it is never quite the geographical setting alone. One senses nearly always the emotional charge behind the words: the sea setting may be quite neutral but it is difficult to feel it quite neutral in an example like:

Gu talla 'n fhir fhéil,
Ceann-uidhe nan ceud,
Cill Ma-Ruibhe fo sgéith a' chuain.

To the hall of the generous one,
destination of hundreds,
Kilmaree under the wing of the bay.

Note how the predominant auditory effect of this image, a great one in its way, is magically transformed to a visual effect in the last line. Obviously, Kilmaree was to Griogar Og MacGriogair a name to conjure with; one cannot imagine that the generosity of the Mackinnon chief was all that was to it; surely the beauty of the geographical setting — and Strathaird is wonderfully beautiful — has something to do with it.

I have begun with sea images that are as near emotional neutrality as a poetic image can be; indeed one of them could be regarded as not neutral but hostile. Mary MacLeod is lamenting that now her only music is the sound of the sea, not the pipe of the MacCrimmons:

Ri fuaim an taibh
Is uaigneach mo ghean;
Bha mis' uair nach b'e siod m'àbhaist;
Ach pìob nuallanach mhór

Bheireadh buaidh air gach ceòl
Nuair a ghluaist' i le meòir Phàdraig.

At the sound of the sea
sad and forlorn my mood,
I was once when that was not my wont;
but a great loud resonant pipe
that would excel all music
when it was moved by the fingers of Patrick.

The resonance and onomatopoeia of the image belies the apparent implicit hostility: it as if the great sound of the sea, so briefly and imaginatively evoked, is yet inferior to the great music of Patrick. There is thus a subtle ambivalence about it, which is all the more emotive because of its reticence. Otherwise the image is a very good example of the evocative power of sound, in which all Gaelic poetry, and not least 17th century poetry, is peculiarly rich, and the whole contrast is well brought out by the rather beautiful and very evocative image of the 'sea-divided Gael' in the grim and powerful poem 'Mac Neachdainn an Dùin' which must be almost exactly contemporary with Mary MacLeod's 'Ri fuaim an taibh':

'S iomadh bàt agus long
Tha le fonn a' dol thairis
Eadar Eirinn an t-slòigh
'S dùthaich bhòidheach Mhic Cailein.

Many a boat and ship
is cheerfully going over
between Ireland of the host
and the beautiful land of Mac Cailein.

These lines are especially effective as a counterpoint to the evil passions of men and women which pervade this great and terrible poem.

There are, of course, hundreds of examples, especially in the popular poetry, of such images, in which the sea is mainly a briefly noted and, generally, emotionally neutral part of the environment; but one can never be too sure of the emotional neutrality or detachment, for the images are generally too beautiful in themselves to indicate indifference to the sea: a typical one is the beginning of the song 'Gura muladach sgìth mi':

Gura muladach sgìth mi
'S mi liom fhìn 'san tìr aineol,

Anns an h-eileanan Diùrach,
'S mór mo dhùil ri dhol thairis.
Chì mi 'm bàta troimh'n chaolas,
Tha mo ghaol oirre dh'fhearaibh;
Tha mo leannan 'ga stiùireadh,
Lùb ùr a' chùil chlannaich,
Lùb ùr a' chùil chùbhraidh,
'S toigh liom fhìn do chaol mhala.

Sorrowful and weary am I,
alone in a land of strangers,
in the islands of Jura,
how I expect to go over the sea!
I see the boat going through the kyles,
my love of men is on her,
my lover is steering her,
the strong young man of the thick hair,
the strong young man of the fragrant hair,
I like your thin eye-brow.

To attribute indifference or neutrality in the face of the natural environment is a very dangerous thing, even in images when the sea is ostensibly only a thoroughfare for the beloved's ship or boat; even in those it is a road to a loved land, to 'dùthaich bhòidheach Mhic Cailein', or

. . . a null a Bhròchaill,
A dh'amharc air maighdean an òr-fhuilt.

. . . over to Brochel,
to see the girl of the golden hair.

To take a parallel example with mountain images: love of the mountains for their own sake is quite explicit in Duncan Macintyre and in Byron and in Western European poetry generally from about 1780 onwards, but round about 1600 it is no less unmistakeable in the Gaelic poetry of Dòmhnall MacFhionnlaigh nan Dàn. Unlike Donnchadh Bàn and Byron, Dòmhnall MacFhionnlaigh does not, as far as I can remember, make a single overt declaration of his love of the mountains in his great poem, 'Oran na Comhachaig', but surely it is as instinct with unspoken love as 'Beinn Dórain' and the Third Canto of 'Childe Harold' are with declared love. As with the mountains, so with the sea. I think the imagery of 17th-century Gaelic poetry has the whole emotional gamut.

I have begun with images on the face of it emotionally neutral or as near neutrality as can be, but I think that they alone (and there are hundreds, even thousands, of them in the literary and folk poetry of the 17th century) would indicate a sensitive awareness of the physical environment, and a great love, if not ostensibly of the sea itself, certainly of its islands and coastlands. Think of the vast number of references in poetry collected in Uist to the other Clan Ranald islands — Rum, Eigg, Canna; or in the mainland Clan Ranald poetry, to Uist itself.

A very natural corollary of this, especially in the earlier poetry of the 17th century, and in the poetry of the late 16th century, was the glorification of the chief's galley or galleys, and, in the poetry of the early 17th century especially, the images picturing the galley retain much of the traditional paraphernalia of the mediaeval court poetry, even the hyperboles about the masts of gold and silver, and about the well of wine in the stern and the well of fresh water in the other end. In most poems of that type the sea is merely the setting or thoroughfare, and the galley might almost be a state barge on a river, so much is the stress on the hyberbolical embellishments and so little on the struggle with the elements. Probably the most famous of all Scottish Gaelic poems of this type is the 16th-century 'Tàladh Dhòmhnaill Ghuirm'. In far more poems the sea is evoked as a worthy foe or at least a splendid battleground for hardy heroes and tough ships, and the images are not hyberbolical conventions but sensuously and acutely realised. Such images are notable in late 16th-century poetry, as in the *iorram* in honour of Iain Og MacSheumais, the noted MacDonald warrior killed in Mull in 1585, and the father of the still more famous Dòmhnall Mac Iain Mhic Sheumais:

> M'eudail a dh'fhearaibh nan àlach,
> Nuair a dheigheadh tu gu d' bhàta,
> Siod an obair nach biodh cèarr dhut:
> Bhiodh do ghillean anns an àlach
> Bhiodh tu fhéin air stiùir do bhàta,
> Fear curanta treubhach làidir.

> *My treasure of the oar-bank men,*
> *when you went to your boat,*
> *that would be no wrong work for you:*
> *your young men would be on the oar-bank,*
> *you yourself at the rudder of your boat,*
> *a brave strong man as your people were.*

Or again:

M'eudail a dh'fhearaibh na seòltachd,
Nuair a shìneadh tu ri seòladh
Ghlacadh i eadar na sgòide,
Cneadan a cléithe bu cheòl dhut,
Stiùir 'na déidh 's fear treubhach eòlach
'Ga stiùireadh 'san iùl bu chòir dhi.

My treasure of the men of skill,
when you began to sail her
she was held between the sheet-ropes,
the groans of her oarbank were your music,
a rudder behind her and an experienced man, brave like his people,
steering her in the direction that was right for her.

The emphasis here is still on the stout ship and heroic sailors, not on the sea itself; but as the century progressed and the poetry became more popular, the environment is more stressed, often with brief powerful evocation:

Fliuch an oidhche nochd 's gur fuar i,
Ma thug Clann Nèill druim a' chuain orr,
Luchd nan ro-seòl 's nan long luatha,
'S nan ulagan cruinne cruaidhe,
'S nam brataichean dearga 's uaine,
'S nan claidheamhna geura cruadhach
Nach laigh smal orr' anns na truaillean.

Wet this night and very cold,
if Clan Neil have taken to the ridge of the sea,
the men of the great sails and the swift ships,
and the hard round pulley-blocks,
and the red and green banners,
and the sharp steel swords
on which no stain lies in the scabbards.

The sense of heroic struggle is, however, more explicit in the imagery of others, where the evocation of environment is brief and powerful, as in one of the songs on the death at sea of Iain Garbh Mac Ghille Chaluim of Raasay:

Bha mi uair nach do shaoil mi
    Ged is faoin bhith 'ga agairt
Gun rachadh do bhàthadh
    Gu bràth air cuan farsainn
Fhad 's a dh' fhanadh a stiùir dhi
    'S tu air cùl a buill bheairte

Dh'aindeoin ànradh nan dùilean
  Agus ùpraid na mara;
'S fhad 's a dh'fhanadh ri chéile
  A cuid dhealgan 's a h-acfhuinn
'S a b'urrainn dhi géilleadh
  Do d' làimh thréin air an aigeann.
Ach 's i 'n doineann bha iargalt
  Le gaoith 'n iar-thuaith 's cruaidh fhrasan,
Thog i 'mhuir 'na mill dhùghorm,
  Smuais i 'n iùbhrach 'na sadan.

I was once when I did not think,
though it is vain to claim it,
that you would ever be
drowned on an open sea,
while the rudder stuck to her
and you behind the ropes of her tackle,
in spite of the distress of the elements
and the uproar of the sea;
while there remained together
her block-pins and tackle
and she could respond
to your strong hand on the ocean;
but it was the surly forbidding tempest
with north-west wind and hard showers,
it raised the sea in dark-blue hills
and smashed the galley in little fragments.

This poem has been ascribed, apparently without much reason, to
Mary MacLeod, while there is a poem on the same theme undoubtedly
by Mary. In Mary's own poem the picture of struggle is briefer but
strongly evocative:

Mo bheud 's mo bhròn
Mar dh'éirich dhò:
Muir beucach mór
A' leum mu d' bhòrd,
Thu fhéin 's do sheòid,
Nuair reub ur seòl,
Nach d'fhaod sibh treòir
  A chaitheamh oirr.

My loss and pain
what his fate was:
a great roaring sea
leaping about your board:

> *that you and your heroes,*
> *when your sail was torn,*
> *that you could not lay*
> *your strength on it!*

Of the two, Mary MacLeod's 'great roaring sea leaping about your board' has greater originality; powerful as the imagery of the other poem is, it has not quite the startling freshness of the great Mary's two lines:

> Muir beucach mór
> A' leum mu d' bhòrd.

In both, the auditory and the visual is combined; but the anonymous poem seems to me to have double movement: of a ship going strongly, and then of a ship overwhelmed. Mary's has only the brief moment of the overwhelming, but with a strangely vivid force. Both seem to me to have a very strong tactile sensuousness.

Indeed tactile and dynamic sensuousness is very remarkable in 17th-century sea imagery. A dynamic sensuousness is generally just another name for a realisation of some movement in sound and rhythm. The *locus classicus* of such in Gaelic sea poetry is Alexander MacDonald's 18th-century poem, the 'Birlinn of Clan Ranald', but the same quality is splendidly achieved in much 17th-century poetry, as in two famous ones: Iain Lom's 'Iorram Dharaich' and Murchadh Mór Mac Mhic Mhurchaidh's 'Làir Dhonn'.

There is evidence that one may have suggested the other, as both have the horse-ship contrast, but MacKenzie's poem is more personal, probably more acutely felt than MacDonald's, which is so much the glorification of the chief and his ship, in the older style. Still Iain Lom's poem, too, contains brief and splendid evocations, images of splendid visual and auditory impact:

> Cha bu mharcach eich leumnaich
> A bhuinnigeadh geall réis ort
> Nuair a thogadh tu bréid os cionn sàile.
>
> Nuair a thogadh tu tonnag
> Air cuan meanmnach nan dronnag
> 'S iomadh gleann ris an cromadh i h-eàrrach.
>
> Nuair a shuidheadh fear stiùir oirr'
> An àm bhith fàgail na dùthcha
> Bu mhear ruith a' chuain dhùghlais fo h-eàrrlainn.

Cha b'iad na lucharmuinn mheanbha
Bhiodh m'a cupail ag èaladh
Nuair a dh'éireadh mór shoirbheas le bàirlinn;

Ach na fuirbirnich threubhach
As deise dh'iomradh 's a dh'éigheadh
Bheireadh tulg an tùs cléith air ràmh bràghad.

Nuair a dh'fhalaichte na bùird di
Is nach faighte làn siùil di
Bhiodh luch-tighe 'sìor lùb air a h-àlaich.

'S iad gun eagal gun éislean
Ach ag freagradh d'a chéile
Nuair thigeadh muir bheucach 's gach àird orr'.

Dol timchioll Rudha na Caillich
Bu ro-mhath siubhal a daraich
Ag gearradh shrutha gu cairidh Chaoil Acuinn.

Dol gu uidhe chuain fhiadhaich
Mar bu chubhaidh dhut iarraidh
Gu Uibhist bheag riabhach nan cràghiadh.

Cha bu bhruchag air meirg i
Fhuair a treachladh le h-eirbheirt
Nuair a thigeadh mór shoirbheas le gàbhadh;

Ach an Dubh-Chnòideartach riabhach,
Luchdmhor àrd-ghuailleach dhìonach,
Gur lìonmhor lann iarainn m'a h-eàrraich.

It is not the rider of a leaping horse
that would win a wager of a race against you
when you raised a sail above the sea.

When you raised a mantle
on the spirited ridgy sea,
to many a glen she would lower her keel.

When a steersman sat on her
in the time of leaving the land
the run of the dark-grey sea was gleeful about her stern.

They were no puny manikins
who crouched about her shrouds
when a great wind rose with high seas;

but the heroic giants
expert in rowing and shouting
who would bend the fore oar at the head of an oarbank.

94

When her boards were hidden
and her sail could not fill
the household men always bent on her oarbank.

Fearless and hale
responding to each other
when a roaring surge came on them from any airt.

Going round the Headland of the Cailleach
her oakwood moved surely
splitting the current towards the yare of Kyleakin.

Going on the voyage of the stormy sea
as it was your way to desire
to little brindled Uist of the sheldrakes.

No little rusted smutty one
battered by her movement
when a great wind rose with its danger;

but the brindled Black One of Knoydart
capacious, high-shouldered, water-tight,
with many an iron rove about her keel.

Murchadh Mór's poem is less consistently splendid than Iain Lom's, but now and again there is a touch in it of greater originality and subtlety, something of a specialised nautical delight:

Cha b'ionann 's mo shaoi
Ri grinneas na gaoith
Gun bhioran r'a taoibh 's i folbh.

Not so my brave one
with the wind that was right,
with no stab in her side as she went.

And again:

Chan iarradh i moll
No fodar no pronn
Ach sadadh nan tonn r'a sròin.

She would not ask for chaff
or fodder or mash
but the spray of the waves against her nose.

It seems to me that the shorter phrases of Murchadh's strophes with their ultimate stresses are finer rhythmically even than Iain Lom's, which is saying much, but Iain Lom's visual sensuousness is better, except for one or two touches where Murchadh seems to hit something beyond Iain Lom's reach, something indicative of a greater personal knowledge and a more personal reaction.

Imagery expressive of heroic struggle, triumph and joy is very common in all 17th century sea poetry, though it does not bulk so big in many single poems as in Iain Lom's 'Iorram Dharaich' and Murchadh Mór's 'Làir Dhonn'. It is not, however, as common as the sea imagery in the poems that are primarily laments for the drowned. There are so many of them and so many of them are wonderful poems that it is impossible to deal with all the types of imagery in this kind of poem alone. Very frequently those images are sharply sensuous and piercingly poignant.

The image of the person looking out to sea is common, looking for a boat or for the right boat. One of the four or five poems extant on the death, in 1671, of Iain Garbh of Raasay begins:

Seall a mach, an e 'n là e,
'S mi ri feitheamh na fàire;
Leis an luasgan th'air m'aigne
Chan eil an cadal 'na thàmh dhomh.

Look outside — is it day? —
as I wait for the horizon;
with the unrest of my spirit
sleep is no rest for me.

Indeed, the image of looking out to sea, especially at day-break, sometimes seems to indicate tragedy and disquiet not necessarily connected with drowning. In a most poignant lament for the death of children not by drowning, a mother says:

A nighean ud thall
A bheil thu t'fhaireachadh?
Seall a mach,
A bheil a' ghealach ann,
No 'm faod am bàta
'Taobh a theannadh ruinn.

Girl over there,
are you awake?
Look out to see
if there is a moon,
or if the boat can
come near us.

96

In this poem, both in Mr Craig's version and as my brother Calum got it, there is no apparent connection between the boat and the death of the children. The looking out for the boat seems an image of disquiet and anguish, perhaps of a despairing seeking for relief or distraction. Whatever it is, it is very moving and even haunting in its context. Commoner, of course, is the image of this type:

> Cha tig bàta mu'n rudha
> Nach tig snigh' air mo ghruaidh.

> *No boat comes round the headland*
> *but a wetness comes on my cheek.*

Or the person may be watching from the eminence, the bare cold eminence, 'o'n tulaich luim fhuair'. In the poem found in Strath in Skye and containing the Strath and Mull name Mac Sìri, the watching image has a marvellous beauty:

> Ach am faic mi seòl bréid-gheal
> Latha gréine 'sa' chuan,
> Ach am faic mi siùil bhàna
> Tigh'nn gu h-àrd air bhàrr stuadh.

> *So that I may see a kertch-white sail*
> *on a sunny day on the sea,*
> *so that I may see white sails*
> *coming high on the top of waves.*

Richest of all in metaphor are the images of the drowned bodies, as in the next examples:

> 'S duilich liom do chùl clannach
> Anns an fheamainn 'ga luadh.

> *Sad, sad am I that your thick hair*
> *is being waulked in the sea-weed!*

> 'S mise 'bhean bhochd
> A th'air mo sgaradh
> Mur h'e Leódhas mhór ur cala;
> Mas e 's bobhstair dhuibh a' ghaineamh,
> Mas e 'n t-slaodach 's aodach-tarruing,
> Mas e na sgairbh ur luchd faire.

> *I am the miserable woman*
> *who is cut to the heart*

if great Lewis is not your harbour;
if the sand is your bolster,
if the serrated seaweed is your pall,
if the cormorants are your watchmen.

Fhaoileag bheag thu, fhaoileag mhar' thu,
Fhaoileag a shnàmhas gach cala,
Thig a nall is innis naidheachd,
Càit an d'fhàg thu na fir gheala?
Dh'fhàg mi iad 'san eilean mhara,
Cùl ri cùl is iad gun anail,
Beul ri beul, a' sileadh fala.
Gur e mise th' air mo sgaradh
Ma tha ur leabaidh anns an fheamainn,
Mas e na ròin ur luchd faire,
Na reultan àrd ur coinnlean geala
'S ur ceòl fìdhle gaoir na mara.

Little gull, gull of the sea,
gull that swims every harbour,
come over here and tell a story,
where have you left the finest of men?
I left them in the island in the sea,
back to back and without breath,
mouth to mouth, dripping blood.
It is I who am heart-broken
if your bed is in the seaweed,
if the seals are your watchmen,
the high stars your white candles,
and your violin music the scream of the sea.

Obviously many poems contain variants of the same image. The candle metaphor of the penultimate line has a finely detailed variant in one of the 'Iain Garbh' poems:

Tha na staimh dhut 'nan lainnir,
Ann an clachan gun tràghadh.

The sea tangles are your torches
in an ebbless graveyard.

There are so many great laments for the drowned in Gaelic poetry, and so many of those that can be historically placed are of the 17th century that is tempting to ascribe to that century some that may be far earlier and many that are later. It may be said that the characteristic style is 17th century, even in a poem like 'Ailein duinn, shiùbhlainn leat', which is evidently of the 18th century. There is in it, however, no image or expression that could not be of the 17th century, in fact that is not paralleled in poems demonstrably of the 17th century, except perhaps:

> M'achanaich-sa, Rìgh na Cathrach,
> Gun mi dhol an ùir no'n anart,
> An talamh toll no àite falaich,
> Ach 'sa bhad 'san deach thu, Ailein,
> Ged a b'ann 'san liadhaig fheamann,
> No am broinn na muice mara.

> *My supplication, King on the Throne,*
> *that I do not end up in dust or linen,*
> *in a hole in the ground or in a hiding place,*
> *but in the place where you went, Allan,*
> *though it were in the sea-tangle leaves,*
> *or in the belly of the whale.*

Laments for the victims of the sea are very common, but in one famous poem the speaker is the victim, the famous "S i 'bhean iadaich thug a'n tràigh mi', a poem localised in many places from the Butt of Lewis to Kerry. I imagine that this song is older than the 17th century, but I think it took its present form in the great century and a half between 1600 and 1750. It is famous for its poignancy of feeling and sharp intense visual imagery:

> Mo chòta bàn am bàrr an t-sàile,
> Mo chuailean donn feadh na làthchadh.

> *My petticoat on the top of the brine*
> *my brown hair amongst the soft sea-shore clay.*

There is a most intense visual sensuousness combined with piercing feeling in the unavailing cry:

> Sìn do chas dhomh, sìn do làmh dhomh.

> *Stretch your foot to me, stretch your hand to me.*

I cannot think of any other poem where the speaker is the victim in such circumstances, nor can I think of any other poem of greater poignancy.

Gaelic folklore ascribed to the sea the counterpart of everything on land, and thus one expects poems of fairy fantasy to have their counterparts in like sea poetry, but, unless I am much mistaken, there are not nearly so many poems of the supernatural on sea as on land. One thinks of the many fairy poems, as, for example, 'A phiùthrag's a phiuthar', 'A Mhór, a ghaoil', 'Fhuair mi lorg an dóbhrain duinn', and one cannot think of nearly as many poems of the supernatural in or on the sea. Yet the old prose stories, with their verse runs, had their sea monsters, such as 'A' Mhuileartach', and in many others the cave by the sea is the scene of weird events, as in the story of Conall Mac Rìgh Cruachain. Is it that the prose tale normally enshrines more archaic traditions, or what is it? For example, there are many prose accounts of the work of witches causing the death of Iain Garbh Mac Ghille Chaluim, but in none of the five poems on his death extant is there any mention of witches, though there is a tradition that it was the chief witch concerned in his death who made at least one of the laments, when she repented. She had been his foster-mother but had been bribed to drown him by the jealous MacDonald chief. It is a fact that by the 17th century the popular poem is less extravagant in imagination than is the prose tale. The most notable example of the supernatural theme I can think of in poetry that looks like the 17th century is the strange mermaid song:

Gur e mise chunnaic ìongnadh:
Sa' mhadainn mhoich 's mi 'g iarraidh chaorach,
Chunnacas gruagach chuailein chraobhaich
'S i 'na suidh air sgeir 'na h-aonar;
Trusgan gorm oirr' air son aodaich
A measg maoraich èalaidh na tràghad.
Ach cha b'fhada siod a' caochladh:
Thog i 'ceann 's gun d'rinn i straonadh;
Sheall i ormsa thar a guailne,
'S och mo thruaighe, mar a thachair:
Chaidh i 'n riochd na beiste maoile
Shnàmhas an cuan mar an fhaoileig,
Sgoilteas an tonn air gach taobh dhith
Troimh Chaol Mhuile, troimh Chaol Ile,
Troimh Chaol Othasaidh Mhic a Phìotha;
'S chàidh i sin air a fiaradh
Gu eilean riabhach na gaineimh,
Gu tìr fharsainn nam fear fialaidh
'S an sgeir mhóir nach gluais a' ghaillionn.

It is I who saw a wonder:
one early morning, looking for sheep,
I saw a girl with flowing hair
sitting on a sea-rock alone;

with a blue mantle as clothing
among the creeping shell-fish of the shore.
But that was not long in changing:
she raised her head and was startled;
she looked at me over her shoulder,
and — alas, alas, the thing that happened! —
she took the shape of the blunt-headed monster
that swims the sea like a seagull,
that splits the wave on each side of her
through the Kyle of Mull, through the Kyle of Islay,
through Kyle Oronsay of MacPhee;
and then she went veering to the brindled island of the sand,
to the wide land of the generous men
and the great rock unmoved by tempest.

It is true that the last six lines I have quoted are heard in versions of other poems, such as 'Moch Di-luain, ghabh i 'n cuan'. If the poem can be taken as a piece as I have heard it, it is a good example of contrasted imagery, the small detail of 'maorach èalaidh na tràghad' standing against the great sweeps of the course through the famous kyles and to the large vagueness of 'tìr fharsainn nam fear fialaidh' and the 'sgeir mhór nach gluais a' ghaillionn'. Is it Ailsa Craig or 'Roc á Barraidh fo thuinn'? Is the 'tìr fharsainn' Ireland or the fabulous Isles of the West?

In his famous and beautiful essay 'Duatharachd na mara' the late Dr Kenneth MacLeod concentrates on the supernatural in sea imagery, and many of the verse examples he gives would be better placed in the 17th century stylistically than in any other century, as for example:

Chunnacas fearra-long mhór a raoir,
Solus oillt is éig 'na crann,
'S thuig mi gun robh m'aon mhac òg
Fuar fo spòig a' chuain ud thall.

I saw last night a great (?) phantom ship,
a light of horror and death in her mast,
and I understood that my one young son
was cold under the paw of yonder sea.

There is no doubt, however, that the origin of this supernatural imagery is far older than the 17th century, although many verses quoted probably took their final form in the 17th century. At the beginning of the same essay, Kenneth MacLeod notes the greater intensity of sea-imagery than most other kinds of imagery and puts it down mainly to the folk nature of most sea poems, saying that the known bards generally avoided the sea, and implying that in the known bards intensity was frequently lost in excessive wordiness and other rhetorical effects, but he also finds a greater intensity in the very nature of sea poetry. In general, I agree, especially with his first thesis, the superior intensity of what is loosely called 'folk poetry', and I think there is something in the second thesis too. Besides the phantom ship, the legendary monsters, the seal, swan and 'Tìr fo Thuinn', Dr Macleod is dealing with themes and images of very great antiquity; in general, the supernatural is older than the 17th century, and I do not think that its imagery is characteristic especially of the 17th century. Still, the 17th century is so great a watershed in Gaelic poetry that almost everything that is older than it, at any rate in orally transmitted poetry, has been linguistically modified during the 17th century.

Most of the poems I have mentioned are in some way or other primarily poems of the sea. What of sea imagery in poems only remotely connected with the sea, or not at all connected as far as we can tell? One would expect the sea image in such poems to be less detailed, less exact, and more conventional, and that is generally the case. About 1600 'Oran na Comhachaig', a poem of the mountains and of hunting, has the converse of the antithesis in Iain Lom's and Murchadh Mór's poems quoted:

Cha mhinig a bha mi 'g éisteachd
Ri séitrich na muice mara,
Ach 's tric a chuala mi móran
De chrònanaich an daimh allaidh.

I was not often listening
to the blowing of the whale,
but I often heard much
of the bellowing of the wild stag.

Following closely is the famous contrast, in which an implied delight in the sea is said to be excelled by the greater joy of the hunt:

Is aoibhinn an obair an t-sealg,
Aoibhinn a meanmna 's a beachd;
Gur binne a h-aighear 's a fonn,
Na long is i a' dol fo bheairt.

A joyous work the hunt,
joyous its spirit and perception,
more melodious its zest and mood
than a ship going under its rigging.

102

Is the implied joy in the ship an individual touch, or is it a measure of the prestige of the ship in Gaelic poetry before 1600?

The conventional sea images are fairly common, the flowing tide of prosperity, and the ebb tide of adversity. Pòl Crùbach says of the death of Iain Mór Mac Leòid in 1649:

Gur mór an sruth-tràghaidh
Thàinig air fir Innse Gall.

How great the ebb-tide
that has come on the men of Innse Gall!

And Eachunn Bacach says of the disaster of Inverkeithing in 1651:

Och, a Mhuire, mo chràdh
Mu Chloinn Ghill-Eain nam bàrc,
Mo chreach mar tha 'n tràghadh seachad oirbh.

O Mary, my pain
about Clan Gillean of the ships,
it is my ruin that the ebb has gone past them.

In the Ciaran Mabach's famous elegy on the death of his brother, Seumas Mór of Sleat, in 1678, the sea tragedy is a metaphor for overwhelming death:

Ormsa rug an t-anrath cuain,
Chuaidh mo riaghailt uam air chall;
Mo sgeul duilich 's mo chàs cruaidh:
'S nì buan gun bhuinnig a th' ann.

Dhìomsa thug an t-eug a' chìs
Is léir dhut, a Rìgh, mar atà;
Ormsa rug gàir-thonn nan sian,
Gun sìth ach dòruinn gu bàs.

Cha robh stiùir no seòl no slat
No ball beirte a bha ri crann
Nach do thruis an aon uair uainn:
Mo thruaigh-sa, an fhras a bh'ann.

I am seized by the distress at sea,
my compass is lost to me;
my sad tale and my hard extreme:
it is a lasting thing without gain.

Death has taken its toll of me,
you see, o King, how things are;

the roaring wave of the elements has seized me,
with no peace but only sorrow till death.

There was no rudder, sail or yard
nor rope of tackle to a mast
that the one hour did not sweep from me:
my misery, the shower it was!

The Ciaran Mabach's imagery is obviously a metaphorical extension of what is, on the whole, rather conventional, but expressed in stately and restrained language, with a noble kind of poignancy. But scattered throughout the folk poetry are sea images, sometimes of startling originality. In a version of the famous 'Chailin òig, an stiùir thu mi?' among the many similes for the fickleness of women we find this one:

Luaithe an aigneadh na 'ghaoth Mhàrtainn,
No muir-tèachd air leacan bàite.

Swifter their mind than the Martinmas wind
or jelly-fish on flagstones under the sea.

This seems to me a complex and subtle image. Sometimes the forlorn condition is symbolised by the 'eilean mara'. Indeed the separation from kith and kin and hereditary splendour is again and again, either literally or figuratively, placed in such an island:

Muladach mi 's mi air m'aineol,
'S mi 'm aonar an eilean mara,
Gun chuideachd ach dithis leanabh —
Caitrìona bheag agus Anna —
'S na geòidh fhiadhaich a' dol seachad;
Faodaidh iad sin 's a bhith fallain:
Tha mo shealgair donn fo'n talamh.

Sad and homesick in a land of strangers,
alone in an island in the sea,
with no company but two young children —
little Catriona and Anna —
and the wild geese passing;
they may do that and be unharmed:
my brown-haired hunter is under the ground.

In the famous song to Dòmhnall Mac Iain 'ic Sheumais, Nic Còiseam bewails that he is immured in Eriskay, 'eilean ìosal eadar Niall agus Ailean', 'eilean ciar gun fhiar gun fhasgadh' — perhaps just an expression of resentment that the great MacDonald warrior did not get his due from the chief of Sleat, a feeling noticeable in other traditions, but it is very much in line with the general attitude to the 'eilean mara', a poor forlorn place, often a symbol for forlorn separation, the last place. Hence it is frequently the place one would share with a lover, the test of great love. Thus it occurs among the imaginative hyperboles of the great song of Seathan:

Chaithris mi là am bàrr nan cranna leat,
Chaithris mi tràth 'san tiùrr fheamann leat,
Chaithris mi oidhche air sgeir mhara leat,
Chaithris, a ghaoil, is liom cha b'aithreach e,
Mi an cirb do bhreacain bhallaich,
Siaban nan tonn sìor dhol tharainn.

I was awake for a day in the tree-tops with you.
I was awake for a time in the sea-wrack with you,
I was awake for a night on a sea-rock with you,
I was, my love, and I was not sorry,
in the fold of your speckled plaid,
the drift of the waves the whole time going over us.

Sometimes, however, the associations are the converse: the 'eilean mara' is not necessarily a bad place, only a strange land of strangers. Thus it is in the poem containing one of the most haunting evocations of the Outer Isles in poetry:

Seòladh leat gu tìr a' mhurain:
B'àird a chluinnte fuaim na tuinne,
Fuaim an t-siabain ris a' mhuran.

Sailing with you to the land of the marram:
loud the noise of the sea,
sound of the sand-drift against the marram.

Old songs and new poetry

A few months ago my brother John, who is as well qualified to give an opinion as anyone I know, said that the greatest of all Scottish works of art is *Cumha na Cloinne*, the 'Lament for the Children', attributed by the tradition of pipers to Patrick Mór MacCrimmon and therefore of the 17th century. I hardly demurred, but suggested that, if it is not *Cumha na Cloinne* or some other one of the great pibrochs, it is one of those Gaelic songs of the two and a half centuries between 1550 and 1800 — the songs in which ineffable melodies rise like exhalations from the rhythms and resonances of the words, the songs that alone make the thought that the Gaelic language is going to die so intolerable to anyone who knows Gaelic and has in the least degree the sensibility that responds to the marriage, or rather the simultaneous creation, of words and music. It may be that a great piper without Gaelic can play a great pibroch supremely; it may even be that a great singer without much Gaelic can be coached into a great singing of one of those songs; but it is certain that no one who does not know Gaelic can really hear one of those songs. Perhaps one or another of the great pibrochs is in itself a greater thing than any single one of the songs, but there are so many more great songs than great pibrochs that I am convinced that Scottish Gaelic song is the chief artistic glory of the Scots, and of all people of Celtic speech, and one of the greatest artistic glories of Europe. I have been of this opinion for nearly 40 years, I have reiterated it *ad nauseam*, and now I am more convinced of its validity than I have ever been. I am no musician, but I can well imagine one of our fine pipers making about me the kind of remark that Gogarty made to Francis George Scott about Yeats, after listening to Scott and Yeats arguing about words and music. Like many others, I believe that there has never been a great song that is not a great poem too, and I believe with Croce that all poetry is 'lyrical', that verse now and again, but rarely, arrives at a point which it utters the 'lyrical cry'.

There are now in the archives of the School of Scottish Studies something like 6,000 separate Gaelic melodies, and it can be taken for granted that many of them can be called 'great'. A song like the Campbell/Morrison 'Ailean Donn', or the MacLean 'Ailean Donn',

'Cairistìona', or the 'Jura Islands' or 'Mac Sìri', or 'Iain Garbh', or 'Young Margaret', or two or three of the MacGregor songs, is an art beyond art when it is well sung, and it is still great poetry to one who has never heard it sung. I am, for instance, quite sure that I thought 'On the level of the road' one of the greatest of all Scottish poems long before I knew that there was extant a melody for it, which I heard for the first time from the late Mrs Buchanan Dunlop (Cathy Clark) in 1948.

If the words only of those old songs were extant, if the melodies were all lost, the songs could not fail to be a perennial stimulus to Gaelic poets. But since both melodies and words are extant for very many of them, the stimulus to some poets is so great as to be almost destructive. In the Thirties of this century something happened to articulate Gaels (by 'articulate' I mean likely to express their views more or less publicly) which had not happened for 100 years before. It was as if a French child of some peasant family near Chartres or Rheims, after being inside these cathedrals, had been taken away to some English industrial town where the only Gothic architecture was a few Victorian churches; as if he had lived there and had never seen a picture of a French or English medieval church until, in his late teens, he went back to the French cathedrals. In 1920 the 'image' of Gaelic song was to almost all articulate Gaels only as mediocre Victorian Gothic is to the Gothic of the 12th or 13th centuries. By 1930 there was beginning to be a difference, and as the Thirties went on, more and more Gaels were boldly proclaiming where the real artistic glories of their people lay. Among those Gaels Hector MacIver was one of the keenest sensibilities, and his eloquence was such that while he was still an undergraduate, or soon after, he was being mentioned with Maxton as one of the foremost Scottish orators of the day. He was also one of the few Gaels whose moral courage equalled his physical courage, and he had as much physical courage as any man I have known.

The Celtic Twilight of the 1890s and its product, the *Songs of the Hebrides*, were to the realities of Gaelic song poetry as Victorian Gothic is to the North French cathedrals. There is, however, in Gaelic song such an intrinsic quality of poetry and music that some of it could not fail to come through again and again, even in the *Songs of the Hebrides*, just as there is such a quality in Gothic architecture that it often shines through sham Gothic. In the 1920s, therefore, much 'educated' Gaelic opinion was right in preferring the *Songs of the Hebrides* to almost all 19th-century Gaelic song, which now seems, to me at any rate, to have been a natural product of the Clearances, the

Evangelical Revival and the Education Act of 1872.

The Clearances removed most of the Gaelic-speaking people to the industrial Lowlands and to Canada and Australia, vastly aggravated the poverty of those left crowded on the poorest patches of land in the Highlands and Islands, and broke their spirit. The Evangelical Revival proved with Fundamentalist and Calvinist logic that this world is only 'a vale of tears' and that the faithful must bear all the iniquities heaped on them by the powers that be, which are ordained by God, and that this world's material acquisitions do not matter at all. When the effects of the Evangelical Revival were abating, the Education Act began to teach children to sing 'Hearts of Oak' instead of 'Cairistìona', 'Cabar-féidh' or 'Beinn Dòrain'. The 'spiritual' leaders who were not Free Church Evangelicals went to Balmoral, and for the sake of the Anglo-Scottish Establishment, of which they were a part, preached nauseous propaganda against their fellow Gaels of Ireland. Even if the Free Church ministers could have brought Victoria and all the Establishment to some Gaelic Canossa, they would not have thought it worthwhile, knowing that she and almost all of her Establishment would soon have to endure fires worse than the Canossa snows.

In the terrible late 18th century and the worse 19th century, the years from 1780 to 1870, when Anglicised land-capitalist Highland chiefs with Gaelic names all but destroyed their blood kindred in order to fill their own pockets, Gaelic song poetry degenerated to a feeble wail and to a feebler pietism; what was healthy became parochial. In those years most of the real spiritual quality of the Gaelic-speaking people was expressed in the almost wholly extempore and unrecorded sermons and prayers of ministers and 'men' to whom all poetry and song except the Psalms of David was one of the more seductive vanities of this vale of tears. If only a moderate fraction of those sermons and prayers had been recorded, however, Scottish Gaelic would have a great 19th-century prose. Even as late as the 1920s it was quite common to hear some minister or elder quoting richly, by oral tradition, from sermons or prayers delivered 70 or 100 years before. Such quotations made it quite plain that in frankness, sincerity and psychological insight, expressed with an astonishing wealth of imagery and illustration, sometimes sonorously eloquent with the incomparable resonances of the Gaelic language and sometimes racily colloquial, Gaelic once had a great prose. If a man of imagination is convinced of the rags of human righteousness and of the desperate wickedness of the human heart, the expression of his conviction cannot fail to be powerful. Even to this day there may be heard Gaelic sermons in which the thought is essentially that of St Augustine, Calvin or even Pascal, and the prose one of great tension and variety. I fully believe that I have never heard or read as great a Gaelic prose as I have heard in the unrecorded sermons of Ewan MacQueen.

I do believe that this almost lost prose had far more impact on modern Gaelic poets than the prose, for instance, of Norman Mac-Leod, who was regarded until recently as the 'greatest' Gaelic prose-writer. I am sure that, compared with the lost prose of John Mac-Donald of Ferintosh, that of Norman MacLeod is merely orotund pietistic parochialism crossed with the parochialism of Balmoral. The Balmoral variety confirmed the parochialism that was imposed on Gaelic literature by the impotence of the 19th-century Scottish Gael in the face of the Clearances, and aggravated that post-1746 sense of inferiority which induced so many educated Gaels to derive an undue amount of comfort from the impact on Europe of James ('Ossian') Macpherson. A few months ago, hearing the doyen of international Celtic scholars exalt James Macpherson largely because of his impact on Europe, I felt impelled to commend to his attention a much greater Macpherson (Mary), of whom he had apparently never heard. One trouble is, or was, that men of industry and critical intellect comparable to the many who had worked on Celtic philology, and Scottish Gaelic philology in particular, had never applied themselves to Gaelic poetry, or at any rate to the Gaelic poetry of Scotland. I vividly remember my own thrill in 1933 when Mr James Caird and Dr George Davie introduced me to *Sangschaw* and *A Drunk Man Looks at the Thistle*, and I found, *inter alia plurima*, that Hugh MacDiarmid had sensed the greatness of Alexander MacDonald. Looking back now, I realise that the native sense of inferiority was part of my gratification at finding some genuine if one-sided appreciation of 18th-century Gaelic poetry in the man, a Lowland Scot, who I then felt, and still feel, had written some of the greatest European poetry of the century. I do not presume to be a judge of comparative European poetry, but the Nobel Laureates, Yeats and Eliot, are both, I think, inferior to MacDiarmid. If I remember rightly, I did not in 1933, nor do I now, put Alexander MacDonald's poetry on the same high level as the obscure or anonymous songs of 1550 to 1800, but it is very difficult to think of those songs as poetry alone. Their impact can never be that of poetry alone, though as such they are great enough for me. Their duality does, however, make them a dilemma to the modern Gaelic poet, whom they may fill with despair.

By the second half of the 18th century Gaelic poetry had known some wonderful triumphs in the realisation of physical nature. In a kind of objectivity it had gone as far as poetry can go, certainly further than any poetry I know in English, French or Latin. But it is deficient in explicit humanity. Duncan Macintyre can realise the great sweep of a mountain or the different motions of stags and hinds on it, or the eddying of a spring on its shoulder; MacDonald can realise the thump and splash of a ship's fore-quarters, or the sob under its aft-quarters, or the squirting race of a rope over its gunwale or through a cleat. Both can do such things as no one else, I believe, has ever done them in any language I know. But the physical scene is in itself far more important than either the explicit human reaction to it or its place as a background to human activity. Its appeal is overmuch to the senses rather than the heart or the brain, and though I do not discount its implicit emotion of joy, I think that it lacks the power to move most people deeply. In essence, its effect is something like a transcendent triumph of the Imagist programme of English and American poets in the first 20 years of this century.

In this same second half of the 18th century, however, the saintly Dugald Buchanan was expressing with a terrible clarity and intensity the Pauline-Augustinian-Calvinist reaction to the dispensation of the universe. His poetry is at the very opposite pole from that of Mac-Donald and Macintyre. It is an explicit expression of human love pitted in acceptance against a pre-conceived theistic view of the universe; it is the inevitable resolution of Calvinist passion. His poetry is at the opposite pole, too, from the inhuman sexual passion of the 16th-century song, though the modern reader may see a likeness:

> You burned my stackyard of oats and barley,
> You killed my father and my husband,
> Yes, and my three young brothers;
> Though you did that, I rejoice that you are alive.
> I like dark Allan from Lundy,
> My love the brown-haired coated Allan
> I like dark Allan from Lundy.

It is a sad and ironic comment on the inadequacy of contemporary evaluations of poetry that in the Eighties and Nineties of the last century Scotland had in Mary Macpherson a major Gaelic poet when Edinburgh, Dublin, London and Paris thought that the vapid Celtic Twilight was the only poetic habitat of the Gael. She, too, is the antithesis of Dugald Buchanan. Nineteenth-century Gaelic poetry is at its best in her when she mingles in it her sorrow and humiliation, the destruction of her people by the Clearances, her great *joie de vivre* and her perplexity that the remnant of her people have grown so 'strange' that 'sorrow is wheat to them', her holding fast to her own worldly pride and 'vanity', the plant that 'satisfies the flesh'. She is one of the few 19th-century Scottish Gaels of stature who did not dismiss the world in exchange for the ecstasies of the Evangelical Revival, or who were not so broken by the breaking of their people that their poetic voices became mouthpieces for parochialism and moralising. In her, echoes of the old songs are heard far oftener and more authentically than in any other 19th-century Gaelic poet. Indeed the old songs, gone underground except in the Catholic Islands, were often more or less secretly in the mouths of people who refused to accept the orthodoxy that no worthwhile 'criticism of life' in glorious words, that was not ostensibly religious, had ever come from Gaelic lips. In Raasay about 40 years ago, an old woman of impeccable Free Church antecedents once said of the Psalmist: 'David, the dirty blackguard, what was he compared with William Ross!' I myself consider William Ross's last song one of the very greatest poems ever made in any language in the islands once called British, but I do not think of it nearly as often as I do of some of the old songs. I think of it, however, more often than I do of any poem by MacDonald or Macintyre.

I suppose the poet is the musician *manqué*, but just as surely the musician is the poet *manqué*, because 'this intellectual being, the thoughts that wander through eternity', are at most only implicit in the musician's art. As poetry, the old Gaelic song has everything except our modern world and the far-ranging, uninhibited, troubled, explicit modern intellect; and because it has what it has, and is the supreme aesthetic product of our Gaelic-speaking people, it is bound to be one of the major influences on even the most modern Gaelic poet who is not altogether *déraciné* and ready to swallow unmixed the latest poetic theory from London, New York, Paris or Moscow. I think that all modern Gaelic poets, even those out at forward observation posts on the European poetical battlefield, would agree with me in this. On the European front itself, it is this necessity for an intellectually satisfying content that remains art which has produced Symbolism, and Symbolism, in its manifestations in Blok, Yeats, Valéry, Rilke, MacDiarmid and Eliot, is the most impressive 'ism' that I know of in this century.

Gaelic song before 1800 has everything except complexity of explicit thought, and it affords a variety of the many kinds of utterance that Arnold calls 'criticism of life'. Think of Fraser of Reelig's daughter

111

regretting the three things that come unasked; or John MacLean holding off his passion for the Campbell woman, with his unbending tree and ebb followed by flood; or the unknown poet accepting his loss of East, West, North and South, and — 'almost' — of his God. It has supreme passion held at the shortest arm's length compatible with art or the longest arm's length consistent with passion. It has the consolation of the woman raped at the shieling and forsaken, that she still has kinsmen and probably a lover among the splendid MacDonalds with the glories of Auldearn on their arms; the bitter grief and mixed love of the Campbell wife of MacLean of Coll hearing the slaughter of her brave kinsmen at Inverlochy by the 'bad' clans, with her husband and son among them, the MacDonalds and the MacLeans; the magical evocations of external nature in such songs as those attributed to Donald of Bohuntin and 'The Braes of Locheil', the 'Heir of Strath Swordale's Daughter', 'Mac Sìri', the song of the Kintail outlaw Farquhar MacRae in his cave in Coire Gorm a' Ghlinne behind Ben Attow, of John MacRae on the run from the Yankees about 1780, remembering his going up and down through Glen Sheil and Torr-Laoisich of the song-thrushes.

In the impressive 'Notes on the Border Ballads' in his book *Latitudes*, Edwin Muir had some significant and even moving things to say about those great Lowland poems. He talks of them as contemplating life in the light of pure passion. More often than not, the Gaelic song does not have this pure passion. It offers a breathtaking evocation of the natural background as well as passion as great as words can hold, and since human life and the human heart are subtle and 'impure', I believe that, partly because of this, the greatest Gaelic songs are greater poems than the greatest of the Lowland Ballads. For those who know Gaelic I need mention only the 'heavy surge and the deep kyle' in 'Cairistìona', or the 'little birch hollow' in 'Come, my love', or the glimpse of moonrise in the song of the woman who has lost her five children, 'Girl over yonder'. There are many examples of such a counterpointing of suffering and of a kind of Yeatsian 'joy'.

Celtic poetry has frequently, and rightly, been accused of rhetoric, of excessive stylisation, of a too elaborate and self-conscious technique. Far too much of the technical virtuosity of the Bardic Schools overflowed into the vernacular Chief-and-Clan poetry of the 16th, 17th and 18th centuries. But it is not so with the old songs. There the poet is talking to himself — herself, more often — walking the tightrope of metre without being conscious of it: and it is never tighter than, until this century, was considered by European practice necessary to poetry. I am not going to enter the question of metre and Free Verse except to say that however slack the rope of auditory shape may be, there has nevertheless to be some kind of tightrope onto which the poet goes. I am not prepared to allow to the word 'rhythm' the vagueness sanctioned by much contemporary theory in Britain, Europe and America. Metre does not make poetry, but I am not satisfied that poetry can exist without it. Perhaps it is as the 'filthy rags of human righteousness' are to the Calvinist Elect.

One seldom or never hears in the old songs of Gaeldom the rhythmic stumblings that one often hears in even the greatest of the Lowland Ballads. It can be argued that these flaws in the Ballads are due to generations of oral transmission, but why do they occur so seldom in Gaelic songs, which have undergone oral transmission for as many generations? In the Gaelic song the obvious corruption is often as breathtaking as the undoubted original — in total imaginative effect as well as in rhythm or metre. One undoubted quatrain on the execution, in 1570, of Gregor of Glenstrae reads as follows:

I reached the meadow of Bealach,
And there I got no peace;
I did not leave a hair of my head unpulled
Or skin on my hands.

That quatrain appears to have 'corrupted' to:

I ascended the great mountain path with no stop for breath,
Before the day greyed (i.e. before morning twilight);
I put the hair of my head to the ground
And the skin of my two hands.

Metrically, the corruption is as good as the original.

Most of the new Gaelic poets are very much aware of the tremendous song poetry behind them, and I suspect that its effect on them is ambivalent. On the other hand, it is an emotional stimulus making for devotion to the marvellous Gaelic language. I frequently re-read Sir Maurice Bowra's remarks on the Russian language in his introduction to *A Book of Russian Verse*, and I can never do so without applying to Gaelic much of what he says about the Russian language, and without being aware of a devotion to the Gaelic language among nearly all Gaelic poets, old and new, traditionalist and *avant-garde*, similar to the devotion to the Russian language which Bowra attributes to Turgenev. Nor can I read Bowra's words without being the more painfully aware of the intolerable situation of Scottish Gaelic today. For there is good reason to fear that the great song may soon be lost because there are no ears left to hear it. Modern Gaelic poetry may be, as an Appin man once put it 25 years ago, 'the last glimmer of the Gaelic sun before it goes down for ever'.

The Appin man's words referred in particular to what was new and vital in Gaelic poetry 25 years ago, but now, with what there is of 'new' as well as of more traditional Gaelic poetry, it looks as if there will be Gaelic Joshuas while there is a Gaelic language. We have the work of William Matheson, the Canna Campbell, the School of Scottish Studies, and of three now dead, my brother Calum, K C Craig and Hector MacIver, to keep all Gaels, and the new poets especially, alert to what is behind them. And we have the inspiring examples of the great tradition-bearers, of whom it is impossible not to mention Mr Calum Johnston. We owe more to him than to anyone else alive.

Of those of whom I am thinking, Hector MacIver was almost unique, in that he was able to respond to the old and the new at the same time, and by virtue of his astonishing moral courage and his eloquence. He always maintained in conversation that what was in Gaelic would be Gaelic if it were worth while at all, no matter what foreign influences had gone to its genesis. That, I feel sure, is true. Certainly the Gael is a mixed, variable human being, and not a pasteboard creation looming in a twilight or anywhere else. Poetry must have some kind of universality in it, no matter what the local habitation and name. It is much the same, but different as well, with prose literature. With some important changes, the central character of Mauriac's fine novel *La Parisienne* could be a West Highland Seceder. The language itself, however, does in poetry constitute a difference so great as to be a difference in kind. I think I can apprehend the greatness of Mauriac fairly well without reading a word of him in French, but I cannot see greatness in Goethe, reading him in translation, and so I have to take it on trust that he is a great poet. By the same token, neither I nor anyone else can ever hope to persuade the non-Gaelic world that William Ross's last song is comparable in quality to the best of Shakespeare's Sonnets. When Iain Crichton Smith talks of 'the infinite resonance' of William Ross, we know what he means, but the phrase is meaningless to anyone who does not know Gaelic.

The old songs may have a destructive influence on the modern Gaelic poet because of the danger that, no matter how many languages and literatures he knows well, the old Gaelic songs will remain for him the supreme hermaphrodite of words and music. It may be true on occasion, as with the 'Cro of Kintail' and the fragmentary words to one movement of *Cumha na Cloinne*, that the words are not anything to the music, but very often the simultaneous growth of both is such that after them one despairs of any human art of the ear. I know perfectly well that this is not fashionable talk nowadays, but to me no poetry, whatever it has of intellect or passion, or of delicacy and subtlety of perception, is great poetry unless it also has an auditory effect in proportion to one or more of its other qualities. Compared with that, 'purity' of diction is just one of the better products of sterility. The reduction to the absurd of the opposite view was achieved by editors who put in their anthologies MacDiarmid's 'Perfect' and rejected his 'Moonstruck'. (Morally, T S Eliot was one of them.) It is primarily this appeal to the ear which makes Yeats and the early MacDiarmid and, at a lower level, Eliot and Auden, such good poets. (I never shared Hector MacIver's reverence for Dylan Thomas.)

The old songs must be a burden on the new Gaelic poet if he has anything at all of Verlaine's feeling that poetry must be *'de la musique avant toute chose'*. I think that George Campbell Hay has felt the burden more lightly in that the music he seems to have most often at the back of his mind is the word music of the Bardic Schools, a more sophisticated, less intense, more attainable music than the 'out of this world' music of 'Cairistìona', 'Little Sister', 'Girl over yonder', 'The Jura Islands', 'Mac Sìri', 'I saw my lover', the two 'Ailean Donn' songs and scores of others. To me George Campbell Hay's poetry has the virtuosity of genius and is an exquisite blend of the Bardic old and the new, but I think that Derick Thomson and I myself are always haunted by the more intense, piercing and lyrical cry of the old songs. Because of that, we feel their burden more than Campbell Hay does. Of Crichton Smith, Donald MacAulay and Donald MacLeod I am not sure. It may be that they do not feel the burden at all, but I hesitate to think that.

Sometimes I feel that people like myself ought to shut up about the old songs: talking about them may be trying to do something to young Gaelic poets that can bring to mind Yeats's pardonable illusion that words of his sent out 'certain men the English shot'. On the other hand, the ceaseless reiteration of the poetic qualities of Gaelic songs which some of us have carried on for about 30 years may at least be an antidote to the dead-pan flatness of contemporary English verse. England is big and near, and liable to be too much of an influence on the new Gaelic poet, especially if he is not the linguist that George Campbell Hay is. And, by the nature of things, the poet is seldom a good linguist.

To insist on the necessity for music in poetry may put one, I suppose, into the category that English Literary criticism calls 'romantic', and it has been said again and again that the modern world and the atom bomb have eliminated romantic qualities from poetry. It seems to me that what 'romantic' means is largely a question of language, and I believe that all poetry may be called romantic in some way or other. The atom bomb, more than anything else, has brought about a change since 1945. But is this a change in kind rather than degree? The world was bad enough, and hopeless enough, between 1920 and 1930 when Scotland and the Anglo-Irish minority produced the great romantic poetry of Yeats and the early MacDiarmid, and certainly the *avant-garde* knew enough about Freud even then. It seems to me that to suggest that the atom bomb has destroyed romantic poetry for ever is equivalent to saying that it has destroyed all poetry except propaganda against the use of the bomb. This is to suggest that the final criterion of all poetry is a political or moral one, which is the same as saying that the final criterion of all human activity is political and moral, since men live in societies. It is also the same as saying that the final criterion is religious, if one believes in personal immortality. For Shelley the poet was the unacknowledged legislator of the world. For Dugald Buchanan he was, implicitly, the legislator for eternity, in which legislature the saintly Dugald Buchanan would have considered himself the obscurest of obscure backbenchers, but yet a member. The question is too big.

For the poet to believe, with the conscious mind at any rate, that the world may soon be turned to rubble by the atom bomb — is that radically different from believing, with the conscious mind, that 90 per cent of humanity, including nearly all those one loves most, are to spend an eternity of spiritual and physical torment? Poets have believed in an eternity of torment for the bulk of humanity and yet have continued to delight in love of all kinds and in external nature — in other words, have continued to be romantics. And I think they will continue to do so and be so even if they believe, with the conscious mind, that the world may soon be destroyed by atomic warfare. In the circumstances of our sub-atomic condition, it is romantic to put into pleasurable form the strange and complex, the mixed, greyish workings of the human heart. In spite of certain implications in Iain Crichton Smith's profound paper to the Gaelic Society of Inverness, poets and human beings will continue to be chancers; the preoccupation with the atomic bomb and with psychoanalytical honesty and linguistic 'purity' will have intervals of romantic voluptuousness. Perhaps these delights will be heightened by the prospect of the atomic holocaust, as those of William Ross must have been by the prospect of his own imminent death and his intellectual acceptance of Calvinism. It was only when he was actually dying that he asked for his poems to be burned.

The honesty that admits to the inhuman sexual passion of the woman who made the song for Allan of Lundy is fit to be an example of honesty in any poetry. If the insincerity of a great deal of Gaelic and English Victorian poetry is a long way from modern sincerity, it is an even longer way from the sincerity of the woman who loved Allan. With all his poses, snobberies and disgusting fascism, Yeats is to me a far more sincere poet than Eliot. Because of this sincerity, there shines through his poetry a deep, and romantic, envy of the noble plebeian James Connolly, not to mention Pearse, MacDonagh, and even his 'drunken vainglorious lout'. Even when Yeats is at his most rhetorical, one can sense the counterpointing of the sincere and the insincere, and I myself cannot see such a sincerity behind the preciously consistent humility of Eliot.

One reason why the old song is likely to be a very dangerous inspiration for the new Gaelic poet is that it is so difficult to separate its poetry from the mysteriously moving melodies that seem to rise spontaneously from the words. That the tunes do rise spontaneously, or that they and the words are simultaneous creations, is, I take it, the opinion of the greatest living authority, Mr William Matheson. When I put the matter to him, he said that of course they did rise spontaneously, and I don't think he misunderstood my words. The moral would seem to be that if a new Gaelic poet is more than ordinarily susceptible to music, he ought to avoid the old songs, just as Rilke travelling through Switzerland, refused to see the Alps and drew down the blinds of his railway compartment. He was afraid that the Alps would disturb his art too much. The old songs are, however, human, as the Alps are not, and the modern poet can hardly shun them entirely. I think that the poet is safer in contemplating an art other than poetry if he cannot avoid 'impurities' that may come into his work from that of others, though the logic of such an insistence on purity would indicate that a poet should not read or hear, or have read or heard, any poetry but his own: this is the essence of D H Lawrence's theories but the very opposite of Eliot's.

No Gaelic poet, at all events, can shun the greatest glory of Gaelic poetry, and make an artistic Origen of himself for the sake of his art. The old songs are 'there', and in a more human way than the mountains were 'there' in Mallory's words. If they are greater than poetry alone, nevertheless the poet cannot avoid them. It may be that there is the same kind of compulsion in the minds of the many who have maintained that if a poem cannot in some way approach the quality of music, if it lacks the lyrical cry, then it is not poetry; that even if it does not sing or chant, it must in some way suggest the song or chant. The question is how to find this suggestion of the song or chant in poetry that satisfies the mixed, troubled modern mind, and carries what is implicit in the old-fashioned phrase, 'criticism of life'. Perhaps, after all, the medley is the most satisfying modern poetic form. Perhaps, in spite of all Croce says, we must accept the 'unpoetic' flats out of which the lyrical peaks arise. Perhaps that is why so many good minds in Scotland consider MacDiarmid's *Drunk Man* and not *Sangschaw* the greatest single book of poetry by one man which has been produced in the British islands in this century. A few years ago I would have said *Sangschaw* myself, but now I am not sure. Probably no modern Gaelic poet will satisfy himself — even on the rare occasion when poets manage to do this — unless he has applied the lesson of the *Drunk Man*, or some similar lesson, as well as having drunk the heady wine of the old songs. A poet can disregard the internal combustion engine, but I doubt if he can disregard Freud and the atom bomb. Nevertheless, I feel that poetry will always resemble Valéry's sun:

> *Soleil, soleil, faute éclatantée,*
> *Tu gardes les coeurs de connaître*
> *Que l'univers n'est qu'un défaut*
> *Dans la pureté de non-être.*

What is in question is whether there can be poetry, or any art, which is fully relevant to the modern world and which at the same time satisfies the instinct for what is called 'beauty'. Psychoanalysis has shaken the belief in the wide divergence of good and bad, right and wrong, and has therefore undermined the basis of strong feeling which has seemed in the past to be essential to all art. Is an amoral delight no longer possible in serious art? Is George Campbell Hay's 'Siubhal a' Choire' the kind of poem that ought to be no longer possible, and is Iain Crichton Smith's 'The Old Woman' the only kind of poem that ought now to be made? To me they are both fine poems, and both have strong feeling in them. George Campbell Hay's has an old delight, and Iain Crichton Smith's has the grey modern mind's profound sympathy for decrepit humanity. His old woman could be, though she is not, the symbol of a post-atomic world, but three out of four people would say that George Campbell Hay's poem is 'beautiful', while not more than one would say the same of Iain Crichton

Smith's. Yeats excluded Wilfred Owen from his Oxford Book of Modern Verse because he felt that none of Owen's poems had in them what he called joy. By the same token he would have rejected 'The Old Woman'. Yeats, I am sure, was wrong about Owen. And I feel that the three out of four would be wrong about this particular poem of Iain Crichton Smith's.

Some Thoughts about Gaelic Poetry

When I hear one of the great song poems, especially those of obscure or unknown authorship, those sometimes called 'folk poems' or 'sub-literary' poems, I ask myself how much of their magic is due to their tunes, including their refrains of choruses of meaningless vocables or mixtures of actual words and meaningless vocables. I am thinking of such obscure or anonymous songs as 'Griogar Cridhe', one or two others of the MacGregor tragedies, 'Cairistìona', 'A Phiùthrag', 'Seathan', 'MacSìri', 'An Crònan Muileach', 'Uamha 'n Oir', one or two of the extant laments for Iain Garbh of Raasay, the two great 'Ailein Duinn' poems, Beathag Mhór's song to Màrtainn Mór a' Bhealaich, 'Nighean Oighre Shrath Shuardail', 'Bràighe Loch Iall', 'Mo Nighean Donn á Còrnaig', 'Iomair thusa, Choinnich chridhe', 'Mo Rùn Geal Og', and many, many more; and of such songs by well-known poets as 'Oran Mór Mhic Leòid', three or four or five of Màiri Nighean Alasdair Ruaidh's, Màiri Mhór's 'Ged tha mo cheann air liathadh' and 'Nuair bha mi òg', Ross's 'Oran Eile', 'Beinn Dórain'; 'Cabar Féidh', and so on.

In many of those song poems, the tunes themselves are great, very great, or simply ineffable; and what is more they seem like exhalations from the words, as if the very words created the tunes. At one time, at any rate, one of the very greatest authorities, Rev. William Matheson, agreed with me that some of the tunes came out of the words in a simultaneous creation. Whether they did or not, they very often seem to, which is the ultimate test. I am thinking of such songs as the versions of 'Cairistìona' and 'A Phiùthrag' that I heard from Calum Johnston; the version of 'Na h-Eileanan Diùrach' that my brother Calum got from Mrs MacCormick from Hàclait in Benbecula; the version of 'MacSìri' that came from the MacInnes family and the MacDonald family in Strath in Skye; the version of ''S mi 'nam shuidh' air an fhaoilinn' that my grandmother had; the version of another Iain Garbh song sung by the late J.C.M. Campbell; the version of Ross's 'Oran eile' as sung by my father; 'Calum Sgàire' or 'A

Choinnich Chridhe' as sung by Katie MacLeod; and many similar examples.

I think, and I have long ago said it publicly, that many Gaelic songs were spoiled by becoming *luadh* songs; that their rhythms and timing were quickened and made less poignant and subtle, and that the verbal accretions of the *òrain luaidh* lessened the intensity of their poetry. For example, the late K.C. Craig's *Orain Luaidh Màiri Nighean Alasdair* made even the greatest of the Iain Garbh songs, ''S mi 'nam shuidh' air an fhaoilinn', an *òran luaidh*; and his versions of 'A Phiùthrag' and 'Mo Nighean Donn á Cornaig' seem to me to have disturbing accretions in their words. Indeed I was told that Dòmhnall Ruadh Mac an t-Saoir said that Màiri Nighean Alasdair was prone to mix the words of songs, many of which she got from Dòmhnall's own mother. That does not alter the fact that many more of her versions are magnificent homogeneous poems and that the loss of K.C. Craig in 1963 was a tragedy for Gaeldom.

Let me give Calum Johnston's version of 'Cairistìona' without the refrain of vocables:

Nach freagair thu, Chairistìona?
Na freagradh tu chluinninn fhìn thu.
Thug mi bliadhna 'n cùirt an rìgh leat;
'S ged theirinn e thug mi trì ann.
Turus thug mi a Ghleann Comhann,
Bha 'n fhairge trom 's an caolas domhainn,
Cha b'urra dhomh mo leum a thomhas;
Cha robh Cairistìona romham.
Chì mi luingeas air Caol Ile
Tighinn an coinneamh Cairistìona,
Chan ann gu banais a dhèanamh,
Ach g'a cur 'san talamh ìseal,
Fo leacan troma gu dìlinn.

Will you not answer, Cairistìona?
If you would answer, I would hear you.
I spent a year in the King's court with you
and, though I myself would say it, I spent three.
Once when I went to Glencoe
the surge was heavy and the kyle deep,
I could not measure my leap;
Cairistìona was not there before me.
I see ships on the Sound of Islay
coming to meet Cairistìona,
not to make a wedding

121

but to put her in the low earth,
under heavy flagstones until Doomsday.

These are all the words I heard from Calum Johnston, and he always sang all the words he knew of a song to an audience keen to hear him. For example, he would sing a very long version of 'A' Bhirlinn Bharrach'.

In Sinclair's *Oranaiche* there are wonderfully fine versions of at least three of the songs I have mentioned: the Campbell/Morrison 'Ailein Duinn'; the Maclean 'Ailein Duinn'; and 'Mhic Ain mhic Sheumais'. These are three of those with great words and great melodies which are also great even without the melodies to which they are sung. In 1955 I was giving a lecture to a big group of Bavarian teachers and student teachers in Munich. It was on something to do with modern English poetry. Knowing that I knew Gaelic, one of the audience asked me without any warning to give them an English translation of a Gaelic poem. I had only my memory and had to choose quickly. I chose the Campbell/Morrison 'Ailein Duinn' and translated it (I think every word in Sinclair's *Oranaiche*) line by line, having to remember the Gaelic and put it into English almost simultaneously. It must have been a very lame performance on my part, but the reaction was in the words: 'What a marvellous poem!' I think the same reaction would have greeted a great number of Gaelic songs even in translation and, of course, without their tunes, which are sometimes beyond all words; and I still think that those songs, words and music together, are the greatest artistic glory of Scotland. My brother John would have said some pibrochs such as the 'Lament for the Children'.

Of the tune of the great MacGregor song-poem ''S mi 'm shuidhe seo m' ònar air còmhnard an rathaid' I have no proper recollection, though I heard it at least once. As far as I remember, the melody to which this song was sung is not at all adequate for the words of this great poem, a poem which seems to have complexities and ironies. The lines beginning ''S ann a rinn sibh 'n t-sithionn anamoch/Anns a' ghleann am bi 'n ceathach/Dh'fhàg sibh an t-Eòin bòidheach/Air a' mhòintich 'na laighe/'Na starsnaich air féithe/An déidh a reubadh le claidheamh' may seem a savage gloating about the killing of John Drummond, King's Forester in Glenartney, but he had summarily hanged seven or eight MacGregors for poaching. What of the word 'bòidheach'? The concession in the word is, I think, ambivalent. How much is it a gloating contrast between his living appearance or his appearance as a mangled decapitated corpse left a stepping-stone over a bog; and how much is there in it of a woman's pity for a handsome man? I think there is a strange density about the word 'bòidheach', and there is surely an irony about the words "S ann a rinn sibh 'n t-sithionn anamoch'. It is dangerous to use the word 'simple' in talking about poetry.

A great many of the anonymous or obscure song poems are high-keyed expressions of tragedy, most often of tragedies of circumstances, but often too the tragedies involve character. I suppose the MacGregor chiefs and clan were unusually reckless in their revenge for the terrible wrongs they suffered, and that they committed barbarities almost as bad as the judicial barbarities of the time. What do we know of Iain Garbh MacGille Chaluim of Raasay except that he was unusually strong and handsome? His death was purely a tragedy of circumstance to his sister, who, according to one tradition, made the songs, one every Friday for a year after his death; but the drunkenness of himself and the crew had something to do with it, according to the letter written by his surviving brother Alasdair. There are also traditions that he was more than ordinarily vain. One is about his wanting to take on a great Matheson strong man, John of Fernaig, and the other is a Skye tradition about his coming to challenge Gilleasbuig na Dìge. Whether Gilleasbuig was a Mac-Donald, MacQueen, Nicolson or Martin I do not know. Whatever Iain Garbh was really like in character and disposition there is nothing in the five extant songs about him to suggest that his death was anything but a tragedy of circumstance. It is interesting however that one of the songs is by a sister who was abandoned by her lover, presumably not the wife of Duncan MacRae of Inverinate. Who the 'mac thighearna 'n Dùine' who was false to Iain Garbh's sister was, we do not know. Was he of Duntulm or of Dunvegan or of Peighinn an Dùine, now called South Cuidreach? At any rate the personal humiliation may give edge to the great songs attributed by some traditions to the sister of Iain Garbh.

A great number of the songs are by no means tragic, indeed anything but. There is the wistful fragrant memory of 'Nighean Oighre Shrath Shuardail', and more than a wistful memory in the quiet triumph of 'Bràighe Loch Iall', both men's songs. There is a great triumph in the woman's song 'A mhic Ain mhic Sheumais' though there is in it too pain because of his wound and regret that he has to stay in the bare exposed Eriskay instead of in lush Sleat or in the rich pasture lands of Trotternish. There is another kind of triumph in the much sought after girl of 'Nochd a' cheud oidhche 'n fhoghair', and in the tolerant and amused gentleness of 'Mac Og an Iarla Ruaidh'. The famous song by Beathag Mhór for Martin of Bealach has

123

love, regret and bitterness, and a triumph in the existence of the son she had from Martin before the time came for him to get an aristocratic wife from Uist or from the Lewis and Raasay MacLeods or from the 'seed of Norman', the MacLeods of Skye and Harris.

Ma théid thu dh'Uibhist an eòrna
Thoir bean bhòidheach dhachaidh leat.
Ma gheibh thu bean a Shìol Leòid
Gun iarr i móran fhasanan;
Ma gheibh thu bean a Shìol Tharmaid
Marbhaidh i le macnas thu.

If you go to Uist of the barley
bring a fair wife home with you.
If you get a wife of the MacLeods
she will ask for many fashions;
if you get a wife of the seed of Norman
she will kill you with wantonness.

I wonder how often the uninhibited sentiments of some of those songs are *luadh* accretions. It was actually a daughter of MacLeod of Raasay that Martin did marry, and there was a tradition that she was uppish and put him out on a wild wet winter night to mend the thatch on their house, saying that in her father's house there would be no such leak. I wonder if the 'móran fhasanan' is an after-the-event extemporisation at a *luadh*, and I wonder if the imputation of wantonness to the 'Norman' MacLeod women is a Trotternish jibe at the women of Dùis Mhic Leòid and Harris by a Trotternish woman other than Beathag Mhór herself.

It may be that the *luadh* accretions were sometimes improvements making the songs franker and more complex. Not that I think complexity is necessarily a poetic virtue, but frankness nearly always is. Was it women's exclusion from the Bardic Schools that made so many of their songs so uninhibited sexually that even incestuous love is heard once or twice in *luadh* songs, and desires to be raped or bear illegitimate sons to some handsome aristocrat are common motifs? Was women's frankness partly a reaction against the fulsome recital of the noblemen's virtues in the poems of the Bardic Schools and the chief-and-clan eulogies of their seventeenth and eighteenth century successors? For instance, what kind of man was the greatly lauded Alasdair Dubh of Glengarry, who died about 1720, and was the subject of so many poems, notably the elegy by Sìleas of Keppoch, herself a woman with few illusions about men? Was he really so wise as she says — as well as brave, strong, handsome and generous? It is said that he spoiled things for the Jacobite army before and after Killie-crankie by gratuitously insulting the Camerons, who had double the numbers of the Glengarry MacDonalds. It was said that after Claver-house's death, the leader ought to have been Ewen of Lochiel, who was very experienced and skilful, instead of Cannon the Irishman. The boy chiefs of Clanranald and Maclean would not have much say, and Donald of Sleat had no love for Glengarry because of jealousy over the headship of Clan Donald. But we cannot be sure. After all, 'the Earl had lost his money and Ewen had lost his God' in the Campbell/Maclean quarrels in the 1670s, when the Macleans were temporarily saved by Alasdair's predecessor Angus and lesser MacDonald chiefs such as Keppoch. Besides, Alasdair was probably much wiser in 1720 than he was in 1689, and probably Sìleas had no axe to grind, and there is some evidence that she considered the Sleat chiefs the heads of Clan Donald.

This is really a digression. There is no doubt at all that the women's songs of the *luadh* are most frank and outspoken and full even of sexual bravado. I wonder how many of them are really by the woman who speaks, and how many are simply words put into her mouth. The desire to bear illegitimate children to some handsome aristocrat, or envy of some woman raped by a handsome aristocrat, is fairly common. Take, for example, the song of the woman who regrets that she was not the 'maighdean cheutach' raped by a Niall Donn who was high enough in the social scale to have a page. Craig has it in his *Orain Luaidh Màiri Nighean Alasdair* (pp. 9-10), and my brother Calum got much the same version in Benbecula.

The frank wish to bear a son or sons to a man higher in the social scale is common, the sons to be bred to be one a duke, one a captain, one a drover, one a scrivener in Perth, sometimes one on 'a big ship in England', the rank unspecified but presumably high. Such a poem does not necessarily involve any question of rape.

But there are poems of rape with a great difference. There is a very different ending in a song with one of the most haunting melodies and refrains. Most authorities say that there are two very different songs with the refrain

> Ho roho hì hóireannan
> Ho ró chall éile
> Ho roho hì hóireannan.

One is by a girl raped on a shieling and one about the MacDonalds at Auldearn in 1645. But a few versions from different parts make them one song. The MacDonald editors say that it was made by a woman in Crossal in Skye, and I have heard a Trotternish tradition that 'bothag na h-àirigh' was in one of the Cuillin corries. If it was, it must have been in one of the corries facing north and west, that is on the Crossal side. If it is really one poem it is a most complex and remarkable poem: first anger and humiliation turning to indifference and then to an exulting compensation in the military glories of her MacDonald kinsman.

In one or two waulking songs there is an almost incomprehensible tragedy of passion. Such is the song on incest between brother and sister recorded by Craig (*Orain Luaidh Màiri Nighean Alasdair*, pp. 25-26). Surely they are words put into the mouth of the young woman by women at a waulking far in time and place from the event out of which the song came? But perhaps not: compare the mad sexual passion of the woman in love with 'Ailean Dubh á Lòchaidh', who had killed her father, husband and three young brothers as well as burning her stackyard of oats and barley.

The ranges of emotion and imagery in these songs are immense. Consider this one, with a dark weird cry in its music:

A nighean ud thall
A bheil thu t'fhaireachadh?
Coimhead a-mach
A bheil a' ghealach ann,
No bheil a' ghaoth an iar
Gun charachadh,
No faod am bàta
Taobh a theannadh ruinn.

Girl over there,
are you awake?
Look out to see
if there is a moon,
or is the wind west
without changing,
or can the boat
manage to come our way.

Then the woman reproaches another woman who was casting up to her that she was losing her children. She will not wish pain to that woman's soul, but she wishes that she will have earthly sorrow.

Poems definitely not waulking songs have a great range of mood, rhythm, music and imagery, if one can ever separate those elements.

Think of the images in the complexity of the poem "'S mi air m'uilinn sa' leabaidh', and of the images conveying the curse on her sister by the deserted wife of MacNeachdainn an Dùin.

Sometimes the song poems with ineffable tunes can even be ironical, as for instance, the mock-heroic 'Mhic Mhaoilein a shaorainn', with its glorious tune and ironical words parodying some women's love songs:

Bidh m'athair is mo mhàthair
A ghnàth ga mo sheòladh,
Mi sheachnadh coinneimh anamoich
Ri sealgair na mòintich;
Do shùgradh a chlaoidh mi,
Do choibhneas a leòn mi:
Gum b'fheàrr liom na fear oighreachd
Bhith oidhche riut pòsda.

My father and my mother are
always giving me guidance,
to avoid a late meeting
with the hunter of the moorland.
Your love-talk did overcome me,
your kindness did wound me;
I would prefer to a landlord
to be one night married to you.

This song was by the Tàillear Crùbach, MacCulloch, of Camas Loighnidh in Kintail about 1850 and it seems to follow the tune and echo some of the words of a love song made before 1800 for my own great-great-grandfather, Tarmad Mór Ain mhic Tharmaid MacLean.

It is true, however, that sometimes the tunes carry middling words with them, as in many passages of the so-called *òrain mhóra*, like passages of 'Beinn Dórain', 'Coire Cheathaich' or 'Allt an t-Siùcair', especially where the adjective-packing is great. Not that adjective packing is necessarily bad. I can think of one great line where five adjectives qualify one noun with wonderful effect: 'An cridhe geal fialaidh aotrom aighearach òg'. It is true that that line is followed by a line with only one adjective, and that a sensuously contrasted one: 'Bu mhilis liom fhéin am beul on tigeadh an ceòl'.

The origins of adjective-packing in Gaelic poetry are, I am sure, the subject of theories and theses which I do not know. Nor do I know how many examples can be traced in Scottish Gaelic before the Harlaw poem. I wonder if it is at all related to the involutions and details of the illuminated manuscripts, but I suppose those also exist in countries with few affinities with Celtic-speaking peoples — if indeed there are in Europe any such nations, when one remembers the central position in Europe of the Celts in their hey-day. Whatever the origins, the adjectival excess is a blemish even on such great poems as 'Beinn Dórain', and more so on many, many others of the eighteenth century nature poems. Of course, the cumulative effect of 'Beinn Dórain' is that of a great poem that achieves something that can be called a realisation of static and dynamic nature, an apotheosis of naturalism. That such an apotheosis of naturalism could be achieved in a most highly stylised series of metres modelled on the movements of pibroch is an artistic miracle. The poem ought to be a *tour de force* and is not, for it is so spontaneous, so lacking in the least suggestion of the laboured, precious or contrived. The movements of each *ùrlar*, *siubhal* and *crùnluadh* seem to come naturally from the great sweep of the mountain, the different movements of stags, hinds, bucks and does on it, the gurgling eddies of springs of water, and, in the last *crùnluadh*, the rush, clangour, clatter and struggles of the hunt. Alasdair MacMhaighstir Alasdair had preceded Donnchadh Bàn with his 'Moladh Móraig'; but splendid as that poem is with its paeans of lust, I do not think that such male reactions to a woman's body go so well into pibroch metres as a mountain and the animals and static scenes and movements on it. This is not a moral judgment. For example, MacDonald's last *crùnluadh* is about an erotic dream and the wakening from it. The movement of the verse is not at all inevitable to such a situation as Macintyre's last *crùnluadh* is to the hunt.

MacDonald's 'Birlinn' has no stylisation of metres and in it there are splendid passages that achieve an apotheosis of naturalism, such as the sea foaming about and into the shoulders of the *birlinn*; the swishing thumps and sob of the sea about her quarters and stern; the rope squirting through a cleat; the twisting of oars in the oxters of high waves; and the splendid contrast between the Incitement to Rowing and the Rowing Song itself; and in the storm scene, marred as it is with frigid hyperboles and sometimes a frigid kind of surrealism. Unlike 'Beinn Dórain' there are no metrical *tours de force* in the 'Birlinn' but the old syllabic metres so modified by speech stress as to give a counterpoint between metre and ordinary speech movement.

What does so much of this magnificent Gaelic nature poetry of the eighteenth century say of the human mind and heart? Not a great deal explicitly, but what is or may be implicit may be very much greater. I suppose there is in MacDonald's poetry a great verve and pride in life — a delight in external nature, and a still greater delight and pride in the heroism of human struggle and human physical and emotional exuberance. In Macintyre there is a quieter joy in the beauty of mountain and corrie and the vegetation and, above all, the wild animals in them; but there is also the skill of the hunter and the excellence of his equipment in killing the handsome stag and the lissom hind. The dichotomy is strange in a man so sensitive in many ways, but Macintyre is given to an acceptance of things, and seems unaware that human pity may be extended to the otherness of wild animals. Nearly two centuries before Macintyre's time, Dòmhnall MacFhionnlaigh nan Dàn had said: 'Moladh gach fear eile 'n cù/ Molaims' an trù tha dol as'. But the hunt was a necessity for food, and a delight in it for its own sake is rather a common human characteristic.

Macintyre was not a contentious man. He accepted his conscription in the Hanoverian militia and his having to run away at Falkirk but he had the compensation that it was from the MacDonalds he was running, for the Macintyres were traditionally of Clan Donald. There was, however, one thing that neither he nor any Gaelic poet for the next hundred years could accept, and that was the Clearances for sheep. I wonder how he would have taken the later Clearances for deer forests. There is a proviso about all such things: we know so little. After all, the fathers and perhaps the grandfathers of the same Breadalbane Campbell lairds had been with the MacDonalds and Macleans on the victorious Jacobite wing or centre at Sheriffmuir and as such had been celebrated by the very Jacobite MacDonald poetess, Sìleas of Keppoch:

Chaidh Clann Dòmhaill an sin an òrdugh
Is Clann Ghill-Eain nan rò-seòl àrd,
Sgioba Bhraid-Albann, a' bhratach bhallabhuidh,
Bu bhuidheann ainmeil bha sin aig Màrr.

Clan Donald then went in order
and Clan Gillean of the great high sails,
the men of Breadalbane, the speckled yellow banner,
that was a famous company of Mar's.

Which raises the question of propaganda in poetry, especially when it involves a one-sided bitterness. One of the most terrible quatrains in Gaelic poetry is that which Professor Watson puts as the last verse of Iain Lom's 'Inbhir Lòchaidh':

Mo chreach mas duilich liom ur càramh
Ag éisdeachd anshocair ur pàisdean

Ag caoidh a' phannail bha san àraich,
Donnalaich bhan Earra-ghàidheal.

Curse you if I pity your condition
listening to the distress of your children
lamenting the womanish band on the battlefield,
the howling of the women of Argyll.

One thinks of the inhuman implications of the words: the rather
muted pity of 'anshocair'; the contempt of the word 'pannal' as against
the great stand of the genuine Campbells deserted by two-thirds of
Argyle's army, the conscripted Lowlanders and the many of Argyle's
own soldiers who were not really Campbells at all but others whom the
policy of Argyle and of his predecessors had forced into the Campbell
muster. Why is a verse of such inhumanity splendid poetry? It
appears from the words of the generous Donald of Bohuntin and still
more from the words of his mordant brother Dòmhnall Gruamach,
that Iain Lom's anti-Campbell snarl was deprecated by at least some
of the Keppoch MacDonalds. I wonder what is behind the story that
Iain Lom was not a MacDonald at all but really a Campbell himself
whose father or grandfather had been forced to flee from the Campbell
country. Of course, terrible things had been done by both factions in
the Montrose wars. We have the words of the MacMhuirich historian
about Auchinbreck's return from Ireland and the fury and madness
that took him when he found his country burnt and plundered. But I
do not know what Auchinbreck himself had done in Ireland. (I have
referred to the 'muted pity' of the word 'anshocair'; but I may be
wrong, for 'anshocair' may have been as strong a word to Iain Lom as
it is to me. Semantics play strange games with stylistic analysis.) It
appears that Florence, sister of Campbell of Auchinbreck, was married to MacLean of Coll, and that her son was in Montrose's army. It is
true that the heart-break of her poem in Vol XXVI of the *Transactions
of the Gaelic Society of Inverness* is crossed with her own wrongs at the
hands of her husband and his paramour 'Seònaid dhona', and that the
poem has that in it to add to her grief for 'Dònnchadh calma cròdha',
i.e. Auchinbreck, and some handsome young Donald, who may also
have been her brother. It seems to me that in the end we have to fall
back on moral judgments, and in old partisan poetry there is so much
of the unknown that the particular judgment is impossible. In poetry
it is dangerous to be bitter against anyone but oneself; but on the other
hand frankness is preferable to insincerity. I remember Norman
MacCaig saying that what human beings have in common is more
important in poetry than what divides them.

Propaganda in poetry there must be where there is strong commitment, and the test of its poetic value cannot be wholly divorced from what one knows of the poet himself apart from his poetry. I doubt if Duncan Macintyre had any very strong political, social or religious convictions. In 'Beinn Dórain', as I have said, there is little explicit feeling for humanity, the *lacrimae rerum*; but there is a great deal of it in 'Cead Deireannach nam Beann'. Politically and socially he appears to have been rather a naive conservative, accepting the dictates of his social and political superiors, whom he liked, until it came to the Clearances. Even then he deplores the result of their actions rather than condemn themselves, and his chief sorrow seems to be that they are substituting sheep for deer, not for people.

If propaganda is really convincing in poetry it must evince either an intense commitment or be crossed with the confessional. There is, as far as I remember, nothing of the personal confessional about the great religious propagandist poetry of Dugald Buchanan except that he accepts the corruption of his own nature in that of all mankind. It is an unmixed poetry of intense commitment to the saving of souls, the poetry of a single-minded devotee. What we know of the man confirms that. He was loved in Rannoch as John MacLachlan of Rahoy was in Morvern and Mull. That is clear from the strife between the people of Rannoch, where he worked and died, and his own kinsfolk, as to whether he was to be buried in Rannoch or in little Leny among his own Buchanans. I wonder how much the example of the life influences our judgments. Would our valuation of Buchanan's poetry be the same if it were anonymous? As to Buchanan, the really fearful intensity and concentration of his poetry grips us and, all the more, because there is external testimony that he was a kind of saint. I have heard a humanist agnostic call Buchanan the greatest of all Gaelic poets, quoting the eight lines beginning 'Ged àir'mhinn uile reulta nèimh' and ending 'Ach mar gun tòisicheadh i 'n dé'.

In some ways, the Gaelic antithesis to Buchanan is Rob Donn, with his humanist sermo-pedestrian verse. He seems to have been a worldly-wise, humorous, rather satirical moralist, with however a courageous sense of honour, although he was capable of lapses like the making of the poem 'Marbhrann Eóghainn' (if John MacKenzie's account is right). Rob Donn poses a question: how can such relaxed poetry be great? Even 'Iseabail Nic Aoidh', a pibroch poem, is relaxed, and in the last *crùnluadh* especially the relaxation is at strange variance with the expertise of the stylised metre.

In the short poem on the three old bachelors of Taigh Ruspainn he is not relaxed but terse and taut, although conversational at the same

time, especially if one knows that the line 'Chaidh stràc dhe'n
t-saoghal thairis orr' is a Bowdlerisation for 'Dh'ith is dh'òl is chac
iad'. Lack of intensity and passion, indeed lack of the *lacrimae rerum*,
is manifest in Rob Donn's poetry, and I think John MacKenzie was
right in attributing a deficiency in pathos to Rob Donn; but I doubt in
attributing to him a lack of invention.

Since every life ends in death and is full of the deaths of others, it
seems that most really great poetry is tragic or suffused with the
lacrimae rerum; but this raises the question: how great is the sorrow if it
goes into articulate words at all and still more into verse? And what if
the verse is stately as well as plangent? I think of the Ciaran Mabach's
noble elegy for his brother Seumas Mór MacDonald of Sleat, who
died in 1679; of William MacKenzie's elegy for his brother Alasdair
Donn, which too is a resonant stately poem; of Sìleas of Keppoch's
lament for the harper with its grace; and above all, of William Ross's
dirge for his loss of love and his approaching death at the age of
twenty-eight or so. Somebody or other has accused Ross of self-pity
and somebody else has accused this great poem of an over-elaboration
of the passion. I think such accusations are superficial and ignorant of
the nature of poetry and indeed of all art. Wordsworth said very truly
that poetry is generated by emotion recollected in tranquillity, and
someone else rejoined, also truly, that it is generated by tranquillity
recollected in emotion. I would say that in each case tranquillity is a
relative term. Even the most sustained and passionate love has its
intervals of relative tranquillity; and I know, having been face to face
with almost certain death in war, that varying forms of human pride
can overcome fear, sometimes at any rate; and it is certain that the
pride of the poet was strong in William Ross, as it is in many poets.
Besides frankness is a necessity for poetry as it is for truth. We do not
know what was the interval of days, weeks or months between the
marriage of Mór Ross and the making of the 'Oran Eile'. I don't think
Montrose is greatly blamed for going to his death in a scarlet coat or
whatever other finery he wore. At any rate, the magnificent rhythms,
cadences and resonances of the poem are not laboured or contrived,
for the words seem to carry the noble tune with them; and it is a noble
tune as I have heard my father and one or two others sing it. The
sublimation of sexual love has been responsible for much of the
world's greatest poetry and notably when the sexual love is crossed
with tragedy.

An Irish critic who knows Scottish poetry well could not see why I
preferred the poetry of Màiri Mhór to that of Neil MacLeod. I think it
is because Màiri Mhór's 'public' poetry is so impregnated with her

individual suffering that it has a rare complex intensity and is more personal and confessional, albeit implicitly so. It appears that all 'public' poetry has to be personal in one way or another; and yet there is very little of the personal in John MacLachlan's 'Dìreadh a-mach ri Beinn Shianta', which I think a great poem.

It is difficult for me to be objective about John MacLachlan's poetry, as I know it is for many others besides myself to be objective about Dugald Buchanan. In Mull in 1938, and later from Alasdair Cameron, 'North Argyll', I heard so much of the splendour of his personality and of the great love that he evoked in others. I tried to express that in a poem published in *The Scotia Review* and I think it says more than anything else I can say.

The difficulty of objectivity in the criticism of poetry is so great that it is impossible unless one applies arbitrary rules that in the next decade or generation are discredited; and then even that limited objectivity is questionable. For instance, Scottish nationalist propaganda is strong in the poetry of that fine poet and man George Campbell Hay; and although I do not consider such overtly Nationalist poetry his finest poetry, yet I value it greatly because I know that he is as pure a spirit as a man can be and that he suffered greatly for his Nationalism at a time when I myself could not agree with his political stand, just as I could not with the stand of others whom I considered some of the finest men I knew. That modern Scottish Gaeldom could produce two such different poets, both such exceptionally fine men as well as such fine poets, as Hay and Iain Crichton Smith is a very great thing, especially as they are so very different as poets.

The poetry of William Livingston

In bulk the most considerable part of William Livingston's poetry consists of heroic medleys on historical, legendary, or imaginary pseudo-historical themes. Of these the two longest are 'Na Lochlannaich an Ile' and 'Blàr Shunadail', both of which deal with fighting between the Gaels and Norsemen in Islay and Kintyre at a very hazy date and both of which have hardly a shred of even legendary basis. Three poems, 'Cath Thom Ealachaidh', 'Blàr Dhail-righ' and 'Blàr Allt a' Bhannaich', deal with the Wars of Independence, while 'Cath Monadh Bhraca' is on Mons Graupius, and 'Blàr Thràigh Ghruineart' on the clan battle between the MacDonalds and the MacLeans in Islay in 1598. There is also a heroic piece on Alma and Balaclava, contemporary events.

Of the heroic poems I think 'Na Lochlannaich an Ile' is the most impressive, though it is much less uniform than some of the others, and more of a medley in form than any of the rest. It is a formless semi-epical fragment, in which the verse varies from strong adequacy to utter wordy formlessness, lit up occasionally by a striking image like that from the opening description of the MacDonald arms:

Bradan 's a shlios mar bhoillsgeadh airgid gun smal
Fo ghluasad samhladh sruth a' ruith 'na chuisle bhras.

A salmon with its side like the gleam of stainless silver
under the movement of the likeness of a stream in an impetuous torrent.

But, as well as the pseudo-historical matter, there is the poignant theme that recurs almost everywhere in Livingston's poetry, namely the contemporary desolation of Islay in the matter of men, in spite of the permanent majesty of nature; the woes of the Gael at the hands of the 'coimhich gun iochd', the barbarian English landlord being a far more effective spoiler than the vanquished Norseman; the lowing brutes lying on the floors of the Gael; the glory of Gaelic hospitality and charity gone; and Islay, 'cathair lagh nan Eileanan Gàidhealach', forlorn; and there is a direct, unveiled attack on the particular landlord, Ramsay of Kildalton. The Gaels are a remnant, but there is the proud assertion that there is still 'fuidheall nach salaich an t-òr 's nach lùb'.

The chaotic formlessness of much of the verse contrasts with parts where it is vigorous, metrically adequate, and even powerful:

Bha 'm freiceadan air Mùr Dhùn Athad
Do'm bu dreuchd an talla choimhead,
'S a chunnaic a' teachd o'n iar-dheas
Càbhlach nam buidhnean fiata,
Sgaothan toirmisgt' tìr na gaillinn,
A bu tearc a stadadh sìon no doireann,
Creachadairean allta lìonmhor,
Iargalta, gun iochd, gun fhìrinn,
Dìorrasach, fuileach, coirbte, dàna,
A dh'fhàg basraich an iomadh àite
Air còrsan Rìoghachdan na h-Eòrpa
O'n Fhairge Mhòir gu Cuan na Reòta.

On the rampart of Dun Athad were the guards
whose duty was to keep the hall,
and they saw coming from the south-west
the fleet of the fierce bands,
the forbidden swarms of the land of tempest,
whom weather or storm would rarely check,
plunderers who were savage and numerous,
frightful, merciless, truthless,
vehement, bloody, wicked, audacious,
who left wringing of hands in many a place
on the coasts of the kingdoms of Europe
from the Great Sea to the Frozen Ocean.

The Norse are heroic barbarians, whose arms have a 'bear with a king in his teeth', a typical Livingston touch, and the verse becomes more than adequate in describing their ships:

Bha 'm brataichean am bàrr nan cranna
Le anail nan neul a' srannail,
Stiallan dubh ri fiodhrach seòlaidh,
Starcaicht' ri fàraidhean còrcaich.

Their banners were at the tops of their masts,
snoring with the breath of the clouds,
black strips against sailing timber
made firm against hempen shrouds.

Such stretches of well knit action verse contrast with the usual irritating formlessness of Livingston's heroic poetry. Not that anything in Livingston approaches real epic. I am afraid that Livingston suggests, at several removes, Walter Scott rather than Homer or the Ultonian Hero Ballads, but now and again there is, if not epic grandeur, a very striking turn of imagery. One hero's eyes flash like the *aurora borealis* — 'mar phlathadh nam Fir-chlis'; and the messenger speeds

> Mar luaths iolair gu dìoladh braid
> An t-sealgair 's e creachadh a nid.

> *With the speed of the eagle (swooping) to avenge*
> *the theft of the hunter who is plundering her nest.*

Livingston inserts lyric into the epic narrative and dialogue. One of these lyrics is the battle-cry of the Norsemen. It is on the whole worthy of its name, 'Ròc a' chasgraidh', but it is spoilt by the refrains, 'Tuagh, tuagh!' and 'Sgian, sgian!':

> Cha téid fear a dh'ìnnseadh sgeòil dibh
>   Tuagh, tuagh;
> Cluinnibh na fithich a' ròcail,
>   Tuagh, tuagh;
> Nì sinne dhaibh cuirm do'r spòltan,
>   Tuagh, tuagh.

> *No one will go to tell a tale of you,*
>   *axe, axe;*
> *Hear the ravens croaking,*
>   *axe, axe;*
> *we will make them a feast of your spoils,*
>   *axe, axe!*

It merits, however, its first name and that other, 'caismeachd nan sgòrnan'. Blair, editor of Livingston, calls it 'a wild and vigorous lyric'.

Fergus, fortieth king of Scotland, appears in a heroic vision and speaks a lyric that is formally fine, with a sonorous clangour:

> Chì mi dreag o'n iar ag éiridh,
> Manadh an-iochd is creich mhóir,
> Basraich bròin is tòir is claidheamh
> Nan Geintleach borb 'gar caitheadh,
> Leis an aighear thu, chreach mhór.

I see a comet rising from the west,
portent of cruelty and of a great foray,
wringing of hands in grief, pursuit and sword
of the barbarous pagans scattering us —
to whom you are a delight, great Plunder.

The narrative verse describing Fergus is typically formless:

Aig deireadh nam briathran so
Thionndaidh e aghaidh rium;
Cha bu tannasg foilleil
An sealladh àigh;
'S an crios a' boillsgeadh
Le spangan òir is neamhnuidean
Air a bhroilleach aibhseach.
Dhearc e orm le caoimhneas
A cheangail ris mi mar gum bithinn
Ann am bannan iarainn;
Bha m'fhuil 'gam thogail
A dhol g'a fhàilteachadh,
'Nuair a tharruing e chlaidheamh,
Lann air fad is leud
Nach 'eil a leithid idir ann,
'S a' deàrrsadh mar ghathan nan reultan
An oidhche reòta.

At the end of these words
he turned his face to me;
no deceiving ghost
the auspicious sight;
the belt sparkling
with spangles of gold and jewels
on his huge chest.
He looked at me with kindness
that bound me to him as if I were
in bands of iron:
my blood was inciting me
to go to welcome him
when he drew his sword,
a blade whose length and breadth
has no equal at all,
and glittering like the beams of the stars
on a frosty night.

Such is unfortunately typical of a great deal of Livingston's heroic verse, though at times, in epic and in lyric, it is fully formed and powerful.

'Na Lochlannaich an Ile' has the epic council of chiefs, and at it MacKay of the Rhinns proves a tactician of a brand unknown to a genuine epic. Finally there is the battle itself, complete with epic single combats. Here and there are fine images, as in

> Chaidh a' cheann-bheairt, an claigeann 's an t-eanchainn,
> 'Nan spreadan dearg gliongrach.

> *His helmet, skull and brains went*
> *in red clangorous spatters.*

There is a complete victory for the Gaels though the Norsemen have a ten to one superiority in numbers.

'Blàr Shunadail', over 1200 lines in length, is somewhat longer than 'Na Lochlannaich an Ile'. It is an account of a fictitious war between a Norse king of Dublin and the men of Kintyre, Islay and Cowal, and it is full of Livingston's anachronisms. Livingston likes a good thing, and those early Gael-Viking wars are enlivened by the bodily presence of two famous rievers of a later date, Ailean nan Sop and Mac Iain Gheàirr, who appear as fine patriotic Gaels. Indeed, the whole thing is amusingly absurd when Mac Iain Gheàirr is feelingly complimented by a mythical Griogar nam Bó from Cowal, whose cattle he has frequently lifted, and when Ailean is provided with faggots to indulge his well known love of arson at the expense of a Norse castle in Man. There is even better than that. Blair notes: 'It may be interesting to know that the Bard has taken the names of decent farmers and cottars who lived in the district in 1865 and transformed them into brave chieftains of the olden time.'

The verse of 'Blàr Shunadail' is mixed, like the verse of 'Na Lochlannaich an Ile'. Some of it consists of strong seven, eight, nine or ten-syllabled lines rhyming in couplets with penultimate assonance, which is Livingston's most successful narrative metre, but most of it is formally like the part I quoted from 'Na Lochlannaich', that is unassonated verse so irregular in length of line as to be formless. The lines vary from four to fourteen syllables. Hence it is clear that Livingston did not solve the problem of an unrhymed Gaelic verse. Indeed his ear for rhythm is generally much poorer than his eye for the visual image, but even then it is only seldom that his action verse has the sharp visual effects of our older Gaelic poetry, notably Iain Lom's.

The battles in Islay and Kintyre are fictitious, or legendary, and Gaelic victory is assured, but in 'Cath Monadh Bhraca' (Mons Graupius) Livingston has to compromise with Tacitus by offering a drawn battle. The poem opens with a midnight soliloquy by a magnanimous and kingly patriot Calgacus, who ruminates on the depredations wrought by the barbarian bands of Rome in a verse that is metrically competent but not very distinguished in rhythm or in imagery, except in an occasional touch like 'stàirn nan sleagh air màillich liath nan sparrag dlùth'. Then Calgacus has the epic dream, in which he sees the doom to be averted from Caledonia. There is a melancholy grandeur about the vision for it is instinct with Livingston's feeling for Scotland and for majestic nature. The battle piece has the customary vigorous unassonated verse, but here it is better patterned than in most of the heroic narratives, the lines being more even in length. As usual, the unqualified vaunting of Highland heroism is rather tiresome.

'Blàr Dhail-righ' celebrates Bruce's defeat at the hands of the MacDougalls of Lorn. It begins in vigorous compact verse with a conversation between the bard and his Muse, in which he reproaches her for dragging him from place to place in quest of historical material, never letting him rest. She answers:

Thug mise dhuit, mar gheall mi,
Sealladh air glinn àigh 's air beanntan,
Air coirean fraoich 's air raointibh alltach,
'S lochain nach traoigh air gach meall diubh;
Muim' altrum nan gèadh 's nan lach,
Far am faigh am fiadh a dheoch,
'S a lòn gu fial air leirg a mach,
De mhìltibh lus ri gréin gu moch,
Air aonach farsuing nan eas caoirgheal
A' steall-ruith troimh chlaisibh craobhach,
A' mire leum 'nan ceudaibh caochan
Nach do thruailleadh riamh 's nach caochail.

I gave you as I promised
a view of glorious glens and mountains,
of heathery corries and fields with burns,
and on every mound of them little lochs that will not dry up;
fostering mother of the geese and the wild ducks,
where the deer will get his drink
and his food generously out on a hillside,
of thousands of herbs in the morning sun,
on the wide mountain of the foam-white cascades
running spouting through tree-lined runnels,
raging and leaping in hundreds of brooks
that were never defiled and will not change.

The Muse concludes her speech by rebuking him for his lateness in wooing her.

Livingston goes on to describe the battle much in the usual manner. The verse is all the more spirited because the poet's full sympathies are with both sides. They are all heroic Scots, and he does not question the rights or wrongs of either side, but he laments that Scots should fight Scots. Its verse is the most uniformly efficient of all the verse in the heroic poems.

'Cath Allt a' Bhannaich' is shorter and not so uniform, but it is a clangorous vituperation of the 'unclean, barbarous English'. There is no lack of strong sensuousness in Livingston's battle poetry but its rather self-smothering noise compares badly with the terseness of Iain Lom, nor does the vituperation have anything like the economy and bite of the earlier poet.

'Cath Thom Ealachaidh', on one of Wallace's skirmishes, is shorter still and rather undistinguished, but it opens with a characteristic invocation of the glories of ancient Scotland, and a rebuke and incitement to contemporary Scots, and a piece of vigorous vituperation, presumably on the evicting landlords of his time.

> An toir gur neò-ghlan
> Nan gàrr mucach bhuait do chiall,
> Do mhaoin, do chòir is do Dhia?
> Eirich, a sheana mhàthair bhuadhach,
> Rìoghail, dhoirbh,
> Ardanach, aintheasach, threòraich, gharbh,
> Thig a mach le d' mhórachd o shean,
> 'S cluinneadh do mhic
> Le seirm nam bàrd carson.

> *Will the foul brood*
> *of the swinish ordure take from you your reason,*
> *your goods, your right and your God?*
> *Arise, old mother who is of great virtues,*
> *royal, stern,*
> *proud, perfervid, mighty, fierce.*
> *Come out with your ancient majesty*
> *and let your sons hear why*
> *from the music of the bards.*

'Blàr Thràigh Ghruineart', like 'Blàr Dhail-righ', describes the encounter of heroic Gael with heroic Gael. Hence, though Livingston's closest sympathies are with the Islay MacDonalds, there is much courtesy and mutual admiration in the poem. The greatest hero is not Sir James MacDonald of Islay but Sir Lachlan MacLean of

140

Duart, who in actual history was probably a great warrior and very certainly a great rascal. In this poem, however, he is the very apogee of heroic Gael, a bit unreasonable in his demands on the Islay men but, nevertheless, bitterly mourned by the same Islay men when he is killed by a bullet from the gun of a dwarf 'of the devil's spawn'. What the battle of Gruineart Bay was like no one will ever know for the MacDonald and MacLean accounts differ so completely, but Livingston makes it the occasion of the very highest European heroism. As a poem the account is indifferent, rhythmically weak and generally undistinguished, and by his frequent irritating over-repetition Livingston spoils even the concluding lyric, the *corranach* for Lachlainn Mór:

Chan fhacas ad latha air talamh
Na h-Eòrpa, na h-Eòrpa,
Air talamh na h-Eòrpa,
Fear eile do shamhuil, do shamhuil,
Fhir àillidh, fhir àillidh,
Cha d'fhàgadh ad dhéidh dhuinn,
Ad dhéidh dhuinn, ad dhéidh dhuinn.
O na rinneadh do d' chreubh
Caisil-chrò, caisil-chrò,
O na rinneadh do d' chreubh
Caisil-chrò!

There has not in your time been seen on the land
of Europe, of Europe,
on the land of Europe
another man like you, like you,
most beautiful man, most beautiful man,
there has not been left to us after you,
to us after you, to us after you,
since there has been made for your corpse
a bier, a bier,
since there has been made for your corpse
a bier!

That seems to me what might have been a fine lyric gone wrong. I have heard in Raasay what purported to be part of a traditional lament for Lachlainn Mór.

Cà facas air thalamh
Boinne fala a b'àille
Na 'n t-oighre bh' air Dubhaird,
Locha Buidh' agus Aros?

'S iomadh bean a bhiodh réidh riut
Ach thu fhéin bhith air mhànran,
'S cha d' fhuaradh beachd-sgeul ort
Ach gun reubadh sa' bhlàr thu,
Mo Lachlainn Mór.

Where has there been seen on earth
a blood-drop more beautiful
that the heir who was on Duart,
Lochbuie and Aros?
Many a woman would be charmed by you
if your talk was amorous,
and no report of you has been got,
save that you were wounded in the battle,
my Lachlan Mór.

This was sung to the tune of 'Mo rùn geal òg'. Now the difficulty is obvious. Apart from the refrain 'Mo Lachlainn Mór', these words are almost the same as a verse of the lament for Red Hector, who was killed at Inverkeithing in 1651. My informant's memory may have played her false and she herself may have inserted the refrain. At any rate, Livingston is probably echoing either the lament for Red Hector or an earlier lament for Lachlainn Mór, which the lament for Red Hector is itself echoing.

Livingston's heroic poetry is complete with a piece on Alma and Balaclava. Of course, there is no mention of Englishmen, Irishmen, French or Turk. The battles are battles between hordes of brave but rather barbarous Russians and Sir Colin Campbell's heroic Scots. I suppose the imperialist rivalry of Britain and Russia meant very little to Livingston. As likely as not, he might well have been on the side of the Russians had the British Army not contained Highlanders. Provided he can prove the Gaels the world's greatest warriors, Livingston does not care much if the war has as little relevance to Scotland as the Crimean had. In verse it is a poor example of his heroic manner, but in all his heroic verse I am afraid that Livingston is merely doing in a poor way what Iain Lom had done splendidly in the 17th century.

Those nine heroic poems comprise more than half the verse in the collected edition of Livingston's poems. There are thirty-six other pieces of great variety in length, technique and quality. Of these there are two long poems, 'Cuimhneachan Bhraid-Alba' and 'Driod-fhortan Imhir an Ràcain'.

Blair, the editor of Livingston's poems, prefaces 'Cuimhneachan Bhraid-Alba' with a note on its matter. 'This,' he says, 'is a sort of medley . . . the poem opens with an address to the country . . . the

Bard descends into the glen. As he approaches a herd of cattle he hears the milkmaid's song, which is perhaps the sweetest piece in his whole works. The Bard approaches the shieling, where he is made welcome by a Highland matron, whose description he gives and whose praises he sings . . . Then follows a lament for the desolations caused by strangers in the Highlands, and a coronach is played by the aged Harper on the same subject. The whole finishes with "Big John's Testament", which consists in a vow laid upon his son to stand by the language and customs of the Gael, and to see the Bard decently buried.'

The poem is in a variety of metres. The opening address to the country is pleasant pastoral poetry in a form modelled on the modification of *sneadhbhairdne* used by MacDonald in the 'Birlinn'. Indeed a line like 'tomach gleannach' is pretty certainly an echo of 'garbhlach thomach' in the 'Birlinn'. It is good verse, though far below its use by the great MacDonald, of whom there are many echoes.

A thalamh àrd nan coilltean uaine
'S nan sruth fìor-uisg',
Cuislean bras nan lochan domhain
Nach gabh dìobradh;
Caochain ghlan na doimhne móir'
A' ruith air uachdar
Do bheanntan gorm, a thìr nan curaidh
'S nam ban stuama;
Neòil ghlas m'a bharraibh stùc a' snàgadh
Is féidh 'nan langan
Ri creachainn a' dìreadh 's a' teàrnadh
Le lùth eangain;
Coilich nan cneas dubh a' turraraich
Air do tholmain,
Is mìltean lus a' fàs 'nam maise
Le brìgh talmhainn.

High land of the green woods
and of the streams of spring water,
impetuous runnels of the deep lochs
that cannot fail:
pure brooks of great depth
running on the surface
of your green mountains, land of heroes
and of modest women;
grey cloud creeping about the tops of peaks
and deer bellowing

against the face of a rocky summit, ascending and descending
with strength of hoof;
black cocks with a strong murmur
on your knolls,
and thousands of flowers in their beauty
because of the goodness of the soil.

The milkmaid's song, which Blair calls 'perhaps the sweetest piece in his whole works', is in a verse form much more typical of the 19th century. It is certainly beautiful, but its beauty is of a kind fairly common in the century:

Chàidh gruaim nan siantan a chadal,
'S tha fèath air talamh 's air cuan;
'S choisg gaoth fhuaraidh na gaillionn
Gu sìth a h-anail o thuath;
Tha neòil shoilleir na h-iarmailt
A' sgaoileadh cian air an cuairt,
'S a' pògadh gathan na gréine,
Chuir blàths a' Chéitein a nuas.

The surliness of the elements has gone to sleep
and there is calm on land and sea;
and the cold wind of the tempest has checked
its breath from the north until it is at peace.
The bright clouds of the sky
are scattering distantly on their round,
and kissing the beams of the sun
that have sent down the warmth of May.

Even it lacks the limpid quality and sure rhythm of John MacLachlan and Neil MacLeod.

The description of the Highland matron is in Livingston's commonest metre for narrative and description, lines generally of eight syllables with penultimate couplet rhyme occurring irregularly. It is idyllic and heroic, but in the address to Macnab there is a plangent autobiographical note:

Ràinig tu leab' a' chruaidh chàis,
Dhiùlt thu teach mear na luath-ghàir,
Is an iargain loisgeach 'gam bhualadh,
'Bu tric agam 's b'annamh uam thu.'

You reached the bed of hardship,
you refused the merry house of the loud rejoicing
as the burning longing struck me:
'Often were you with me, and seldom were you away from me.'

144

And again:

>'S trom an t-eallach gaol dùthcha
>'S fòirneart aindeoin.

>*A heavy burden is the love of a country*
>*and forced oppression.*

He goes on to a contemplation of the doing of evictors in Breadalbane:

>Braid-Alba le gàmhlas foilleil
>Air a sguabadh;
>Sglamhaiche gun iochd 'ga rùsgadh
>'Na lom-fhàsaich,
>'S a mic laochail fad o'n dùthchas
>A' caoidh na dh'fhàg iad.

>*Breadalbane with treacherous spite*
>*swept bare:*
>*a merciless vile fellow stripping it*
>*to a bare desert,*
>*and her heroic sons far from their country*
>*mourning for what they have left behind.*

The Harper's lament follows in fine strophes:

>Cuimhne na bhà
>Ghluais mi gu dàn
>'S sinn claoidhte le cràdh fòirneirt:
>'Gar sgiùrsadh le smachd
>Fo'n smàig nach do chleachd,
>'S sinn gun dùthaich fo reachd fògraidh.

>*The memory of what was*
>*has moved me to a poem,*
>*oppressed and exhausted as we are with the strength of tyranny:*
>*scourged and subjected*
>*under the paw to which we were not used,*
>*without a country, under the edict of exile.*

As a whole the poem is lit with Livingston's feeling for Scotland, pride in its ancient heroism and sorrow for its contemporary impotence and desolation:

>Alb', an seun thu mo ghlaodh,
>Nach dùisg thu, Mhàthair mo ghaoil,

Mun toir mallachd na daorsa buaidh ort?
Na sean fhineachan treun
Air an sgapadh an céin,
Sliochd nan saoi d'am bu bheus cruadal.

Scotland, will you bless my cry,
will you not waken, beloved mother,
before the curse of slavery will overcome you?
The brave old clans
scattered afar,
stock of the good men who had the virtue of hardihood.

Here the cadences of Mary MacLeod are echoed in the lament for the loss of what was Livingston's image of ancient Scotland:

Cha robh do dheamhain 'san t-slochd
Le gur Shasuinn fo'n smachd
Na chuir do shaorsa fo reachd nàmhaid.

There were not enough devils in the pit,
with the brood of England under their control,
to have put your freedom under the law of an enemy.

But now Gaelic Scotland is at the mercy of the later evictor:

Chithear cumhachag bròin,
Is ialtag nam fròg,
Gun eagal an còmhnuidh dhuaichnidh
Far an d' àraicheadh laoich,
Sliochd nan Crìosduidhean saor
Tha nis feadh an t-saoghail fuadaicht'
Le màgaich ghreannach tnù,
Lior nan garrachain brù,
'S nan cràin sliopach gun chliù,
O'n d'fhàs iad;
Pòr salach na foill,
Ris an dubhairt ar n-athraichean Goill,
'S trom acain na roinn a dh'fhàg iad.

There are seen a piteous owl
and the bat of the crannies
without fear in a loathsome dwelling
where heroes were reared,
stock of the free Christians
who are now exiled throughout the world
by morose-faced toads,

litter of the bloated bellies
and of the blubber-lipped ill-famed sows
from which they grew —
the foul treacherous seed
called 'Goill' by our forbears:
heavy is the moan of those they have left.

The masterly use of the strophes gives an edge reminiscent of Iain Lom or John Roy Stewart, an edge which the formlessness common in Livingston's verse fails to achieve. 'Tiomnadh Iain Mhóir' concludes the poem with Livingston's hopes for what is left of Scotland.

'Cuimhneachan Bhràid-Alba' is a very uneven poem; but, on the whole, it is a fine expression of Livingston, for into it he puts most of his vehement personality.

In content, 'Còmhradh air Fàsachadh na Gàidhealtachd' is closely akin to 'Cuimhneachan Bhràid-Alba'. The poem is formless but it contains much of Livingston's fiercest anger against the Anglo-Saxon exploiter.

Faic a' chreag àrd chorrach ud thall,
Air deis-thìr thonnaich,
Aon uair sealbh Mhic Dhòmhnuill;
Am balla briste 'na chàrn,
An sàmhchair linntean fada,
Gun ghuth ceann-feadhna no gaisgich,
Gun sgal mìol-choin, gun fhoirm clàrsaich;
Ach lombair nàduir mu charraig an Dùin
A thug fasgadh 'na theinn do Rìgh Raibeart:
Sin ceart samhladh cor nan Gàidheal
'San àite so anns nach eil iad a nis.
O shannt chruaidh-chridhich,
Càit am bheil crìoch do mhallachd
An aghaidh nan curaidhean dìleas?
Bheir fìrinn fathast buaidh 'nan aobhar.

See yonder high rock of unsteady foothold
on a surfy southern land,
once owned by MacDonald;
the broken wall a cairn
in the peace of long generations,
without voice of chief or warrior,
without howl of deer-hound, without flourish of harp,
but the bare face of Nature about the rock of the Dun
that gave shelter in his peril to King Robert;
that is the true image of the state of Gaels
in this place where they are not now.

O hard-hearted greed,
where is the end of your curse
on the faithful heroes?
Truth will one day triumph in their cause.

But the concluding speech, by Uilleam Ileach, is far stronger:

Is gann a gheibhear air fad na talmhainn
Samhladh ghuir o'n Diabhal
A rinn fàsach do Thìr nan Gàidheal.

There can scarcely be found throughout the earth
the like of the Devil's brood
who have made a desert of the Land of the Gaels.

Those who have evicted the Gael are

Alach nan *Cràin* Sasunnach!
Bior taghairm dheamhan is shiùrsach!

Tribe of the Saxon swine,
roasting-spit for raising demons and whores.

They are

Luchd comuinn chon,
Is brùidean crodhanach an fheòir,
Mic mhallachd an t-saoghail fharsuing.

The mates of dogs,
cloven-hoofed brutes of the grass,
the most accursed sons of the wide world.

It is Livingston's most angry complaint about 'cor muladach leth àrd na h-Alba'.

Though 'Còmhradh air Fàsachadh an Gàidhealtachd' is formless, Livingston wrote at least one perfect poem on the same theme. 'Fios thun a' Bhàird', a poem in which his perennial theme was perfectly expressed. It is perhaps the finest poem of the century and, with 'Eirinn ag Gul' and passages from other poems, quite unmistakeable evidence that, whatever he generally was, Livingston is not a minor poet. In conception the poem is simple and usual; in it the permanent grandeur of nature is set against human desolation. Now Livingston's poetry of external nature is not generally arresting. The poetry of natural scenery had reached its climax in Macintyre and MacDonald: it had become a dynamic realisation, a realisation that is a great impressionism, and in that Livingston is not of the same order. In 'Fios thun a' Bhàird' there is an occasional magic touch like:

Tha 'n linne sleamhuinn sìochail
O na chiùinich strì nan speur.

The kyle is slippery and tranquil
since the strife of the skies has calmed.

Admittedly, there is not much of this quality, but throughout the poem the description of nature has a fine gravity, and clearness of line, which, with the sonorous plangency of the description of human desolation, make it a perfect poem. Now there are a few poems of the Clearances, as for example MacLachlan's 'Dìreadh a mach ri Beinn Shianta', that have a greater intensity than 'Fios thun a' Bhàird', but its grandeur and perfection of grave music has a kind of finality that perhaps no other poem of the Clearances has. It may have no real originality of thought, image or even music, but its total effect of majestic sadness and restrained anger, grandeur and simplicity makes it, as it were, the last word on the theme. The poem is so well known that I need not quote, and also its excellence is uniform. I myself think the sixth, eighth and thirteenth stanzas especially fine.

In 'Eirinn ag Gul' there is essentially the same feeling, but this time for Ireland. This sympathy for Ireland is very rare in other 19th century Gaelic poetry. 'Eirinn ag Gul' has a greater economy than 'Fios thun a' Bhàird', and it is even more fully charged with the burden of history, and is even more limpidly perfect in form. There is the same contrast between the lasting beauty of nature and human desolation, wrong and shame. Ireland is the green land of poetry, music and heroism, which has broken its own strength and has fallen a prey to the English foxes. There is a final blending of feeling for Ireland and for its neighbour, Livingston's own Islay. The poem has a wonderful evocative beauty of phrase and music very unusual in Livingston, and in a line like 'Luathghaireach sona mar sin' there is a fully charged magic. Though the last two quatrains are a remarkable echo of the pregnant simplicity of Iain Lom and John Roy Stewart, the whole poem is Livingston's own. Like 'Fios thun a' Bhàird' it is individual, and it, even more than the other, shows what evocative splendour Livingston could sometimes achieve when he curbed his formless abundance with brevity and rigid metrical form.

'Soraidh Dhonnchaidh do Chomhal', on the same theme as 'Fios thun a' Bhàird', has beauty of a kind more common in the 19th century. It too shows that Livingston could use regular verse forms very well when he chose.

The worth of Livingston's poems on the contemporary state of Scotland is surely a very effective reply to the doubts as to the real worth of his nationalism expressed by his editor, Blair. If Livingston had been just an egocentric crank with a merely antiquarian feeling for Scotland, he could not have written such fine poetry on the Scotland of his own day, for Livingston is important to Scotland where he is dealing with contemporary themes and not where he is the amateur of the antiquarian heroic.

Anger and sorrow for the state of Scotland provoked Livingston's finest poetry, but he wrote a few poems in which there is splendidly expressed joy. Such are the three fine expressions of delight in the sea to be found in 'Oran Bean a' Bhàird', 'Tigh Chailein' and 'Rannan do Uilleam MacGhille Chrìosda'. In 'Oran Bean a' Bhàird' a fine old measure is used with the clear beauty that is so frequent in the sea poetry of the Scottish Gael:

'S fad thu o linne nam beuc
Far an cluinnear séitrich thonn,
Cuisle sruth cuain 'na still
A' cothachadh ri strì nan long.

You are far from the roaring kyle
where is heard the neighing of waves,
the stream of ocean current in spouts
fighting against the striving ships.

A similar beauty pervades some of the verses of 'Tigh Chailein':

O'n tha sinn ann chan àm gu stad e,
Gus an tog sinn séist an Rannaich,
Stiùradair na birlinn Ileach,
A dh'fhalbh a thoirt na rìbhinn thairis.

Tha 'm bàta gnìomhach luath fo h-aodach,
A' dol 'na deann troimh chaoirean steallach,
Miann maraich' a siùil gheala sìnte,
'S bior-snaois a' snìomh ri ceann a saidhe.

Eibhneas eileanaich a gluasad,
Nuair thogas na fuaraidh a darach,
'S taobh an fhasgaidh leagt' a crònan,
Fo chòbhrach a sròin a' gearradh.

Since we are here, it is no time for stopping
until we raise the chorus of the Rinns man,

steersman of the Islay birling
who went to take the maiden over the sea.

The boat is fast and does well under her sails,
going with great speed through spouting wave-crests,
a mariner's desire her white sails stretched
and bowsprit twisting at the top of her stem-post.

The joy of an islesman her movement
when waves to windward raise her oakwood
and her hum on the lowered lee-side,
under the foam from her cutting prow.

The third of these three poems, 'Rannan do Uilleam MacGhille Chrìosda,' has a great vigour and originality of rhythm, with something of the vivid visual and auditory effects of 18th century poetry. In this poem Livingston has made an addition of importance to the technique of Gaelic verse, and, strangely enough, it is to that type of poetry that realises dynamic nature, the type that is one of the chief glories of 18th century poetry. In the inset lyric, a traditional and simpler metre is finely used.

Besides a few elegies and humorous poems, there remain three or four occasional poems written in honour of various people and bodies. Such are the poem to 'Comunn nam Fineachan', 'Rannan do Uaislean Comunn nan Gàidheal' and 'Comunn nam Fiann'. None of them is a notable poem, and they have nothing more than the usual expression of pride in ancient Scotland mingled with regret for its modern state, and some praise for good Gaels.

The elegies are finer poems. 'Rannan mu Bhàs Neill Strachan' is a noble sonorous poem in the best tradition of Gaelic elegy, the tradition of Rob Donn's 'Marbhrann Iain Mhic Eachainn' and Ewen MacLachlan's 'Marbhann Sheumais Bheattie'. It shows Livingston's fine command of strict verse form when he chose to use it. 'Rann Marbhthaisg Dhonnchaidh Bhlair', an impression of the contrast between permanent nature and mortal man, is formless. The poem on the death of the Arran stranger is full of Livingston's love for his own country. There remain two tributes to Gaelic poets of another day. 'Rann Marbhthaisg Iain Luim' is in the adjective-packing style. 'Leacan Uaighean nam Bàrd' records in the familiar couplet verse Livingston's admiration for Oisein, Deirdre, Crimine, Am Bard Aosda, Dòmhnall MacFhionnlaigh nan Dàn, Màiri Nighean Alasdair Ruaidh and Iain Lom. He adjures Màiri:

Thoir do chàch mar is àill do dhìleab
Ach tilg do thonnag air an Ileach.

Give to others your legacy as you wish
but throw your plaid on the Islay man.

But the best of it is the lines on Iain Lom:

Teanga nach do ghluais ri càirean
A leithid eile o'n latha dh'fhàs i;
Their càch 'Iain Lom' riut; ainm is feàrr ort,
Sùisde greadaidh Earra-Ghàidheil.

A tongue the like of which has not moved
against gums since the day it grew:
Some call you 'Bare John'; a better name for you:
the flail for drubbing Argyll.

Livingston's temperament would not seem to have been eminently suited to humorous poetry, but he did write some humorous verse. His earliest known poem, 'Bran', written to his dog when he was a shepherd lad has rare grace and restraint in its unusual and ingenious humour, while the last verse is a notable animal picture drawn with a few strokes.

Bheir mise dhuit teisteas sgrìobhta,
Thu bhith dìleas air mo chùl,
'S nach innis thu gum bi mi cadal
No 'g iarraidh nead air an Dùn;
Tha thu sleamhainn, dubh, 's do chluasan
A' lùbadh a nuas mu d' shùil,
'S a dh'aindeoin na their luchd an tuaileis
'S companach duin' uasail thu.

I will give you a written testimonial,
that you are loyal at my back,
and that you will not tell that I sleep
or go bird-nesting on the Dun.
You are sleek and black, and your ears
bend down about your eyes,
and in spite of what the reproachful say,
you are the companion of a gentleman.

'An t-Oircean' has a similar neat grace. The last verse, and especially the last line, is notable.

Chàidh gach bruach is gleann is allt
A rannsachadh le siubhal chas;

152

'S mas fìor 's an t-oircean gun fhaotuinn,
Thòisich caoineadh 's greadadh bhas.

Every bank and glen and burn
was searched with travelling feet;
and when the little pig was still unfound
there began weeping and beating of palms.

'Sùisde Chonain' is a strikingly humorous and kindly poem on an antiquarian who accumulates articles stolen from the Fiann, and 'Mocheirigh Fhinn' is similar. In it Fionn distributes Fingalian relics such as Diarmid's spear and Oscar's plaid among Livingston's worthy friends, and the description of Angus of Killin under a heavy load of Fingaliana is particularly good. All these poems are kindly in their humour, but in one, 'Eóghain, bhuail thu' there is a characteristic triumph in an Islay man's discomfiture of a Lowland miller. Of the humorous poems, however, the most notable is that mystifying medley of farcical adventures, 'Driod-fhortan Imhir an Ràcain', a poem of over 500 lines in a verse form that is well adapted to its amusing absurdity, an absurdity that is, however, expressed with a restraint and purity of idiom not seen in Livingston's heroic poetry.

Neither the elegies nor the humorous poems will count for a very great deal in the estimate of Livingston's place among Gaelic poets. He will be judged largely on those poems that deal with the contrast between the old Highlands and the Highlands of the post-Clearances period, which is after all the most central theme in the poetry of his century. All the considerable Gaelic poets of the time, John Mac-Lachlan, John Smith, Neil MacLeod, Ewan MacColl, Calum Campbell MacPhail, Dugald MacPhail and Mary MacPherson, are full of this, but it preoccupied no one of the rest, except Mary MacPherson, as it preoccupied Livingston. In many ways he has an extraordinary individuality. While he had nothing like the tender intensity and the lyric perfection of the best of MacLachlan's poetry, nothing like the large passionate intellectual humanity of John Smith, and nothing like the glowing intimacy and racy tenderness of Mary MacPherson, nor the polish of Neil MacLeod, he is at his rare best unapproached by any other of the 19th century poets in a terse, manly, indignant and sad eloquence, and always he gives the impression of heroic personality to whom the sufferings of Scotland were sufferings that would not let him rest. This heroism is reflected in his life: his passionate researches into Scottish history, his struggles with languages like French, Greek, Latin and Hebrew, carried on with all the disadvantages of poverty, exacting daily work, and a very poor education in his youth, and all with the purpose of adding to Scotland's glory and protesting against her wrongs. There is nothing parochial in Livingston; everywhere he is national in interest and scope. I think it probable that his failures are in some way due to his restless preoccupation with the advancement or maintenance of Gaelic culture. Probably it was this that led him to experiment with novel verse forms that he was not artistic enough to make his own. The chaotic energy of most of his heroic poems probably reflects his nationalist, propagandist aim, for he had not the patience nor self-criticism necessary to find a satisfactory new technique. Thus Livingston is weak in the sphere in which most 19th century poets are at least competent. This common failure to achieve form, so marked in Livingston's poetry, is strange when set against his few triumphs. A few poems such as 'Eirinn ag Gul' and 'Fios thun a' Bhàird', poems of splendid finality, stand out against great waste lands where there are only very rare blossoms of real beauty. The evocative economy of the two poems I have just mentioned seems strange when set against the clumsy wordiness of 'Blàr Shunadail' and 'Na Lochlannaich an Ile' and the other heroic poems. It is not that there are no intermediate stages, for Livingston did write a fair number of poems that are all fine or contain fine passages, but the difference between the rare best and the great average is huge.

Livingston's poetry did suffer from his always feeling it incumbent on him to glorify Scotland, and especially the military virtues of the Scots, and it must be admitted that his poetry is very often crude and indiscriminate protestation, which is seldom even good argument. While all would agree with him that the sufferings of the Gaels in the 19th century could be ultimately attributed to the accession of strength landlordism received from its backing by the force of the English Empire, Livingston does not develop the theme but merely protests and not always very convincingly. Of course, it may be said that the development of political and economic argument is not the sphere of poetry, but Livingston is so obsessed with the theme that one would expect more than nationalistic vituperation from him. His nationalism ignores all factors but the purely national. Nor is his history very careful. Thus he is prepared to exalt Gaels like Lachlan Mór MacLean of Duart, whose doings in Ireland were flagrant treachery to the cause of the Gael that is championed in 'Eirinn ag Gul', and he rejoices that Highland soldiers are smashing Sebastopol when, according to his own thesis, they ought to have been smashing Highland landlordism. Livingston is so intent on proving Highland heroism that he does not examine the exercise of this heroism. Thus his heroic poetry has little value in political content and is, at any rate, very poor poetry. In his elegies and humorous poems and in poems like 'Rannan do Uilleam MacGhille Chrìosda' he did very well what others had done better long before his day, but in a few poems his passionate contemplation of the actual state of the Highlands in his own day is crystallised in verse of noble and moving eloquence, which I think just misses being great poetry beause it is slightly rhetorical, but I suppose that is a failing which is inherent in the nature of all political poetry. It remains true that Livingston made a heroic attempt to enlarge the scope of Gaelic poetry in his day, and while his innovations were not successful enough to make a big contribution to Gaelic poetry, he did in a few poems reach a degree of perfection in traditional modes that warrants a claim that he was a considerable poet; and in no other poet of his day is there such a sustained and passionate plea against the sad fate of the Gael in the 19th century.

Clach Air a' Chàrn — Uilleam Mac Dhùn-Léibhe

Anns an naoidheamh linn deug, thàinig latha na dunachd air cloinn nan Gàidheal. Cha robh an linn ach glé òg — ma thòisich i idir — nuair a chualas glaodh cruaidh o Ailean Mac Dhùghaill, Ailean Dall, an Gleann Garadh:

Thàinig oirnn a dh'Alba crois,
Tha daoine bochda nochdte ris,
Gun iochd, gun airgead, gun chluain:
Tha'n Aird a Tuath air a sgrios.

'S iomadh glaodh de'n t-seòrsa sin a chualas o bhàird nan Gàidheal anns a' cheithir fichead bliadhna a bha ri teachd; ach cha robh glaodh dhiubh uile cho cruaidh, sgairteil, neo-sgàthach ris an iomadh glaodh a rinn an t-Ileach curanta, Uilleam Mac Dhùn-Léibhe. Ma dhleasas dithis sam bith an t-àrd urram air son gaol dùthcha agus cinnidh am measg bàird na Gàidhlig, 's ann aig Uilleam agus aig Màiri Mhór nan Oran a tha e; agus chan e aon chlach ach móran bu chòir a dhol air a' chàrn, nan robh carraghan-cuimhne nam fíor Ghàidheal cho àrd-cheannach ri gach colbh as lugha toillteanais.

Rugadh Uilleam Mac Dhùn-Léibhe faisg air a' Bhodha-mhór an Ile, anns a' bhliadhna 1808. Bha e de theaghlach mór agus cha d'fhuair e ach beagan sgoile — ciamar a gheibheadh e móran anns na làithean a bh'ann — ged a dh'fheuch athair, a bha 'na shaor, air a chomas a dhèanamh. A réir Uilleam fhéin, cha robh móran cùiram aige 'na òige de fhoghlum na sgoile, agus rinneadh tàillear dheth.

Cha bu dona a' cheàird sin dha oir bha an tàillear air shiubhal o thigh gu tigh, agus far an robh an tàillear, chruinnicheadh sean is òg gu tigh-céilidh; ach chuir tubaist do uircein muice Uilleam agus a mhaighstir gu carraid, agus dh'fhàg am bàrd òg Ile gu teachd-an-tìr fhaighinn air a' Ghalldachd no, có dhiùbh, air Tìr-mór. Bha e greis an Dùn Breatunn; greis an Arrochair agus am Both-chuidir; greis mu thaobh Loch Eireann an siorrachd Pheairt. Phòs e té bho Strath

156

Eireann, agus rinn ise a dìcheall 'ga chuideachadh 'na shaothraichean móra, oir cha robh e fada air Ile fhàgail nuair a lìonadh e le eud mór agus dìorras chum seirbhis na h-Albann, agus gu h-àraid nan Gàidheal. Chàidh e dh'obair an Grianaig, agus an sin a Ghlaschu. Thàinig bàs aithghearr air anns a' bhliadhna 1870, dusan bliadhna mun tug 'fir mhóra' Bràighe Thròndairnis Gàidheil na h-Albann gu car dùsgaidh. Chaochail a bhean beagan mhìosan roimhe, agus cha robh teaghlach aca. Thiodhlaiceadh iad anns a' chladh ris an abrar 'Janefield Cemetery' an taobh an ear Baile Ghlaschu. Chuireadh clach air an uaigh troimh obair Dhonnchaidh Mhic Ghille Bhàin agus Chaluim Mhic Mhuirich, agus anns a' bhliadhna 1882 chuir an Comunn Ileach *Duain agus Orain* Uilleim an clò fo stiùireadh an Urramaich Raibeart Blàr. Dlighidh an Comunn Ileach urram mór a thaobh na h-obrach, agus rinn Raibeart Blàr seirbhis shònraichte d'a luchd dùthcha. Thug e cunntas air beatha Uilleim ann an roimh-ràdh an leabhair. Anns a' chunntas sin thug e, ar leamsa, cus molaidh do'n bhàrd, ach cha tug e leth gu leòir do'n duine. Tha mise de'n bharail nach bu toigh leis a' mhinistear a' chainnt bhorb, sgaiteach leis an do sgiùrs Uilleam na slaightearan a thug sgrios air na Gàidheil, agus na sliomairean nach fosgladh am beòil mar a rinn Uilleam.

Tha Blàr a' cur as leth Uilleim gun robh e buailteach air iadach agus nach robh e suilbhir ri daoine eile a bha a' strì ann an aobhar na Gàidhlig. Faodaidh sin a bhith, ach feumar cuimhneachadh gun robh sliomairean 'nam measg-san cuideachd. Cha chuala mise gun robh 'Caraid nan Gàidheal' e fhéin a' toirt a' chraicinn de uachdarain agus de chinn-chinnidh sgrèamhaidh na Gàidhealtachd nuair a bha e a' sliomaireachd ri Bàn-righinn Victoria am Bràigh Mhàirr agus cha robh móran comain aig curaidhean an t-sluaigh air ministeirean Eaglais Mhór na h-Albann anns na làithean sin. Mar a thubhairt Màiri Mhór:

> Tha luchd teagaisg cho beag cùraim
> A' faicinn allaban mo dhùthcha,
> 'S iad cho balbh air anns a' chùbaid
> 'S ged bu bhrùidean bha 'gan éisdeachd.

Ged nach robh Uilleam Mac Dhùn-Léibhe air rann a dhèanamh riamh, bhiodh a shaothair air sgàth na h-Albann mìorbhaileach. Gun ach sgoil thruagh 'na òige, agus a' strì ri obair fhada làitheil, dh'ionn-saich e Greugais, Laideann, Fraingeis agus eadhon Eabhra feuch am biodh am barrachd tuigse aige air eachdraidh an t-saoghail gus an cuireadh e an céill glòir a dhùthcha agus gus an seasadh e a còir.

Bha a pheann gun sgur anns na pàipearan-naidheachd is e ag agairt cliù is math a dhùthcha.

Ged nach robh e riamh 'na sgoileir coimhlionta no 'na fheallsanach — agus ciamar a b'urrainn gum biodh — thug e oidhirp shònraichte air bàrdachd na Gàidhlig a leudachadh agus a leasachadh le dòighean agus cuspairean ùra, agus ged nach deach leis mar bu trice, dh'fhàg e iomadh rann coimhlionta, iomadh rann mìorbhuileach, gu h-àraidh nuair a lasadh an fhearg uasal agus am bròn uasal a mhac-meanmna.

> Braid-Alba le gàmhlas foilleil
> Air a sguabadh,
> Sglamhaiche gun iochd 'ga rùsgadh
> 'Na lom-fhàsaich,
> 'S a mic laochail fad o'n dùthchas
> A' caoidh na dh'fhàg iad.

Chan ioghnadh ged a their e:

> 'S trom an t-eallach gaol dùthcha,
> 'S fòirneart ain'eoin

agus

> Ràinig tu leab' a' chruaidh chàis,
> Dhiùlt thu teach mear na luath-ghair;
> Is an iargainn loisgeach 'gam bhualadh,
> 'Bu tric agam 's b'annamh uam thu'

agus a rithist

> Is gann a gheibhear air fad na talamhainn
> Samhladh ghuir o'n Diabhal
> A rinn fàsach do Thìr nan Gàidheal.

'S ann o 'Chuimhneachan Bhraid-Albann' agus bho 'Chòmhradh air Fàsachadh na Gàidhealtachd' a tha na rainn air an tug mi iomradh, ach chan eil anns an dà dhàn sin ach fear no a dhà de na dàin a tha làn feirge is bròin mu thogail na tuatha agus mu 'chor muladach leth àrd na h-Alba'. Tha dàn eile fada nas trice air na bilean aig a bheil ùidh ann am bàrdachd ar dùthcha. Is e 'Fios thun a' Bhàird' as òirdheirce dhiubh uile, agus 'na cheithir rannan deug chan eil e furasda rann seach rann a thaghadh. Anns an dàn seo tha am bròn nas truime na tha an fhearg. Seo agaibh a' cheud rann, an siathamh rann, an t-ochdamh rann, an treas rann deug, agus am fear mu dheireadh.

Tha 'mhaduinn soilleir grianach
'S a' ghaoth 'n iar a' ruith gu réidh;
Tha 'n linne sleamhuinn sìochail
O na chiùinich strì nan speur.
Tha 'n long 'na h-éideadh sgiamhach,
'S cha chuir sgìos i dh'iarraidh tàmh;
Mar a fhuair 's a chunnaic mise:
Thoir am fios so thun a' Bhàird.

Tha bogha-mór an t-sàile
Mar a bha le reachd bith-bhuan
A' mórachd màise nàduir
'S a' cheann-àrd ri tuinn a' chuain;
A rìombal geal seachd mìle,
Gainmhean sìobt' o bheul an làin;
Mar a fhuair 's a chunnaic mise:
Thoir am fios so thun a' Bhàird.

Ged a roinneas gathan gréine
Tlus nan speur ri blàth nan lòn,
'S ged a chithear spréidh air àirigh
'S buailtean làn de dh'àlach bhó,
Tha Ile 'n diugh gun daoine:
Chuir a' chaor' a bailtean fàs,
Mar a fhuair 's a chunnaic mise:
Thoir am fios so thun a' Bhàird.

Chan fhaigh an déirceach fasgadh
No 'm fear astair fois o sgìos,
No soisgeulach luchd éisdeachd:
Bhuadhaich eucoir, Gaill is cìs;
Tha 'n nathair bhreac 'na lùban
Air na h-ùrlair far an d'fhàs
Na fir mhór a chunnaic mise
Thoir am fios so thun a' Bhàird.

Lomadh ceàrn na h-Oa,
An Lanndaidh bhòidheach 's Roinn Mhic Aoidh,
Tha 'n Learga ghlacach ghrianach
'S fuigheal cianail air a taobh,
Tha 'n gleann 'na fhiathair uaine
Aig luchd fuath, gun tuath, gun bhàrr,
Mar a fhuair 's a chunnaic mise:
Thoir am fios so thun a' Bhàird.

Ile no Braid-Albann, no roinn sam bith eile anns an robh Gàidheil a
dh'fhuiling sannt is fòirneart nan uachdaran, le cumhachd riaghaltas
Bhreatainn air an cùl, bha iad uile fo bheachd sùil Mhic Dhùn-

Léibhe, agus cha tug breugan is cealgaireachd riaghladairean Bhreatainn air a chùl a chur air Gàidheil Eirinn:

A' maduinn neo-chiontachd na h-òige
Fhuair mi sgeòil nan linn a dh'fhalbh
Aig cagailtean Ile Chlann Dòmhnuill
M'an d'fhògradh na Gàidheil o'n sealbh.

A' chòisridh fhuranach le'm b'éibhinn
Aithris sgeulachd Innis-Fàil,
Uirsgeulan nan aoighean còir,
An séisdean ceòlar nam bàrd.

Shaoileadh na macain gum b'fhìor
Na dh'innseadh dhaibh o bheul nan sean;
'S gun robh thus' a ghnàth mar chualas
Luath-ghàireach, sona, mar sin.

Tha mi 'n diugh mar a b'àbhaist
A' faicinn t'fhaire thar an lear
O chladach tonnach deas-thìr Ile,
'S is dubhach ri innseadh do chor.

Sgeula mulaid, cuing is fògraidh,
Gort is bròn is ana-cheart,
'S gun dòigh air t'fhurtachd od' phéin
O na bhrist thu féin do neart.

Thug mi iomradh a nis air 'Fios thun a' Bhàird', 'Eirinn ag Gul', 'Cuimhneachan Bhraid-Albann' agus air an dàn ris an abrar 'Còmhradh air Fàsachadh na Gàidhealtachd', an dàn as treasa cainnt is càineadh nan uachdaran: 'samhladh ghuir o'n Diabhul', 'àlach nan cràin Sasunnach', 'bior taghairm dheamhan is shiùrsach', 'luchd comuinn chon', 'mic mallachd an t-saoghail fharsaing'.

Thuirt mi fhìn roimhe so gun robh Màiri Mhór agus Uilleam ceàrr ann a bhith cur na coire air Sasuinn 's a' dìochaineachadh gum b'e Gàidheil mór roinn nan ceann-cinnidh agus nan uachdaran a rinn fàsach de ar dùthaich agus a sgrios ar daoine. 'Se mise bha ceàrr, cha b'e Màiri is Uilleam. Dé bha anns na cinn-cinnidh sin agus na h-uachdarain sin ach Sasunnaich, air an oileanachadh an sgoiltean Shasuinn, le cumhachd Shasuinn air an cùl. Is tric a smuainicheas mi air amaideas nan saighdearan Gàidhealach is Eireannach a choisinn gach blàr an aghaidh Napoleon. Nan robh air a dhol le Napoleon, dh'fhaodadh gun robh e air Mac Nèill Mhic Eachainn a chur 'na riaghladair air a' Ghàidhealtachd. Cha b'urrainn esan gun a bhith fada na b'fheàrr na'n fheadhainn a bh'ann, mur robh an donas buileach air, agus tha a h-uile coltas nach robh. Ma bha gealtairean is sliomairean am measg Gàidheil Ghlaschu agus Ghrianaig r'a linn, chan ioghnadh idir gun robhas ag ràdh gum bu duine corrach Uilleam Mac Dhùn-Léibhe.

'Is trom an t-eallach gaol dùthcha,' arsa Uilleam. Cha b'ioghnadh idir ged a bhristeadh e gach druim Gàidhealach air an robh e anns an linn eagalach eadar 1782 agus 1882. Feumaidh duine, ge dìleas e, an t-eallach a chur dheth agus anail a leigeil an dràsda 's a rithist. B'fheudar do Uilleam Mac Dhùn-Léibhe sin a dhèanamh, mar as fheudar do dhaoine eile, agus thàinig iomadh dàn as an leigeil analach sin. Mas d'fhàg e Ile, nuair a bha e 'na bhalach òg, rinn a rannan cuimir, grinn d'a chù Bran:

Bheir mise dhut teisteas sgrìobhta:
Thu bhi dìleas air mo chùl,
'S nach innis thu gum bi mi cadal
No 'g iarraidh nead air an Dùn.
Tha thu sleamhainn, dubh, 's do chluasan
A' lùbadh a nuas mu d' shùil;
'S a dh'aineoin na their luchd an tuaileis,
'S companach duin' uasail thu.

Bha Uilleam Mac Dhùn-Léibhe éibhinn, neònach iomadh uair. Chì sinn sin anns na dàin a leanas — 'An t-Oircean', 'Sùisde Chonain', agus gu h-àraidh ann an treamasgal fada, 'Driod-fhortan Imhir an Ràcain', dàn anns a bheil gach seòrsa neònachais air a chur an Gàidhlig bheothail, ghlain, ghrinn, agus tha còig ceud sreath ann dheth. Bha còir barrachd eòlais a bhith aig Gàidheil air an dàn so.

Is toigh leam 'Oran Bean a' Bhàird', 'Tigh Chailein', agus 'Rannan do Uilleam Mac Ghille Chriosda'. Tha aighear na mara annta; ach chan eil móran agam mu na dàin fhada mu chogaidhean a bha ann 's nach robh ann: 'Na Lochlannaich an Ile', 'Blàr Shunadail', 'Blàr Dhail-righ', 'Cath Thom Ealachaidh', 'Cath Allt a' Bhonnaich', 'Blàr Thràigh Ghruinneart', agus càch. Dh'fheuch Mac Dhùn-Léibhe dòigh ùr no a dhà anns na dàin sin, ach mar as trice tha iad ro-bhriathrach agus gun an dealbhadh snaidhte a tha anns na dàin éibhinn no an cuid de na dàin mu chor a dhùthcha.

Ma tha Ilich 'gam éisdeachd, tha mi ag ràdh riutha gu bheil mi duilich nach eil mi cho eòlach air beul-aithris mu'n bhàrd 's a tha iadsan; ach gun tubhairt mi fada bharrachd m'a dhéidhinn ann am pàipear m'a dhéidhinn a thig a mach am bliadhna bho Chomunn Gàidhlig Inbhirnis; gu bheil mi an dòchas gun cuir na h-Ilich a mach clò-bhualadh eile de dhàin Uilleim, agus gun cum iad a' dol an deagh obair a rinn an Comunn Ileach anns a' bhliadhna 1882.

Mairearad Nighean Lachlainn

Tha Mairearad Nighean Lachlainn air aon de na ban-bhàird a bha beò mu dheireadh na seachdamh linn deug agus mu thoiseach na h-ochdamh linn deug. A réir an Ollaimh MacBhàtair, rugadh i mu 1660 agus chaochail i mu 1730, ach tha MacGill-Eain Mac na Ceàrdaich, 'na leabhar *Na Bàird Ghàidhealach eadar 1715 agus 1765*, ag ràdh: 'She lived to an extreme old age. It is impossible to fix the date of all her poems. One of them, however, was composed in 1702 and another in 1751. The year of her death is not known. It seems impossible to find out as a matter of certainty where she is buried.' Is e an dàn a rinn i an 1751 'Oran do Shir Eachann MacGill-Eain', a chaochail anns an Ròimh an 1751. Am b'i Mairearad a rinn an dàn seo? Tha Mac na Ceàrdaich cinnteach gum b'i. Tha Pàdraig Mac an Tuairneir de'n cheart bharail, agus tha e soilleir nach robh Mac na Ceàrdaich ag aithris air Mac an Tuairneir a mhàin oir tha iomadh eadar-dhealachadh bhriathran eatorra. Mar eisimpleir, tha Mac an Tuairneir a' tòiseachadh mar a leanas:

> Thì tha 'n cathair nam feartan,
> Cum ceart agus còir ruinn
> 'S cuir deagh sgeul thugainn dhachaidh
> Air Sir Eachann nan ròiseal;
> 'S ma chaidh thu as t' fhearann
> 'S tu bhith tamull air fògradh,
> Gur h-e sgeula mo sgathaidh:
> Càch ag aithris nach beò thu.

Agus tha Mac na Ceàrdaich mar seo:

> Fhir tha'n cathair an Fhreasdail,
> Cum-sa ceart agus còir ruinn
> 'S cuir deagh sgeul thugainn dhachaidh
> Air Sir Eachann nan rò-seol.
> Tha e fad uainn á fhearann
> Agus tamull air fògradh;
> Gur h-e sgeula mo sgaraidh:
> Càch bhith 'g aithris nach beò e.

Chan eil rann seach rann ag ràdh gu deimhinneach gu bheil Eachann marbh, 's cha mhotha tha rann eile anns an òran ag ràdh a leithid, ach a mhàin gun dànaig a sgeul bàis; ach tha an siathamh rann (anns gach clò-bhualadh) a' nochdadh gum b'ann an déidh Blàr Chuil-lodair a rinneadh an t-òran:

> Dh'fhairich latha Chuil-lodair
> Gum bu dosgach na Gàidheil,
> 'S gun robh thus' ann an Sasuinn
> Air do ghlacadh le d'nàmhaid.

Uime sin, ma tha Mac an Tuairneir agus Mac na Ceàrdaich ceart ann a bhith ag cur an òrain seo as leth Mairearaid, bha i beò an 1746 agus, a réir gach coltais, an 1751.

A thaobh an òrain a rinneadh an 1702, chan urrainn nach e seo an t-òran do Shir Iain MacGill-Eain a tha a' tòiseachadh:

> O fhuair mi sgeul 's chan àicheam e,
> Gu bheil e dhomh toirt gàirdeachais,
> Gur binne leam na clàrsaichean
> Bhith 'g innse mar a thànaig sibh,
> Gu bheil Sir Iain sàbhailte
> 'S gun tug a' Bhan-righ'nn cùirt dha.

B'i Anna a' bhan-righinn oir tha an dara rann ag ràdh, 'Nam b'fhiosrach Ban-righ'nn Anna.'

Ged a thuirt e 1702 anns na *Bàird Ghàidhealach*, tha Mac na Ceàrdaich ag ràdh anns an leabhar *The Clan Gillean*: 'Sir John MacLean returned to London about the beginning of 1704.' Gidheadh, faodar a bhith cinnteach gu robh Mairearad ris na h-òrain roimh 1702, agus cha mhór dà bhliadhna anns an aois mhóir a fhuair Mairearad a réir beul-aithris. Dh'fhaodadh gun d'rugadh i mu 1660 agus gun robh i beò an 1751, gu h-àraidh a chionn nach eil òran air a chur as a leth roimh 1689 no 1692, agus tha beul-aithris ann gun robh i 'na meadhon aois mun do shìn i air bàrdachd.

Anns a' bhliadhna 1821 chlò-bhuaileadh an Inbhirnis le Seumas Friseal *Co-chruinneachadh Dhàn, Oran, etc.*, agus tha dà òran ann air an ainmeachadh air Mairearad: 'Gaoir nam Ban Muileach', agus duan beag eile, 'Do chloinn Ghill-Eain air do na Caimbeulaich buaidh fhaotainn orra'. Seo mar tha an duan a' tòiseachadh:

> Cha choma leam fhéin no co dhiù sin,
> Aon mhac Sir Lachun na lùireach,

Cuilean leomhan nan long siùbhlach,
Bhith cur lasair ri aitreabh Dhuibhneach.

Có 'aon mhac Sir Lachun'? Cha robh ach aon Lachlann 'na
cheann-cinnidh air Cloinn Ghill-Eain eadar bàs Lachlainn Mhóir an
1598 agus 1751. B'esan Lachlann, am 'fear bu mheasaile 'n campa
Mhontrois'. Chaochail e an 1648, ach bha dithis mhac aige, Eachann
Ruadh, a mharbhadh aig Inbhir-chéitein an 1651; agus Ailean, athair
Shir Iain. Bha Ailean 'na cheann-cinnidh eadar 1651 agus 1674. Tha
an 'duanag' aig Mac na Ceàrdaich mar seo:

Cha choma leam fhìn co dhiù sin,
Aon mhac Sir Ailein nan lùireach,
Cuilean leóghainn nan long siubhlach
A bhith bhuainn le cluain nan Duibhneach.

Chan eil teagamh nach eil Mac na Ceàrdaich ceart anns a' chùis seo.
B'e Sir Iain an 'cuilean leóghainn', aon mhac Shir Ailein. Bha Iain 'na
cheann-cinnidh eadar 1674 agus 1714, agus gu dearbh is iomadh latha
bha e 'bhuainn le cluain nan Duibhneach'. An 1674 thòisich na
Caimbeulaich air milleadh a dhèanamh air Muile, agus a rithist an
1679 agus an 1680. Cha robh Iain ach ceithir bliadhna a dh'aois an
1674, agus eadar 1674 agus 1686 b'e Lachlann Bhròlais fìor cheannard
Chloinn Ghill-Eain. Chaochail Lachlann Bhròlais an 1686, agus
ghabh Lachlann Thorrloisg an ceannas. Cha b'ann gus an do
chaochail Lachlann Thorrloisg, an 1687, a b'urrainn do neach a ràdh
gun robh Sir Iain 'na cheann-feadhna da-rìreadh, agus cha robh e ach
seachd bliadhna deug an uair sin fhéin. An 1688 theich Rìgh Seumas
do'n Fhraing. Chaidh Sir Iain as a dhéidh, ach thill e a Mhuile an
1689, dh'éirich Clann Ghill-Eain leis, agus bha iad air deas làimh an
airm Sheumasaich aig Cath Raon Ruairi (Coille-chnagaidh). Ach
mharbhadh an Greumach, agus chaidh an t-ar-a-mach bun os cionn,
agus b'fheudar do Shir Iain tilleadh a Mhuile. Dh'éirich na Caimbeulaich a rithist, agus an 1690 thàinig Gilleasbuig, an deicheamh
iarla, a Mhuile le arm mór. Ghabh Sir Iain dìon an Càrn-Burg, ach
anns a' mhios Mhàrt 1692 ghéill e do'n Riaghaltas agus thill e do'n
Fhraing beagan ùine an déidh dha Càrn-Burg fhàgail. Theagamh gum
b'ann eadar 1692 agus 1704 no 1702 a rinneadh an duanag agus gur i
an t-òran as sine a tha air fhàgail de bhàrdachd Mairearaid. Uime sin,
faodar a h-obair a chur eadar 1692 agus 1751.

Chan eil fhios againn ach air fìor bheag mu a beatha. Ré iomadh
bliadhna cha robh cinnt mu a h-ainm, am bu Dhòmhnallach no
Leathanach i. Tha Mac na Ceàrdaich ag ràdh: 'It is generally sup-

posed that the famous Mairearad was a MacLean. On behalf of this opinion it may be argued that the earliest reference to her in a printed work is in Duncan Kennedy's collection of hymns, which was published in 1786, and that in that work she is called "Mairearad Nighean Ailein, or Margaret MacLean". As Kennedy was a schoolmaster in Kilmelford in Lorn, he had a good opportunity of knowing who she was. It is certain, however, that he was mistaken in calling her Mairearad Nighean Ailein. It is possible, then, that he was mistaken in speaking of her as Margaret MacLean. She may, of course, have been married to a MacLean. There is a poem in Dr MacLean's MS which is said to have been composed by "Nighean Lachlainn mhic Iain mhic Lachlainn". That Mairearad Nighean Lachlainn is the authoress referred to is in our opinion a matter which cannot be called in question. But Dr MacLean must have been acquainted with her. We may take for granted then that he gives her genealogy correctly. We are inclined to think that Mairearad Nighean Lachlainn was a MacDonald. We got the following account of her, October 14, 1873, from a daughter of John MacLean, the poet, who told us that she had received it from her father: "Mairearad Nighean Lachlainn was born in Mull, and lived and died there. Her father was a MacDonald, and her mother a MacLean. She was married and had a large family. All her children died before herself. She nursed sixteen MacLeans of the best families in Mull. All these, like her own children, predeceased her. She used to go very frequently to the grave of the last of them and sit there. She was a very old woman, and much bent by old age." John MacLean took down several of her poems from oral recitation about the year 1816. In the heading of one of these poems he calls her "Mairearad Dhòmhnullach, da'm bu cho-ainm Mairearad nigh'n Lachinn".'

Tha dearbhadh air a' chùis do nach tug Mac na Ceàrdaich an aire. Rinn Mairearad marbhrann do Ailean, mac Lachlainn Bhròlais, a chaochail an 1722. Ann an rann de'n òran seo, air dhi bhith a' moladh Ailein agus chloinn Ghill-Eain, tha i ag ràdh:

Càit a bheil an Albainn
No thall anns an Olaind
Leithid cinneadh mo mhàthar
Mach o àrdan Chlann Dòmhnaill?

Chan eil aon teagamh nach e Clann Ghill-Eain 'cinneadh a màthar'. Ann an 'Gaoir nam Ban Muileach', ann a bhith ag caoidh bàs Shir Iain, tha i ag ràdh:

Is mairg rìoghachd de'n deachaidh
An triath calm' ud is Caiptean Chlann Raghnaill.

Agus an rann eile de'n aon òran tha i ag ràdh:

Tha mi faondrach, gun fharraid,
Gun cheann-cinnidh thaobh athar no màthar.

Tha e soilleir gum b'e Ailean Mùideartach a 'ceann-cinnidh thaobh athar'. Uime sin, tha e soilleir gum bu Bhan-Dòmhnallach de Chloinn Raghnaill Mairearad, agus gum bu Nic Gill-Eain a màthair. Chan eil teagamh sam bith nach robh Mairearad pòsda aig fear de chloinn Ghill-Eain, agus tha e cuideachd cinnteach gun do chaith i a beatha am Muile, agus gum b'e Clann Ghill-Eain cuspairean a dàn, có dhiùbh anns na dàin a tha againn fhathast.

Cha do chuir Iain MacCoinnich ach seachd rannan de 'Ghaoir nam Ban Muileach' ann an *Sàr Obair*. Cha b'fhiach leis an còrr de a bàrdachd a chur 'na leabhar, ged tha e ag ràdh: 'We have seen twenty-five pieces of (her) composition.' Cha robh aige ach fìor dhroch bharail air bàrdachd Mairearaid. Cha robh i, 'na bheachd-san, idir faisg air Diorbhail Nic a' Bhriuthainn, mu'm bheil e ag ràdh: 'She is the only poetess who at all approaches Màiri Nighean Alasdair Ruaidh.' Tha sinne a' dìoghladh air an dì-meas a rinn MacCoinnich air Mairearad, oir chan eil againn ach a h-aon deug de a dàin, ged a chunnaic Iain MacCoinnich cóig ar fhichead. Seo an fheadhainn air a bheil lorg agamsa:

(1) Duanag do Chlann Ghill-Eain, 'Cha choma leam fhìn . . .' Rinneadh i eadar 1692 agus 1704.

(2) Oran do Shir Iain, 'Ged is stoc mi air crìonadh'. Ar leam gun d'rinneadh e seo cuideachd eadar 1692 agus 1704.

(3) Oran do Shir Iain, 'O fhuair mi sgeul 's chan àicheam e'. Rinneadh an t-òran seo mu 1704, a' bhliadhna a thàinig Sir Iain gu cùirt Ban-righinn Anna.

(4) Oran do Shir Iain, 'Dh'fhalbh mo chadal . . .' Tha cinnt gun d'rinneadh e eadar 1714 agus 1716, oir tha iomradh ann air Rìgh Deòrsa.

(5) 'Gaoir nam Ban Muileach', marbhrann Shir Iain, a chaochail anns a' mhios Mhàrt 1716.

(6) Oran do Ailean mac Fear Bhròlais. Chaochail Ailean an 1722. B'e mac an Lachlainn a chaochail an 1686, agus b'e bràthair athar an Ailein a fhuair ceannas Chlann Ghill-Eain nuair a chaochail Sir Eachann, mac Sir Iain, an 1751.

(7) Oran do Ailean Bhròlais, triath Chlann Ghill-Eain an déidh 1751. Tha an t-òran a' tòiseachadh: 'Mo rùn an t-Ailean, marcach allail'. Rinneadh e eadar 1725 agus 1749.

(8) Oran eile do Ailean Bhròlais, 'Mo cheist an Leathanach mòdhar'.

(9) Oran do Shir Eachann, 'Fhir tha 'n cathair an Fhreasdail'. Rinneadh an t-òran seo mu 1751, a' bhliadhna a chaochail Sir Eachann.

(10) Oran, 'Gur h-e mheudaich mo chràdh'. Tha Mac na Ceàrdaich ag ràdh: 'We have no means of determining who the subject of this lament was. It seems, however, to have been composed about a grandson of Allan of Ardtoirnish.' A réir Mhic an Tuairneir b'e a chuspair 'Eachunn mac Iain Diùraich'.

(11) Cumha do Lachlann Mac Gill-Eain, 'Gur h-e mise th' air mo leònadh'. Is e seo cumha fir a bhàthadh, ach có e agus cuin a rinneadh an t-òran dà cheist nach soirbh am fuasgladh. Dh'fhaodadh gun d'rinneadh e roimh fhear sam bith de chàch.

Tha mi air geàrr iomradh a thoirt air na tha air mhaireann de dhàin Mairearaid, a h-aon deug dhiubh. Cha mhór an àireamh, ach chan eil againn ach mu shia deug le Màiri Nighean Alasdair Ruaidh, agus faodar teagamh a chur ann am fear no a dhà dhiubh. Chan eil air fhàgail ach glé bheag de'n ionmhas mhór a bha ann am bàrdachd na Gàidhlig mu thoiseach na h-ochdamh linn deug, agus 's ann a dh'fhaodas iongnadh a bhith oirnn gun do mhair na mhair de òrain Nighean Lachlainn.

(1) 'Se a' cheud òran air an d'rinn mi iomradh an Duanag do Chloinn Ghill-Eain. Tha sia rainn innte, ceithir sreathan air an rann, agus gheibhear i aig Mac na Ceàrdaich agus aig Seumas Friseal. Chan eil teagamh ann nach e Mac na Ceàrdaich a tha ceart mar is trice. Tha Mairearad ag caoidh 'aon mhac Shir Ailein nan lùireach' a bhith air choigreachas 'le cluain nan Duibhneach'. B' e an t-aon mhac seo Sir Iain, a bha 'na thriath air Dubhaird eadar 1674 agus 1716 ged nach d'ràinig e ìre gu 1687. Choisinn Sir Iain agus Clann Ghill-Eain urram mór aig Cath Raon Ruairi agus aig Blàr Sliabh an t-Siorraim. Tha Mairearad ag urnuigh gun 'tionndaidh an roth'. Tha i a' toirt iomraidh air gaisge a cinnidh anns na làithean a dh'aom agus ag ràdh gum b'e 'am dol sìos do'n dream Dhuibhneach am dol suas' do Chloinn Ghill-Eain, ach a nis tha i ag caoidh 'cinneadh làidir nan lann rùisgte' a bhith 'truagh roimh na Duibhnich'. Tha i an dòchas gum faic i rithist an latha 'am bi dol suas air sìol an taighe', taigh Mhic Ghill-Eain. Chan eil móran eadar-dhealachaidh eadar Mac na Ceàrdaich agus Friseal ach anns a' cheud rann, far a bheil 'aon mhac Shir Lachuinn' aig

Friseal. Tha 'Lachuinn' ceàrr có-dhiùbh, ach theagamh gu bheil 'bhith cur lasair ri aitreabh Dhuibhneach' ceart, oir dh'fhaodadh gun d'rinn Sir Iain sin mu 1686, 1689 no mu 1715. Ach carson a chaoidheadh Mairearad 'dol sìos' Chlann Ghill-Eain dìreach aig aon de na h-amannan goirid anns an robh seòrsa dìoclaidh de 'dhol suas' orra? Faodar nach robh moran earbsa aice gum maireadh an rath, ach is e mo bharail fhìn gun d'rinn i an duanag anns na làithean dorcha eadar 1690 agus 1704. Mar dhàn, tha neart agus grinneas agus caomhnadh air faclan anns an duanaig. Tha an caomhnadh fhacal 'na bhuaidh nach beag. Tha sìmplidheachd éifeachdach anns na briathran. Tha iomadh earrann nas miosa ann an *Sàr Obair*.

(2) An dara òran a chuir mi sìos, Oran do Shir Iain, 'Ged is stoc mi air crìonadh'.

Tha mi de'n bheachd gum b'ann eadar 1692 and 1704 a rinneadh e seo cuideachd, eadar do Shir Iain Càrn Burg fhàgail agus tighinn do chùirt Anna an 1704. Ach carson a ghabhadh Mairearad 'stoc crìon' oirre fhéin nuair nach robh i, aig a' char bu mhotha, móran a bharrachd air dà fhichead bliadhna a dh'aois. Theagamh nach ann gu litireil a tha i a' labhairt.

Tha sia rannan anns an òran, agus ochd sreathan air an rann. Tha Mairearad ag caoidh cor a cinnidh agus fuadach a cinn-cinnidh. Tha i ag ràdh gun robh iad 'sàr mhath' nuair a dh'fhàgadh Sir Iain 'na leanabh; gun tug e 'sòlas dhaibh', ach gun do 'ghabh e fògradh á fhearann'; tha a 'dhùthchannan bochd dheth/Làn de ghort is de ainnis'. Ar leam gum b'fhìor dhi sin. An déidh sin tha am moladh àbhaisteach. 'S e Iain 'mac-samhailt do'n reul — do 'n ghréin no do'n ghealaich', 'iuchair, gàrradh is daingeann nan Gàidheal'. Tha luaidh air cuachagan òr-bhuidh a ghruaige; air a thalla rìoghail, le 'fhìon, le uisge-beatha, le leann 's le éibhneas'. Chan eil an dà rann mu dheireadh idir cho math ri càch. Tha Mairearad nas treasa anns a' chumha na tha i air aithris air an t-sòlas. A dh'aindeoin an lagachaidh seo, tha drùidhteachd thiamhaidh anns an òran, agus a chionn gu bheil iomradh air 'gort is ainnis' a luchd dùthcha, theagamh gu bheil barrachd brìgh anns a' bhàrdachd seo, ann a leithid a chur an céill, na tha an iomadh rann nas glòrmhoire an cainnt le Màiri Nighean Alasdair Ruaidh. Bha mì-fhortan air triathan Dhubhaird nach robh air triathan Dhùn Bheagain, agus cluinnear o Mhairearad mu 'ghort is ainnis' an t-sluaigh far nach cluinnear o Mhàiri ach 'gleadhraich nan còrn' anns an 'talla mhór phrìseil'.

(3) Tha òran eile do Shir Iain a' tòiseachadh 'O, fhuair mi sgeul 's chan àicheam e'. Rinneadh e air do Iain tilleadh as an Fhraing an 1704. Tha aon rann deug ann, agus sia sreathan anns gach rann. Tha

Mairearad aoibhneach a chionn's gu bheil 'Sir Iain sàbhailte 's gun tug a' Bhan-righinn cùirt dha'. Bhiodh Anna 'aoidheil geanail', nan robh fhios aice mar a thugadh 'fhearann bhuaidhe' is 'gun chron ri aithris air/Ach leantuinn a rìgh dùthchais'. Is truagh nach fhaigheadh Mairearad fhéin cothrom air facal no a dhà a chur an cluais Anna, ach chan eil 'Beurla Shasunnach' no 'Fraingeis mhìn gu fasanta' aice. Thug 'teann lagh strìochdadh' as na Leathanaich. 'Is mairg a bha cho dìleas riutha'; b' fheàrr a bhith 'cealgach innleachdach' mar a bha an nàimhdean. Is e sin a 'dheanadh gnothach cinnteach dhaibh/A bhith cho faicleach crìonda/'S gum b'fhiach leo a bhith tionndadh'. Anns na rannan seo tha Mairearad nas leimhe ris na triathan Caimbeulach na chaidh Iain Lom riamh: tha ise socair sgaiteach; 's ann a tha Iain Lom borb. Bha uair a bha Clann Ghill-Eain 'nam 'bàdhan' do na bha mu thuath. Is beag an t-iongnadh an ionndrainn a tha orra. B' iadsan 'an fhine mhór bha àrdanach, urramach, buadhach, sgairteil'. Ged a thill Sir Iain, tha Mairearad 'diombach cianail' oir tuigear gur h-e a smuain dìomhair gu bheil latha Chlann Ghill-Eain air tréigsinn. Tha deagh bhàrdachd anns an òran, gu h-àraidh far a bheil Mairearad a' toirt tarraing leamh air fortan nan Caimbeulach.

(4) 'S ann do Shir Iain a tha an ceathramh òran 'nam chunntas: Dh'fhalbh mo chadal a' smaointinn'. Rinneadh an dàn seo eadar bàs Anna an 1714 agus bàs Shir Iain an 1716. Tha naoi rannan ann, is ceithir sreathan anns an rann. Tha cadal Mairearaid air falbh le iomagain. Cha d'fhuirich Sir Iain ann an Lunnainn 'a' feitheamh air furan Rìgh Deòrsa', ach is beag an t-iongnadh Iain a bhith 'àrdanach beachdail' is a 'liuthad fuil bhras' a bha 'na phòraibh'. Tha i a' luaidh a chàirdeis do Ruairi Mór MacLeòid agus do Chailean Cam Mac-Coinnich a measg chàich, agus ag ràdh gum b'e dalta a seanar agus 'nighean Ruairi 's na h-Earadh'. (Am b'i nighean Ruairi seanmhair Mairearaid?) Tha i ag guidhe gun tionndaidh Dia riutha ged nach eil iad 'cho mùinte 's bu chòir dhaibh'.

Tha loinn agus grinneas Màiri Nighean Alasdair Ruaidh air an dàn seo.

(5) Is e 'Gaoir nam Ban Muileach' an cóigeamh òran, an t-òran air an ainmichear Mairearad mar is trice. Tha cóig rannan ar fichead dheth aig Mac an Tuairneir, agus dà rann ar fhichead aig Mac na Ceàrdaich, ach chan eil aig Sàr Obair ach seachd, agus a h-aon deug aig Seumas Friseal. Chan eil e soirbh a ràdh am feàrr an dòigh aig Mac an Tuairneir no aig Mac na Ceàrdaich. Ar leam gu bheil seòl Mhic an Tuairneir nas fheàrr uaireannan, ach an iomadh àite tha e soilleir gu bheil Mac na Ceàrdaich ceart, agus tha sreath no a dhà mhath aig MacCoinnich no aig Friseal nach eil aig càch.

Tha neart is uaisle cainnte anns an dàn seo, agus saoilidh mi gu bheil blas na fìrinne air ann an tomhas nach eil cumanta ann an dàin de a sheòrsa. Faodar gun robh cothrom aig Mairearad nach robh gu tric aig na bàird a bha ag caoidh nan triath. Bha Sir Iain mì-shealbhach fad a bheatha agus dh'fhaodadh gum b'e a dhìlse neo-chumanta a b'aobhar air sin. Tha comharraidhean ann gun robh e 'na dhuine a b'fheàrr na càch de chinn-chinnidh a linn; gun robh esan agus Ailean Mùideartach air leth a measg chàich agus gun robh meas anabarrach aig an dithis air a chéile. Uime sin, theagamh gu bheil barrachd de'n fhìor bhròn ann an 'Gaoir nam Ban Muileach' na tha ann an iomadh cumha eile, agus ge b'e deagh bheusan no droch bheusan Shir Iain, tha cinnt gun robh dìlse a chinnidh sònraichte agus gun do dh'fhuiling iad móran air a shàileabh eadar 1688 agus 1692 agus a rithis an 1715, air 'turus na truaighe', 'am briosgadh thug Màrr as'. Tha blàth na dùrachd air an dàn uile: cha d'fhalbh Sir Iain 'air an luingeas le càch'; cha b'e 'neart dhaoine thug bhuainn e'; dh'fhàg a bhàs a chinneadh 'an cruaidh-chàs os cionn tuigse agus smuaintinn'; agus cha tugadh dhachaidh an corp.

> Och is mis' th'air mo sgaradh
> Nach tug iad thu thairis
> Dhol air tìr air an Ealaidh,
> Dhol fo dhìon anns a' charraig,
> Ann an réilig nam manach,
> Mar ri t'athair 's do sheanair
> Is ioma treun laoch a bharrachd,
> Far am faodamaid teannadh mu d'chàrnan.

Chan eil cumha cinn-chinnidh ann am bàrdachd na Gàidhlig anns a bheil fìor ghuth a' chinnidh gu léir cho cinnteach drùidhteach is a tha e ann an 'Gaoir nam Ban Muileach', agus gabhaidh e a choimeas ris an fhear as fheàrr dhiubh ann an snas uasal cainnte.

(6) Is e an siathamh òran air an toir mi iomradh 'Chunnaic mis' thu, Ailein', do Ailean mac Fear Bhròlais. B'e an t-Ailean seo dara mac Lachlainn Bhròlais, a chaochail an 1686, agus b'e bràthair athar an Ailein Bhròlais ris an abradh triath Dhubhaird an uair a chaochail Sir Eachann, mac Shir Iain, an 1751. Bha cuspair an òrain 'na chòirneal anns an arm Bhreatannach ged a bha a bhràthair, Dòmhnall Bhròlais, 'na dhara còirneal air Cloinn Ghill-Eain aig Sliabh an t-Siorraim. Cha do phòs Ailean riamh agus chaochail e ann an Sruighlea an 1722. Tha an t-òran aig Mac an Tuairneir agus aig Mac na Ceàrdaich. Tha i ag caoidh bàs Ailein agus a' moladh a chumaidh agus a ghaisge. An sin tha i ag cuimhneachadh mar chàidh athair Ailein agus Lachlann

Thorrloisg gu Dùn-Eideann a sheasamh còir Chlann Ghill-Eain an 1680; mar a ghabh gach 'morair a b'àirde' iongnadh de'n coltas agus de'n gliocas. Tha i ag aithris air seann dòighean a cinnidh, tha i greis air an t-sloinneadh, agus tha i ag caoidh bàs Ailein 'eadar Ghallaibh', agus nach eil a chorp an Innis Choinnich no an I Chalum Chille. Tha an t-seann ghearan ann air mar a 'dh'fhalbh Clann Ghill-Eain nan cruaidh chath mar an raineach', mar tha 'an t-oighre air fògradh' agus 'a chòir aig Mac Cailein'. Tha am marbhrann ag crìochnachadh le rann a nochdas gu bheil i fhéin ag coimhead fada nas sine na tha i.

(7) Tha dà òran aig Mairearad do'n Ailean Bhròlais a bha 'na cheann-cinnidh eadar 1751 agus 1783. B'e seo mac bràthar an Ailein do'n robh an siathamh òran. Tha e coltach gun d'rinneadh na dhà eadar bàs Dhòmhnaill Bhròlais an 1725 agus tilleadh Ailein do Mhuile an 1748. Tha a' cheud fhear a' tòiseachadh: 'Mo rùn an t-Ailean, marcach allail'. Tha ochd rannan ann is ceithir sreathan anns gach rann. Chan eil anns an òran seo ach am moladh àbhaisteach, a' chaoidh àbhaisteach mu chaochladh cor Chlann Ghill-Eain, agus a mulad fhéin; ach tha tionndaidhean agus cuir neo-chumanta air gluasad na rannaigheachd.

(8) Tha an t-òran eile do'n Ailean cheudna, 'Mo cheist an Leathanach mòdhar', fada nas fhaide, ochd rannan deug le ochd sreathan anns gach rann. Anns an t-sloinneadh tha iomradh air an Eachann a mharbhadh aig Inbhir-Chéitein agus air an 'fhoill' a rinn Hòbrun, an fhoill air an robh daor an ceannach aig Cloinn Ghill-Eain is 'le MacCailein cha bu dubhach'. Tha cuimhne aig Mairearad fhathast air Sir Iain, 'an t-iarla a b'fheàrr bha an Albainn' agus air a mhac, Sir Eachann, a tha thall air fògradh, agus tha i ag ràdh nach robh i 'chòir cinneadh m'athar/Bho'n a dh'fhògradh Clann Ghill-Eain'. Tuigear gu bheil Mairearad cho breòite tre dheuchainnean nan Leathanach 's gu bheil i air na Dòmhnallaich a dhìochaineachadh.

(9) 'S ann mu sgeul bàis Shir Eachainn a tha an t-òran 'Fhir tha 'n cathair an Fhreasdail'. Rinneadh e an 1750, nuair a bha Eachunn glé thinn, no an 1751, a' bhliadhna a chaochail e. Bha Eachann 'na 'sgiath air uileann Phrionnsa Teàrlaich', agus 'dh'fhairich latha Chuil-lodair' gun do ghlacadh e mas do thog e a dhaoine. A nis tha caistealan Eachainn 'fo luchd adachan dubha', agus tha Mairearad ag guidhe gun robh iadsan anns 'a' Chaillich fo àrd chaithream an lìonaidh'. Tha Mac na Ceàrdaich ag ràdh gur h-i a' Chailleach an rudha de'n ainm sin am Muile, ach tha e gu tur ceàrr; is e Coire Bhreacain a' chailleach seo. Tha rann anabarrach a' leantuinn 's ag iarraidh gun robh Diùc Uilleam agus a shluagh air an 'tilgeil mu chasan' an Rudha Mhurchanaich 'ann am braisead a bhuaireis'. Tha an ath rann ag

guidhe gun robh 'Fir Shasuinn' a' faotainn an duaise bho 'làimh chruaidh' baintighearna móire 'stràiceil' nach caraich an rìgh. A réir Mhic na Ceàrdaich, is e Coire Bhreacain a' bhaintighearna, ach tha fhios gu bheil e ceàrr. Dh'fhaodadh gur h-i an rudha am Muile ris an canar a' Chailleach. Tha e coltach nach robh fhios aig Mac na Ceàrdaich gun robh dà 'Chailleach' ainmeil air còrsa Earra-ghàidheal.

Tha rann cumhachdach drùidhteach a rithist a' togail a' chumha. Tha a cridhe 'air a shracadh mar seann phàipear a fhliuchteadh' is i a' smaoineachadh air Cuil-lodair, far an robh na h-eich dhonna is dubha ''gur bruthadh 's 'gur prannadh'. Tha dà rann uasal ag cur urram air Teàrlach mac mhic Ailein mhic Theàrlaich, a bha 'na chomanndair air Cloinn Ghill-Eain aig Cuil-lodair. Tha dòchas aice fhathast nach eil Sir Eachunn marbh.

(10) Tha an deicheamh òran a' tòiseachadh, 'Gur h-e mheudaich mo chràdh.'

Tha sia rannan deug ann, is seachd sreathan anns gach rann. Tha Mac na Ceàrdaich ag ràdh: 'We have no means of determining who the subject of the lament was. It seems, however, to have been composed about a grandson of Allan of Ardtornish, possibly about Hector son of Charles of Ardnacross.' Tha an t-òran aig Mac an Tuairneir agus tha e air a chur sìos: 'Do Eachunn mac Iain Dhiùraich.' Feumar beagan sloinnidh, ged tha eagal orm nach gabh a' cheist a fuasgladh, oir tha Mac an Tuairneir ceàrr, agus tha Mac na Ceàrdaich ann an imcheist. A réir an t-sloinnidh àbhaistich, b'e Ailean Aird Toirinis dara mhac Iain Duibh na Morbhairne, bràthair Lachlainn Mhóir Dhubhaird: agus b'e Iain Diùrach mac Theàrlaich, ceathramh mac Iain Duibh. Tha an siathamh rann (mar a tha e aig Mac na Ceàrdaich) ag ràdh: ''S ogha Ailein nan lann 's nan steud thu', agus tha an deicheamh rann ag ràdh: 'Iar-ogha dìleas mo ghràdh do Iain Dubh a bha 'n làimh'; ach tha aig Mac an Tuairneir ''S iar-ogha Ailein nan lann 's nan steud thu' agus 'ogha dìleas mo ghràdh do Iain Dubh . . .' A réir sloinnidh Mhic na Ceàrdaich b'e Ailean Aird Toirinis bràthair seanar Eachainn mhic Iain Diùraich.

Tha an cumha uasal snaidhte am briathran mar a tha iomadh cumha a rinneadh aig an am, agus ann an aon rann tha e neo-chumanta:

. . . marcaich nan stuadh
Ri là frionasach fuar:
'S tu gun iarradh i suas
Ged a bhiodh i 'n sàs cruaidh na h-éiginn.

Tha crìoch an dàin ag caoidh cor muladach Chlann Ghill-Eain.

(11) Ma tha e duilich a ràdh có bu chuspair an deicheamh òrain, tha e fada nas duilghe a ràdh có cuspair an òrain mu dheireadh. Rinneadh e mu bhàthadh Lachlainn air choireigin. B'e an Lachlann mac Eachainn air choireigin, agus chailleadh e a' dol a Chanaidh no a' tilleadh á Canaidh. Tha Mac na Ceàrdaich ag ràdh: 'It is slightly probable that the lines were composed about Lachlan son of Hector son of Charles of Ardnacross.' Tha rud annasach anns an òran seo. Tha Mairearad ag ràdh anns an t-siathamh rann:

> Mur bu dhomhsa bhith òg leanbail
> Is nach eòl domh do sheanchas,
> Bheirinn umad làn iomradh.

Ach tha rann eile ag ràdh gum b'e an Lachlann a bhàthadh 'ogha bràthair a seanar', agus shaoilinn nach biodh e doirbh do'n bhan-bhàrd ogha bràthair a seanar a shloinneadh, gu h-àraidh ma bha e de theaghlach cho ainmeil ri teaghlach Theàrlaich Aird na Crois; agus tha i a' dèanamh ròp mór sloinnidh air cheana, ag innse gu bheil e càirdeach do Thriath Dhubhaird, do Iarla Andruim, do Mhurchadh Locha Buidhe, do Mhac Fhionghuin an t-Sratha, do Mhac Mhic Ailein, do Mhac Mhic Eóghain, do Mhac Nèill Bharraidh, agus do Lachlann an Rois.[1]

Tha Mairearad ag innse dhuinn gum b'e an Lachlann seo

> . . . ogha do dh'Ailean
> Thug an long o MhacCailein
> Ris an oidhche ghil ghealaich,
> Is a luchd innte chrodh ballach
> Ged nach b'ann gu crò earraich a' gheumnaich.

Có an t-Ailean seo? Am b'e Ailean Aird Toirinis? Ach nam b'e, shaoilinn gu bheil 'ogha' ceàrr agus gur h-e 'iar-ogha' bu chòir a bhith ann.

Tha aon rann deug anns an òran, agus cóig sreathan anns gach rann. Tha a dhà dhiubh glé àlainn:

> Och, mo thruaighe do mhàthair!
> 'S daor a cheannaich i 'phàirtidh
> Nuair a bhristeadh do bhàta
> 'S a bha bloigh air gach tràigh dhith:
> Bha mo dhiubhail mu'n chàrn gun chead éirigh.

> Och, mo thruaigh i 's thus', Eachainn,
> Le do mhoch-éirigh mhaduinn,

Ri siubhal gach cladaich
'S nach d'fhuaras leat Lachlann
Og ùr a' chùil chleachdaich mar theudan.

Uime sin, tha air mhaireann de bhàrdachd Nighean Lachlainn aon
dàn deug: Duanag do Chloinn Ghill-Eathain; trì òrain do Shir Iain
agus a mharbhrann, 'Gaoir nam Ban Muileach'; seòrsa marbhrann do
Shir Eachann; marbhrann do mhac Lachlainn Bhròlais; dà òran do
Ailean Bhròlais; agus dà mharbhrann eile, fear do Eachann air
choireigin agus fear do Lachlann air choireigin. Cha bhi móran dùil ri
annasan ùra 'na bàrdachd, gu h-àraidh a chionn gun robh i an déidh
Nighean Alasdair Ruaidh, Eachainn Bhacaich, Iain Luim agus
iomadh fir eile a bha ris an aon sheòrsa bàrdachd dà fhichead bliadhna
mun do thòisich ise. Tha e nas fhasa coimeas a dhèanamh ri Iain Lom
na tha e ri Màiri Nighean Alasdair Ruaidh, oir tha Mairearad agus Iain
Lom 'nam bàird cinnidh agus Màiri 'na bàrd cùirt a' chinn-chinnidh,
ach tha Mairearad nas fhaisge air a cinneadh gu léir na tha Iain Lom.
Bha Iain Lom air bhoile le aobhar nan rìghrean Stiùbhartach, ach 's
ann a bha Mairearad air a sìor chlaoidh leis na h-àmhghair a dh'fhuiling Clann Ghill-Eain air lorg an dìlse do'n teaghlach Stiùbhart. Chan
eil an gamhlas borb innte-se a tha ann an Iain Lom, ach tha am bròn
drùidhteach:

Ach có an neach air nach tig muthadh
Mar na neòil 's na speuraibh dubh-ghorm?
Cinneadh làidir nan lann rùisgte,
'S truagh mar tha iad roimh na Duibhnich.
Gu bheil m'inntinn-sa fo smalan
Is mo shùilean gum bi galach
Gus am faic mi rìsd an latha
Am bi dol suas air sìol an taighe.

Agus:

Tha do dhùthchannan bochd dheth
Làn de ghort is de dh'ainnis.

Ann an 'Gaoir nam Ban Muileach', tha i ag gearain air dealas Shir
Iain:

Gur e turus na truaighe,
Gun bhuidhinn, gun bhuannachd,
Thug thu'n uiridh nuair ghluais thu
Le do dhaoine ri d'ghualainn:

Dh'fhàg e sinne 'n cruaidh-chàs
Os cionn tuigse is smuaintinn:
Tha sinn falamh lag suarach,
Dh'fhalbh ar sonas mar bhruadair gun stàth bhuainn.

Tha gaoir ghoirt aice mu chall eagalach nan Leathanach aig Cuil-
lodair:

Chan e cumha nan caorach
Tha mi caoineadh fo smalan;
Gur h-e m'iargain na daoine
Ris am faodainn mo ghearan.
Ormsa thàinig an t-ànradh
An tùs samhraidh na gaillinn:
Na h-eich dhonn' agus dhubha
Bhith 'gur bruthadh 's 'gur prannadh.

Tha cor a cinnidh a' drùdhadh air aigne agus air cridhe Mairearaid,
agus tha briathran 'ga chur an céill le cumhachd thiamhaidh. Sin am
pong as trice 'na dàin, ach air uairean tha i briathrach le feirg:

Tha do chaistealan geala
Is do thallachan prìseil,
Am biodh òl agus aighear
Aig luchd caithimh an fhìona,
Fo luchd adaichean dubha —
Mo sgeul duilich gur fìor e —
Rìgh, nach robh iad 's a' Chaillich
Fo chaithream an lìonaidh.

B'urrainn dhi a bhith leamh cuideachd. Tha i a' toirt comhairle air
Cloinn Ghill-Eain, mar gum b'ann gum bu chòir dhaibhsan a bhith
'cho faicleach crìonda' ri an nàimhdean. Cha tug Iain Lom riamh
tarraing cho leamh ri seo air na Caimbeulaich:

Gum b'fheàrr bhith cealgach innleachdach
Mar bha ur nàimhdean mìorunach:
'S e dh'fhàgadh làidir lìonmhor sibh,
'Se dhèanadh gnothach cinnteach dhuibh
A bhith cho faicleach crìonda
'S gum b' fhiach leibh a bhith tionndadh.

Theirinn gu bheil rian agus gearradh annasach air a' mhagadh sin.
Tha e nas fhaisge air Voltaire na tha e air Iain Lom.
Saoilidh mi gu bheil gnè anabarrach de mhac-meanmna dùthchasail

175

ann an cuid de rannan Mairearaid. Far a bheil càch ri draoidheachd leis an ainm fhéin, tha Mairearad ag cur ris le facal no a dhà a tha a' beothachadh dhealbhan anns an aigne as baoithe. Tha a' bhuaidh seo iongantach ann an caithream lìonaidh na Caillich agus ann am braisead buaireis an Rudha Mhurchanaich; ach 's aithne do Mhairearad ceòl-sìdhe an ainm leis fhéin — 'nuair a chruinnich do shluagh ann an Aros'. Tha gach seòrsa samhladh beothail 'na beul. Tha

> Clann Ghill-Eain air an dìobradh,
> Iad gun iteach gun linnidh,
> Ach mar gheòidh air an spìonadh.

Ach nuair a tha iad fo'n armaibh is e a tha annta:

> Fir mar gharbh fhrasa fuara
> Bheireadh leotha na fhuair iad.

Cha tug Iain MacCoinnich móran urraim do Mhairearad Nighean Lachlainn, ach bha meas mór aig Seumas Mac Ghille-Mhìcheil Mac Bhàtair oirre. Cha do chuir mise mo chorrag air a buaidh àraidh; cuiridh fear-eigin fhathast, ma mhaireas blas ar cànain ann am beòil na tha air fhàgail de ar daoine.

EARR-NOTAICHEAN

1 Dh'fhaodadh gu bheil Mairearad a' bualadh air moitif a bha stéidhichte anns a' bhàrdachd molaidh, is e sin gu bheil càirdeas Lachlainn cho farsaing 's nach glac inntinn a' bhàird e: cf. 'chan aithne dhomh fad a-mach ort/'s nì math m'eòlas' anns an Duanaig Ullaimh; Bard Thighearna Loch nan Eala ann an *Comh-chruinneachadh nan Stiùbhartach*, t.d. 132; etc. Mar sin cha ruigte a leas seagh ro-litireil a chur air facail Mairearaid an seo. Mur eil sin ceart, is dòcha gum bu chòir dhuinn *seanchas* a ghabhail mar 'chòmhradh', an àite 'sloinneadh' mar a rinneadh shuas.

Margaret daughter of Lachlan

Margaret daughter of Lachlan was one of the women poets who flourished about the end of the seventeenth century and the beginning of the eighteenth. According to Professor Watson she was born about 1660 and died about 1730, but MacLean Sinclair, in his book *Gaelic Bards 1715-1765*, says: 'She lived to an extreme old age. It is impossible to fix the date of all her poems. One of them, however, was composed in 1702 and another in 1751. The year of her death is not known. It seems impossible to find out as a matter of certainty where she is buried.' The poem she made in 1751 is 'Song for Sir Hector MacLean', who died in Rome in 1751. Was it Margaret who made this poem? MacLean Sinclair is certain that it was. Patrick Turner is of the same opinion, and it is clear that Sinclair was not drawing on Turner alone, for there are many verbal differences between their versions. For example, Turner starts as follows:

> Thou Being who art on the throne of miraculous powers,
> keep right and justice for us,
> and send us home good news
> of Sir Hector of the great ways;
> and though you went from your land
> and have been for a space an exile,
> the tale that breaks my heart is
> that others say that you are dead.

Sinclair's first verse runs:

> Thou One who art on the throne of Providence,
> keep right and justice for us
> and send us home good news
> of Sir Hector of the high sails.
> He is long away from us and his land,
> and for a while an exile;
> the tale that cuts my heart is
> that others say he is dead.

Neither version says definitely that he is dead, and no more does

177

any other verse in the song say as much, but only that news of his death has come; but the sixth verse (in each imprint) indicates that it was after the Battle of Culloden that the song was made:

> The day of Culloden knew
> that there was misfortune and grief for the Gaels
> and that you were in England
> captured by your enemy.

Therefore, if Turner and Sinclair are right in ascribing this song to Margaret, she was alive in 1746 and, in all likelihood, in 1751.

As to the song made in 1702, it can hardly be other than the song to Sir John MacLean that begins:

> O I heard a story and do not deny it,
> it makes me rejoice,
> sweeter to me than harps
> the telling how you came,
> that Sir John is safe
> and that the queen has received him (at court).

Anne was the Queen, for the second verse says, 'If Queen Anne knew'. Though he opted for 1702 in *Gaelic Bards*, Sinclair states in *The Clan Gillean*: 'Sir John MacLean returned to London about the beginning of 1704.' Nevertheless, one can be certain that Margaret was making songs before 1702, and two years is not a long time in the long life that Margaret enjoyed according to tradition. It could be that she was born about 1660 and that she was alive in 1751, especially since there is no song ascribed to her before 1689 or 1692, and there is a tradition that she was middle-aged before she began to compose poetry.

In the year 1821 there was printed in Inverness James Fraser's *A Collection of Poems, Songs etc*, which contains two songs bearing Margaret's name: 'The Cry of the Mull Women', and another little poem entitled 'To Clan Gillean when the Campbells had overcome them'. This is how the second poem begins:

> I am not indifferent at any rate,
> that the one son of Sir Lachlan of the hauberks,
> lion cub of the swift ships,
> is setting fire to a Campbell dwelling.

Who was 'the one son of Sir Lachlan'? There was only one Lachlan who was Chief of the MacLeans between the death of Lachlan Mór in

1598 and 1751. That was Lachlan, the 'most esteemed man in the camp of Montrose'. He died in 1648 but he had two sons, Hector Roy, who was killed at Inverkeithing in 1651; and Allan, father of Sir John. Allan was Chief between 1651 and 1674. Sinclair has the little poem thus:

> I at any rate am not indifferent,
> that the one son of Sir Allan of the hauberks,
> lion cub of the swift ships,
> is an exile from us through the deceit of the Campbells.

There is no doubt that Sinclair is right in this case. Sir John was the 'lion cub', the one son of Sir Allan. John was Chief between 1674 and 1716, and he was indeed for many a day 'an exile from us through Campbell deceit'. In 1674 the Campbells began to do injury to Mull and again in 1679 and 1680. John was only four years of age in 1674, and between 1674 and 1686 Lachlan of Brolas was the real leader of Clan Gillean. Lachlan of Brolas died in 1686 and Lachlan of Torloisk took the leadership. It was not till Lachlan of Torloisk died, in 1687, that Sir John could really be called the chief, and he was still only seventeen at that time. In 1688 King James fled to France. Sir John went after him, but he returned to Mull in 1689, the Clan MacLean rose with him and they were on the right wing of the Jacobite army at the Battle of Killiecrankie. But Claverhouse was killed, the rising collapsed, and Sir John had to return to Mull. The Campbells rose again, and in 1690 Archibald, the tenth Earl, came to Mull with a big army. Sir John took refuge in Carnburg, but in March 1692 he submitted to the Government and returned to France shortly after leaving Carnburg. Perhaps this poem was composed between 1692 and 1702 or 1704, and is the oldest song left of Margaret's poetry. On that basis her work may be put between 1692 and 1751.

We know only a very little about her life. For many years there was no certainty about her name, whether she was a MacDonald or a MacLean. It is worth quoting Sinclair in full. He says: 'It is generally supposed that the famous Mairearad was a MacLean. On behalf of this opinion it may be argued that the earliest reference to her in a printed work is in Duncan Kennedy's collection of hymns, which was published in 1786, and that in that work she is called "Mairearad Nighean Ailein, or Margaret MacLean". As Kennedy was a schoolmaster in Kilmelford in Lorn, he had a good opportunity of knowing who she was. It is certain, however, that he was mistaken in calling her Mairearad Nighean Ailein. It is possible, then, that he was mistaken in speaking of her as Margaret MacLean. She may, of course, have been married to a MacLean. There is a poem in Dr MacLean's MS which is said to have been composed by "Nighean Lachlainn mhic Iain mhic Lachlainn". That Mairearad Nighean Lachlainn is the authoress referred to is in our opinion a matter which cannot be called in question. But Dr MacLean must have been acquainted with her. We may take for granted then that he gives her genealogy correctly. We are inclined to think that Mairearad Nighean Lachlainn was a MacDonald. We got the following account of her, October 14, 1873, from a daughter of John MacLean, the poet, who told us that she had received it from her father: "Mairearad Nighean Lachlainn was born in Mull, and lived and died there. Her father was a MacDonald, and her mother a MacLean. She was married and had a large family. All her children died before herself. She nursed sixteen MacLeans of the best families in Mull. All these, like her own children, predeceased her. She used to go very frequently to the grave of the last of them and sit there. She was a very old woman, and much bent by old age." John MacLean took down several of her poems from oral recitation about the year 1816. In the heading of one of these poems he calls her "Margaret MacDonald, who was also called Margaret, daughter of Lachlan".'

There is a proof of the matter that Sinclair did not notice. Margaret made an elegy for Allan, son of Lachlan of Brolas, who died in 1722. In a verse of this song, after praising Allan and Clan Gillean, she says:

> Where is there in Scotland
> or over in Holland
> the like of my mother's clan
> except for the pride of Clan Donald?

There is no doubt at all that Clan Gillean is her 'mother's clan'. In the 'Cry of the Mull Women', in lamenting the death of Sir John, she says:

> Pity the kingdom from which have gone
> that hardy chief and the Captain of Clan Ranald.

And in another verse of the same song, she says:

> I am friendless, unasked for,
> without a chief on father's or mother's side.

It is clear that Allan of Moidart was her 'chief on her father's side'. Thus it is clear that Margaret was a MacDonald of Clan Ranald, and that her mother was a MacLean. There is no doubt at all that Margaret was married to a MacLean, and it is also certain that she spent her life in Mull, and that MacLeans were the subjects of her poems, at any rate in the poems that we still have.

John MacKenzie put only seven verses of the 'Cry of the Mull Women' in *The Beauties of Gaelic Poetry*. He did not think it worthwhile to put more of her poetry in his book, though he says: 'We have seen twenty-five of (her) composition.' He had only the lowest of estimates of the worth of Margaret's poetry. She was not in his opinion anywhere near as good as Dorothy Brown, about whom he says: 'She is the only poetess who at all approaches Mary Daughter of Red Alasdair (MacLeod).' We suffer from MacKenzie's depreciation of Margaret, for we have only eleven of her poems, though MacKenzie saw twenty-five. These are the ones I can trace:

(1) 'Little poem' (*duanag*) to Clan Gillean, 'I am not indifferent . . .' It was made between 1692 and 1704.

(2) Song to Sir John, 'Though I am a withered stock'. It seems to me that this one too was made between 1692 and 1704.

(3) Song to Sir John, 'O, I heard a tale and do not deny it'. This song was made about 1704, the year Sir John came to Queen Anne's court.

(4) Song to Sir John, 'My sleep has gone . . .' It is certain that it was made between 1714 and 1716, for King George is mentioned in it.

(5) 'The Cry of the Mull Women', the elegy for Sir John, who died in March, 1716.

(6) Song to Allan, son of MacLean of Brolas, 'I saw you, Allan'. Allan died in 1722. He was the son of the Lachlan who died in 1686, and he was the paternal uncle of the Allan who got the chiefship of Clan Gillean when Sir Hector, son of Sir John, died in 1751.

(7) Song to Allan of Brolas, chief of Clan Gillean after 1751. The song begins: 'My love Allan, the famous horseman'. It was made between 1725 and 1749.

(8) Another Song to Allan of Brolas, 'My love the gentle MacLean'.

(9) Song to Sir Hector, 'Thou who art on the throne of Providence'. This song was made about 1751, the year Sir Hector died.

(10) A Song, 'What has increased my pain'. Sinclair says: 'We have no means of determining who the subject of this lament was. It seems, however, to have been composed about a grandson of Allan of Ardtoirnish.' According to Turner, its subject was Hector, son of John from Jura.

(11) Lament for Lachlan MacLean, 'It is I who have been wounded'. This is a lament for one who was drowned, but who he was and when the song was made are two questions not easy to solve. Perhaps it was made before any of the others.

I have given a brief notice of those that are extant of Margaret's poems, eleven all told. The number is not great, but we have only about sixteen by Mary MacLeod, and one or two of them can be doubted. There is left only very little of the great wealth that was in Gaelic poetry about the beginning of the 18th century, and we may wonder that so many of Margaret's lasted as they did.

(1) The first song I mentioned is the *Duanag* to Clan Gillean. It has six verses, four lines to the verse, and it is found in Sinclair's and James Fraser's collections. There is no doubt that it is Sinclair who is generally right. Margaret laments that the 'one son of Sir Allan of the hauberks' is an exile 'through the deceit of the Campbells'. This one son was Sir John, who was chief of Duart between 1674 and 1716 though he did not come to maturity until 1687. Sir John and the MacLeans won great honour at the battles of Killiecrankie and Sheriffmuir. Margaret prays that the 'wheel will turn'. She talks of the heroism of her clan in bygone days and says that 'the time of going down for the Campbells was the time of going up for the MacLeans'; but now she laments that the 'strong clan of the drawn swords' was 'wretched in the face of the Campbells'. She hopes that she will again see the day 'in which the seed of the house will go up', the house being that of MacLean. There is not much difference between Sinclair and Fraser except in the first verse, where Fraser has 'one son of Sir Lachlan'. 'Lachlan' is wrong at any rate, but perhaps 'putting a Campbell house in flames' is right, for perhaps Sir John did that in 1686, 1689 or 1715. But why should Margaret lament the 'going down' of Clan Gillean just at one of the brief times when they had a kind of respite of 'going up'? Perhaps she did not have much confidence that the good fortune would last; however, my own opinion is that the *Duanag* was made in the dark days between 1689 and 1704. As a poem, the *Duanag* has strength, grace and an economy of language. The economy is no small virtue. The words have an effective simplicity. There is many a worse piece in the *Beauties of Gaelic Poetry*.

(2) The second song I noted was the Song to Sir John, 'Though I am a withered stock'.

I am of the opinion that it was between 1692 and 1704 that this one too mas made, between Sir John's leaving Carnburg and his coming to Anne's court in 1704. But why should Margaret call herself a 'withered stock' when she was, at most, not much more than forty? Perhaps she was not speaking literally.

The song has six octaves. Margaret laments the condition of her clan and the expulsion of her chief. She says that they were 'most prosperous' when Sir John was left as a child; that he gave them 'great joy', but that he was driven from his lands: 'His lands are poor because of it, full of famine and poverty.' I imagine those words of hers were very true. After that there is the usual praise. Sir John is 'the likeness of the star, of the sun or of the moon', and 'key, garden and stronghold of the Gaels'. There is mention of the gold-yellow curls of his hair, and of his royal hall 'with its wine, whisky, beer and joy'. The last two verses are not at all as good as the rest. Margaret is stronger in elegy than she is when talking about happiness. In spite of this weakening, there is an eerie poignancy in the song, and because there is an account of the 'famine and poverty' of the people of her country, perhaps there is more pith in this poetry, in the expression of such, than there is in many a verse more glorious in language by Mary MacLeod. The chiefs of Duart had a misfortune that the chiefs of Dunvegan did not have, and the 'famine and poverty' of the people is heard from Margaret, where there is heard from Mary only the 'clatter of the drinking horns' in the 'great precious hall'.

(3) There is another song to Sir John, that beginning: 'O, I heard a tale and do not deny it'. It was made when Sir John had come back from France in 1704. It contains eleven six-line stanzas. Margaret is happy because Sir John 'is safe and the Queen has received him at court'. Anne would be 'affable and kind' if she knew how his 'land was taken from him' when 'no fault could be ascribed to him, save his following of his rightful hereditary king'. A pity that Margaret herself would not get a chance to put a word or two in Anne's ear, but she has no English or 'smooth fashionable French'. A 'stringent law' has made the MacLeans yield. 'Pity those who were as loyal as they were'; it would be better to be 'deceitful and ingenious' as their enemies were. That is what would assure the success of their affairs — 'to be so circumspect and prudent' that they would 'deign to be turncoats'. In these verses Margaret is more galling to the Campbell chiefs than Iain Lom ever was: she is quiet and sarcastic; Iain Lom is barbarous. There was a time when the MacLeans were 'a fortress' to all who were in the North. Little wonder that they are so much missed. They were 'the great clan who were proud, honoured, victorious, of great force'. Though Sir John has returned Margaret is 'dissatisfied and sad', for it may be understood that her secret thought is that Clan Gillean's day has gone. The song has good poetry, especially where Margaret makes galling mention of the good fortune of the Campbells.

183

(4) The fourth song in my enumeration is also to Sir John: 'My sleep has gone with thinking'. This poem was made between Anne's death in 1714 and Sir John's death in 1716. It has nine quatrains. Margaret's sleep has gone with anxiety and distress. Sir John did not stay on in London 'waiting for King George's welcome'; but it is little wonder that Sir John is 'proud and high-minded' when there is 'so much impetuous blood in his veins'. She talks of his kinship with Rory Mor MacLeod and with Colin Cam MacKenzie among others, and states that he was the foster-son of her grandfather and the 'daughter of Rory in Harris'. (Was Rory's daughter Margaret's grandmother?) She prays that God will turn to them though they are not 'as well-instructed as they ought to be'. This poem has the beauty and grace of Mary MacLeod.

(5) 'The Cry of the Mull Women' is the fifth song, the song by which Margaret is most often remembered. Turner has twenty-five stanzas of it, and Sinclair has twenty-two, but *The Beauties* has only seven, and James Fraser has eleven. It is not easy to say if Turner's way or Sinclair's is better. I think that Turner's way is better sometimes, but in many places it is clear that Sinclair is right, and MacKenzie and Fraser each have one or two good lines that the others do not have.

This poem has a strength and nobility, and it seems to me that it has the taste of truth to a degree that is not common in poems of its kind. It may be that Margaret had a chance that poets lamenting chiefs did not often have. Sir John was unfortunate all his life and it may be that his uncommon loyalty was the reason. There are indications that he was a better man than the other chiefs of his generation; that he and Allan of Moidart stood apart and that the two liked one another very much. Therefore, it may be that there is more real grief in the 'Cry of the Mull Women' than there is in many another elegy, and whatever the virtues or failings of Sir John, it is certain that the loyalty of his clan was outstanding, and that they suffered much for his sake between 1688 and 1692 and again in 1715, on 'the wretched trip', 'the brief jump made by Mar'. The whole poem is tinged with fervour: Sir John did not go 'on the ship with the rest'; it was not 'the strength of men that took him from us'; his death has left his clan in 'hardship above understanding and thought'; and his corpse was not taken home.

> O it is I who am broken
> that they did not bring you over
> to land on the Eala,
> to go for refuge in the rock,

in the graveyard of the monks,
with your father and grandfather
and many more brave heroes,
where we might come close about your little cairn.

There is no elegy for a chief in Gaelic poetry in which the real voice
of the whole clan is so poignant and certain as it is in 'The Cry of the
Mull Women', and it could be compared with the best of them in a
noble perfection of language.

(6) The sixth poem I will talk about is 'I saw you, Allan', to Allan
son of MacLean of Brolas. This Allan was the second son of Lachlan
of Brolas, who died in 1686, and he was the paternal uncle of the Allan
of Brolas who was called Chief of Duart when Sir Hector, Sir John's
son, died in 1751. The subject of the song was a colonel in the British
army, though his brother, Donald of Brolas, was second-colonel of
the MacLeans at Sheriffmuir. Allan never married, and he died in
Stirling in 1722. Turner and Sinclair have the song. Margaret laments
Allan and praises his form and his courage. Then she remembers how
Allan's father and Lachlan of Torloisk went to Edinburgh in 1680 to
maintain Clan Gillean's right: how 'all the greatest lords' wondered at
their appearance and wisdom. She talks of the old ways of her clan,
she dwells briefly on genealogy, and she mourns for Allan's death
'among Lowlanders', and that his body is not in Inchkenneth or Iona.
There is the old complaint about 'how Clan Gillean of the hard fights
have gone like the bracken', how 'the heir is in exile' and his 'right
with Argyll'. The elegy ends with a verse that divulges that she herself
looks far older than she is.

(7) Margaret has two songs for the Allan of Brolas who was Chief
between 1751 and 1783. This Allan was brother's son to the Allan for
whom the sixth song was composed. It appears that both were made
between the death of Donald of Brolas in 1725 and Allan's return to
Mull in 1748. The first begins: 'My love Allan, the famous horseman'.
There are eight quatrains. This song has only the customary praise,
the customary lament about the changed condition of the MacLeans,
and the poetess' own sorrow; but there are unusual turns and twists in
the movement of the versification.

(8) The other song to the same Allan, 'My love the gentle Mac-
Lean', is far longer, consisting of eighteen octaves. In the genealogy
there is mention of the Hector who was killed at Inverkeithing and of
the 'treachery' of Hoburn, the treachery for which the Clan MacLean
suffered greatly and which 'was no grief to Argyll'. Margaret still
remembers Sir John, 'the best earl who was in Scotland' and his son,

Sir Hector, who is an exile over the sea; and she says that she was not 'near her father's clan/since the MacLeans were exiled'. It is to be understood that Margaret is so stricken and frail because of the trials of the MacLeans that she has forgotten the MacDonalds.

(9) The news of the death of Sir Hector is the subject of the song 'Thou who art on the throne of Providence'. It was made in 1750, when Sir Hector was very ill, or in 1751, the year he died. Hector was 'a shield on the elbow of Prince Charles', and 'the day of Culloden was affected' by the fact that he had been captured before he could raise his men. Now Hector's castles are under 'the men of the black hats' and Margaret wishes that they were 'in the Cailleach under the raging triumph of the flood-tide'. Sinclair says that 'the Cailleach' is the headland of that name in Mull, but he is completely wrong: this Cailleach is Coire Bhreacain (Corryvreckan). There follows a remarkable verse wishing that Duke William and his army were 'thrown about the feet' of Ardnamurchan Point 'in the vehemence of its turbulence'. The next verse wishes that the 'men of England' were getting their reward from 'the hard hand' of a 'great haughty lady' whom the King will not move. According to Sinclair, Coire Bhreacain is the lady, but it is certain that he is wrong. It may be that she is the headland in Mull called the Cailleach. It seems that Sinclair did not know that there were two famous 'Cailleachs' on the coast of Argyll.

A poignant and powerful verse again raises the lament. Her heart is 'torn like old paper made wet' as she thinks of Culloden, where the brown and black horses were 'bruising and pounding you'. There are two noble stanzas in praise of Charles son of the son of Allan son of Charles, who was commander of the MacLeans at Culloden. She still hopes that Sir Hector is not dead.

(10) The tenth song begins: 'What has increased my pain'. There are sixteen stanzas and seven lines in each. Sinclair says: 'We have no means of determining who the subject of the lament was. It seems, however, to have been composed about a grandson of Allan of Ardtornish, possibly about Hector son of Charles of Ardnacross.' Turner has the song, but designates it: 'For Hector son of John from Jura'. A little genealogy is necessary, though I fear that the question cannot be solved, for Turner is wrong and Sinclair is perplexed. According to the usual genealogy, Allan of Ardtornish was the second son of Black John of Morvern, brother of Lachlan Mor of Duart; and John from Jura the son of Charles, the fourth son of Black John. The third verse (as Sinclair has it) says: 'You are the grandson of Allan of the swords and the steeds', and the tenth verse says: 'My faithful beloved great-grandson of Black John who was in prison'; but Turner

has: 'You are the great-grandson of Allan of the swords and steeds' and 'My faithful beloved grandson of Black John . . .' According to Sinclair's genealogy Allan of Ardtornish was the brother of the grandfather of Hector son of John from Jura.

The elegy is noble and chiselled like many another elegy made at the time, and in one stanza it is unusual:

> . . . rider of the waves
> on a cold vexed day:
> you would wish to keep her to the wind
> though she would be in the hard grip of extremity.

The end of the poem laments the sad state of the MacLeans.

(11) If it is difficult to say who was the subject of the tenth song, it is far more difficult to say who the subject of the last song was. It was made about the drowning of some Lachlan. The Lachlan was the son of some Hector and he was lost going to Canna or returning from Canna. Sinclair says: 'It is slightly probably that the lines were composed about Lachlan son of Hector son of Charles of Ardnacross.' There is a strange thing in the sixth stanza of this song, where Margaret says:

> Were it not that I am young and childish,
> and do not know your genealogy,
> I would give a full account of you.

But another stanza says that the drowned Lachlan was 'the grandson of her grandfather's brother', and I would think that it would not be difficult for the poetess to give the genealogy of the grandson of her grandfather's brother, especially if he was of a family so noted as that of Charles of Ardnacross; and she is in fact already weaving a long rope of genealogy for him, telling that he is a kinsman of the Chief of Duart, of the Earl of Antrim, of Murdoch of Lochbuie, of MacKinnon of Strath, of Clanranald, of MacLean of Ardgour, of Macneil of Barra, and of Lachlan of the Ross.[1]

Margaret also tells us that this Lachlan was

> . . . grandson of Allan
> who took the ship from Argyll
> on the bright moonlit night
> with its cargo of speckled cows,
> though the lowing was not towards a spring cattle-fold.

Who was this Allan? Was he Allan of Ardtornish? But if he was, I would think that 'grandson' is wrong and that it ought to be 'great grandson'. There are eleven five-line stanzas in the song. Two of them are very beautiful:

> O, how I pity your mother!
> She dearly bought the party
> when your boat was broken
> and there was a piece of it on every shore:
> my lost one was about the cairn and could not rise.

> O, how I pity her and you, Hector,
> with your early morning rising,
> traversing every shore
> and that you did not find Lachlan,
> young man in the bloom of life, with the curly hair like harp strings.

Therefore, there are extant of Margaret's poetry eleven poems: the *duanag* to the Clan MacLean; three songs to Sir John and an elegy for him, 'The Cry of the Mull Women'; a kind of elegy for Sir Hector; an elegy for the son of Lachlan of Brolas; two songs to Allan of Brolas; and two other elegies, one for some Hector or other and one for some Lachlan or other. One would not expect any great novelties in her poetry because she came after Mary MacLeod, Lame Hector, Iain Lom and many others who were making the same kind of poetry forty years before she started. It is easier to make a comparison with Iain Lom than with Mary MacLeod, for Margaret and Iain Lom are clan bards and Mary a bard of the chief's court; but Margaret is nearer her whole clan than Iain Lom. Iain was passionately obsessed with the cause of the Stewart kings, but Margaret was weighed down and wearied all the time with the great distresses that Clan Gillean suffered because of their loyalty to the Stewart family. She does not have the barbarous rancour that there is in Iain Lom, but the grief is poignant:

> But who is there on whom no change comes,
> like the clouds in the dark-blue skies?
> The strong clan of the bare swords,
> how miserable they are before the Campbells!
> My mind is in gloom
> and my eyes always full of tears
> until I see again the day
> when there is a going up for the seed of the house.

And again:

> Your lands are poor because of it,
> full of poverty and famine.

In 'The Cry of the Mull Women', she complains of Sir John's fervour:

> It was the wretched journey,
> without profit, without gain,
> that you made last year when you moved
> with your men at your shoulder;
> it has left us in hardship
> beyond understanding and thinking:
> we are empty, weak, despised,
> our happiness has gone from us like a dream without substance.

She has a sore cry about the terrible losses of the MacLeans at Culloden:

> It is not a lament for the sheep
> that makes me weep in deep gloom,
> but mourning and longing for the men
> to whom I could make my complaint.
> On me there came the height of misfortune
> in the beginning of the summer of storms:
> the brown and black horses
> bruising and pounding you.

The condition of her clan pierces Margaret's mind and heart, and her words express it with an eerie power. That is the note most frequent in her poems, but at times she is full of angry words:

> Your white castles
> and your costly halls,
> where there was once drink and high spirits
> among the drinkers of wine,
> are under the black-hatted ones —
> my sad tale that it is so —
> God, that they were in Coire Bhreacain
> under the raging triumph of the flowing tide.

She could be galling as well. She advises the MacLeans as if it were that they too ought to be as 'circumspect and prudent' as their enemies. Iain Lom never made such a galling thrust as this at the Campbells:

> Better to be deceitful and ingenious
> as your malicious enemies were:

that is what would leave you strong and numerous,
that is what would assure your success,
to be so circumspect and prudent
that you would deign to be turncoats.

I would say that there is a remarkable cutting restraint about that
mockery. It is nearer Voltaire than Iain Lom.

I think that there is a most remarkable kind of indigenous imagination in some of Margaret's verses. Where others make magic of the
name itself, Margaret adds a word or two that can kindle pictures in
the most vapid mind. This quality is wonderful in the triumphant
flood-tide of the Cailleach and in the impetuous turbulence of Ardnamurchan Point; but Margaret knows the musical evocation of the
name alone — 'when your host gathered in Aros'. There is every kind
of lively image in her mouth:

Clan Gillean are forsaken,
without feathers or brood,
but like geese who are plucked.

But when they are in arms, they are

Men like cold stormy showers
who would take with them what they found.

John MacKenzie did not give much honour to Margaret daughter
of Lachlan, but James Carmichael Watson had a great liking and
esteem for her. I have not put my finger on her individual quality;
somebody will sometime, if the taste of our language remains in the
mouths of those left of our people.

NOTES

1 Possibly, Margaret is touching on a conventional motif of Gaelic praise
   poetry, to the effect that Lachlan's relationships are so widely ramified
   that the poet's mind cannot comprehend them: cf. 'Chan aithne dhomh
   fad a-mach ort/'s nì math m'eòlas' in the Duanag Ullamh; James Shaw in
   the Stewarts' Collection, p. 132; etc. In that case Margaret's words would
   not need to be taken too literally here. Otherwise, we should perhaps
   take *seanchas* (rendered 'genealogy' above) to mean simply 'talk'.

Alasdair Mac Mhurchaidh

In the Fernaig Manuscript, which was compiled in 1688 by 'Donochig Mack Rah', now generally believed to have been Duncan MacRae of Inverinate, Donnchadh Mór nam Pìos, there are four poems attributed to 'Allister McCurchj', and six poems to 'Murchig Maighk vyck cùrchj'. In Ranald MacDonald's 'Eigg' Collection there are also two poems attributed to 'Murcha Mór Mac Mhic Mhurcha, fear Eichildi'. These two poems in the Eigg Collection do not exist in the Fernaig Manuscript, but there has never been, to my knowledge at any rate, any suggestion that the 'Murchadh Mac Mhic Mhurchaidh' implied by the Fernaig Manuscript is not the same person as the 'Murcha(dh) Mór Mac Mhic Mhurcha(idh), fear Eichildi' of the Eigg Collection; and I do not think there is any doubt at all that they are the same person, and that he has been correctly identified as Murchadh, the fifth Mackenzie of Achilty, in Contin. As to Alasdair, there has been some doubt, for Professor Mackinnon identified the 'Alasdair Mac Mhurchaidh' of the Fernaig Manuscript as Mac Mhurchaidh Mhic Iain Ruaidh, a Kintail poet. He says, in a paper in Volume XI of the *Transactions* of the Gaelic Society, ' "Allister McCurchi" was probably a local bard still remembered by the name of "Mac Mhurchaidh 'ic Iain Ruaidh".' I do not know who first identified the Alasdair Mac Mhurchaidh of the Fernaig Manuscript with Murchadh Mór's father, the 4th Mackenzie of Achilty, but in his Notes to *Bàrdachd Ghàidhlig* Professor Watson appears to be in no doubt at all about it. And bearing in mind the internal evidence in the poem 'Tùirseach dhùinne ri port', I myself have no doubt that Professor Watson is right. Even in the unlikely event of his not being Alasdair, the fourth Mackenzie of Achilty, I think it certain that he is not the 'Mac Mhurchaidh Mhic Iain Ruaidh' conjectured by Professor Mackinnon, but I think it more than likely that he was Alasdair of Achilty. I think I have now made it clear that I do not see any valid reason for doubting that Alasdair and Murchadh are father and son, the fourth and fifth Mackenzies of Achilty.

Not being by any means very 'far seen' in the history of the Mackenzies, I have to accept without question what Alexander

Mackenzie says of the lairds of Achilty in his clan history. According to 'Clach-na-Cùdainn', Rory Mór, the first of Achilty, was the third son of Kenneth, the seventh Mackenzie of Kintail. Rory Mór died in 1533 and was succeeded by his eldest son, Alasdair, the 2nd of Achilty, who died in 1579, and was succeeded by his eldest son, Murchadh, the 3rd of Achilty, who died in March 1609, and was succeeded by his eldest son, Alasdair, the 4th of Achilty, who is generally taken to be the poet Alasdair Mac Mhurchaidh.

Of this Alasdair, the 4th of Achilty, 'Clach-na-Cùdainn' says that he married a daughter of David Chambers, had three sons, Murdoch, John and Thomas, and some six daughters, that he died at Kildin, was buried at Dingwall, and was succeeded by his eldest son, Murdoch, the fifth of Achilty. As far as I can find out, 'Clach-na-Cùdainn' makes no mention of either Alasdair or Murdoch as poets, nor does he evidently know the year of either's death, but Professor Watson says that Alasdair's poem, 'Tùirseach dhùinne ri port', was composed between 1636 and 1648, and I myself believe that the earlier date can be changed to 1643, thus making it clear that Alasdair was alive in 1643. Internal evidence in the poem mentioned also makes it clear that Alasdair was an old man when the poem was written, but that could be conjectured without any such evidence. Thus we can say of the period of Alasdair's life that he succeeded his father in 1609, and was alive certainly in 1636 and very probably in 1643.

There is, however, a little more known of Alasdair's life than Alexander Mackenzie records in his chapter on the lairds of Achilty. The first reference that I know is repeated in the general part of the history of the Mackenzies. It is to the year 1602. In the Autumn of that year it is recorded that Glengarry, with Allan of Moidart, reached Kyleakin with 37 birlinns intending to attack Loch Broom. They sent before them to reconnoitre the famous warrior cousin of Glengarry, Alexander MacGorrie, whose father had been murdered by the Mackenzies. Alexander MacGorrie landed at Applecross on his reconnaissance with about 80 men. Word of their arrival was brought to Kenneth of Kintail, who was visiting his relative of Gairloch in the latter's house on Island Rory in Loch Maree. Kintail sent Alasdair Mac Mhurchaidh with 16 men and eight oarsmen to Applecross on a counter reconnaissance. They landed and surprised MacGorrie when apparently he and a few others were detached from their main body. MacGorrie was killed chiefly through the agency of a certain John Dubh Mac Choinnich Mhic Mhurchaidh. The remainder of Mac-Gorrie's men put to sea and were pursued to Loch na Beiste by the Mackenzies, but when the latter approached that loch they saw the whole MacDonald fleet coming out against them, and were so closely pursued that they had to put in again in Applecross, whither the MacDonalds followed them on land so hotly that, were it not that a certain of Mackenzie's men, John Mac Roy Mhic Mhurchaidh Matheson, knew the ground so well, the whole Mackenzie band would have been overtaken by the greatly superior forces of the enemy. It is recorded in *Highland Papers* that, during the flight of the Mackenzies, 'Alasdair Mac Mhurchaidh, though otherwise a very pretty man, was so heavy that he was not able to bear up with his company; whereupon John Dubh Mac Coinnich drew his sword and vowed to kill him before the enemy would have to say that they killed him. At last, by throwing cold water upon him, they carried him with them'. Now this account seems to indicate that as early as 1602 Alasdair Mac Mhurchaidh was a trusted and intimate follower of Kintail, but it is strange that, if he indeed lived till about 1640, he should have been inordinately heavy in 1602, when he could hardly have been more than forty years of age at most. The phrase 'a very pretty man' indicates, of course, that he was of some considerable account as a warrior. The *New Statistical Account* says that Mac Mhic Mhurchaidh, viz Murchadh Mór, Alasdair's son, was the first factor sent to Lewis by Mackenzie; but Professor Watson, going, I think, on the very strong internal evidence in Alasdair's poem, 'Tùirseach dhùinne ri port', says that several of the Achilty Mackenzies, including Alasdair and Murchadh, acted as representatives of Seaforth in Lewis. It is known, of course, that Murchadh's son was chamberlain of Lewis about the beginning of the 18th century. The history of the Mackenzies says that Kenneth, the first Lord Mackenzie of Kintail, brought the whole island of Lewis except Berisay, where Neil MacLeod was still holding out, to submission in 1610, the year before he died, and that the famous Tutor of Kintail, Sir Roderick of Coigach, Kenneth's brother, reduced Berisay in 1613, the year in which Neil MacLeod was executed. Now it is unlikely that Murchadh Mór would have been old enough in 1610 or in 1613 to become chamberlain of such an important territory, and it is therefore quite likely that the *New Statistical Account* is wrong, and that Alasdair, and not his son Murdoch, was the first factor sent by Kintail to Lewis; but I shall deal with that when I consider the poem 'Tùirseach dhùinne ri port'.

As I have already said, there are extant only four poems by Alasdair, three of which are religious, while 'Tùirseach dhùinne ri port' is, in Professor Mackinnon's words, 'somewhat the reverse'. Professor Mackinnon goes on to say: 'Here the poet represents himself as in early life a sailor, a jolly bachelor, and a general favourite in society.

His patrons are now gone, and his company is despised, so he will turn a religious man, apparently because he cannot make better of it.' I shall take this poem first because, while it is certainly a poem of his old age, there is every probability that the other three poems are also poems of old age, especially as the normal order is for the irreligious poetry to precede the religious in time. Besides, 'Tùirseach dhùinne ri port' is packed with historical and biographical matter, which it would be as well to have cleared up a little before going on to the other poems, which contain no historical allusions, and in which biographical matter is at most only implicit.

'Tùirseach dhùinne ri port' is a poem of twenty quatrains, and is one of the two of Alasdair's poems included in *Bàrdachd Ghàidhlig* by Professor Watson, who, by the way, does not print the second last quatrain; but of that later. The metre is the classic *rannaigheacht dialtach mhór*, with *aicill* general in both couplets, a verse form used by Alasdair with fine grace and sense of form. Of the twenty stanzas, twelve contain historical references, while almost all the rest raise biographical questions. I am, therefore, afraid that I shall have to quote almost the whole poem, verse by verse. Twenty people are mentioned, seven of whom Professor Watson has not identified. On that score alone my work is, as they say, 'cut out for me'.

The first verse contains no difficulties:

> Tùirseach dhùinne ri port,
> Chan iongnadh mo dhos bhith liath:
> Thug mo chridhe troigh air ais
> Mar Oisin an déidh nam Fiann.

> *It is a sad thing to be kept waiting on the shore,*
> *no wonder my forelock is grey;*
> *my heart has gone a foot back,*
> *like Ossian surviving the Fiann.*

The second verse is:

> Is mi an déidh Choinnich an àigh,
> Nach ceileadh air càch an t-òr;
> Làmh a mhalairt nan seud
> Iomadh ceud da dtug se fòir.

> *I survive the great good Kenneth*
> *who would not hide gold from other men;*
> *hand that gave jewels in exchange:*
> *to many a hundred he gave help.*

194

'Coinneach an àigh' is, of course, as Professor Watson points out,
Kenneth, the first Lord Mackenzie of Kintail, whom I have already
mentioned as conquering Lewis and as visiting the laird of Gairloch in
1602. He died in 1611. The third quatrain is biographically interesting, especially when compared with the second and fourth. The third
reads:

Nì air mhaireann Cailin ùr,
B' allail a chliù is e òg:
Ge do ghabh se ruinne fearg,
Ghiorraich e gu dearbh mo lò.

Strong young Colin is no more,
great was his fame when he was still young;
though he was angry with me,
his death certainly shortened my days.

'Cailin ùr' is, as Professor Watson says, Colin, the first Earl of
Seaforth, the son of 'Coinneach an àigh'. He succeeded his father in
1611, but the vast Mackenzie territories, and other territories as well,
were administered by his uncle, the great Sir Roderick of Coigach, the
Tutor of Kintail, until he died in 1626. Colin himself died in 1633.
Now what Alasdair says and what he does not say is very interesting. It
appears that Colin was very extravagant, especially with his drink,
and therefore it would be expected that he would be praised by
Alasdair for generosity, but he is not. The praise is the most general
and noncommittal possible in eulogistic verse. I gather from the
History of the Mackenzies that Colin, even more than his uncle, the
Tutor, made himself obnoxious by gross increases of dues and rentals.
I wonder if that has anything to do with Alasdair's relative faintness of
praise; and what was the anger he had conceived against Alasdair?
Was it something connected with the factorship of Lewis, and was
Alasdair's period as factor a short one, if indeed he was ever factor, as
it is pretty certain he was? Those are questions that I cannot resolve,
but probably some expert in Mackenzie history can.
  The fourth quatrain refers to the Tutor himself:

Nì air mhaireann Ruairidh Mór,
Bhrostnadh fa trom dhùinn air thùs:
Och òn nach maireann na suinn
Choisinn le 'n loinn dhuinn gach cùis.

Rory Mór is dead,
who gave me encouragement in my youth;

> *alas, alas that the good men are dead,*
> *whose skill (or swords) won every cause for us.*

The second line is very ably interpreted by Professor Watson as meaning: 'His incitement to us at the outset was weighty', i.e. 'he encouraged me greatly at the beginning of my career'. This interpretation, which seems to me a very good one, is put forward only tentatively by Professor Watson. One question arises: is the first person plural a real plural, referring to the Mackenzies in general; or is it, as Watson takes it, the plural used for the singular, which is quite likely? Obviously, if it is a real plural, the line is of less importance biographically. That it may be a real plural, in spite of Professor Watson's interpretation, is possible, especially because the *dhùinn* in the fourth line is almost certainly a plural referring to the whole Mackenzie clan. By the way, the word which Watson reads as *loinn* in the fourth line is read by Cameron and Macbain in *Reliquiae Celticae* as *lainn*, but that is a matter of importance not historically but textually. The Fernaig Manuscript seems to have 'laijn'. If Watson's reading of the second line is correct, it would seem that Alasdair owed more to the Tutor than he did to Colin.

The fifth quatrain contains a great historical difficulty. It reads:

> Nì air mhaireann Ruairidh Geàrr,
> Do chumadh spàirn ris gach neach;
> Laoch nach géilleadh ach san chòir,
> B' éibhinn leis slòigh agus creach.

> *No longer lives Short Rory,*
> *who would hold his own against any man;*
> *a hero who would yield only when he ought,*
> *he delighted in armies and forays.*

Textually there is no difficulty: the verse is as clear as any in the Fernaig Manuscript; but who was Ruairidh Geàrr? Professor Watson has not identified him. I have searched all Alexander Mackenzie's Mackenzie genealogies of the period, and can find no 'Ruairidh Geàrr'. There is, however, one Ruairidh Beag, who was a younger son of Ruairidh Mór, the first Mackenzie of Achilty, and therefore Alasdair's own grand-uncle. He is mentioned as one of the Mackenzie gentlemen who accompanied Kenneth of Kintail to Mull in 1602, when he went to get help against the great MacDonald confederacy from his brother-in-law, Eachann Og MacLean of Duart, and it is mentioned that he was parson of Contin. It is indeed strange that one of Alasdair's grand-uncles should be still alive in 1602, the year in which Alasdair himself was evidently so heavy that he could not run away fast enough from the MacDonalds in Applecross, but it is possible. There is, however, no special mention of this Ruairidh Beag as a warrior, and his holy orders would seem to preclude that. Finding no suitable Ruairidh Geàrr or Beag among the Mackenzies of the period, I turned to the other Ross-shire clan with whom Ruairidh was a favourite name, i.e. the Mathesons. Now the chief of the Mathesons in 1602 was Ruairidh of Fernaig, the son of Murchadh Buidhe. He made the famous bond with Kintail in 1602, giving the superiority of all his lands in Lochalsh, except Fernaig and Balmacara, to Kintail in return for the latter's help against Glengarry, against whom the Mathesons had many bitter scores to pay. This Ruairidh of Fernaig appears to have been a considerable warrior himself, but, as far as I know, he was never called Geàrr or Beag. He had, however, a grandson, Ruairidh Beag, who though only a fourth son of his father, John of Fernaig, was one of the most famous of all the warriors of his time. The *History of the Mathesons* quotes a verse about his prowess:

Ruairidh Beag Mac Iain Mhic Ruairidh Mhic Mhurchaidh Bhuidhe,
Dha math thig clogaide cruadhach is pìc iubhair,
Bheireadh creach á tìr an nàmhaid gun aon umhail.

Ruairidh Beag son of Iain son of Murchadh Buidhe,
who well suits steel helmet and yew bow,
who would lift a spoil from enemy territory without thinking twice.

It is noticeable that Alasdair's line 'B'éibhinn leis slòigh agus creach' has some resemblance to the last line of the verse about Ruairidh Beag Mac Mhathain. Both MacBain and Alexander Mackenzie, in their histories of the Mathesons, say that this Ruairidh Beag fought with Kintail in his conquest of Lewis, and that he was 'invariably the leader in the pursuit of the Lochaber men who on occasions paid a visit on the business of cattle-lifting to the west'. They also, say, however, that Ruairi Beag challenged Iain Garbh Mac Ghille Chaluim of Raasay to single combat, but that is hardly possible if Ruairidh Beag fought in Lewis before 1613, as Iain Garbh became chief of Raasay in 1648 while still a very young man. It is, of course, barely possible, but then Ruairidh Beag must have been about sixty and Iain Garbh about twenty. That it is said of him that he challenged Iain Garbh may mean only that he was considered the equal of the most famous warrior of the generation. I do not think that Ruairidh Beag's being not a Mackenzie is against my supposition, as the relation between Mathesons and Mackenzies at the time was so very close. It may, however, be objected that there is a great social disparity between the fourth son of the chief of the Mathesons and such Mackenzies as the two chiefs of Kintail and the great Tutor, such a disparity that Alasdair would not have mentioned them together. That may be true, but the disparity is not so very great between Ruairidh and some of the rest mentioned, such as Mackenzie of Fairburn, etc. It is to be remarked that everything said by Alasdair about Ruairidh Geàrr refers to his warlike qualities, and as Ruairidh Beag Mac Mhathain was pre-eminent in that, I think it very possible that he may be the Ruairidh Geàrr of the poem.

The sixth verse refers to 'ceannard an Tùir, bho 'n d' fhuaras mùirn is mi òg'. Professor Watson identifies the 'Tùr' as the Tower of Fairburn, and the 'ceannard' is therefore either Alexander, the second Mackenzie of Fairburn, who died about 1620, or his son John, the third of Fairburn, who died in 1645. Alexander, the second of Fairburn, was a grandson of Ruairidh Mór, the first Mackenzie of Achilty, and therefore a near relation of Alasdair Mac Mhurchaidh.

The seventh quatrain mentions two men, the first of whom Professor Watson has not identified. The verse is:

Nì air mhaireann mac Ruairidh fhéil,
Neach nach d' fhuiling beum fo eud;
No fear-tighe Chille Chrìosd:
Allail an dithis chaidh eug.

The son of the generous Roderick is dead,
a man who did not suffer a blow from envy;
likewise the head of the house of Kilchrist:
a famous pair whom Death took.

'Fear-tighe Chille Chrìosd' is almost certainly Kenneth, the third Mackenzie of Kilchrist. The date of his death is unknown, but his marriage was in 1605, according to the *History of the Mackenzies*. 'Mac Ruairidh fhéil', unidentified by Professor Watson, may very well be one of two people: either Murdoch, the second Mackenzie of Redcastle, who died sometime between 1615 and 1629, the son of Ruairidh Mór, the first Mackenzie of Redcastle; or Kenneth, the third Mackenzie of Davochmaluag, who died in 1618. His father's name was also Roderick. Murdoch of Redcastle was much the more famous man in Mackenzie history, but Kenneth of Davochmaluag was an uncle of Alasdair Mac Mhurchaidh, whose mother was a daughter of Ruairidh, the second of Davochmaluag. Those are the only two Mackenzie potentates of the period whose fathers were called Ruairidh, and it is, I think, pretty certainly one of them, but which it is impossible to say.

The next two verses allude to two or three persons who are hitherto unidentified, but I think I have managed to solve the difficulty. The first of the two is:

> Smuainmid aon ogha Eachainn fhéil,
> Neach nach d'eur cara mu nì:
> Bu luath leam do ghoin am bàs
> An urra dh'fhàg se 'na thìr.

> *Let us think of the only grandson of the generous Hector,*
> *a man who would refuse nothing to a friend;*
> *for me death wounded all too soon*
> *the nobleman he left in his land.*

'Ogha Eachainn fhéil' immediately suggests the Gairloch family, and John Roy, the fourth Mackenzie of Gairloch, died in 1628. John Roy was the grandson of Eachann Ruadh, the first Mackenzie of Gairloch. John Roy succeeded, in 1566, his elder brother, Hector, who died childless. There is, however, one difficulty, namely, in the word 'aon' before 'ogha'. Eachann Ruadh, the first of Gairloch, had four legitimate sons, besides a few illegitimates; he must, in all likelihood, have had more than one grandson. It is, however, possible that in 1628 John Roy was the only surviving grandson of Eachann Ruadh. Indeed, it is extremely likely, as John Roy survived his own elder brother by 62 years. In that case, the phrase 'aon ogha' might be used of the one surviving grandson, especially if he survived his cousins by many years. There is, again, another factor. The word which Malcolm MacFarlane reads as 'oon' in his translation of the Fernaig Manuscript is read as 'fon', with a question mark after it, by Cameron and Macbain. I do not, therefore, think that the reference to John Roy of Gairloch can be ruled out on the strength of a reading which is extremely doubtful, especially since the third and fourth lines of the quatrain fit the Gairloch family:

> Bu luath leam do ghoin am bàs
> An urra dh' fhàg se 'na thír.

> *For me death wounded all too soon*
> *the nobleman he left in his land.*

John Roy was succeeded in 1628 by his son, Alexander, who died in

1638. The ten years Alexander enjoyed as chief of Gairloch was a very short time compared with the 62 years his father had. I therefore take it that 'an urra' refers to Alexander, the fifth of Gairloch. The succeeding quatrain reads:

Mo chompán is mo charaid ghaoil,
Neach nach cuireadh fo sgaoil rùn:
Goirid leam do ghléidh a mhac
A' ghlac fhuair se anns an Dùn.

My comrade and my beloved kinsman,
one who would not betray a secret;
In my eyes, his son kept far too briefly
the prize (?) he got in Duntulm.

I read 'mo chompán', etc., as referring to Alexander, not John Roy. Alexander was an elderly man when he succeeded his father in 1628; he therefore, rather than John Roy, was of an age with the poet. The third and fourth lines of the quatrain seemed to me to contain an allusion utterly impossible to explain until I noticed Alexander's son, Kenneth, afterwards the 6th of Gairloch, married, in 1635, the daughter of Sir Donald of Sleat, the very man who is hailed by Iain Lom as:

A Dhòmhnaill an Dùin,
Mhic Ghilleasbuig nan tùr . . .

Donald of the Dun (i.e. of Duntulm),
son of Archibald of the towers . . .

She was dead by 1640, because in that year Kenneth married again. I anticipate the objection that this is a strange use of the noun *glac*, but I think it possible, especially because 17th century poets are fond of the verb *glac* in that connection: cf. *Ghlac e 'n éiteag mar mhnaoi*. Altogether, I am pretty certain that the two verses refer to the Gairloch family.

The next quatrain says that he remembers the deaths of many gentlemen in Ross whom he cannot now mention, and that he survives them 'gun phrìs'. It would be interesting to know just how much biographical significance there is in the piquant 'gun phrìs', but in view of the conclusion of the poem, there is probably a great deal.

In the eleventh verse he turns to 'fir Innse Gall', and mentions the deaths of Donald Gorm, almost certainly Dòmhnall Gorm Mór, who died in 1617, and Ruairidh Mór of Dunvegan, who died in 1626. In the succeeding verse he mentions William MacLeod of Talisker, and says then, 'An Ratharsair bha an t-slat fhial', referring most probably to Gille Calum Garbh, who died about 1616, the author of the poem on 'Na trì làmha bu phailte', and therefore likely to be himself celebrated for generosity. (It is interesting that Duncan MacRae spells the Gaelic for Raasay as 'Ra-ersher', thereby giving 17th century authority to the way the name of the island is pronounced by the islanders themselves and their nearest neighbours in Skye and on the mainland.) The third line of the quatrain refers to the 'fear pailt' of Strath, probably the Lachlan Mackinnon who died shortly after 1628.

The next quatrain I had better quote, as it contains a name, or two names, unidentified by Professor Watson. It is:

Nì air mhaireann Eachann Òg,
Mac Ailein nan seòl 's nam pìos,
No Raoghalt bha air Dùn Bhuirbh,
No Domhnall Gorm tòir do phill.

No longer lives Hector Og,
the son of Allan of the sails and silver cups,
nor Ronald who was on Dun Bhuirbh,
nor Donald Gorm who turned a rout.

The difficulty is in the first and second line. Professor Watson identifies 'Raoghalt' as Ranald MacDonald of Benbecula, who died in 1636. That is, of course, certain. Of the fourth line, Professor Watson says: 'This may be Sir Dòmhnall Gorm Og of Sleat, who died in 1643, or it may be a repetition of the earlier reference to a Dòmhnall Gorm Mór.' I myself think it almost certain that it is not a repetition, and that therefore the poem can be placed in 1643 or later. As to the first two lines, Professor Watson takes 'Eachann Òg Mac Ailein nan seòl 's nam pìos' as one man, and says he has not identified him, but I do not think that there is really any difficulty. In spite of the lack of a conjunction between them, I take 'Eachann Òg' and 'Mac Ailein' as referring to two different men. I admit that to have a conjunction would be more in accordance with Gaelic usage, but then Duncan MacRae is very careless with his articles and prepositions, omitting then almost as often as not, and I do not therefore see why it is to be assumed that he would not drop a conjunction here and there. Mention of 'fir Innse Gall' makes it all but certain that Murchadh would refer to chiefs of the Macleans and Clan Ranald, and, happily for the elucidation of the stanza, there is one of each who fits. Eachann Og Maclean of Duart, who was married to a sister of Kenneth, first

Lord Kintail, and who gave effective help to the Mackenzies against the MacDonalds in 1602, died in 1623. I am certain that he is the Eachann Òg mentioned. Sir Donald, the chief of Clan Ranald, died in 1619. As his father was Allan, it is fairly certain that he is 'Mac Ailein nan seòl 's nam pìos'. The only other historical person in the poem is 'Seòras Òg', in the eighteenth verse. He is, of course, George, the second Earl of Seaforth, who went into exile early in 1649 and died in Holland in 1653, having never come back. The verse makes it clear that the poem was composed before George's exile.

The seven remaining quatrains have no allusions to definite people except, as I said, to George, 2nd Earl of Seaforth, but autobiographically they are somewhat difficult. In the one immediately following the last one discussed, he bewails the many friends gone from whom he was wont to get 'cuairt is lòn'; to-night he is 'gun chuirm':

> Mo dheoch is e bùrn ri òl.

> *My drink is nothing but water.*

In the quatrain following that he continues in the same strain about his cheerlessness, his empty-handedness: 'Mo làmh lom ri dol an cùirt', and he says that for all he spent on others, he gets now only bare boards. After that he bewails what seems to be his lack of earning or employment, and the youth in which he did not provide for his old age.

> Do na chrann cha dtugas fonn:
> B'annsa leam long agus fìon.

> *I had no liking for the plough:*
> *I preferred a ship and wine.*

There is certainly an engaging frankness about Alasdair. By the way, the line last quoted hints that the passion for the sea, which is so wonderfully expressed in Murchadh Mór's poem 'An Làir Dhonn', was inherited from Alasdair. The verse after that I must quote in full because there is a very definite question of its real meaning:

> Is minig do dh'òl mi sabhs
> De'n fhìon as mìlse thig bho'n Fhraing;
> Bho'n sguir mi sgrìobhadh nan trosg
> A nochd chan fhiach mo dheoch plaing.

> *I often drank a sauce*
> *of the sweetest wine that comes from France;*

since I stopped keeping an account of the cods,
to-night my drink is not worth a plack.

Professor Watson explains 'sgrìobhadh nan trosg' as 'keeping a written account of the cod-fish' for Lord Seaforth, in connection with the extensive fishings round the coast of Lewis. I think, of course, that there is no doubt of this interpretation, and to me the lines seem to imply that Alasdair was acting for Seaforth in Lewis for a considerable time. What of the first two lines of the verse? Do they mean that the practice of cooking fish in wine obtained in the Highlands in the first half of the 17th century? I am inclined to think that, if it did, it would have been in the house of Colin, the first Earl, who appears to have been inordinately extravagant in that way, but 'sabhs' may be only a picturesque metaphor for wine itself suggested by the word 'trosg' in the third line.

The autobiographical complication comes in the verse after that:

Bidh mi a nis ri mo bheò
Aig Seòras òg an ceann bhùird:
Le clàrsaich ge ghabhainn dàn,
Olaim gach tràth làn a' chùirn.

Now I shall be, as long as I live,
with young George at the head of a table;
though I might treat a poem with a harp (accompanying),
at every meal-time I drink the fill of a horn.

As the Fernaig MS goes, the reading is clear; but what does it all mean? Does not his being 'aig Seòras òg an ceann bhùird' seem to contradict what he has been saying of his forlorn, wineless state? And does the 'olaim' in the last line express a wish or is it a statement of fact? And why the concessive 'ge ghabhainn dàn'? Does it show a turn for the better of his fortunes under the regime of George? But George had succeeded to the earldom in 1633, and if, as I think, the poem was not written until 1643, it can hardly mean that. As I have already said, the post-dating to 1643 depends on the second Dòmhnall Gorm mentioned being Domhnall Gorm Og, who died in 1643. It may, of course, be a repetition of the reference to Domhnall Gorm Mór, who died in 1617. But the poem cannot be before 1636 if that is the corrrect date of the death of Ranald of Benbecula, and I think it cannot be before 1638, if 1638 is the date of the death of Alexander, the fifth laird of Gairloch. At any rate, the quatrain shows that the bottle was very much on Alasdair's mind in his old age, even if he did mix piety with it. It also shows that he must have been of repute as a singer or reciter.

We now come to the nineteenth stanza, which is omitted by Watson. It has a blank in the penultimate word of the third line. The metre would require a word of one syllable. The first two lines are:

Nì air mhath mo ghnothach 'na chùirt
Nach faighinn mùirn bho na mnài.

My business is no good in his court
where I get no joy from the women.

In the MS the third line is, according to MacFarlane, 'Di zhi snach eil mi — kroy', and, according to *Reliquiae Celticae*, 'Di zhe snach heil . . .', the only difference being that MacFarlane reads 'zhi' where Cameron and Macbain read 'zhe'. *Reliquiae Celticae* does not write the verse in normal Gaelic, but MacFarlane does. I give it, and its successor:

De dhìth 's nach eil mo — cruaidh
'S e gheibhim fuath air son gràidh.

Because of the lack of hardness of my —
what I get is dislike, not love.

Alasdair seems to be very disgruntled. I myself have little doubt that the blank space was deliberately left by Duncan MacRae in order to veil a piquant obscenity, a sardonic comment on life, morally neutral if a little cynical, but probably very neatly turned.

The last verse is irreproachably pious, even if it is the kind of piety that makes, as Professor Mackinnon says, a virtue of necessity.

'Tùirseach dhùinne ri port' may not be one of the greatest poems of the 17th century, but it is certainly one of the most interesting. It is a great pity that Duncan MacRae's extraordinary orthography makes it even more difficult to appreciate than it might necessarily have been.

The other three poems by Alasdair extant are free from the historical and biographical difficulties of 'Tùirseach dhùinne ri port', but they are all very interesting both because of their fine command of phrase, their grace and finish, and their implications. There is also that characteristic frankness. Alasdair is apparently always a battle-ground between the world and the flesh on the one hand, and the claims and promises of religion on the other. With Alasdair the victory of religion is always uncertain. The fine opening stanza of one of them says just that:

204

Tà cogadh oirnne do ghnàth,
Toradh mo ghràidh dhuit, a Dhé:
Tà mo spiorad da mo rian,
Nam biodh srian 'sa' cholainn chré.

We are forever at war,
because of my love for you, God:
my spirit is for ruling me,
if there were a bridle in my body of clay.

Mankind has been given 'airm eagnaidh': 'creideamh, ùrnaigh agus gràdh', but they are sorely exercised by ill-will, deceit, anger and pride of body. There follows a very affecting series of warlike metaphors dependent on the fine paradox 'buidheachas dò ge do thuit'. Those metaphors may nowadays seem commonplace enough, but they must have been very real to men like Alasdair, who had taken part in the dreadful wars waged by his clan for Lochalsh and Lewis.

Beiridh mo chaiptein-se buaidh,
Ceannard sluaigh le 'm pillear tòir.

My captain will have the victory,
the head of a host by whom a pursuit is turned.

The compact strength and economy of the language is a quality rather lacking in a great deal of what is commonly considered the greatest Gaelic poetry.

Alasdair remarks on the blindness and the short views of humanity, a blindness and shortness of view that he knew best in himself. He concludes:

Crìoch a' chogaidh bho 's e an t-eug,
Chan obainn-s' e, cia eadh fàth,
Ar n-uile aoibhneas do bhith thall:
Saoghal a bhos meallta atà.

Since the end of the war is death,
I would not deny that, whatever the cause,
all our joy is beyond:
the world here (below) is deceitful.

The poem is rounded off with the *ceangal,*

M'anam do Chrìosd mar sgrìobh na h-ostail gu léir,
M'anam a rithist bhrìgh bhaistidh bho na chléir,

An t-aran 's am fìon 's am pìos an càirichear éad,
Is lughaide m'fhiamh go m'anam a dhìon a péin."

My soul to Christ as all the apostles have written,
my soul again because of baptism from the clergy,
the bread and the wine and the pyx in which they are placed,
because of them my fear is the less that my soul will not be protected from pain.

It is a remarkable thing that the *ceangal*, so common in Irish, is used only twice, as far as is now known, in Scottish Gaelic poetry — in this poem by Alasdair, and in the elegy for Dòmhnall Gorm Og, by Murchadh Mór.

The conflict between soul and body is the theme of another short poem by Alasdair, this time one of only five quatrains, all marked by the same economy and compact grace of language:

Treòraich m'aigneadh, a Dhé:
Aidmhim nach réidh mo thoil;
Tàim aimh-ghlic ann an strì:
Amhairc, a Rìgh, air mo chor.

Guide my spirit, God;
I confess that my will is not at peace;
I am unwise in strife:
Look, o King, at my state.

The strife is very simply and pungently stated in the third:

Mo spiorad ag amharc gu geur
Air athair féin tha chon teachd;
'Cleachdmaid ar cothrom an sionn,'
Deir a' cholainn rium gu beachd.

My spirit looking keenly
at his own father who is to come;
'Let us make use of our opportunity here,'
says my body to me with decision.

The body is piquantly emphasising the claims of this world. Alasdair is perplexed by their strife:

Gu bheil leadairt orm is sgìos
Eadar an dìs d'am bheil mé:
Miann na coluinn do bhith bhos,
M'anam air làimh dheis Mhic Dhé.

206

I am mangled and weary
between the two of which I am:
the body desires to be here,
my soul on the right hand of God's Son.

The concluding stanza is a prayer to God for succour in the conflict with himself, in which he is otherwise certain to be the loser:

A Rìgh, a bhuadhaicheas 's gach cath,
Bho'n d' fhuaras gach math de d' dheòin,
Dìon mi san iomarbhaigh ghairbh
Gun t'iomairt bho is meirbh mo threòir.

O King, who will be victorious in every battle,
from whom I have got every good thing of your own free will,
protect me in the dire struggle
since my strength is feeble without your doing.

The only other poem by Alasdair extant is a dream vision of Judgement, which begins simply, directly and vividly:

Eibhinn mo shuain an raoir:
Chunnacas féisd bu mhór meadhair,
Cathair òir is Rìgh geal,
A mhac agus mìle aingeal.

Sluagh ri teachd air mhagh mìn
Fa chomhair cathair an àrd-Rìgh;
Aon mhac ri teachd gu deas
'Nan ceann mar ghrinn bheairt sholuis.

Claidheamh òraidh 'na làimh,
Na slòigh roimhe 'gan iomain;
Buidheann thagh e ri làimh dheis
Fa mór meadhair is aoibhneas.

Buidheann eile fo lionn dubh
'Nan coluinn 's iad an eug-chruth;
Eubh an guil — is truagh an gàir —
Is aon fhear mór d'an iomain.

Joyful my sleep last night:
I saw a feast of great ecstasy:
a throne of gold and a white King,
His Son and a thousand angels.

A host coming on a smooth plain
in the presence of the throne of the High King;

One Son coming to the right
at their head, a fine suffusion of light.

A gilded sword in His hand,
driving the hosts before Him;
a band He chose on His right hand
in great mirth and joy.

Another band in great melancholy
in their bodies, which were in the form of death:
the cry of their weeping — piteous their din —
and one big fellow driving them.

After the striking directness and simplicity of the beginning, Alasdair goes on to moralise on the folly of man and the high praise of the Divine Law, and mankind's lack of excuses. There are three stanzas on the pains of Hell, and the poem ends with an exhortation to the young.

As I have indicated, these are the only poems by Alasdair that have come down to us, and they do not, of course, form a very considerable body, but I think that their historical and intrinsic importance is greater than their bulk suggests. In the first place, their matter and outlook on life make them very different from the vast majority of Gaelic poems that survive from the first half of the 17th century and, indeed, from the whole of the 17th century. Broadly speaking, what is the content of most of 17th-century Gaelic poetry? On the one hand, we have the surviving verse of the well-known poets such as Iain Lom, An Clàrsair Dall, Pòl Crùbach, Diorbhail Nic a' Bhriuthainn, Mairearad ni Lachainn, Sìlis na Ceapaich, Am Pìobaire Dall, Niall Mór Mac Mhuirich, Lachlainn Mac Theàrlaich Oig, Iain Dubh Mac Iain Mhic Ailein, Màiri Nighean Alasdair Ruaidh, An Ciaran Mabach, Eachann Bacach, Iain Mac Ailein, and many more. On the whole, it is what could be called a poetry of chief and clan, extolling the traditional virtues of bravery, generosity, loyalty. When it goes beyond chief and clan, it is usually strongly political, the political bent usually depending on the clan part in the political struggles of the age. When such poetry is religious, it is such usually in a simple but partisan way. A great deal of this poetry is splendid in visual imagery and more of it is splendid in its auditory appeal, but, on the whole, it is a simple, unperplexed poetry, and therefore it is, broadly speaking, rather deficient in abiding human appeal. Besides that great body of poetry by known poets, there is in the 17th century what I consider a far finer body of poetry, those innumerable songs by unknown or obscure poets, in which the abiding human interest is enthralling, but again, very broadly speaking, this great bulk of glorious song is an expression of highly pitched passion, generally of the rapture of love or of piercing sorrow. It is gloriously lyrical, with the inevitable simplicity that goes with the gloriously lyrical.

The four poems by Alasdair Mac Mhurchaidh are obviously very different. There is, of course, much of the clan and chief motif in the first half of 'Tùirseach dhùinne ri port', but I think with a difference, the difference being a more marked personal note. Alasdair is not, even in the first half of that poem, just a Mackenzie, as Iain Lom is so often just a MacDonald, or Màiri Nighean Alasdair just a MacLeod. The Mackenzies had plenty of great victories in the first twenty years of the 17th century, but Alasdair is not greatly concerned with them. One feels that he is primarily a human being, not a clansman. Again, if he celebrates generosity and open-handedness, especially with wine, one feels that he is doing that not just to celebrate such poetically conventional virtues, but in order to record his own gratitude and to bolster his own defeated self-esteem. And his religious poetry is not at all the polemical and political type so common in the age. It is the poetry of a human being primarily concerned with the battle over the very mixed soul of Alasdair Mac Mhurchaidh. His poetry is also at the very opposite pole from the high-keyed lyricism of the anonymous song of the period. Alasdair is not lyrical; he does not deal in glowing colours, in very white whiteness, or very black blackness. His verse is very much of the very much mingled yarn of human life. It is, therefore, a sophisticated, middle-aged kind of *sermo pedestris*: restrained, economical, ironic and paradoxical. And it is perennially human on that account. Now Alasdair was preceded by two very remarkable religious poets, MacCulloch of Park and Duncan McRyrie, both of whom are represented in the Fernaig Manuscript, and he was succeeded in his type of verse by his son Murchadh Mór, and by Duncan MacRae himself. The question, of course, arises: how many poets like MacCulloch, McRyrie, the two Mackenzies and MacRae were in other parts of Gaeldom at the time without a Fernaig Manuscript to record them? Possibly there were very many, but we have to go on what is left to us, and thus the poetry of the four mentioned is of proportionately greater importance.

It is not, of course, that Alasdair's religious poetry is doctrinally original or even of very great interest. The interest is in its candour, universality and, of course, in its terse, unstrained expression of conflict between the soul and body, between the desires of the flesh and the demands of the spirit. In spite of the occasional references to forays, hawks, wine and spoils in 'Tùirseach dhùinne ri port', Alasdair's poetry is not the expression of a simple, primitive stage of society. There is a middle-aged maturity and a kind of disillusion with the world in it. Curiously enough, the combination of frank sensuality and spiritual struggle in Alasdair is somewhat like that expressed in the English poetry of John Donne, the great Dean of St. Paul's, who was probably an exact contemporary of Alexander, though nothing could be more different than Donne's metaphysical conceits and Alasdair's unpretentious imagery. In imagery Alasdair has not the variety and originality of his son, Murchadh Mór, nor does he have anything like that splendid lyrical abandon that Murchadh Mór reveals in the 'Làir Dhonn', but he is lucid, terse, unaffected, has a fine economy and grace, and frequently a surprising turn of irony, and a felicity of paradox which is more real than a merely verbal turn of paradox.

Domhnall Donn of Bohuntin

In the 17th century the Keppoch MacDonalds were more than ordinarily lawless, but very notable for their many poets, especially for the many poets who were of their chiefs' families or closely related to them. Of these poets the most picturesque figure and the one to whom most stories clung was Dòmhnall Donn. Indeed Dòmhnall Donn became such a focus of stories that probably many of the traditions about him are really older traditions. Of these the most widespread is that of 'Oran an Amadain Bhòidhich', the famous song beginning 'A Mhairearad Og' or 'A Chaitrìona Og', but there are others.

Most of what we know of Dòmhnall Donn comes from MacLean Sinclair, from William MacKay and from Alexander MacDonald ('Gleannach'). It is known that MacLean Sinclair kept up a vast correspondence with bearers of tradition in Scotland, but for the traditions of Keppoch, and especially of the Bohuntin family, he had no need to come or write to Scotland, as there was in Nova Scotia a great *seanchaidh*, Alexander MacDonald of Ridge, Antigonish, who was himself of the Bohuntin family. Accordingly neither the authors of *Clan Donald* nor Keith Norman MacDonald have much to tell of Dòmhnall Donn that MacLean Sinclair did not have in print before their books appeared.

MacLean Sinclair says that Angus Mór, third MacDonald of Bohuntin, had three sons, of whom the eldest was Iain Dubh, who married a daughter of Cameron of Glenmallie. (This Iain Dubh, alleged fourth of Bohuntin, is not to be confused with Iain Dubh, the first of Bohuntin, Angus Mór's grandfather.) But the authors of *Clan Donald* are not so sure. After coming to Angus Mór, they say that it is 'quite impossible to reconcile the conflicting statements given in several manuscript genealogies of this family'. They quote one authority who gives the succession after Angus Mór as his son Alexander, his son Alexander, his son Angus, his nephew Angus, who they say was the last legitimate MacDonald of Bohuntin. This genealogy makes no mention at all of Dòmhnall Donn. It contains one Donald, father of the last Angus, but obviously he is not Dòmhnall Donn.

211

Clan Donald quotes 'other authorities' who give John as the son and successor of Angus Mór and ascribe to John three sons, Alasdair Mór, Dòmhnall Donn and Dòmhnall Gruamach. This is MacLean Sinclair's version, but after Alasdair Mór this genealogy goes further than MacLean Sinclair's and is rather different, but neither *Clan Donald* nor MacLean Sinclair mentions any legitimate sons of Dòmhnall Donn or of Dòmhnall Gruamach. MacLean Sinclair says that Dòmhnall Donn's two brothers were good poets. In support of the part of the genealogy that makes Dòmhnall Donn a son of Iain Dubh, it can at least be said that he was traditionally known as Dòmhnall Donn, 'Mac Fhir Bhoth-fhionntainn', and that one of the poems attributed to him calls on an Iain Dubh for help, but it is by no means certain that the Iain Dubh of the poem is any poet's father. The second Bohuntin genealogy given by *Clan Donald* has it that a daughter of Angus Mór of Bohuntin married Alasdair Buidhe, the chief of Keppoch who profited by the murder of his nephew in 1663. This would make Dòmhnall Donn a first cousin of Archibald of Keppoch, and a first cousin at one remove of Colla nam Bó, Archibald's son. Tradition says that Dòmhnall Donn was on very bad terms with Colla nam Bó, and it may be inferred that he was on bad terms with Archibald as well. All traditions make Dòmhnall Donn notable for his cattle raids and amours as well as for his poetry.

There is another conflicting genealogy, that given in 1877 by John MacDonald, Antigonish, known as An Tàillear Abrach, who gives himself as John, son of Archibald, son of Angus, son of Alasdair Mór, son of Angus Mór and says: 'B'e Dòmhnall Donn Bhoth-fhionntainn agus mo shìnseanair, Alasdair Mór, clann an dà bhràthar.' This makes Dòmhnall Donn a nephew, and not a grandson, of Angus Mór of Bohuntin; but Dòmhnall Donn is traditionally known as 'Mac Fhir Bhoth-fhionntainn' which means that his father was MacDonald of Bohuntin.

The authors of *Clan Donald* say that Alasdair Buidhe of Keppoch was drowned in the Spean in 1669 and that his son Archibald died in 1688. MacLean Sinclair, however, says that Archibald died in 1682. If MacLean Sinclair is right, at least one known poem by Dòmhnall Donn is prior to 1682. The poem in question is 'Moladh a' Phìobaire', in which Dòmhnall Donn praises Donald Campbell, piper to Archibald of Keppoch. According to MacLean Sinclair, whose *Glenbard Collection* is the only source I know, Donald Campbell, Dòmhnall mac a' Ghlaisrich, Am Piobaire Mór, was a nephew of Dòmhnall Donn. The poem praises 'an Caimbeulach suairc' and 'an Caimbeulach sìobhalta', who was handsome and brave:

Nàile, dh'aithnichinn thu romham
Dol an domhaltas blàir,
Bhiodh do phìob mhór 'ga spreigeadh,
'S cuid de h-eagal air càch.

Indeed, I would know you in front of me
going into the throng of battle;
your great pipe being blown into life,
and some of the fear of it in others.

In the same collection there is a reply to Dòmhnall Donn and abuse of the Campbell piper by Archibald himself. Two octaves are devoted to twitting Dòmhnall Donn for 'cur nan Duibhneach an àirde':

'S mór a bhleid is an ràbhart
A rinn blàirean ri ghoistidh,
Cur nan Duibhneach an àirde;
'S mór gum b'fheàrr leinn fo'r cois iad.
Ach nan cumadh iad blàr ruinn
An éirig làraichean loisgte,
Chuireadh faobhar ar greidlein
Iad am freasdal an coise.

There was much adulation and nonsense
spoken by 'white face' to his gossip,
exalting the Campbells;
we would far prefer them under our feet.
But if they did battle with us
in requital of burnt ruined houses,
the blades of our swords would make them
dependent on their feet.

The second octave finds fault with Dòmhnall Donn's Cameron blood.

A Mhaoil-onfhaidh, mhaoil-onfhaidh,
Tog dhe t'onfhail 's dhe t'shéitrich,
Ruig a null Loch a' Mhàilidh
Agus teann-sa ri geumnaich.
'S ann ri cinneadh do mhàthar
Chaidh do mhàsan 's do shléisdean;
'S chan agair Clann Dòmhnaill
Mìr ri 'm beò ach am beul dhiot.

MacGillonie, MacGillonie,
stop your raging and snorting,

go over to Loch Mallie
and start lowing.
It is from your mother's clan
that you take your buttocks and thighs;
and Clan Donald will not, while they live,
claim any bit of you but your mouth.

He calls Dòmhnall Donn 'Maol-onfhaidh' because of his Cameron mother and grandmother, of Clann Mhic Mhaoil-onfhaidh (later Clann Mhic Ghill-onfhaidh, the MacGillonies).

After the two octaves on Dòmhnall Donn, Archibald turns on the piper, whom he abuses with the kind of abuse a few MacDonald bards occasionally directed against the Campbells, but it may be noted that his phrasing is much more pointed than usual. As this was levelled at a Campbell who was, by tradition at any rate, his own piper, it may be asked whether it is as serious as it appears. It could be that Archibald, conscious that the chiefship had come or reverted to his father by foul means, was anxious to be regarded as more vehement against the Campbells than any other MacDonalds were.

As to the date of the poem, the line 'Chaidh an ceann dhe 'r àrd-thraoiteir' could refer to the Argyle executed in 1661, but it is far more likely that it refers to his son, who was executed in 1685, which would mean that MacLean Sinclair's 1682 date is wrong. I infer that Dòmhnall Donn was not as anti-Campbell as many of his clan were. Indeed there is no bitter clan feeling evident in any poem ascribed to Dòmhnall Donn, while his brother, Dòmhnall Gruamach, is openly scathing about Iain Lom's anti-Campbell snarl:

Thugadh greis air Greumaich leat
Gu'n euchdan a chur suas;
Is thugadh greis air Duibhnich
'S air muinntir an taoibh tuath.
Chan eil feum do Dhòmhnallach
Ri bheò bhith ort a' luaidh:
'Se donnal a' choin bhàdhail ud
Dh'fhàg bodhar mo dhà chluais.

You spent some time on the Grahams
to put on high their deeds;
and you spent a time on the Campbells
and on the people of the North.
There is no need for a MacDonald
to mention you while he lives:
It is the howling of that stray dog
that has deafened my two ears.

214

Dòmhnall Gruamach had little to learn in vituperation: Dòmhnall Donn's extant poems indicate a sweeter temper than his brother's, but it is also probable that he was more interested in playing his lone hand than in any front against Argyle. It may be significant that Archibald of Keppoch was the only other MacDonald chief who went with Angus of Glengarry in 1675 to help the MacLeans against the Campbells. Whether he did it to stand well with Glengarry or not is another matter. At any rate, it may be one of the reasons why Iain Lom appears to have been completely reconciled to Archibald's chiefship of Keppoch, for Iain Lom did not forget that he had a MacLean grandmother. Generally it appears that Archibald of Keppoch was anti-Campbell, while Dòmhnall Donn and his brother may very well have been pro-Campbell.

One of the finest poems associated with Dòmhnall Donn is one that appears in MacLean Sinclair's *Glenbard Collection*:

> 'S ann air feasgar Di-haoine,
> Dh'fhalbh mo ghaol thar a' Mhàim.

> *It was on Friday evening*
> *that my love went away over the Mam.*

MacLean Sinclair has a very interesting note: 'Tha am fear bho'n d'fhuair sinn an t-òran so ag ràdh gur h-ann do Dhòmhnall Donn Bhoth-fhiunntain a chaidh a dhèanamh, agus gur h-e nighean do Thighearna Ghlinne-Moireastan a rinn e. Tha e ag ràdh cuideachd gun do thogadh Dòmhnall Donn an teaghlach Dhiùc Gordan, gun robh e 'na chlàrsair fìor mhath, agus gur h-i a' chlàrsach a tha air a ciallach le "inneal a làmh".'

The poem, which consists of seven octaves, contains some difficulties, especially in the fifth verse:

> 'S mas a beag leat mo thochradh
> Gu bheil m'fhortan aig Dia:
> Gura lìonmhor mo chinneadh
> Gus na shireadh tu dhìol.
> Mas e lughad mo nichean
> A bhrist orm do ghràdh,
> 'S mairg mis' thug cion-falaich
> Dhut-sa thairis air càch.

> *If my dowry seems little to you*
> *my fortune is with God:*
> *my clan is numerous*
> *for rendering all you would ask.*

If it is the smallness of my goods
that broke off from me your love,
all the worse for me who gave you
secret love before all others.

That Dòmhnall Donn would boggle at the smallness of the dowry
that a daughter of Grant of Glenmoriston would bring is unthinkable.
Besides, the implication that he left her is very much at variance with
all other traditions about Dòmhnall Donn and whatever Grant lady he
wooed. It may be, of course, that this verse is an interpolation from
another poem; for the third verse is more like what is generally said in
tradition about the material differences between them:

Cha ruig thu leas a bhith 'm barail
Gur h-e do bharantas cùil
Bheireadh dhomhs' a bhith 'm barail
Gum bu leannan dhomh thu;
Ach thu bhith shìol nam fear móra
'S tu cho bòidheach 's cho cuimt':
'S mi gun deanadh do phòsadh
Ged bhiodh do stòras air crùn.

You need not be of the opinion
that it is your guaranteed backing
that would make me think
that you are a lover for me:
but that you are of the seed of the big men
and so handsome and well-formed:
I would certainly marry you
though you had only one crown-piece.

Two other quatrains sustain the inference that the disparity in
wealth was on her side, and that the opposition was from her father:

Gur e m'athair rinn an dò-bheairt
Mise chumail gun do phòsadh;
Shiubhlainn leat ge b'ann do'n Olaind
Ach do chòir a bhuannachd.

'S iomadh nìonag a tha 'n tòir ort
Eadar Inbhirnis is Mórair:
Ged bhiodh tu air crùn de stòras
Phòsainn anns an uair thu.

It is my father who did the evil
keeping me from marrying you;

I would travel with you though it were to Holland
but to gain your right.

Many a girl pursues you
between Inverness and Morar:
even if you had only a crown's worth of goods,
I would marry you at once.

Other verses refer to his prowess and good looks, while the last has a reference, which may be a coincidence, to the Duke of Gordon:

Ged a gheibhinn-sa gu m'òrdugh
Na tha dh'fhearann aig Diùc Gordan,
'S mór gum b'annsa leam na 'n stòras
Sin làn chòir air m'uaibhreachd.

Though I would get to my desire
all the land of the Duke of Gordon,
I would far prefer to all that wealth
a full right to my pride.

It is the sixth verse that has the alleged reference to his skill on the harp:

'S daor a cheannaich mi 'n grinneas
Bha air inneal do làmh.

I dearly bought the elegance
that was on the instrument of your hands.

The seventh verse compliments himself and his clan on their prowess in battle.

Ten years after the publication of the *Glenbard Collection*, MacLean Sinclair himself, in a paper now in Vol XXIV of the Gaelic Society's *Transactions*, gives eleven quatrains of a song to Dòmhnall Donn by 'Nighean Tighearna Ghrannd'. Its *luinneag* is the famous one:

Tha mo rùn air a' ghille:
'S mór mo dhùil ri thu thilleadh;
'S mi gun siùbhladh leat am fireach
Fo shileadh nam fuar-bheann.

My love is for the young man:
I greatly hope you will return;
I am the one who would traverse the hillside with you,
under the rains of the cold mountains.

217

There are three explicit references to Dòmhnall Donn:

Tha thu 'd mhac do dh'fhear Bhoth-fhionntainn
'S mise nighean tighearna Ghrannda,
'S rachainn leat a null do'n Fhraing
Ged bhiodh mo chàirdean gruamach.

Nàile, 's e mo cheist am fiùran,
Dòmhnall Donn mac fhir Bhoth-Fhionntainn;
'S fad is farsaing a tha cliù
Air mùirnein nam ban uasal.

Nàile, 's e mo ghaol an t-òigear,
Dòmhnall Donn an leadain bhòidhich:
Tha thu 'n fhine àrd gun fhòtus,
Dòmhnallaich a' chruadail.

You are a son of the tacksman of Bohuntin,
and I the daughter of the chief of the Grants,
and I would go over to France with you
though my kin would be frowning.

Indeed, my love is the handsome youth,
Donald Donn son of the laird of Bohuntin,
far and wide is the fame
of the darling of the noble women.

Indeed, my love is the young man,
Donald Donn of the beautiful hair:
you are of the high uncorrupted clan,
the MacDonalds of the hardihood.

All traditions agree that Dòmhnall Donn was a great cattle-lifter and ladies' man, and that his forays and amorous adventures were far flung. It appears therefore that the exploits of other men were sometimes ascribed to him, especially if those exploits were mentioned in song. In Vol VII of the *Transactions* of the Gaelic Society Mr William MacKenzie, in the first of his valuable series 'Leaves from my Celtic Portfolio', says of the song 'An Nighean Donn a bha 'n Cataibh': 'I may remark that the exploits of Dòmhnall Donn, as related in Lochaber, coincide with those of Alasdair Sgoileir, as related in the West of Ross-shire. It appears that on some predatory ramble in Sutherland, Donald met the "Nighean Donn" and kidnapped her. Through some cause or other — the "Nighean Donn" made her escape, and hence the song.' William MacKenzie's words imply that the song is also attributed to Alasdair Sgoileir, as is another predatory poem he gives in the same paper. Of the 'Nighean Donn' song he has only four quatrains, and the last of them does not suit the handsome Dòmhnall Donn:

Ged is crom leibh mo cheann
'S ged is cam leibh mo chasan,
Thogainn creach bho Thighearna Ghrannd
'S dh'òlainn dram 'san dol seachad.

Though you think my head bent
and though you think my legs crooked,
I would take a spoil from the Grant chief
and I would drink a dram in passing.

The second quatrain is similar in all existing versions:

Latha dhomh 's mi siubhal fraoich
Fhuair mi 'n fhaodail bha taitneach:
Fhuair mi caileag bhòidheach dhonn
Feadh nan tom buain nan dearcag.

One day as I traversed the heather
I found the attractive treasure-trove:
I found a beautiful brown-haired girl
among the hillocks picking berries.

Much the fullest version I know is contained in Mr K C Craig's *Orain Luaidh Màiri Nighean Alasdair*. This version consists of forty-six lines, but two of those lines certainly, and probably four others as well, look like interpolations from another song. Mr Craig has, moreover, one quatrain, which Keith Norman MacDonald also has, that suggests Alasdair Sgoileir:

Bu bheag orm duine còir
'S móran stòir 's i bhith aige,
Nach do chuir Beurla 'nad cheann
Agus danns' ann ad chasan.

I would not like a good kind man
who had much of the world's goods
and did not put English in your head
and dancing in your feet.

He has also a line 'Bheirinn ruaig do Loch Carthann', which may suggest a Wester Ross origin, but Dòmhnall Donn went farther than Wester Ross, and there is a line about raiding the Munro country that is paralleled by a line or two in another poem attributed to Dòmhnall

Donn. Mr Craig's version has at least four lines in which the girl replies:

> 'S nam bithinn 'nam ghruagaich òig,
> Dhianainn pòsadh gun fhadal:
> B'fheàrr leam seann duin' na duin' òg —
> 'S e bu dòcha bhith beairteach.
>
> *And if I were a young maiden*
> *I would marry without delay:*
> *I would prefer an old man to a young —*
> *he would be more likely to be rich.*

MacLean Sinclair says that Dòmhnall Donn had a son by the Sutherland girl and a daughter by another girl; that the daughter visited him in prison and that it was to her he made the famous song 'Is truagh, a rìgh, mo nighean donn', the song confused with 'Oran an Amadain Bhòidhich'.

The weight of detailed tradition about 'An nighean donn a bha'n Cataibh' inclines to Alasdair Sgoileir rather than to Dòmhnall Donn. Mr Alexander MacDonald, 'Gleannach', has a version of it in *Song and Story from Loch Ness-side*. That version, though not so long as Mr Craig's, is more obviously homogeneous. Like other versions, it makes much of a Lachlan whose carelessness allowed the girl to escape. Indeed so much is made of Lachlan that Mr William Matheson has pointed out to me that it is probable that the song is by Lachlan himself whoever he was.

Mr William MacKenzie says that the song 'Faodaidh am fear bhios fuar falamh', addressed to certain cattle-lifters, has also been ascribed to Dòmhnall Donn. It begins:

> Faodaidh am fear bhios fuar falamh
> Cruaidh smearail foinneamh fearail
> Fead a thoirt air cluais balaich,
> Mur a bi e réidh ris
>
> *The man who is cold and empty,*
> *hardy, vital, active and virile*
> *may give a tingling blow in the ear to a peasant*
> *if the peasant does not agree with him.*

This song calls on Lochaber raiders — Camerons, MacPhees, MacMillans, Kennedys, etc. — to be up and doing:

Fios gu Eóghan, fios gu Ailean,
Fios gu Dòmhnall Bàn an Caillich,
Ciod e 'n truaighe chum aig bail' iad
'S a' ghealach ag éirigh.

A word to Ewen, a word to Allan,
a word to Fair Donald in Caillich:
what mischief kept them at home
with the moon rising?

In the third of his 'Leaves from my Celtic Portfolio', in Vol VIII of the Society's *Transactions*, William MacKenzie says that his friend Farquhar MacDonnell, late of Plockton, writes to him from New Zealand, saying that the author is neither Dòmhnall Donn nor Alasdair Sgoileir, but Coinneach Dubh Mac Dhon' ic-Coinnich, a grand-uncle of the notable Matheson, Ruairi an Iomaire, and that it was made to gall a certain band of Lochaber *ceatharnaich* or 'cattle-lifters'. The whole tone of the song suggests that MacDonnell is right, and that Dòmhnall Donn, at any rate, is not the author.

MacLean Sinclair has a beautifully evocative song of hunting and raiding that is attributed by most to Dòmhnall Donn, but of which many lines may very well be by Stewart of Ach Ghobhail, who murdered Macintosh of Tirinie and whose capture by Atholl men in the north has certainly been confused with the capture of Dòmhnall Donn. (See the note-books of Lady Evelyn Murray, in the archives of the School of Scottish Studies in Edinburgh University).

The first half-strophe runs as follows:

Cha taobh mi na strathan,
Cha bhi mi 'gan tathaich,
Fhad 's a chumas Fir Athaill am Mòd.

I will not go near the straths,
I will not frequent them,
while the men of Atholl hold their court.

It is probably by Stewart; if it is by Dòmhnall Donn, it raises many questions and implies that Dòmhnall Donn's activities were greatly hampered by the Atholl men. MacLean Sinclair has a note on the song, which is very pertinent if those three lines are by Dòmhnall Donn, but quite irrelevant if they are by Stewart. The note is about Atholl's Lord-Lieutenancy of Argyll from 1681 to 1688 and it says that after Argyll was beheaded in 1685, the Marquis of Atholl and his followers, who 'seem to have kept bounds' until 1685, 'plundered the

Campbells and their followers of everything that they could lay hold of'. If the lines are by Dòmhnall Donn, do they mean that Atholl was more efficient in checking other raiders than Argyll himself had been, or do they mean that the Atholl men had taken so much from the Campbells that they had little left? As I have mentioned, Dr. William Mackay has a tradition that Dòmhnall Donn never wronged a poor man. Perhaps this could be extended to imply that he had a generous feeling for the Campbells in their distress.

Of course, even if the lines are by Dòmhnall Donn, they may have nothing to do with Argyll at all; they may simply mean that it was no time to make a descent on Atholl itself. After all, Ben MacDhui is nearer Atholl than Argyll:

> Mi aig sàil Beinn Muic Duibhe
> 'S neo-shocrach mo shuidhe
> 'S mi coimhead srath dubh uisge 'n eòin.

> *At the heel of Ben MacDhui*
> *my seat is most uncomfortable*
> *as I view the dark strath of the Water of Eunaich.*

The succeeding lines contain so many geographical difficulties that it is very improbable that they are all by the same person as made the lines about Ben MacDhui. Most of the places mentioned are north of the Great Glen and include the Munro country, but one seems to be the Cobbler above Arrochar. Most of the other places seem to be Dòmhnall Donn's reputed haunts, Strath Farrar, Glen Loyne, Glen Garry, Glen Cannich and Glen Moriston. There is an apology for his raids and an implication that he kept well away from his own kinsmen:

> 'S mairg a mhaoidheadh a' mheàirl' orm,
> Fhad 's a dh'fhuirinn bho m' chàirdean,
> Airson loth thoirt o àrd bheinn a' cheò.

> *A bad thing for one to denounce me for robbery —*
> *as long as I kept away from my kinsmen —*
> *for taking a filly from the high misty mountain.*

Some evocative strophes suggest that Dòmhnall Donn's activities were chiefly at the expense of the Grants, Chisholms and Frasers, but perhaps they mean only that he passed through their lands on his way to the North; otherwise they could mean that he sometimes raided Glengarry, which would be unlikely in view of Glengarry's dominating position among the MacDonalds at that time.

'S ro mhath b'aithne dhomh Farar,
Far an rachainn ann thairis;
Uisge 'n Lòin agus Garaidh dhubh mhór.

Strathghlais a' chruidh cheann-fhionn,
Far an robh mi car tamuill;
'S ro mhath b'eòl dhomh Gleann Canaich an fheòir.

Dol air Moireasdan thairis
Fo Cheanna-chnoc a' bharraich,
'S tric a fhliuch mi ann gearra chasan 's bròg.

I knew Farrar very well,
where I would go over into it,
The Water of Loyne and big dark Garry;

Strathglass of the white-headed cattle,
where I was for a while;
and very well indeed I knew Glen Cannich of the grass.

Going over the Moriston
under Ceannachnoc of the birches,
often have I wet in it my feet on tip-toe and shoes.

The end of this poem, like the beginning, suggests that the author has to keep to the hills. He tells of his former lavishness with the drink, but now he is cold and wet and has to send a boy, who may not be successful:

Tha mo bhreacan air sileadh
Gus na dhrùidh air dà fhilleadh,
Uisge ruith as nas mire na lòn.

Mo dheoch mhaidne air a fuairead
Uisge 's biolair an fhuarain,
'S bhiodh an eilid air uairibh 'ga chòir.

Rìgh, bu mhath mo bhean rùin i:
Ged a chitheadh a sùil mi
'S i nach cuireadh orm cùis san tigh mhòid.

My plaid is dripping
until the two folds are soaked,
water running out of it more briskly than a burn.

My morning drink in spite of its coldness
the water and water-cress of a spring,
and the hind was sometimes near it.

God, how good a woman she was for keeping my secret!
though her eye would see me
she would not put a case against me in the courthouse.

Twenty-seven lines of this poem are given by Rev. Thomas Sinton in a paper in Vol XXIV of the Society's *Transactions*. In a note he refers to MacLean Sinclair's 'very fine version', but says that it has the fault that it 'identifies the song with places and affairs in Argyllshire, a part of the country which it is highly probable was never visited by Dòmhnall Donn, whose haunts and interests lay in the North'. I think that this assertion of Sinton's is rather sweeping though it may very well be based on a very correct interpretation of tradition. Keppoch is not far from Argyll, but it may be that Dòmhnall Donn had special reasons for not raiding the Campbell country, and the version given by MacLean Sinclair seems to have big geographical discrepancies, perhaps due to an accretion of lines by Stewart of Ach Ghobhail or referring to Stewart. Anent the line 'Fhad 's a chumas fir Athaill am mòd', Dr Sinton says that it refers to the 'extraordinary raid by the Atholl men on the Lovat country in Stratherrick', which he says was 'one of Dòmhnall Donn's favourite haunts'. Dòmhnall Donn appears to be fond of the Frasers, and, if the line is really by him, it may have been prompted by friendship for the Frasers rather than for the Campbells.

Like many famous men, Dòmhnall Donn is more celebrated for his death than for his life. Besides the fragments printed by Dr William Mackay in an appendix to *Urquhart and Glenmoriston*, there are four poems published which deal with Donald's capture and execution. Naturally the traditions about his capture and death are varied and confused, as are the traditions about the most famous of the songs dealing with the last phase of his life.

MacLean Sinclair, Dr William Mackay and 'Gleannach' are the chief authorities. MacLean Sinclair's note says that Donald was in love with a daughter of the chief of the Grants, apparently the chief of the whole clan, who was then living in Glen Urquhart. Grant was unwilling to give Donald his daughter but she was determined to elope with him. Donald was in a cave near Reilig Ghoirridh, waiting for an opportunity to snatch her away. The Grants, however, got to know of his hiding place and sent him a false message to meet the girl at a certain house. There he was made drunk, put to sleep in a barn, and his sword and targe were taken away. When he was attacked his gun missed fire and he was imprisoned. He expected that his clan would interfere on his behalf, but he was not on good terms with Coll of Keppoch, Archibald's son, nor with the influential Iain Lom, whose son Donald had killed in a duel at the High Bridge, eight miles from Fort William, and so there was no effort made to save him. An illegitimate daughter paid him a visit in prison and it was to her he addressed the poem 'Is truagh, a rìgh, no nighean donn'. His sister Kate was present at his execution, and tradition says that as his head was being severed his tongue uttered the words, 'A Cheit, tog an ceann.' The date was about 1691.

It would appear from MacLean Sinclair's account that the Grant chief was more concerned with his daughter's attempt to run away with Donald than he was with Donald's raids. Dr William Mackay has a more detailed account. After saying that Dòmhnall Donn never wronged a poor man and never wantonly shed blood, Dr Mackay says that Donald raided from Breadalbane to Caithness; that his custom was to make rapid journeys, with a few kindred spirits, by the least known tracks, and to swoop upon the cattle of the lairds and tacksmen; that he was aided and abetted by the smaller tenants and cottars, to whom he 'extended his protection and lavish generosity'. He was a frequent and friendly visitor to Glen Urquhart, for he was in love with Mary, daughter of the Laird of Grant, who resided at the time in Castle Urquhart. Her father forbade their meetings, but they did meet secretly. During one of their meetings, Donald had left his companions at Borlum with cattle he had lifted in Ross-shire. The owners appeared and identified the cattle. The Laird of Grant, angry that stolen cattle should be found so near his residence, vowed Dòmhnall Donn's death. 'Bheir an Diabhul mise á mo bhrògan mur téid Dòmhnall Donn a chrochadh.' Donald had to hide in an almost inaccessible cave in Glaic Ruigh Bhacain on the Ruskich side of Allt Saigh, still known as Uaimh Dhòmhnaill Dhuinn. Dr Mackay's account of the capture is much the same as MacLean Sinclair's, but much more detailed. He ends it by telling that Donald asked that he should be beheaded, like a gentleman, and not hanged, which was granted, whereupon he declared that the Devil would take the Laird of Grant out of his shoes. Donald was executed at Craigmonie according to Dr Mackay's tradition, but the authors of *Clan Donald* say that it was in Inverness. Dr Mackay says that the tongue in the severed head uttered the words, 'Tog mo cheann, a Mhàiri.'

The traditions recorded by 'Gleannach' in *Song and Story from Loch Ness-side* are even more detailed than Dr Mackay's. They stress Dòmhnall Donn's prodigious strength and ingenuity and his popularity in Glen Urquhart. It is implied that Donald did not like to shed blood. Different accounts of his capture are given, but all agree that he was made drunk. Those accounts also imply that Donald came to Glenurquhart for the sole purpose of absconding with the Grant lady, and that he deliberately planted stolen cattle near the Grant chief's residence in order to annoy him. Inverness is given as the place of execution, the words from the severed head are 'A Cheit, tog an ceann', and they are addressed to Donald's sister, as MacLean Sinclair had recorded twenty-four years before the publication of *Song and Story from Loch Ness-side*. Of course, 'Gleannach' is quite frank about mingling oral tradition with written tradition, so that anything he says to confirm MacLean Sinclair may be partly or wholly derived from MacLean Sinclair.

Whatever truth there is in the various legends, there are some poems that are ascribed to the space of time between Donald's capture and his execution. MacLean Sinclair has two in his *Gaelic Bards*, and one in a paper in Vol XX of the Society's *Transactions*, while there are many versions of the famous song 'Is truagh, a rìgh, mo nighean donn'. One of the poems in *Gaelic Bards* clearly refers to the expected help from his own clan and perhaps from his Cameron kinsmen:

> Beir an t-soraidh seo bhuam
> Do Ghleann Ruaidh le fear-eigin
> Gu buidhinn mo ghaoil:
> 'S iad nach saoilinn mhealladh orm.
>
> Is truagh nach robh cóig ceud
> Air aon sreud 'sa bhaile seo:
> Gum biodh saighdearan an rìgh
> 'S dà thrian ag gal dhiubh ann.
>
> Chailleadh an salann a phrìs
> 'S cha bhiodh miadh air anartan.

> *Let some one take this greeting*
> *from me to Glen Roy*
> *to the band whom I love:*
> *they are the men who I think would not deceive my hopes.*
>
> *It is a pity that there were not five hundred*
> *in one band in this town:*
> *of the soldiers of the King*
> *two thirds would be weeping here.*
>
> *The salt would lose its price*
> *and there would be no demand for shrouds.*

After that MacLean Sinclair's version goes on to condole with a Ruairi MacLeòid on the death of his brother. MacLean Sinclair evidently knew of no tradition about this Ruairi or he would have annotated the lines, which he does not. One never knows with such things, but the fourteen lines about MacLeod and his brother look like an interpolation from another song.

MacLean Sinclair has forty-five lines of another poem with references to the actual capture. Dr MacKay has twelve lines of it with very little difference from the corresponding lines in MacLean Sinclair's version, but the Menzies Collection of 1870 has also forty-five lines of it almost exactly the same as MacLean Sinclair's, with the only difference that each has three lines not in the other. Menzies, however, has a note that shows he attributes the poem to an 'Athole gentleman', probably Stewart of Ach Ghobhail, 'who had to leave the country on account of a fatal duel . . . He afterwards got a situation in the north, as tutor in a gentleman's family, where he was betrayed by a countryman by the name of Ferguson, who had absconded after stealing hens, the property of the Earl of Athole'. The poem has also been ascribed to a Peter Roy MacGregor, a noted riever in Strath Spey, but the oldest written authority, Stewart's Collection, says that it was by a 'gentleman of Clan Donald taken by treachery in the north'.

The poem begins:

Mìle mallachd do'n òl,
'S mairg a dhèanadh dheth pòit:
'Se mo mhealladh gu mór a fhuair mi.

Mìle marbhphaisg do'n dram
Chuir an daorach am cheann
Nuair a ghlac iad 'san àird a tuath mi.

Mun d'fhuair mi bhith mach
'S bhith 'm armaibh gu ceart,
Bha rag mheàirlich nan cearc mun cuairt dhomh.

Bha trì fichead 's a triùir
'Ga mo ruith feadh nan lùb
Gus na bhuin iad mo lùth 's mo luaths uam.

Bha Seumas Dubh ann air thùs:
Rìgh, bu làidir a dhùirn;
'S chuir mi Uilleam gu ghlùn 'san fhuaran.

A thousand curses on liquor,
pity him who would drink it:
How greatly I was deceived!

227

A thousand death-shrouds on the dram
that put the drunkenness in my head
when they seized me in the North.

Before I managed to be out
and be properly armed
the arrant hen-thieves were around me.

Sixty and three were
chasing me among the bends (of the river?)
until they took my strength and my speed from me.

Dark James was in the forefront:
God, how strong his fists were;
and I put William to his knee in the spring (of water).

Neither Menzies nor MacKay have those last three lines, but they
have the following nine:

'Rìgh, gur mise bha nàr
Nuair a ghlac iad mi slàn
'S nach dug mi fear bàn no ruadh dhiubh.

Bidh mo mhallachd gu bràth
Aig a' ghunna mar arm
An déidh a' mheallaidh 's an tàire fhuair mi.

Ged a gheibhinn dhomh fhéin
Làn buaile de spréidh,
B'annsa claidheamh is sgéith 'san uair ud.

God, it is I who was ashamed
when they seized me unwounded
and that I had not taken a fair or red-haired man of them.

My curse will for ever be
on the gun as a weapon
after the betrayal and shame I suffered.

Though I would get for myself
a fold full of cattle,
I would prefer a sword and shield at such a time.

Then there follow, in MacLean Sinclair's and Menzies' versions,
twelve lines calling on Iain Dubh for help:

Iain Dubh, tog a mach
Thoir na dh'fhaodas tu leat,
Agus cuimhnich a' bheairt bu dual dhuit.

Na seall air do nì,
Faic t'fhuil a' dol dhìot,
'S na bi na do chìleig shuaraich.

Nam biodh tusa fo ghlas
Agus mise bhith as,
Nàile, chumainn mo chas glé luaineach.

Bhiodh an t-osan glé gheàrr
Is am féile glé àrd.
'S balgan piollach os cionn a' chruachain.

Dark John, get on your way,
take all you can with you,
and remember the deeds of your people.

Do not look to your cattle,
see your own blood going from you,
and do not be a base feeble old woman.

If you were under lock
and I were free,
by God, I would keep my foot very restless.

The hose would be very short
and the kilt very high
and shaggy pouches above the hip.

If the poem, or this part of the poem, is really by Dòmhnall Donn,
Iain Dubh may be his father, and it is quite possible that his father was
still a vigorous man at the time. There are, however, the conflicting
genealogies of the Bohuntin family, but it is safe to assume that
MacLean Sinclair had more than this poem to go on when he gave Iain
Dubh as Dòmhnall Donn's father. Is it possible that Iain Dubh is
John, son of Ewen of Lochiel, or a mistake for Eóghan Dubh? If
Dòmhnall Donn knew that his MacDonald kinsmen would not help,
might he not be calling on the most powerful of his Cameron
kinsmen? There are nine lines in which he says women would send
money to reprieve him if they knew of his plight:

'S iomadh maighdean ghlan ùr,
Chluinnte farum a gùin,
A chuireadh na crùin gu m'fhuasgladh.

Gu bheil té dhiubh 'n Srath Spé
'S nam biodh fhios aice fhéin,
Nàile, chuireadh i ceud gu luath ann.

Tha téile 'm Bràigh Màrr
'S nam biodh fios aice mar tha,
Nàile, chuireadh i dhà ri cluas sin.

Many's the girl in the bloom of youth,
— whose gown could be heard rustling —
would send crown-pieces to free me.

One of them is in Strath Spey
and if she herself knew,
she would certainly send a hundred and soon.

There is another in Brae Mar
and if she knew how things are,
she would indeed send two for every one of those.

Those last three lines are found only in the Menzies Collection as far as I know.

The authors of *Clan Donald* say quite definitely, but without quoting their authority, that Dòmhnall Donn was executed in 1692. In his *Gaelic Bards*, published in 1890, MacLean Sinclair says it was about 1691, but in a paper given to the Gaelic Society of Inverness in 1894, and published in Vol XX of its *Transactions*, he has another poem composed by Dòmhnall Donn in prison, which would seem to indicate that his death was not before 1698. It indicates too that his place of execution was Inverness and not Craigmonie. The poem has that kind of spare athletic vigour so characteristic of Donald and of Iain Lom:

Gur mi th'air mo sgaradh
Bho thoiseach an earraich:
Tha mo chas air a sparradh fo dhéile.

B'fheàrr gun digeadh an t-aiteamh
'S gum falbhadh an sneachda
'S gun teannadh gach aigneadh ri chéile.

B'fheàrr gum faicte mo chàirdean
Tigh'nn a stigh le Creag Phàdraig
'S cha b'fhada bhiodh cabhsair 'ga réiteach

'S iad a chuireadh an gradan .
Ri dùthaich nan adag:
Chan fhàgadh iad caisteal ri chéile.

'S iad gun cuireadh an sgùradh
Fo luchd nan gruag fùdair:
Chan fhàgadh iad lùth an cóig ceud dhiubh.

Bhithinn cinnteach a'r cruadal
'N ám an claidheamh a bhualadh:
Chuirteadh laigh' air na Tuathaich nach éireadh.

Bhithinn earbsach a'r dìlseachd,
Nach fàgte mi 'm prìosan,
'S gum faighinn a rìsd air an réidhlein.

How cut up I am
from the beginning of Spring:
my leg is thrust under a deal board.

I wish the thaw would come
and that the snow would go
and that every mind would come to accord.

I wish my kinsmen were seen
coming in down Craig Patrick
and the causeway would soon be put in order.

They would be the men to set fire
to the land of the corn-stooks:
they would not leave a castle in one piece.

They would put the scouring
under the men of the powdered heads:
they would not leave strength in five hundred of them.

I would be sure of your hardihood
at the time of striking with the sword:
the men of the North would be laid low, not to rise again.

I would be confident in your loyalty,
that I would not be left in prison
and that I would be again on the plain.

Then he tells his friends to be good to a smith, one of the clan of that excellent chief Lovat, who may now appear lost to his clan but will yet be honoured in Edinburgh. The men of Atholl will then suffer, which they deserve, according to the poet. MacLean Sinclair's note says that the smith, a Fraser, was in jail with Dòmhnall Donn; that the feud between Lovat and Atholl began in 1696; and that the lines about 'Sìm agaibh caillte' refer to Lovat's attainder in 1698, and that therefore Dòmhnall Donn's death was not before 1698. The unfriendly reference to Atholl is doubly significant if the line in another poem, 'Fhad 's a chumas fir Athaill am mòd', is really by Dòmhnall Donn.

By far the most famous poem attributed to Dòmhnall Donn is the glorious song which is generally begun:

A Mhairearad òg, 's tu rinn mo leòn,
Gur cailin bhòidheach lurach thu.

O young Margaret, it's you who wounded me:
you are a beautiful and handsome girl.

That is the beginning in Sinclair's *Oranaiche*. 'A Chaitrìona òg' is
the beginning in Finlay Dun's *Orain na h-Alban* and the beginning
known to that great Mull *seanchaidh*, the late Conn Duiligh Rankin
MacLean Morrison. The Gesto Collection has no girl's name.

It is, of course, quite obvious that two songs have been inextricably
confused: 'Oran an Amadain Bhòidhich', in which the young aristocrat is deluded by his mother into shooting the bathing girl, ultimately
a variant of the international folk tale used in 'The Swan Lake'; and a
song by Dòmhnall Donn or by someone else in his predicament.

The *Oranaiche* has an amalgam of the two poems and, at the very
least, four lines of the folktale, which could not fit into the Dòmhnall
Donn story at all:

> Och, 's i mo mhàthair rinn an call
> Nuair chuir i shealg na tunnaig mi
> 'S nuair a ràin mi linne chaol
> 'S ann bha mo ghaol a' sruthladh innt.

> *O, it is my mother who caused the ruin*
> *when she sent me to hunt the duck,*
> *and when I reached the narrow sound*
> *it was my love who was bathing there.*

The lines that follow those and curse the 'gunna caol' could fit
either Dòmhnall Donn or the folktale, if one assumes that the earlier
arrow could become the gunshot. The lines about being air 'cnoc leam
fhéin' do not fit Dòmhnall Donn unless 'cnoc' is a substitute for some
other word. But the following lines fit Dòmhnall Donn but not the
folktale; for as far as I know the young man of the folktale is not
himself in danger of his life for killing the girl:

> Ged théid mi suas do'n bhail ud shuas
> Cha bhi mo chuairt ach diomain ann.

> *Though I go up to yonder town*
> *my trip will be but short-lived there.*

There are lines that could fit both stories, but that seem to me to go
better with the Dòmhnall Donn story, e.g.:

> Air leabaidh làir chan fhaigh mi tàmh
> 'S air leabaidh àird cha chuir iad mi.

On a bed on the ground I will get no rest
and on a high bed they will not put me.

There are, of course, two traditions about Donald's 'Nighean Donn', the girl of this song. MacLean Sinclair's is that she was his illegitimate daughter, who visited him in prison. She is not named, but it could be that she has been confused with the sister who appears in the story behind 'O Cheit, tog an ceann'. There is also the tradition that the poem is addressed to the daughter of Grant, who in Glen Urquhart tradition is Màiri; and indeed Dr MacKay has in his appendix to *Urquhart and Glenmoriston* the following quatrain ascribed to Donald:

Bidh mi màireach air cnoc gun cheann
Is cha bhi bàigh aig duine rium —
Nach truagh leat fhéin, mo chaileag bhrònach,
Mo Mhàiri bhòidheach mheall-shuileach.

I will be to-morrow headless on a hill
and no man will feel kindly to me —
how pitiable for you, my sad girl,
my beautiful Mary of the alluring eyes.

The third and fourth lines do not fit any other versions of the song metrically, which is awkward.

The Gesto Collection has sixteen lines, ascribes the poem to Dòmhnall Donn, has no girl's name, and all its lines could suit the Dòmhnall Donn story, and two of them do not fit the folktale. The version in *Orain na h-Alban* fits the Dòmhnall Donn story.

Of the marvellously beautiful fourteen or sixteen lines in the first part of the *Oranaiche* version, it is impossible to say whether they are by Dòmhnall Donn or by an older poet. Why Donald would make Mull his refuge has not, as far as I know, been traditionally explained, but it could be explained very well. If he was indeed a friend of the Campbells, as I strongly suspect he was, he would be safe with them, and they were dominant in Mull after 1689. Any Keppoch or Glen-garry MacDonald would as such be well received by the MacLeans, and Dòmhnall Donn's mother was a MacGillonie, between whom and all MacLeans there was an age-old bond, although the bond was with the Coll MacLeans especially.

In conclusion, I feel that I have been inclined to minimise the amount of poetry that can be ascribed with probability to Dòmhnall Donn. After all, he was far more famous as a poet than Alasdair

Sgoileir, Stewart of Ach Ghobhail and others, and it may be that lines locally attributed to them are by Donald. At any rate, there can, with fair probability, be ascribed to him some things of a rare beauty, the beauty of the peerless Gaelic popular song of the 17th century, and he remains one of the most attractive figures of all Highland tradition.

Sìlis of Keppoch

Sìlis na Ceapaich, variously known as Sìle or Sìlis or Sìleas Nighean Mhic Raghnaill or Ni Raghnaill, is one of the four celebrated poetesses of the period between 1650 and 1750. Of the four, Màiri Nighean Alasdair Ruaidh and Dìorbhail Nic a' Bhriuthainn are of an older generation, both in their maturity during the Montrose wars, though Màiri survived till 1705 at least. John MacKenzie of *Sàr Obair* says that Sìleas lived from the reign of Charles II to that of George I (that is during the period from 1660 to 1727), and in a paper to the Gaelic Society of Inverness in 1900, MacLean Sinclair says: 'It is probable that Sìle na Ceapaich was born about 1660, and that she died about 1739. She was married to Gordon of Beldornie. Her husband died in 1723.' It seems that there is little dispute about Sìle's dates and that she was a contemporary of Mairearad Ni Lachlainn, who lived some time longer than Sìlis, that is if it was really she who made the elegy for Hector MacLean of Duart, who died in Rome in 1751. John MacKenzie says that Sìlis lived to a good old age, and MacLean Sinclair's conjecture would give her 79 years, but there are many traditions that Mairearad lived to a very great age. I fancy that MacLean Sinclair's '1739' may be due to a temporary lapse on his part, confusing Lachlan MacKinnon, the blind harper, with the poet Lachlainn Mac Theàrlaich Oig, who, according to MacLean Sinclair, died in 1734. It is possible that Sìlis has been ante-dated and that she was not born till 1670. It is more or less certain, however, that Sìlis was married some years before 1695.[1] Nevertheless none of the poems attributed to her shows evidence of having been made before 1715, whereas the earliest of Mairearad's is about 1690. The authors of *Clan Donald* say quite definitely, but on what authority I do not know, that Sìlis was born at Bohuntin in 1660 and that she died in 1729.

There is more known about Sìlis than about Dìorbhail and Mairearad, for Sìlis was the daughter of Gill-easbuig, 'ninth' chief of the Keppoch MacDonalds and sister of the celebrated Colla nam Bó. At the time Keppoch was fertile in poets, among them Iain Lom, Dòmhnall Donn, Dòmhnall Gruamach, Gill-easbuig himself and Aonghas Odhar, his son. Thus Sìlis was daughter and sister of poets and relative of poets, but the family of her grandfather Alasdair Buidhe was still under the cloud of the Keppoch murder of 1663. Even the authors of *Clan Donald*, who are normally chary of admitting anything against a MacDonald chief, say: 'Of the part acted by Alasdair Buidhe, it may be said that there always has been a suspicion that he was deeply implicated, although no actual proof, as far as we know, was ever brought against him. Of the guilt of his eldest son, Allan, there is no doubt whatever, the Privy Council record being witness.' MacLean Sinclair has no doubt of Alasdair Buidhe's guilt and says that two sons of Alasdair Buidhe, Ailean Dearg and Dòmhnall Gorm, together with Alasdair Ruadh Mac Dhùghaill and his six sons, actually perpetrated the murder. MacLean Sinclair is a strong authority on Keppoch traditions as he had as neighbours in Canada several Keppoch families who were very rich in old lore. One man in particular, Alexander MacDonald of Ridge, appears to have been a great mine of information to MacLean Sinclair. It therefore appears that two of Sìlis' uncles, if not her grandfather as well, were guilty of a grim murder of their own cousins, the *de facto* chiefs of Keppoch, thus bringing the chiefship into their own family.

From MacLean Sinclair's account, Gill-easbuig, Sìlis' father, was the third son of Alasdair Buidhe, Ailean Dearg having fled the country and the second son, Alasdair Dearg, having been accidentally killed; but *Clan Donald* says that Gill-easbuig was the second son. Alasdair Buidhe died about 1669 and was succeeded by Gill-easbuig, who was chief until his death in 1682, when he was succeeded by his son Colla nam Bó, who died about 1729. Whatever kinds of men Alasdair Buidhe and Ailean Dearg were, it seems that Gill-easbuig was never accused of having anything to do with the murder of his cousins, and he was praised even by Iain Lom, who never mentions Alasdair Buidhe. Colla nam Bó was turbulent, but by the time he became chief, it seems that most of the Keppoch men were quite reconciled to the family of Alasdair Buidhe, although there were dissensions, as when Colla nam Bó made no attempt to save Dòmhnall Donn from the Grants; but Dòmhnall Donn was an enemy of Iain Lom too. One may infer from contemporary MacDonald poetry that at the time the Keppoch chiefs were not regarded as among the major glories of Clan Donald; but that is not surprising, when Glengarry, Clanranald and Sleat had such famous chiefs as Alasdair Dubh, Ailean Beag and Dòmhnall a' Chogaidh. Sìlis herself assessed her contemporaries by their prowess in the Jacobite cause and not by their prowess in feuding.

It is known that Sìlis was a fervent Jacobite and a Catholic, and that she composed hymns in her old age. It is also pretty certain that she was married to Gordon of Beldornie, who was accused of dying of a fit of intoxication 'while on a visit to Inverness'. John MacKenzie says that her husband was 'a gentleman of the family of Lovat', that she lived with him 'in Moraghach MhicShimidh', and that 'after the death of her husband she was nearly cut off by a severe illness, and upon her recovery engaged her muse in the composition of hymns, some of which are still in use, as appears from a hymn book printed at Inverness in 1821'.

MacLean Sinclair says that her husband died in 1723, but there are difficulties about the text of the poem 'Marbhrann air bàs a fir', and it is clear that the bulk of it is not about her husband at all, but about Sir James MacDonald of Sleat (James of Oronsay), who died, according to *Clan Donald*, in 1720. According to MacLean Sinclair Sir James died in 1723, and of a spree at Forres; but of that later.

Of the ten or dozen poems by Sìlis that are extant, the earliest are four dealing with the 1715 Rebellion: two of them appear to have been made before Sheriffmuir, one of them is about the battle itself, and the fourth was probably composed after the battle. Of the poems before the battle, it is hard to say which is the earliest. The one I take first is 'Oran do Fheachd Mhorair Màr', of which the first verse is:

> Tha mulad, tha gruaim orm, tha bròn
> On dh'imich mo chàirdean air falbh:
>   On chàidh iad air astar
>   Gun chinnt mu'n teachd dhachaidh
> Tha m'inntinn fo airtneal gu leòr.

> *I am in sorrow, in gloom and in grief*
> *since my kinsmen have gone:*
> *since they went on a journey*
> *with no certainty of their coming home*
> *my mind is weary in depression.*

The second verse expresses some anxiety, and then she greets Sir Donald of Sleat and his brothers William and James (James of Oronsay), Alasdair Liath of Glengarry, and Allan of Moidart, about whom she has a piece of biography not elsewhere recorded as far as I know:

> Beir soraidh gu Ailean o'n chuan,
> Bha greis anns an Fhraing uainn air chuairt:
>   'S e ro-mheud do ghaisge
>   Chum gun oighre air do phearsa,
> Craobh chosgairt air feachd nan arm cruaidh.

Bear a greeting to Allan from the sea,
who was away from us in France for a while.
It is the excess of your valour
that kept your person without heir,
tree of slaughter of the host of the hard weapons.

She then mentions the men of Keppoch:

Ceannard a' Bhràghad
'S a' chuid eile de m' chàirdean.

The chief of the Brae (of Lochaber)
and the rest of my kinsmen.

A MacDonald begins with the MacDonalds. After the Mac-
Donalds, she has:

Tha ùrachadh buidhinn tigh'nn oirnn:
MacCoinnich, MacShimidh 's MacLeòid,
  MacFhionghuin Strath Chuailte
  'S an Siosalach suairce:
'S e mo bharail gum buailear leò stròic.

New bands are coming for our side:
MacKenzie, Lovat, MacLeod,
MacKinnon of Strath Swordale
and the affable Chisholm:
it is my opinion that they will strike and rend.

It is significant that she gives two verses to the Gordons, which
alone would be fair evidence that her husband was a Gordon and not a
Fraser. She then goes on to mention Robertson of Struan, Mar
himself and the Forbeses. A difficult verse follows:

Tha mo ghruaim ris a' bhuidhinn ud thall,
A luaithead 's mhùth iad an t-sreang;
  Tha mi cinnteach a'm aigne
  Gum bu mhiann leò bhith againn
Mur bhith Chuigse bhith aca mar cheann.

I have a surly look for the band over yonder,
for their quickness in changing the string;
I am sure in my mind
that they would like to be with us
if they did not have a Whig as a head.

In spite of the previous verse about 'MacCoinnich, MacShimidh 's

MacLeòid', MacLean Sinclair has no doubt that 'a' bhuidhinn ud thall' refers to the Frasers. Perhaps, of course 'MacShimidh' in the previous verse is an error that has crept in, or it may be that the verse that I have just quoted was added later, when Lovat had shown his hand. After all, it was fully expected that Lovat was to be on the Jacobite side, and this verse may have been added sometime after the Braemar meeting. On the other hand, could not the verse apply to the Macintoshes, especially as the verse following refers to Cluny? The Macintoshes were the special enemies of the Keppoch clan, and it may be that Sìlis would be pleased to rebuke them, or at any rate their chief. It is significant for the dating of the poem that MacLeod of Dunvegan is mentioned with Seaforth and Lovat, and that there is no mention of the MacLeans, who, with the MacDonalds and the Breadalbane Campbells took the most distinguished part on the Jacobite side in 1715. It seems that the poem — or part of it — was made before it was clear who were going to rise and who were not.

The last two verses are very confident and have an anticipation of looting unusual in Jacobite poetry. Technically the poem is in the Limerick measure. I do not know that this metre is used in any previous poem that is extant.

The other poem made almost certainly between the death of Queen Anne and Sheriffmuir is called 'Oran do Righ Seumas nuair bha e anns an Fhraing'. It has a refrain, of which Sìlis was fond:

'S binn an sgeul so tha iad ag ràdhainn,
  Mo Mhàlaidh bheag ó,
Ma sheasas e gun fhàillinn,
  Mo nighinn rùin ó;
Rìgh Seumas bhith air sàile
'S a' tighinn a steach gun dàil oirnn
Chur misneachd 'na chàirdean,
  Mo Mhàlaidh bheag ó.

Sweet this tale they are telling,
  my little Màlaidh ó,
if it stands without failure,
  my dear girl ó:
that King James is on the sea
and coming in on us without delay
to put courage in his friends,
  my little Màlaidh ó.

This poem is very bitter against the Whigs and their clergy, and appeals strongly to Scottish national sentiment against the English and the Union of 1707:

Ach, Alba, éiribh còmhla
Mun geàrr Sasunnaich ur sgòrnain:
Nuair thug iad airson òir uaibh
Ur creideas is ur stòras,
Nach eil e'n diugh 'nur pòca,
   Mo Mhàlaidh bheag ó.

Gur goirt leam thug iad sgrìob oirbh
Nuair dheasaich iad ur dinneir,
Nuair chuir iad uinnean puinnsein
'G a ghearradh air gach truinnsear:
Mas fhiach sibh bidh e cuimhnicht',
   Mo Mhàlaidh bheag ó.

But, Scotland, rise together
before the English cut your throats:
when they have taken from you for gold
your credit and your wealth,
so that it is not in your pocket to-day,
   my little Màlaidh ó.

It is a sore thing to me that they furrowed through you
when they prepared your dinner
and put a poisonous onion/union
to be cut on every plate.
If you are worthy it will be remembered,
   my little Màlaidh ó.

The swine taunt is made against the house of Hanover.

Of the two other poems on the 1715 Rising, 'Oran do Fheachd Rìgh Seumas' with the refrain 'Tha mi 'nam chadal 's na dùisgibh mi' may have been made before Sheriffmuir, but on the whole I think it is later than the battle. The other is called, in Turner's Collection, 'Oran air Latha Sliabh an t-Siorraim', but in Volume XX of the *Transactions of the Gaelic Society of Inverness*, MacLean Sinclair has a version so different as to be a different poem. The Turner version consists of eight octaves. The first four lines has a sentiment strange in such a Jacobite as Sìlis:

Dh'innsinn sgeula dhuibh le reusan
A b'fhiach éisdeachd anns an am,
bhith murt a chéile as leth Rìgh Seumas
Agus e fhéin bhith anns an Fhraing.

> *I would tell you a tale with good reason*
> *that would be worth hearing at this time,*
> *people murdering each other on behalf of King James*
> *and he himself in France.*

In the next four lines, however, she is very contemptuous of King George and says that it was the money that put the crown on his head. The next verse, which sounds like the words of an eye-witness, mentions the burning of homesteads and stackyards before the battle, which it is said the Jacobites found necessary to keep the enemy from getting extra cover. The third and fourth verses are impressive, with the brief and vivid lines about the beginning of the battle and her pride in Clan Donald, MacLeans and Breadalbane Campbells, the clans on the victorious right wing:

> Chàidh Clann Dòmhnaill an sin an òrdugh
> Is Clan Ghill-Eain nan rò seòl àrd;
> Sgioba Bhraid-Albann, a' bhratach bhallabhuidh:
> Bu bhuidheann ainmeil bha sin aig Màrr.

> *Clan Donald then went in order*
> *and Clan Gillean of the great high sails;*
> *the men of Breadalbane, the speckled yellow banner:*
> *that was a famous band with Mar.*

One verse is devoted to those Jacobites who did not do so well, and though she is contemptuous of Huntly and Seaforth, she expresses the hope and belief that Locheil, Stewart of Appin and Robertson will do better next time. There is the almost inevitable reference to Glengarry and to the dead Allan of Moidart, and a mention of Thomas the Rhymer's prophecy that the Gaels will be victorious in the great battle 'thall aig Cluaidh' and that England will submit. In the last verse there is an apology for forgetting John of Breadalbane, though his clan had been glowingly mentioned. She says that if he were only fifty years old and had his Frenchmen, things would have been different. The reference to the French is rather obscure to me.

The two most complimentary notices of the Breadalbane Campbells and their chief seem to indicate that Sìlis did not hold them responsible for the Massacre of Glencoe. In a very able paper to the Celtic Union two years ago, Mr Arbuckle of the Scottish Education Department came to the conclusion that John of Breadalbane had no responsibility for the Massacre, and that it was not a Campbell affair at all, in any clan sense. That confirmed my own general impression from MacDonald poetry.

The 'version' of the poem contributed by MacLean Sinclair to Volume XX of the *Transactions* has nothing corresponding to the first four stanzas of the Turner version. Of its seven verses, five are devoted to the matter contained in one verse, the fifth, of the Turner version. Thus it gives one whole verse to Seaforth; one to Locheil; one to the Gordons, Stewarts and MacKinnons; one to the men of Atholl and Badenoch, and one to Rob Roy.

Those five verses about the reverses suffered by various clans at Sheriffmuir are very inconsistent with the general tone of Jacobite poetry, and especially with Sìlis' poetry. It is almost unthinkable that Sìlis should dwell so tauntingly on the failures of certain clans and chiefs. One cannot say definitely that Sìlis did not make this poem. Obviously it is a poem by a MacDonald, for the other two victorious clans are not mentioned; and we do not know enough about Sìlis to be certain that she was not the author; but it is, at any rate, a different poem from that of Turner's Collection, as it is in a different metre. I do not know MacLean Sinclair's authority for ascribing it to her, but if it is by her, it has accretions. For example, her attitude to her husband was such that she could hardly have dismissed his clan with the two contemptuous lines:

> Theich Gòrdanaich uainn
> Le luas an casan.

> *Gordons fled from our side*
> *with all the speed of their legs.*

In the same verse as that about the Gordons and the Stewarts there are four lines on the MacKinnons:

> Clann Fhionghuin bu luath
> Air ruaig na gealtachd:
> Theich buidheann nam faochag
> Gun aodach dhachaidh.

> *The MacKinnons, how fast they were*
> *in the cowardly rout!*
> *the band of whelks fled*
> *home without clothes.*

These lines make it all the more probable that the poem was not by Sìlis, or has been so corruptly transmitted as to be unrecognisable. According to all that I can gather, the MacKinnons were with the MacDonalds on the victorious right wing, and it is unthinkable that

Sìlis did not know that.[2] The fifth verse refers to Rob Roy. As he and his men were only spectators at the battle, it is possible that even the most prudent Jacobite might say of 'Raibeart nam Bó':

Cha b'fhiach iad am biadh
An t-aon cheud a bh'agad.

*They were not worth their food
the one hundred you had.*

Although one never knows what pique might have caused Sìlis to be hard on the clans who formed the defeated left wing at Sheriffmuir, it is most improbable that the poem as it stands is by her.

The fourth poem on the '15 Rising, called by Turner 'Oran do Fheachd Rìgh Seumas', appears to have been made after the breaking of the rebellion. It begins, 'Gur diombach mi 'n iomairt chuir gach fine air fògradh', and it is formally interesting as it consists of three stanzas with an unusual arrangement. There are ten lines in each, with the refrain 'Tha mi 'nam chadal 's na dùisgibh mi' after the second, fourth and last lines of each. This poem has no difficulties of matter, but it is an interesting example of Sìlis' style, which can sometimes be very easy and colloquial. It is interesting, too, as the reflection of an ardent Jacobite woman's feelings about 1715, the disappointment with the difference between promise and result being very evident.

Those four poems are the earliest that can be dated. If Sìlis were really born as early as 1660, it is strange that no extant poem by her can be dated before 1715. The next that can be dated are of the early 1720s. They are 'Marbhrann air bàs a fir' and 'Alasdair á Gleanna Garadh'. *Clan Donald* says that Alasdair Dubh of Glengarry died in 1721, but MacLean Sinclair says 1724. In the lament for Glengarry, Sìlis has what is taken as a reference to her own widowhood. Of Glengarry's wife she says:

Ge nach b'ionann dhomhsa is dhìse,
Is goirt a fhuair mi fhìn mo chàradh.

*Though it was not the same with me as with her
I myself was in a most sore condition.*

If this assumption is right, Gordon of Beldornie was dead before Glengarry. In Volume XX of the *Transactions of the Gaelic Society of Inverness*, MacLean Sinclair implies that Gordon died the year before Glengarry's death, that is 1720 or 1723. The fourth verse of the 'Marbhrann air bàs a fir' has some problems. It is:

Mas beag leam sud, fhuair mi bàrr air:
Ceann mo stuic is pruip nan càirdean,
A leag na céid le bheum 's na blàraibh,
'Ga chur fo'n fhòid le òl na gràisge.

If that is a small thing to me, I got a thing that topped it:
the head of my stock and the prop of the kin,
who laid low hundreds with his blow in battles,
being put under the sod through the rabble's drinking.

In the paper to which I have so frequently referred, MacLean
Sinclair says of this poem: 'The first two verses are about Julia's
husband, the third is about her daughter, whilst the remainder of the
poem is about Sir James MacDonald of Sleat, who died at Forres from
the effects of a spree on wine in 1723.' Now the *Clan Donald* authors
say that Sir James died in 1720, but where MacLean Sinclair got his
information that Sir James died of a spree I do not know. The *Clan
Donald* authors do not mention it, but they are inclined to gloss over
such things. The question really hinges on the words 'ceann mo stuic'.
I am of the opinion that Sìlis would use the phrase only of a chief of
Sleat, for I think it is quite clear that the various branches of Clan
Donald, except Glengarry and Clan Ranald, regarded the chief of
Sleat as, in some way or other, the head of all Clan Donald. It is
strange that a poem of twelve quatrains came to be entitled as it is,
when only two verses of the twelve refer to her husband; but as the
poem stands in Gillies' Collection, it cannot be otherwise interpreted.
If this interpretation is correct, then the story that Gordon of Beldornie died of a spree is due to a misreading of this poem by John
MacKenzie. On the other hand, MacLean Sinclair's assertion that it
was Sir James MacDonald who died of the spree may be due only to
his reading of this poem, and an error in transmission may be
responsible. As the verse stands, it appears to me to be applicable only
to MacDonald. There is a minor difficulty in the fifth verse, where
Inverness, not Forres, is mentioned as the place, but such an error
only confirms the impression that MacLean Sinclair had information
other than the poem. The tenth quatrain makes it certain that the bulk
of the poem refers to Sir James. The verse reads:

Nise on dh'fhalbh na bràithrean,
'S nach eil ach Uilleam a làthair,
A Rìgh mhóir, mas deònach, dàil da
Gus an diong an t-oighre 'n t-àite.

Now since the brothers are gone
and only William remains,

Great King, if it is Thy will, delay him (i.e. his death)
until the heir is equal to his place.

Sir James had a brother William, while his elder brother was
Dòmhnall a' Chogaidh, who died in 1718, leaving an heir Donald, the
fifth baronet, who died in 1720, and was succeeded by Sir James, his
uncle, who died, according to *Clan Donald*, only a few weeks later,
leaving a minor, Sir Alexander, to succeed.

MacLean Sinclair says that the third verse refers to Sìlis' daughter,
and certainly the tone of it makes that almost certain; but he has
additional evidence in twelve lines of verse, which he prints in the
same paper under the title 'Rannan, le Sìle na Ceapaich':

> Chaoidh chan urrainn mi gu bràth
> Dol thoirt cunntas ann do chàch
> Air na rug orm eadar dà Dhi-sathurna.
>
> Chiad Di-sathurna bha dhiubh
> Chuir mi Anna bhuam do'n ùir,
> Bu tric a ghluais mi gu sùgradh aighearach.
>
> 'N ath Dhi-sathurna 'na dhéidh
> Thug e malairt dhomh am chéill,
> Gun do liubhair mi Mhac Dé m'fhear-taighe bhuam.
>
> 'S tric a shuidh thu, ghaoil, 'gam chòir,
> Thu ag amharc 's mi leth-bheò,
> 'S cha chaomhnadh tu an t-òr a chaitheamh rium.

> *Never shall I be able at any time*
> *to give an account to others*
> *of what came on me between two Saturdays.*
>
> *The first Saturday of them*
> *I put Anna away from me to the earth,*
> *Anna who often moved me to mirth and high spirits.*
>
> *The next Saturday after it,*
> *it put a change in my reason*
> *that I rendered to the Son of God the man of my house.*
>
> *Often did you sit, my dear, beside me,*
> *looking on me half alive,*
> *and you would not spare to spend gold on me.*

After the poem, Maclean Sinclair has a note that 'the poetess was
nearly cut off by a severe illness some time before the death of her
husband'. In *Sàr Obair*, John MacKenzie says of Sìlis: 'After the
death of her husband she was nearly cut off by a severe illness, and

upon her recovery engaged her muse in the composition of hymns, some of which are still in use, as appears from a hymn book printed in Inverness in 1821.' The phrase 'nearly cut off by a severe illness' looks like an echo of John MacKenzie by MacLean Sinclair, but MacLean Sinclair, presumably on the authority of the 'Rannan', says 'before', not 'after' her husband's death. In this case, I think MacLean Sinclair is more reliable than MacKenzie, and I imagine he had very good authority for ascribing the 'Rannan' to Sìlis.

The 'Rannan' have a directness and poignancy, which Sìlis could have, and which, in a way, is like the directness and poignancy which the great Màiri Mhór had two hundred years or so later. I am dubious, however, of the effect of the dactylic ending of the last lines.

The famous elegy for Alasdair Dubh of Glengarry can be dated in 1721 or 1723. It contains only one difficulty in historical or biographical reference:

Nam b'ionann do chàch is do Gholl
An uair a dh'imich an long a mach,
Cha rachadh i rithist air sàl
Gun fhios dé 'm fàth mu'n d'thàin' i steach.
Ach nuair chunnaic sibh 'san tràth sin
Bhith 'gur fàgail air faontradh,
Bhrist bhur cridheachan le mulad:
Is léir a' bhuil, nach robh sibh saoghlach.

If it had been the same with others as with Goll
when the ship went out,
she would not go again on the sea
without knowing why she came in.
When you saw at that time
that you were being left neglected
your hearts broke with sorrow:
the effect is clear, that you were not long-lived.

Of this 'somewhat obscure stanza', Professor Watson thinks the reference is to the 'abortive affair of Glenshiel in 1719, in which Glengarry took no part'. I would suggest that it refers to the Pretender's sailing back to France in December 1715. Since Glengarry took no part in the Glenshiel rising, how was he left 'air faontradh' by it, and how did his heart 'break with sorrow' because of it? Of course, Glenshiel was only two or four years before his death, whereas 1715 was six or eight years, and it is possible that Professor Watson was right. I do not, however, think that Sìlis would commend Glengarry for his non-participation in Glenshiel. It is possible that there is a kind

246

of *double entendre* in the image of the ship going out and coming in, one literal and the other figurative. If this is so, it is all the more likely that the verse refers to the Old Pretender's coming from France and sailing back, having accomplished nothing.

There is no way of dating the famous elegy for Lachlan Mac-Kinnon, the blind harper, except that it was made some years or decades after her marriage. Whatever the date, the poem is, apart from its exquisite artistic quality, one of the most interesting poems of the period. It consists of nine octaves, the second of which makes it certain that Sìlis was married some time before 1695. If she was born in 1660, she may very well have been married 15 years before 1695. She says that when Lachlan came to her on his visits, their talk would begin with Sleat, with Donald and Margaret. It would be like Sìlis to begin with the 'head' of the Clan Donald, even if Lachlan were not a Skyeman. The Donald must be the third baronet of Sleat, and the Margaret must be his wife, the daughter of the Earl of Morton. This Donald, father of Dòmhnall a' Chogaidh, died in 1695. Sìlis mentions the MacDonald lands that Lachlan visited: Sleat, Moidart, Knoydart, Morar, Glengarry and Glencoe; and Mór and Seònaid, who lived in Argyll. *Clan Donald* says that one of Sìle's sisters was married to Macintyre of Glen Noe; and another, as far as I remember, to MacLean of Ardgour.[3]

The sixth verse is charmingly personal and revealing:

An uair a ghlacadh tu do chlàrsach
's a bhiodh tu 'ga gleusadh làmh rium,
Cha mhath a thuigte le ùmaidh
Do chuir chiùil-sa 's mo ghabhail dhàn-sa.
Bu bhinn do mheòir air a cliathaich
An uair a dh'iarrainn Cumha 'n Easbuig,
Cumha Ni Mhic Raghnaill làmh ris,
Cumha Màiri 's Cumha Ghill-easbuig.

When you took your harp
and were tuning it beside me,
no clown could well appreciate
the turns of your music and my singing of poems.
Melodious were your fingers on her side
when I asked for the Lament for the Bishop,
the Lament for Keppoch's Daughter with it,
the Lament for Mary and the Lament for Gillespie.

It appears that Professor Watson did not identify the poems mentioned, for he gives no note on them. Two questions arise. Is

'Cumha Ni Mhic Raghnaill' a lament for or by some daughter of a chief of Keppoch? Normal Gaelic usage would indicate a lament for, but if not, is it the famous lament for her brothers by a sister of the two murdered in 1663? If it is, how much did Sìlis know of the guilt of her grandfather and two uncles? The other question is whether the Gill-easbuig is her own father, and I am inclined to think it is. As he died about 1682, the matter is not of much chronological importance.

In the verse following there is the famous reference to *socair dhàna*, which raises very tantalising questions as to the relation between poetry and music at the time. But there is no certainty at all about the meaning of the phrase. 'Cumha Lachlainn Mhic Fhionghuin' is an intriguing and charming poem in which there is a most rare blend of grace and poignancy, a blend that is particularly noticeable towards the end of the 17th century. The other examples of that blend that rise most immediately to my mind are the elegies by the Ciaran Mabach for his brother, the Sir James of Sleat who died in 1678. The Ciaran's poems have, perhaps, a more chiselled and noble perfection of form, but Sìlis' elegy for Lachlan MacKinnon has a curious conversational intimacy in its grace and fine feeling. Apart from its rare artistry, the poem is a most interesting and attractive social document, with most suggestive and evocative glimpses of the relationship between artist and patron in the Gaelic world just when the relationship was about to be broken for ever.

The lament for Lachlan MacKinnon is far more personal and in some ways far more intimate and tender than the usual run of Chief-and-Clan poetry, if indeed it can be put in that class at all. There are extant a few more poems by Sìlis that are certainly not in that class. There are two poems of advice to young women, one of which is called 'Oran le Sìlis Ni Mhic Raonuill an aghaidh na h-Obair Nogha'. The 'Obair Nogha' is clearly a new sexual laxness (shades of the Restoration!). This poem is obviously the one referred to by John MacKenzie as 'an answer to a song by Mr MacKenzie of Gruinard called "An Obair Nogha".' In the last verse of the poem by Sìlis there is a direct reference to a 'Ruairi' who has glorified the 'Obair Nogha'. This Ruairi is probably MacKenzie of Gruinard, whom John MacKenzie, with his special knowledge of the verse of the MacKenzies, would easily identify. Sìlis' poem is a piece of rather humdrum versification counselling prudence and, Catholic though she was, calling the attention of girls to the terrors of the ministers, elders and session. Again, it has that conversational turn of speech so marked in some of her poems. Turner's Collection has another poem on the same theme but in a different measure, and also ascribed to Sìlis. This poem, which is to the same tune as 'Mi shuidhe 'm ònar air tulaich bhòidhich', consists of eight octaves and has a deeper personal and imaginative note. It does not have the phrase 'an Obair Nogha' at all, and appears to speak sadly from experience, saying that only those with real experience can know. It seems to accept as inevitable the seduction of the young and inexperienced. It is a far more impressive poem, but both have that frank, personal, even intimate, note of much of Sìlis' poetry.

Of the hymns mentioned by John MacKenzie, I have been able to lay hands only on one, 'Laoidh Mhoire', printed in the collection by Hugh MacDonald in Oban in 1893, and, as far as I know, believed to have come mostly from Father Allan MacDonald. 'Laoidh Mhoire' is a long hymn on the life of Christ, and though it is mainly a simple re-telling of the New Testament story, it has the quality of Sìlis' poetry, a cumulative effect of sincerity and unpretentious tenderness.

Mr Calum Johnston has told me that he thinks the hymn 'An Eaglais' in the same book is also by Sìlis. On that, as on so many matters, there is no more dependable opinion than Mr Johnston's; as I write this, I have no access to the book in question and cannot discuss the matter and Mr Johnston's opinion, but there is no opinion for which I have greater respect.

NOTES

1 Dr Jean Dunlop has shown that Sir Donald, the third baronet of Sleat, died in 1692 not 1695, and Dr Colm Ó Baoill has shown that Margaret, and not Mary, was the name of the wife of his son, Dòmhnall a' Chogaidh, chief from 1692 to 1718. I was following *Clan Donald*. My essay on Sìleas was written 15 years before the appearance of Colm Ó Baoill's excellent *Bàrdachd Shìlis na Ceapaich* and so I could not take advantage of his painstaking research, though even he has not solved all the difficulties of text, biography, chronology and interpretation.

2 Ó Baoill has shown that the MacKinnons were not with the MacDonalds during the battle.

3 Several details in the foregoing paragraph require revision in the light of Ó Baoill's findings.

Màiri Mhór nan Oran

A dominant theme, perhaps the dominant theme, of 19th century Scottish Gaelic poetry is the Clearances and the condition of the remnant of Gaels congested on the poorest land. Whatever else may be said of the 19th century Gaelic poets they cannot be accused of an escapist silence.

Before the end of the 18th century Duncan Macintyre had realised what was happening. He praised the foxes for destroying the sheep that were going to destroy his people. About the very beginning of the 19th century Allan MacDougall was stating the theme with intensity, terseness and finality:

> There has come on us in Scotland a cross,
> Poor people are naked against it,
> without food, clothes, solace,
> the North is utterly destroyed.

Somewhat later, a Mull poet has it thus:

> The land of our love is under bracken and heather
> and every field and plain untilled,
> and soon there will be no one in Mull of the Trees
> but non-Gaels and white sheep.

The famous Islay poet, William Livingston, says:

> The speckled adder lies in coils
> on the floor where grew
> the big men whom I saw:
> bring this message to the poet.

> Islay is to-day without people:
> the sheep has made her glens waste.
> As I heard and as I saw:
> bring this message to the poet.

From Sutherland to Breadalbane and to South Argyll it is the same story, but of all 19th century Gaelic poets no-one said so much in song about the Clearances and later, about the Land League, as Mary MacDonald (Mrs MacPherson), Màiri Nighean Iain Bhàin or Màiri Mhór nan Oran.

Mary was born in Skeabost in 1821, and her mother was from Uig in Trotternish. Her father and mother had gone to Glasgow on refusing to emigrate, but they had returned to Skye before Mary was born. Because of her birthplace and heredity, Mary knew best the Mac-Donald lands, where the Clearances were later than they were in the MacLeod districts of Bracadale and Minginish and not so severe. It has been reliably estimated that though the MacDonald estates were bigger in population than the MacLeod estates, three people were cleared from the MacLeod lands for every two cleared from the MacDonald lands.

Mary lived in Skeabost until 1848, when she married Isaac Mac-Pherson, a shoemaker of Skye parents living in Inverness. He died in 1871, leaving her with four children, and in 1872 she suffered the cruel wrong and humiliation 'that made (her) poetry live'. The first of her songs heard publicly were in support of Charles Fraser Macintosh in the Inverness election of 1874, but she had left Inverness in 1872 and was training as a nurse in Glasgow Royal Infirmary. She worked as a nurse in Glasgow, Greenock and in their vicinity until 1882. By this time she was famous for her songs and her championship of the crofters. For several years before 1882 she had visited Skye once a year. MacBain says that in Skye 'it is no exaggeration to say that every house was open for her reception'. Her principal hosts in Skye were the MacRae family of the big farm of Ose, Kintail people who had a great feeling for Gaelic songs and poetry.

1882, when Mary came home to Skye for good, was the year of the Battle of the Braes and the crofter resurgence in Glendale and Staffin, a great year in the history of Skye and of the Highlands and Islands. Lachlan MacDonald, the benevolent laird of Skeabost, gave Mary a rent-free cottage and in 1891 paid for the publication of about 9,000 lines of her poetry, with a preface by Alexander McBain, a Celtic scholar of European reputation. MacBain says that Mary carried in her head 'at least half as much more of her own, and twice as much which she is able to repeat, of floating, unpublished poetry, mainly that of Skye and the Western Isles'. The vast amount of poetry that she knew by heart is significant for the study not only of Gaelic poetry but the study of the genesis of all poetry and especially the relationship of oral and 'sub-literary' traditions.

Mary could not write Gaelic but she could read her own poetry when she saw it in print. It is not clear if she could do the same with the 18,000 or so lines of poetry by others that she knew by heart, but MacBain says that all this other poetry was unpublished. Surely some of it would have been printed in rare collections like Turner's and Gillies', which Mary probably never saw, although she had probably seen MacKenzie's *Sàr Obair*, at any rate the outside of it.

It is known that Màiri Mhór never made a song until the year of her great suffering and humiliation, 1872. She was then fifty. Apart from the more or less dedicatory poem in honour of Lachlan of Skeabost, which appears to be of the year of Victoria's Jubilee 1887, the first poem in the book of 1891 is the famous song 'Eilean a' cheò', probably made in 1872 from the evidence of the first verse, and with one or two verses added about 1875, the year of Ronald Archibald's accession to the MacDonald lordship or the year of his marriage (which I do not know). Of its 22 octaves, the first is magnificent and some of the rest are alive with the great warm pride that was in Màiri. Her own land, the land between the lochs of Snizort, Bracadale and the Sound of Raasay is in her blood and every loved name is charged with memories of her youth, her own agony, and is at the same time resonant with the heroic and romantic nature of the landscape itself, for the landscape itself is at once image and symbol. It is part of the romantic film over Màiri's eyes in the contemplation of the pre-Clearance state of her people. The romantic quality is uniquely robust and materialistic. Who else but Màiri would have romanticised the rush ropes and rush bags, the built up heap of potatoes, the barrel full of beer or mutton, the stock well tended and the crops gathered in, the glories of Skye in Màiri's youth?

The great 13th octave about the misery of the thousands cleared is followed by a kind of optimistic economic survey of iron and coal resources, strangely like the new oil panacea, but the 15th octave says the wheel will turn, with cattle in the folds and the 'Sasunnaich' driven from the Green Isle of Mist. The complimentary octave on Lord Ronald Archibald's wedding reminds him of his duty to his people. The last two lines of the poem is the first and most memorable reference to the humiliation 'that made my poetry live'.

The third poem in the book, 'Civil War', is a dialogue between Mary and Mrs MacRae, a plea for songs and poetry as part of the failing ethos of the Gael and a bulwark of his failing language, and an optimistic assertion that Winans (of the Pet Lamb case) and others of his like will be driven away to spend their gains in London, and that the Crò of Kintail will again be filled with good men. But Mrs MacRae reminds Mary of the psychological change in the Gael himself as a result of the great Evangelical movement:

> The people have become so strange
> that sorrow is wheat to them,
> and if you do not go into a whelk for them
> you will not be suffered to live.

Mary's reply is in two splendid octaves ending:

> But since vanity is a plant
> that satisfies the flesh,
> it clings to me as firmly
> as the lace to the shoe.

'Civil War' is thus partly a conflict between Màiri's natural *joie de vivre*, the many thousands of beloved 'vain' songs that she carried in her head, and the asceticism of the Evangelicals, who regarded this world as a 'vale of tears' and all poetry except religious as a vanity of vanities. The tone of the 'Civil War' is hostile to the more showy Evangelicals, but in some later poems Mary's attitude is ambivalent, perplexed and inconsistent, for in them the name of Roderick Mac-Leod is a poignant symbol. Roderick MacLeod, Maighstir Ruairi, was not only inordinately hard on the 'vanities' of the world but also a fearless champion of the common people, and the love he evoked on that account was heightened by the realisation that he was a grandson of a MacLeod chief of Raasay and regarded by some as a traitor to his own class.

'Eilean a' Cheò' ('The Isle of the Mist') and 'Cogadh Sìobhalta' ('Civil War') are not really typical poems in that Mary's own private suffering is not even implied in the second poem, and implied only in the first octave of 'Eilean a' Cheò' and explicitly mentioned only as a poignant irrelevancy in the last octave. Most of Mary's poetry can be called social poetry but because most of it is impregnated with her own individual suffering, it can be called confessional poetry as well. Its greatness consists in the fusion of social and private passion (and passion means primarily suffering), with extraordinary vitality and natural *joie de vivre*; for of all Gaelic poets not even Alexander MacDonald had more vitality and *joie de vivre* than Màiri Mhór. During her life-time her people had felt the full impact of the Clearances, the emigrations overseas and to Glasgow and the industrial Lowlands, and the miserable congestion of those who remained on the poorest of lands. With this there came the great Evangelical movement with its insistence that this world is only a worthless vale of tears and there ought to be no resistance to the ordinated powers, however bad they might be, for their spiritual blood was on their own heads. It is true that from about 1847, and especially from 1882 to the end of Mary's life in 1898, there was a resurgence and the new hope from the Land League, and Mary's brave heart responded to that with an optimism that is almost unbelievable in a person of her age who had suffered so much herself.

Mary's courage impresses the best minds among the Gaels of her day. In 1891 Alexander MacBain talked of her 'good work and her brave heart'. There was also the great pride in her own people, again and again, implicit or explicit, sometimes just thrown out with the most resonant of names, MacDonald. 'That roused wounded pride in the blood of the Clan Donald.' Unequal as her poetry is, the fusion of public and private suffering, courage, pride, warm-heartedness, great vitality and *joie de vivre* in it makes it universal, even if it can be called territorial or even parochial. Her own country was in her blood, and such parochialism is very often a mark of the universal.

It would entail a great deal of research to establish the chronology of Mary's poetry. For instance, 'An Nollaig Ur' ('The New Christmas') is the fourth poem in order in her book, but it cannot be before 1888, when the passions of 1882 were subsiding and when it was clear that the Crofters' Act of 1886 was only a poor palliative, though it removed the very worst of the abuses of the miserable status quo. It did not restore the cleared lands to the people, giving only security of tenure and lower rents in the existing crofter lands. 'An Nollaig Ur' is a restrained and very poignant poem, but in it the great social wrongs of the century are hardly implicit. The very well known song 'Soraidh le Eilean a' Cheò' ('Greeting to the Isle of the Mist') is full of pathos, but it too has the great evocative effects of the roll-calls of Skye names, the angular elbucky Norse sounds lengthened and made wonderfully resonant. 'Ath-ùrachadh m' eòlais' ('Renewing my acquaintance') is somewhat similar. Sometimes the noble sorrow and noble pride find perfect words, as in the quatrain on cleared Sgoirebreac, but this is followed by the disquisition on William Stewart's well-slated shop. 'Fios gu Clach Ard Uige' ('Message to the High Stone of Uig') has the flame of social anger fanned by her own private mortification. It contains the famous quatrain about the silence of the ministers in the face of the social wrong:

Preachers have so little care
seeing the condition of the people of my land,

and they are so dumb about it in the pulpit
as if their audience were brute beasts.

This poem has fierce denunciation of particular landlords and factors and expresses the solidarity with the people of Skye (and of Bernera in Lewis) of many a stalwart Gael in Glasgow and Greenock, who will go up to help them. It ends with two quatrains about the private wrong that 'put the edge on her nature/making it sharp with the oil of pain', when she fell 'on the field of battle far from her kinsmen'. As well as 'The High Stone of Uig' there are many other songs such as 'The Song of Ben Lee', 'The Hardy Men of Bernera', 'Letters to the Gaels of Canada', and the 'Meeting of the Crofters', alive with a sanguine courage and hope.

Màiri Mhór had one foot in Eden, but it was her own robust Eden of pre-Clearance Skye, 'going in winter to waulkings and weddings/with no lantern light but the (burning) end of the peat' or when she was 'foolish' going over the moorlands with the heather 'tearing her petticoats'. There is no remorse for the 'folly', which is not the Evangelical 'folly' of the unconverted, but the lost 'folly' of youth, which she would have again if she could. I can think of few poems of comparable length that have implicit in them more of human life than 'Nuair bha mi Og' ('When I was Young'), the most famous of all Mary's songs, and one of the great Gaelic songs that are also great poems. It has nothing of the 'humiliation' that made her poetry live and the Clearance motif is only vaguely implicit. There are many songs of sorrow in Gaelic but the sorrow and nostalgia of 'Nuair bha mi Og' is that of one who is still full of the world, *joie de vivre* and the pride of life. No poem of nostalgia has more of the 'objective correlative', more of a strange counterpoint of joy and sorrow, and the language has as much consistency as is possible in poetry that is in any way Dionysian (and all poetry is Dionysian) and not just a laboured distillation in the top of the head.

Her sufferings in Inverness in 1872 were largely at the hands of English monoglots, and that may be one reason why she again and again talks as if the wrongs of Skye and the Highlands were the work of the English, but in one poem, 'Airgead-cinn Alasdair Bhàin' ('The Head-money of Alasdair Bàn') she says that all the responsibility did not lie with the English but with 'bad worthless landlords' who got into debt in London. I wonder if she vaguely felt that the Clearances could not have been imposed on the Highlands without the backing of English force. Probably she implies that the anglicised landlords, chiefs among them, and their agents, were English in all but name.

And, of course, English was the habitual language of the landlord class and their chief agents, and the landlords acceptable to crofters were, like MacPherson of Cluny and MacDonald of Skeabost, great friends of Gaelic. Màiri Mhór was not politically acute except where her own people were concerned. I do not remember that she expressed any sympathy with the Lowland working class or with the victims of colonial exploitation in any of her poetry, but one has to remember that about a third of her poetry was never published and is, as far as I know, completely lost, for I have never heard any fragment attributed to her that was not published in 1891. I simply do not know whether John Whyte, who took down her poems from her own dictation, had social and political reasons for omitting anything.

As far as Gaeldom itself is concerned, Màiri Mhór was uncompromising. The Crofters' Act of 1886 was to her only a small beginning. All cleared lands ought to be restored, and would be restored, to the descendants of the crofters who had been driven out over the sea. The last poem in her book is the brave sanguine 'Prophecy and Blessing to the Gaels':

And when I am in the boards
my words will be a prophecy.

They will return, the stock of the crofters
Who were driven over the sea.

And the aristocratic 'beggars'
will be routed as they (the crofters) were.

Deer and sheep will be carted away
and the glens will be tilled;

A time of sowing and a time of reaping,
and a time to reward the robbers.

And the cold ruined houses
will be built up by our kin.

That song is significantly to the tune of one of Alexander Mac-Donald's indomitable Jacobite songs envisaging the return of Charles Edward Stewart to the land of Clan Ranald. Nowadays it is strange in our ears but it is a measure of the high hopes of the Land League of the 1880s and of its best known poet.

Any big body of poetry that is at the same time social, confessional, discursive, with passionate criticism of life, is bound to be sometimes trivial in content, inconsistent in diction and conventional in imagery. Sometimes may mean very often, and Màiri Mhór's unequalities are

256

many and sometimes ludicrous; but the fire of passion in some words, lines or verses has a way of burning up the clichés in and around them so that the very clichés are weed-killers of the precious and contrived; and as for 'purity' and homogeneity of diction, especially in a language with so much dialectical fragmentation as Gaelic had even last century, and with such a rich oral tradition of poetry as Gaelic, 'purity' of diction is just a flower of a never-never land.

Màiri's poetry is rich in image and symbol although it is not very rich in metaphor. The images are very often of the natural scenery, the animals, especially cows and calves, sheep ambivalently, plants, implements, utensils, food, dress and so on. Very often those images are symbols as well, symbols of the lost Skye of her youth or what is left of it, or of the sad change, or the new hope. Very likely, she herself did not realise how often her images became symbols. The scenery of Skye is spectacular and breeds the heroic romantic symbol, and therefore even the great roll-calls of Skye names are resonant in many ways and symbols of what was, what is left, and what she hopes may be. There is thus a strange complexity in the 'simplicities' of Màiri Mhór's poetry. Perhaps it is wrong to use the word 'subtle', but there are complexities that are deep if not broad. It is question-begging to use the word 'simple' of what is greatly moving, and Màiri Mhór's poetry has always been greatly moving to some of the 'sophisticated' as well as to a great many of the 'unsophisticated' among those who know her language.

Am Misgear agus an Cluaran

Chuir Mgr. Blackwood agus a Mhic a mach *A Drunk Man Looks at the Thistle* an 1926, ach theirig na chlò-bhuail iad, agus fad chóig bliadhna deug cha b' urrainn duinn an leabhar iongantach so a cheannach am bùthan na h-Albann. Am bliadhna thogadh am masladh so de ar dùthaich le Caledonian Press Ghlaschu, agus tha an dara clò-bhualadh againn. Bu chòir do na h-uile aig a bheil spéis do bhàrdachd na Roinn Eòrpa a bhith glé fhada an comain nan deagh Ghàidheal ris an abrar an Caledonian Press, oir chan ann a h-uile linn a bhuilichear air dùthaich sam bith bàrdachd de'n ghnè a gheibhear anns a' 'mhisg' a thàinig air Uisdean MacDhiarmaid no, a réir ainm a bhreith, Crìstean Moireach Mac a' Ghréidheir.

B' anabarrach da-rìreabh an dà bhliadhna ud, 1925 agus 1926, am filidheachd ar dùthcha, oir annta chunnacas reul ag éirigh am measg bàird Machair Albann nach fhacas a leithid o bhàs Burns. Thàinig trì leabhraichean an deaghaidh a chéile o MhacDhiarmaid: *Sangschaw*, *Penny Wheep*, agus *A Drunk Man Looks at the Thistle*. Thug a' Bheurla Ghallda Albannach leum aisde o'n làthaich anns an robh a bàrdachd fad iomadh bliadhna, agus sheas i air àrd-mhullaichean ealain na Roinn Eòrpa. Is còir dhuinne mar Ghàidheil a bhith uasal as ar càirdean, ar comh-cheiltich air a' Ghalldachd.

Tha mise mi-fhìn de'n dream a tha a' cur teagaimh anns an dàn fhada. A réir mo bheachd, chan fhaighear fìor bhàrdachd an dàn fada ach a mhàin an sgurrachan a tha ag éirigh an sud agus an so os cionn machair nan rann. Uime sin, 'se mo bharail gur e nì glé ainneamh a tha anns a' bhàrdachd, eadhon am measg ranntachd nam bàrd as fheàrr a bha agus a tha air an t-saoghal. Tha *A Drunk Man Looks at the Thistle* air àireamh bhig nan dàn fada a tha a' cur teagaimh 'nam theagamh.

Tha MacDhiarmaid e fhéin ag aideachadh gur e treamasgal ('se 'gallimaufry' am facal aige-san) a tha anns an *Drunk Man Looks at the Thistle*. Ar leam-sa gu bheil so do-sheachnadh agus gu tur ionmholta, oir dé an cruth ach cruth an treamasgail a chumadh bàrdachd na 'misge'? Cha ghabh 'a' mhisg' agus an treamasgal an dealachadh. 'Se gleusadh mór air a' mhac-meanmna a chuir cuideachd iad anns an t-saothair so: agus tha dian-theas agus neart agus gleusdachd mhìor-

258

bhuileach anns an inntinn agus anns a' mhac-meanmna a chum còmhla iad anns an t-siubhal-shìthe a tha aca troimh'n domhain mhór gus an gabh iad fois anns an t-sàmhchair dho-labhairt a tha iad a' ruigheachd aig crìch an ànraidh is am mire air cuan is tìr is speur is nèamh is iutharna anns an dàn:

Yet ha'e I silence left, the croon o' a'.

Mas e treamasgal a tha aig a' 'Mhisgear' 'se treamasgal samhlachail, no mar their na Frangaich 'symboliste' a tha ann; agus tha a' 'mhisg' a' toirt saorsa do'n t-samhlachadh. Tha iomadh samhladh anns an dàn, ach tha a dhà no trì ann o thoiseach gu crìch. 'Se an cluaran Alba anns a' cheud dol a mach; agus an toiseach, co-dhiùbh, gu h-àraidh na tha sgreamhail, oillteil, bochd gu spioradail, rag, duaichnidh, danarra an Albainn. Ach 'se an cluaran cuideachd na tha treun do-chìosnaicht' an Albainn. An uair sin tha an cluaran 'ga sgaoileadh fhéin a mach gus a bheil e a' gabhail a steach beatha an duine gu léir; chan e mhàin beatha an duine, ach beatha Nàduir uile. 'Se a' ghealach seann ghealach a' mhisgeir; ach, aig a' cheart ám, 's i tuigse no inntinn an duine fa chomhair na sìorruidheachd; no eadhon, mar gum b'eadh, inntinn na sìorruidheachd fhéin. Tha sin a' nochdadh cho ladarna agus a tha smuain an dàin; ach feumar aideachadh gu bheil an ladarnas so air a sheasamh le mac-meanmna d'a réir; le a leithid de phòsadh eadar mac-meanmna agus breithneachadh 's nach fhacas, 'nam bheadhd-sa có-dhiùbh, am bàrd eile anns an Roinn Eòrpa ri ar linn.

Tha MacDhiarmaid, mar gum b' ann, a' sgrìobadh poll an Domhainn; a' sglàbadh nan reultan leis, agus air a' cheann thall, 'ga chur 'na theine geal le teas àrd nan reultan. Agus chan eil e a' dìochaineachadh airson tiota, gu bheil am poll agus na reultan ann còmhla agus dealaichte, an ceann agus a dh' aindeoin a chéile. Tha fhios againn gu robh comas sònraichte riamh aig bàrdachd Machair Albann air aon chas a chumail air fearann tioram cruaidh as aithne do na h-uile, agus cas eile a bhith aice, aig an aon ám, air fearann dìomhair fad as; gu bheil a mac-meanmna talmhaidh agus spioradail le greim dìon air an t-saoghal so nuair a tha e a' siubhal slighean uaignidh dorcha. Tha a' bhuaidh so barraichte am bàrdachd MhicDhiarmaid; tha i 'ga nochdadh fhéin an iomadh cruth agus fonn: uaireannan sgaiteach, éisgeil, feargach; uaireannan truacanta le truas drùidhteach; uaireannan làn fuath is tàire is sgreamh; uaireannan àbhachdach, neònach, fìor; uaireannan eile toibheumach, no cràbhach; mar as trice, anabarrach, anameasarra; an còmhnaidh a' sireadh eòlais gun shuim do'n chosgais. So an t-anabarr:

I'll ha'e nae hauf-way hoose, but aye be whaur
Extremes meet — it's the only way I ken
To dodge the curst conceit o' bein richt
That damns the vast majority o' men.

So e a rithist, agus an sgreamh 'na cheann:

In wi' your gruntle then, puir wheengin saul,
Lap up the ugsome aidle wi' the lave,
What gin it's your ain vomit that you swill
And frae Life's gantin' and unfaddomed grave?

Agus a rithist:

For less than a' there is to see
'll never be owre muckle for me.

Cutty, gin you've mair to strip,
Aff wi' it lass — and let it rip!

Ach tha mìle eisimpleir de'n anabarr ladarna so anns an dàn, agus
chan urrainn dhòmhsa ach iomradh glé ghoirid a thoirt air iomadaidh
fuinn is gleusan a mhic-meanmna. Tha e sgaiteach:

Rabbie, wad'st thou were here — the world hath need,
And Scotland mair sae, o' the likes o' thee!
The whisky that aince moved your lyre's become
A laxative for a' loquacity.

Tha e a' dol sìos gu doimhne an eu-dòchais:

Grey sand is churnin' in my lugs,
The munelicht flets, and gantin' there
The grave o' a' mankind is laid bare
— on Hell itsel' the drawback rugs.

Nae man can ken his hert until
The tide o' life uncovers it,
An' horror-strack he sees a pit
Returnin' life can never fill!

Tha e làn truais is feirg:

Glesca's a gless whaur Magdalene's
Discovered in a million crimes.

Christ comes again — wheest, whatna bairn
In backlands cries betimes?

Hard faces prate o' their success,
And pickle-makers awn the hills.
There is nae life in a' the land
But this infernal Thistle kills. . .

Tha e fad as, air saoghal eile:

But ilka evenin' fey and fremt
(Is it a dream nae wauknin' proves?)
As to a trystin'-place undreamt,
A silken leddy darkly moves.

Tha e anns an t-sìorruidheachd, agus air an talamh as cumanta:

I tae ha'e heard Eternity drip water
(Aye water, water) drap by drap
On the a'e nerve, like lichtnin', I've become,
And heard God passin' wi' a bobby's feet
Ootby in the long coffin o' the street.

Tha an gaol ag éirigh os cionn a' chuirp:

Clear my lourd flesh, and let me move
In the peculiar licht o' love,
As aiblins in Eternity men may
When their swack souls nae mair are clogged wi' clay.

Be thou the licht in which I stand
Entire, in thistle-shape, as planned.
An no' hauf-hidden and hauf-seen as here
In munelicht, whisky, and in fleshly fear.

Aig amannan tha an saoghal agus na tha ann air an còmhdach le
solus biothbhuan:

These are the moments when my sang
Clears its white feet frae oot amang
My broken thocht, and moves as free
As souls frae bodies when they dee.
There's naething left o' me ava'
Save a' I'd hoped micht whiles befa'.

Agus a rithist:

> And as at sicra times am I
> I wad ha'e Scotland to my eye
> Until I saw a timeless flame
> Tak' Auchtermuchty for a name,
> And kent that Ecclefechan stood
> As part o' an eternal mood.

'Se dàn glé fhada a tha anns an *Drunk Man Looks at the Thistle*; tha mu thrì mìle sreath ann. Uime sin, cha b' urrainn gum biodh a h-uile bloigh cho math ris a' bhloigh eile. Nam biodh, cha bhiodh a leithid eile air an t-saoghal. Faodar aideachadh gu bheil beagan ath-aithris air an aon rud ann; agus faodar aideachadh cuideachd gur treamasgal e, agus a chionn gur treamasgal e, chan urrainn do'n mhac-meanmna a tha 'ga dhealbhadh a bhith daonnan cho teann 's a tha e glé thric. Faodaidh cuideachd gu bheil cus ainmean coigreach ann — seorsa de fhearas-mhór inntinne. Chan eil mi a' talach air Dostoevski, Blok, agus Melville, agus air an tarruing a tha MacDhiarmaid a' dèanamh orra-san agus air am buaidh. 'Se mialan móra an cuan an spioraid a tha annta-san; tha feum aig an dàn orra, agus cha mhisde e iad; ach tha cus spéis air a thoirt do chuideigin beag eile a bha anns an fhasan an uair a rinneadh an dàn. Nam b' e tarruing magaidh a rinneadh orra, mar a rinneadh air Carlyle is air Sir Harry Lauder, bhiodh an dàn nas cunbhalaiche. Chan eil an so ach gnothach beag, ach bheir e oilbheum do'n fheadhainn a tha àilleasach mu fhearas-mhór chàich. Tha fàilling nas miosa anns an dàn — dìmeas air a' chreutair chumanta dhaonda, gu h-àraidh air a' chreutair chumanta Albannach, Cruivie no Gilsanquhar. Tha an dìmeas so a' fàs nas doimhne agus nas farsainge:

> Millions o' wimmen bring forth in pain
> Millions o' bairns that are no' worth ha'en.

Ach faodar a bhith gu bheil an tàire so do-sgaradh o'n iomairt ladarna do-chlaoidhte inntinne a tha air siubhail MhicDhiarmaid; agus feumar cuideachd cuimhne a bhith againn gu bheil seòrsa de sgreamh dheth fhéin a' dol cuide ris an tarcuis a tha e a' dèanamh air càch; agus gur h-ann spioradail, agus nach ann idir saoghalta, a tha a freumh.

> My self-tormented spirit took
> The shape repeated in the thistle
> Sma' beauty jouked my rawny banes
> And maze o' gristle.

Chan eil e sàsaichte leis a' mhórachd a bhreithnicheas inntinn fhéin no inntinn sam bith eile; tha e a' spàirn gu faighinn cuidhteas gach teadhair a tha nàdur an duine a' cur air a spiorad. Tha a' ghleachd anabarrach so a' mairsinn fad trì mìle sreath de'n ranntachd as iongantaiche a chunnaic ar linn.

Cha b'urrainn gum biodh gach earrann de dhàn de'n mheud uile 'na bàrdachd (tha mi an dràsda a' cleachdadh an fhacail anns an t-seagh as àirde); air cho iongantach is a tha còmhradh ranntachd, agus tha an *Drunk Man* loma-làn de so, tha mullaichean ann de bhàrdachd a tha ag éirigh suas os cionn bàrdachd eile ar latha-ne gu àirde nach ruigear ach le MacDhiarmaid fhéin ann an *Sangschaw*, ann am *Penny Wheep* agus ann am bloigh no a dhà eile ann an *Cencrastus* agus ann an *Scots Unbound*. Mar a tha e fhéin ag ràdh:

> These are the moments when my sang
> Clears its white feet frae oot amang
> My broken thocht. . .

Am measg nan sgurrachan so tha an dà iasad a ghabh e o'n bhàrd Ruiseanach, Blok; agus an dàn a tha a' tòiseachadh, 'Drums in the Walligate. . .'; am fear a tha a' tòiseachadh, 'O wha's been here. . .'; am fear a tha a' tòiseachadh, 'The wan leafs shak atour us. . .'; agus na dhà mu dheireadh, 'The stars like thistle's roses floo'er. . .', agus 'Yet ha'e I silence left. . .'.

Ma tha bàrd nas fheàrr na MacDhiarmaid beò anns an Roinn Eòrpa chan aithne dhòmhsa. Cha chreid mi gu bheil a leithid an Sasainn, no san Fhraing, no an Albainn no an Eirinn.

Lament for The Makar

Poetry transfigures but does not fog reality or the Kantian phenomenon. Poetic orginality is relative but one can postulate many
degrees of originality even if there is no such thing as absolute
originality. In poetry originality is most important.

Romantic is one word often used in a pejorative sense to mean
fog-making. In poetry Hugh MacDiarmid transfigured many things
and, although the word 'Romantic' has been used of some of his
poetry, it has never been used but with admiration and approbation.

As different languages are the vehicles of poetry, and as ultimately
poetry cannot be translated, it is vain to call someone 'the greatest
living poet in Europe', as I would have called MacDiarmid; but I
think that if I knew thoroughly ten times the number of European
languages that I know inadequately, it would be difficult to convince
me that his poetic equal has existed in Europe this century.

Hugh MacDiarmid frequently decried the lyric, and having written
not a few but many supreme lyrics, he could do so without a 'sour
grapes' accusation. He wrote also *A Drunk Man Looks at The Thistle*,
which is surely a very great long poem with an astonishing variety and
an astonishing number of Crocean lyric peaks rising out of its 'flats',
and, to vary the metaphor, many crevasses of the unconventional and
the grotesque; for MacDiarmid's 'flats' are mostly very different from
nearly all 'flats' that had appeared before in European poetry.

It would be derogatory to use the normally complimentary word
'modern' of the sensibility of MacDiarmid's great lyrics, for 'modern'
suggests something less subtle, less universal, less original, almost the
following of a fashion, like an engine in which one sees the wheels
going round.

If ever a poet reached frontiers of perception, the MacDiarmid of
the great lyrics did, and it is most significant that almost at once acute
critics recognized their 'high seriousness' as well. They reach frontiers
at many points, and to me the frontiers are recognizable and real. Of
MacDiarmid's lyrics one can use the words intellect, imagination,
originality, a splendid use of language, however 'synthetic' his Scots
may be, and breathtaking rhythms.

I would be very surprised to learn that there has been a greater long poem written anywhere this century than MacDiarmid's *A Drunk Man Looks at The Thistle* with, among many other things, its daring, subtle, marvellously sustained and, as it were, organic symbolism, its *vis comica* and (if I may repeat Arnold's words) its high seriousness.

The almost universal recognition of the greatness of *A Drunk Man Looks at The Thistle* and the doubts about the subsequent long poems by MacDiarmid pose questions: how far can the imagist and symbolist go intellectually without a big counterpoise of the discursive; and how much imagery and symbolism is necessary when the long poem is mainly discursive.

I assume that symbolism was necesary to the intellectualization of poetry; whether it is still necessary, and to what extent, is a big question, made imperative in the Scotland of our day by the inordinate spiritual or, if you like, humanist courage and ambition of MacDiarmid, and his special brand of elitism, which makes so much other elitism look petty and vulgar.

His elitism led MacDiarmid to desire a poetry that would be self-conscious to the *n*th degree and at the same time welling from the depths of the subconscious, a poetry that would take in everything, compared with which the work of Lenin would be 'child's play'.

That much of MacDiarmid's later poetry suffered from its attempts on the impossible, being the work of a genius defying the limitations of the humam condition, must not make us forget that much of his poetry after *A Drunk Man Looks at The Thistle* would be impressive by any standard except that set by the three volumes of 1925-26 and the finer passages of *To Circumjack Cencrastus*, which came in 1928.

Those books of the Thirties and later contain many astonishing poems and some masterpieces, and some of them are in English, to which he gradually turned in the Thirties. I mention only a few of them and those not in order as to language or time: 'The Seamless Garment', 'Milk-Wort and Bog-cotton', 'Water Music', 'Tarras', 'At My Father's Grave', 'The Skeleton of the Future', 'On a Raised Beach', 'On The Ocean Floor', 'Second Hymn to Lenin', and many more.

MacDiarmid's intellectual and creative energy was immense, as is evident from the great corpus of his poetry and prose and his long and enduring political commitment. He became an avowed and active Socialist at the age of 16, and a Scottish Nationalist about the age of 35; but he was almost certainly one long before that.

When he was about 40, that is in the early Thirties, he became a Communist, and he remained a Communist and a Scottish Nationalist to the end. For over 50 years he was, and will remain, an intellectual and spiritual dynamo in Scotland.

He has been called a gadfly to Scotland, but the metaphor is unworthy of him, for he combined a supreme poetic sensibility, and astonishing intellectual energy, with a social and political activism rare in the, intellectual, and still rarer in the artist. The writer of ineffable lyrics could, in the words of Keats, usurp the height of the greatest committed poetry:

> 'None can usurp this height,' returned that shade,
> 'But those to whom the miseries of the world
> Are misery, and will not let them rest.'

MacDiarmid's courage was immense. I found his generosity very great.

Beul na h-oidhche

Bha beul na h-oidhche ann nuair a ràinig Dòmhnall mullach Bealach a' Mhàim. Thug e aon sealladh thar a' ghualainn dheis mun do dhùin slios fada Bruach na Frìthe Coire na Creiche air a chùlaibh. Anns an t-sealladh sin, mhothaich e ceann mór Sgùrr a' Ghreadaidh mar gum b' ann 'ga leanail. Bha gnè de ghaol àraidh aig Dòmhnall air Sgùrr a' Ghreadaidh, riamh o'n cheud uair a chunnaic e e dubh-ghorm ann an ròs an fheasgair, ri a cheud chuimhne, air dha dìreadh gu mullach bearraidh Achadh na h-Annaid. Bha cóig bliadhna deug air triall o'n oidhche sin, ach bha cuimhne aig Dòmhnall gu robh seòrsa de ghràin anns a' ghaol a bh'aige air Sgùrr a' Ghreadaidh; gràin a chionn gun do ghabh e farmad ris air sgàth Sgùrr nan Gillean, oir b'e Sgùrr nan Gillean a' cheud ghaol agus chaidh innse dha gun robh Sgùrr a' Ghreadaidh na b' àirde, agus an oidhche gheal chian ud, b'fheudar do shùilean fhéin sin aideachadh. Ach bho thoiseach bha an gaol anns an fhuath agus cha b' fhada gus an robh dà shealladh aig a mhac-meanmna air a' Chuilithionn: an sealladh faisg, far am b' àille Sgùrr nan Gillean; agus sealladh fad as: Sgùrr a' Ghreadaidh, geàrrte gorm anns an àird an iaras. Dh'fhàs Sgùrr a' Ghreadaidh gu bhith 'na ìomhaigh air a' Chuilithionn gu léir: bha e mar gum b' ann 'na rìgh air na h-ioghnaidhean dìomhair ùdlaidh a bha ag cuartachadh Coire na Creiche agus Coir' an Uaigneis.

Ghabh Dòmhnall roimhe gus an d' ràinig e an t-àite far a bheil an ceum a' ruigheachd an Uillt Dheirg — 'se bu chòir dha ràdh, far a bheil Allt an Fhionna-choire ag gabhail nan allt beaga, 's a' tionndadh an ear 's an eairreas sìos gu Loch Shligeachain. Nuair a chuir e seachad am Meall Odhar dh'éirich na cóig binneinean caola do-labhairt — Sgùrr nan Gillean. Bha Sgùrr a' Ghreadaidh air a dhol fo fhàire air a chùl — ach, a dh' aindeoin, bha e ann, far an robh e riamh. Sgùrr nan Gillean agus Sgùrr a' Ghreadaidh! Bha Dòmhnall air tobhtaichean móra na h-òige. Bha e ochd bliadhna deug.

Bha Glàmaig m'a choinneamh — mór maol an ciaradh na h-oidhche. Thàinig òran fhir-cinnidh a dh'ionnsaigh a bheòil:

Mi air m'uilinn ann an Glàmaig
'S esan làn agam air tulaich,

Ag gabhail seallaidh air na sléibhtean
Far am bi na féidh a' fuireach.

'S gann gun dìrich mi chaoidh
Dh' ionnsaigh frìth àrd a' mhunaidh,
'S gann gun dìrich mi chaoidh.

Thàinig litir o na h-uaislean
Nach fhaodainn luaidhe chur á gunna.
'S gann gun dìrich mi chaoidh.

Thàinig litir á Dùn-éideann
Nach fhaodainn fhéin a dhol do'n mhunadh.

Ach on dh'fhàs an lagh cho làidir . . .

Tigh na galla do na h-uaislean, 's do litrichean Dhùn-éideann, 's
do'n lagh a dh'fhàs cho làidir! Bha Dòmhnall cinnteach gum b'e sin a
bh' ann. Bha fhios aige nach tugadh Tarmod MacNeacail hó-ró orra
uile, a dh'aindeoin 's na thuirt an t-òran. Carson a bheireadh esan,
Dòmhnall MacNeacail, an còrr orra? Bha fhios aig an t-saoghal ciamar
a chaidh leotha-san a rinn an t-sabaid mu dheireadh ri 'fir mhóra a'
Bhràighe'. Bha Beinn Lì an siod mu choinneamh Glàmaig. Bha cas
Dhòmhnaill aotrom sìos an ceum, 's an t-Allt Dearg a' plumanaich 's
a' slugadh 's a' deocadh fichead troigh no dà fhichead troigh fodha.
' "Fir mhóra a' bhràighe" — chan eil móran dhiubh ann an diugh;
tha fhios agadsa air sin glé mhath nan leigeadh t'uabhar baoth òg
cothrom sam bith le t'eanchainn. . .'
Stad Dòmhnall gu grad. Thàinig guth tiamhaidh na feadaig-
mhonaidh:

Cha tog mi fonn aotrom
Bho Dhi h-aoine mo dhunaidh . . .

Ao, ao, ao . . . gun fhaoilte, gun fhuran . . .

'S gann gun dìrich mi chaoidh.

An robh Tarmod a' tuigsinn dé thuirt e? Mura robh, bha fear eile:

Cha dìrich mi bealach nan àrd
Le suigeart mar bha mo nòs. . .

Cha togar leam fonn air clàr,
Cha chluinnear leam gàir nan òg.

'Uabhar! t'uabhar baoth òg! Nan leigeadh t'uabhar baoth òg an
cothrom le t'eanchainn 's le do chridhe, thuigeadh tu. . .'

268

'S ann an uairsin a chunnaic Dòmhnall gu robh fear eile mu fhichead slat air thoiseach air. Bha an coigreach a' gabhail sìos rathad Shligeachain — mar a bha Dòmhnall fhéin, ach cha robh e idir a' tionndadh. Ghabh Dòmhnall seòrsa de ioghnadh 's chaidh gaoir neònach troimhe nuair a thuig e gun robh am fear eile a' bruidhinn ged nach robh e a' tionndadh fiù's a chinn.

'Tha thusa coltach ri do sheòrsa, agus 's ann mar sin a bhitheas tu. Cha ghabh thu comhairle sam bith gus an toir an saoghal ceann cruaidh a' bhata dhut mu'n t-sròin, ach tuigidh tu, tuigidh tu.'

'Dé thuigeas mi?' arsa Dòmhnall, 's e beothachadh a cheuma an tòir air an fhear eile. 'S e gnothach iongantach a bh' ann. Cha robh fhios aige có bh' ann. Bha an guth Sgitheanach gu leòr — bha iomadh guth de a sheòrsa sa' Bhràighe, ann an Sgonnsair, ann am Peighinn-nam-Fìdhleir, sa' Ghleann Mhór, mu Phort-rìgh, no mu Shnigheasort. Ach có bh' ann? Smaoinich Dòmhnall air an fheadhainn a bha aig an tigh á Glaschu no Grianaig no á àite sam bith eile.

'Tha fhios gun cuala e mi a' seinn,' arsa Dòmhnall ris fhéin. 'Tha fhios gur e sin a thug air gnothach a ghabhail rium. Dh'fhaodadh gur h-e seòrsa de Thòiridh a th'ann.' Thàinig seòrsa de dh' fhiamh a' ghàire mu bheul Dhòmhnaill nuair a smaoinich e air seo, ach dh' eubh e: 'Dé thuigeas mi? Fan 's inns' dhomh. Dé chabhag a th' ort?'

'Tuigidh tu an garradh-crìche a tha do nàdur fhéin ag cur mu do thimchioll, agus am buarach a tha mu d' chasan 's mu d' chridhe 's mu t'eanchainn — am buarach a tha thu fhéin 's an saoghal a' fighe — am buarach a dh' fhigheadh tu fhéin ged nach cuideachadh an saoghal idir thu. Ach 's esan a chuidicheas, agus bheir thu a chreidsinn ort fhéin gur ann aige-san a tha a' choire gu leir. . .'

'A' choire gu léir . . .,' dh'aithris Dòmhnall. ' 'S e ablach ceisteir a th' ann,' ars' esan ris fhéin.

'Bheil thu an dùil gur ann ag éirigh air a' Cheist am Port-rìgh no ann a Holoman a tha thu?' dh' eubh Dòmhnall àird a chlaiginn as déidh an fhir a bh' air thoiseach air.

Ach air a shon sin, cha robh coltas ceisteir idir air an fhear eile. A réir na dhèanadh Dòmhnall a mach dhe chumadh agus cuideam a cheuma, bha e eadar cóig deug ar fhichead agus dà fhichead bliadhna, agus cha robh an ad dhubh no an còta dubh air idir. Bha seacaid shoilleir ghlas air, 's cha robh ceap no bonaid idir air. Saoil an ann ri fealla-dhà a bha e?

'Tuigidh tu. . .'

Bha an coigreach mar gun robh e a' bras choiseachd seachad air a ghuth fhéin; bha a ghuth a' tighinn air ais air Dòmhnall mar gum biodh e a' tilgeil smugaidean seachad mullach a chinn 's a' gabhail air adhart, e fhéin coma càite 'n robh iad a' tuiteam.

'Tuigidh tu nach eil an gnìomh co-ionann ris na smuaintean no ris na briathran, agus gu bheil na smuaintean glé sheòlta gu iad fhéin a dhalladh. Tuigidh tu nach eil brìgh anns an dùrachd mur 'eil an gnìomh 'na cois; agus dé do ghnìomharan-sa? Chan fhiach iad hó-ró. Chan eil an gnìomh 'nad dheagh dhùrachd agus tha cus dheth 'nad iodhal-aoraidh; agus 'nad dheagh dhùrachd — ma tha beagan annad — tha a' chruithneachd 's am moll an ceann a chéile 'nam brochan lag truagh, ach tha t'iodhal-aoraidh a' dèanamh cùis-bhùrta dhìot — cùis-bhùrta bhochd ghrànda — miannan t' fheòla 'nad bharail fhéin mar fhàile driùchd air blàth an spioraid. Blàth an spioraid! Tùis bhreugach do d' chuinnlean maol!'

'Dé'n t-iodhal-aoraidh?' ghlaodh Dòmhnall, 'Dé'n tùis? Dé'n t-iodhal-aoraidh?'

Dh'éirich an guth, agus thàinig e o mhullach cinn an fhir eile.

'Iomadh iodhal-aoraidh: fear an dràsda, fear a rithist. An dràsda aon nighean. Laogh òir glé robach. Tha i caran suarach agus glé bhreugach, agus b' fheàrr leatha airgead na thusa, ach mura b'e gu bheil i air a dhol iomrall le fearas-mhór agus sannt an airgid, bhiodh barrachd tuigse aice na th' agad-sa; ach chan eil agaibh còmhla na chartadh bàthach aon mhart. Tha ise nas breugaiche ri càch na thusa, ach tha thusa nas breugaiche riut fhéin.'

'Dùin do bheul, a mhic . . . ' Stad Dòmhnall agus chaisg e an guidhe Sgitheanach a bha 'na bheul. Ghrios e cheum, ach rinn am fear eile an rud cianda. Bha peilearan nam facal is sian aca seachad mullach a chinn. 'Dé rinn thu riamh le do bhòilich bruidhne? Chan eil croitear no mart a bharrachd am Bràighe Thròndairnis no an Tròndairnis eile an lorg do sgoilearachd. Chan eil greim bidhe a bharrachd aig truaghain an cùiltean groda Ghlaschu. Chan eil facal Gàidhlig a bharrachd air sràidean Phort-rìgh. Chan eil làmh a bharrachd air a togail air sgàth còir an duine bhochd sa' Ghearmailt, sa' Spàin, 'san Eadailt, an Abisinia no 'san t-Sìn mhóir do bhrìgh do sheòrsa feall-sanachd, agus, ma tha, chan i do làmh-sa. Chan eil an Alba no an Sasuinn no an Eirinn. Goileam, goileam, goileam! Chan eil fhios agad dé tha bhuat — agus nan robh, cha bhiodh e bhuat — ach cha bhi, cha bhi, cha bhi!'

'Fuirich, a gharraich, ge bith có thu; fuirich!'

Ach éigheadh Dòmhnall mar a thogradh e, bha an aon shruth smugaidean no pheilearan fhacal a' tighinn seachad mullach cinn an fhir a bha a' griosad roimhe.

'Tha thu air latha a chosg a' streap am measg creagan a' Chuilithinn, feuch an toir thu a chreidsinn ort fhéin nach tu an gealtair as math is aithne dhut. Cha ruig thu leas. Biodh fir a' Bhràighe mór no beag. Ged a bheireadh tu a chreidsinn ort fhéin gum b'e Iain Garbh Mac Ghille Chaluim bràthair do sheanar agus Dòmhnall Mac Iain Mhic Sheumais bràthair do sheanmhar chan eil annadsa ach an cladhaire dhìot. Chan aithne dhutsa strì cogadh an anama. Chan eil eòlas agad air cogadh sam bith.'

'Dé'n t-eòlas a th' agad fhéin air cogadh, ma tha?' arsa Dòmhnall. 'Cha robh thu an cogadh a' Cheusair, chan eil thu an aois.'

'Cogadh a' Cheusair, cogadh a' Cheusair! 'S iomadh cogadh a bh' ann 's tha ann o sguir cogadh a' Cheusair. Tha mise ochd deug air fhichead, fichead bliadhna nas sine na thusa. Chunnaic mi cogadh gu leòr, gu leòr dhòmhsa co dhiùbh. Cha ruig mi a leas m' fheuchainn fhìn air creig no muir. 'S aithne dhomh mi fhìn, a thaobh sin, math gu leòr — ach thusa, chan eil annadsa ach an gealtair — an gealtair — an gealtair.'

Thòisich Dòmhnall air ruith as a dhéidh ag éigheachd. 'Ge bith de th' annam, gheibh thusa mach nach e 'n gealtair a th' annam.'

Cha robh tìde aige smaoineachadh dé dhèanadh e nam beireadh e air. Chan e gu robh e dol ga bhualadh. Cha tàinig sin suas air idir, ach bha e airson beireachd air, airson greim a dhèanamh air cùl amhaich air 's a chumail 's foghlum có bh' ann is dé bha bhuaithe. Bha am fear eile cuideachd 'na ruith, agus gu math luath cuideachd. Bha an ceum a nis air fàs glé chas an siod 's an seo, agus mar bu trice bha e cunnartach leis cho faisg 's a bha e air bruaich chais an Uillt Dheirg.

'Se Dòmhnall bu luaithe a réir choltais. Cha mhór nach robh e aig an fhear eile, nuair a thàinig sian pheilearan fhacal thar a dhà ghualainn.

'Amadain, cha bheir thu ort fhein.'

Dìreach an uairsin, rug fraochan bròg Dhòmhnaill air sgealb creige, agus chaidh e 'n comhair a chinn thar na bruaiche. Cha robh i glé àrd far na thuit e ach bhuail a cheann air cloich.

An uair a thàinig Dòmhnall gu bhreannachadh bha beul na h-oidhche air dùnadh gus na bhiodh ann de dhorchadas. Dh'éirich e 's e feuchainn a chinn. Bha beagan goirteis agus móran tuainealaich ann, ach cha robh e air tuiteam glé fhada. Gu fortanach thuit e far a b' isle a' bhruach. Bha an t-Allt Dearg mu dheich troighean bho'n àite 's na bhuail a cheann. An uair a dhìrich e dhruim bha Sgùrr nan Gillean mór, dìreach, làidir m'a choinneamh — na cóig binneinean air a dhol 'nan aon bheinn chuimir iargalta. Cha robh creutair beò ri fhaicinn, no fuaim ri chluinntinn ach eubh na feadag-mhonaidh, agus osagan na gaoithe mu fhaobhair a' Chuilithinn, plubartaich an Uillt Dheirg agus torrunn an uillt a tha brùchdadh troimh ghlomhar gàbhaidh a mach á Coire Bhàisteir, ach cha d' rinn Dòmhnall móran mothachaidh orra. Bha guth a' dol timchioll ann an tuainealaich a chinn: 'Amadain, cha bheir thu ort fhéin.' Ach an dràsda 's a rithist, thigeadh mar gum b'e a ghuth fhéin 's e ag ràdh, 'Thachair mi rium fhìn . . . Thachair mi rium fhìn . . . Thachair mi . . . '

Cha do sheas an Cuil-lodair

Cha robh e, mar a bha Uilleam Siosal, slinneanach leathann. Cha mhotha bha e, mar a thuirt Màiri Bhàn 'ain MhicLeòid an Camus Dianabhaig mu fhear eile, beag buaidheach no mór grànda. Cha robh mealladh sam bith ann; cha bu sgàthan òinsich e. Cha robh ann ach an truaghan dheth: beag, plamach; gun leud 'na ghuailnean; aodann dearg builgeineach; guth àrd caol. Bha speuclanan air, agus tha seòrsa de chuimhne agam gu robh a ghlùinean a' bleith a chéile. 'S e Sasunnach a bha ann, mar a bha anns a' mhór chuid de 'n réisimeid uaibhrich anns an robh e 'na oifigeach. Theireadh na saighdearan: ' 'S iomadh creutair caca tha 'na oifigeach anns an Arm Bhreatannach ach có 'n aon truaighe a rinn oifigeach de Mhgr. Lodan?' Cha toireadh saighdear feairt air, mur robh oifigeach a b' àirde 'san éisdeachd. Choimhideadh NCO thar a ghuailne feuch có bha faisg, agus 's e 'taigh na galla dhut' a gheibheadh Lodan, ma bha e ag iarraidh rud nach còrdadh, agus mur robh cluas inbheach a' cluintinn. Cha ghearaineadh Lodan bochd ri còirnealair, oir bha eagal air gun robh na h-oifigich a cheart cho beag truais ri fear nach cumadh smachd is a bha na saighdearan; cha robh a choltas na a ghiùlan fhéin 'na fhàbhar; cha robh e air a bhith riamh ann an cath, agus bha ceud reusan eile ann 'ga chumail 'na thosd, ged nach aithne dhomh-sa iad.

Bha dùil ri ionnsaigh latha sam bith. Anns a' cheud seachdain no dhà air dhuinn Libia a ruigheachd, b' e a' bharail gun robh sinne a' dol g'a dèanamh; gun tugadh na tancan móra Granndach againne fead air tancan Roimeil; ach ciamar a bheireamaid ionnsaigh troimh na mèin-ean eadar Gasàla is Bir Haicheim? Mu fhìor dheireadh na Céitein 1942 chaochail ar beachd. Bha a nis iomadh comharradh ann gum b' e Roimeal a thòisicheadh, ach ciamar? Bha na raointean mhèinean cho doirbh dhà-san is a bha iad dhuinne; agus có an seanalair air an t-saoghal a thigeadh timchioll deas air Bir Haicheim?

Bha Mgr. Lodan 'na chomanndair air trùp de cheithir gunnachan sia puinnd air carbadan. Bha sia gunnachan deug anns a' bhataraigh seo, a' cheud té de 'n t-seòrsa an Libia. Bha a h-uile coltas ann nach b'e an ceòl-gàire a bhiodh aig Lodan agus a leithid; agus gu h-àraidh mur robh na tancan Granndach cho math ri tancan Roimeil, no mur làimhsichteadh iad mar a dhèanadh Roimeal, bhiodh na gunnachan sia puinnd anns a' cheud shreath mu choinneamh armailt Roimeil. Theireadh saighdear, 'Dé nì Lodan anns a' chath?' Bha aon chomhfhurtachd aig na gunnairean a bha an trùp Lodan: 'Bidh cus eagail air fhéin; cha dèan e dad idir.'

Bha sinne air an làimh chlì de'n arm Bhreatannach. Bu sinne na tancan agus na gunnachan móra Breatannach a b' fhaisge air Bir Haicheim. Bha na Frangaich agus na Spàintich a bha am Bir Haicheim cho tapaidh ri fir air an t-saoghal, ach cha robh tancan no a bheag de ghunnachan móra aca-san.

Air an 27mh de'n Chéitein thàinig am fios, tràth 'sa' mhadainn, gun robh an t-arm Gearmailteach le mór-roinn an tancan, an carbadanairm is an gunnachan móra a' tighinn timchioll deas air Bir Haicheim. Air ball ghluais sinne 'nan coinneamh agus thòisich blàr thancan is ghunnachan móra; agus is iomadh barail a dh' atharraich r'a linn.

Choimhlionadh droch amharus no a dhà. Cha robh na Granndaich againne cho math ri tancan móra Roimeil; air neo cha robh seòltachd Roimeil aig ar comanndairean. Bha na Granndaich 'gan sìor chall; agus mar bu mhiosa call nan tancan, b' ann bu dorra do na gunnaichean, agus b'e gunnachan nan sia puinnd a chrean gu h-àraidh air call nan tancan. Bha iadsan a nis a' dìon ar tancan-ne bho thancan Roimeil, agus bha sgrios eagalach am measg nan gunnairean.

Bha mi fhìn mar bu trice air O.P. Uaireanan bhithinn faisg air ar gunnachan, ach iomadh uair 's ann a bhithinn còmhla ris na tancan. Cha d' fhuair mi ach sealladh an dràsda is a rithist air Lodan fad na ceud seachdaine; ach bha e soilleir gun robh gunnachan nan sia puinnd is gaisgich air an cùl; agus thuig mi nach b' e trùp Lodan bu tàire.

Thàinig aiteal soirbheachaidh roimh dheireadh na seachdaine. Bha sinne a' dol air ar n-adhart, agus bha beagan faochaidh ann. Bha dùil againn gun robh an latha leinn. De cheithir chomanndairan nan trùp sia puinnd, bha dithis marbh cheana, ach bha Lodan agus fear eile beò. Latha a bh' ann, an uair a bha deàrrsadh na gréine 'na h-àirde a' toirt seòrsa de sgur air na gunnachan móra le cion fradhairc, thàinig NCO de thrùp Lodain a nall far an robh mi. Bha e air gnothach, ach fhuair mi beagan mhionaidean 'na chòmhradh, agus bha mo cheistean 'nan sruth; có bha beò is có bha marbh is có bha leòinte? Bha móran marbh is móran air an leòn; agus cha robh dùil aige fhéin ri sìneadh saoghail. Chuir mi a' cheist nach gabhadh seachnadh mu Lodan fhéin. Chrath an NCO a cheann agus thuirt e beagan: 'Duine uamhasach! Chan 'eil a leithid anns an fhàsaich. Chan 'eil eagal idir ann. Chumadh e a ghunnachan far nach cumadh oifigeach eile air an t-saoghal iad.

Nan leigteadh leis, sheasadh e le aon ghunna ri réisimeid thancan. Mur b' e gu bheil ciall aig a' mhàidsear is aig caiptean na bataraigh, cha bhiodh duine dhinne beò an diugh. Gille glan laghach a tha an Lodan, ach curaidh — curaidh diabhlaidh! Mur téid a mharbhadh an là no dhà, chan fhàg e duine beò 'na thrùp.'

Thuig mi gun d' fhuair Lodan a chothrom. Thàinig an cogadh da-rìribh agus b' e dìol-déirce na réisimeid a prìomh ghaisgeach. Cha robh sgeul a bhàis fada gun tighinn. Dà latha 'na dhéidh, thug itealain Ghearmailteach le bombachan is frasan pheilear ruaig air bataraigh nan gunnachan sia puinnd. Ghabh gach oifigeach is gunnar gu dìon, agus cha robh an call mór. Mar bu nòs, b' e Lodan am fear mu dheireadh a chuir mu dhìon a ghabhail. Bha gach oifigeach is gunnar eile air am broinn an trainnsean no air a' ghainmhich luim, 'nuair a dh' éirich Lodan gu socair gu teàrnadh as a' chàr. Fhuair e fras pheilearan mu 'n stamaig.

Cha d' fhuair Lodan duais no bonn-suaicheantais. Ma chunnaic sùil inbheach dad de na rinn e ann an deich latha, cha do leig i oirre. Cha bu toigh leis a' chòirnealair Lodan. Bha am màidsear, fìor dhuine uasal, ri uchd bàis e fhéin; cha robh anns a' chaiptean ach an trusdar. Tha Mgr. Lodan anns an uaigh staoin faisg air Bir Bel Hamaid. Chan 'eil duslach na 's tréine an gainmhich Libia.

Dh'fhuirich Clann Domhnaill

Glé thric — cha mhór nach canainn, mar as trice — tha rud glé bhoireann anns a' churaidh. Cha robh teagamh nach bu churaidh an Caiptean Iarmar: chumadh e a cheann cho àrd neo-chùramach ri Seoc mór Caimbeul fhéin, nuair bu tighe na spealgan agus na peilearan; choisicheadh e a-measg shligean a' spreadhadh mar gum bu lòineagan sneachda iad. Ged a theireadh cuid gum biodh crithean a' tighinn air Iarmar nuàir a chiaradh an oidhche agus a bha strì an latha seachad, chan fhacas riamh air ach aogas a' ghaisgich 'ri uchd buailte'. Bha e 'na dhuine dreachmhor: mu chóig troighean is deich òirlich a dh'àirde: air a dheagh chumadh, le deagh aodann, ach gun robh a bheul cho boireann 's a chunnacas air fireannach — boireann ann an cumadh, chan ann am briathran no an guth. Bha e soilleir gun d' fhuair Iarmar àrach a-measg bùirdeasaich Shasuinn, 'na buic mhóra'; agus bha móran de bhuadhan an stuic ghràineil sin air. Cha robh ann an mór-roinn an Ochdamh Airm Bhreatannaich ach gràisg an sùilean a' Chaptein Iarmar; ach nuair a thogradh e fhéin, chluicheadh mealladh nam ban òga m'a shùilean agus m'a bheul boireann.

Cha robh Iain Howard 'na oifigeach, agus cha robh e 'na churaidh; cha bu mhò bha e 'na ghealtair. Cha do chaill e a thoinisg anns an fhìor chunnart, ach bha e 'faiceallach'. Chan fhàgadh esan a chorp ann an gainmhich Libia nan rachadh aige. Nan tilleadh MacLeòid, thilleadh Iain Howard, nam b' urrainn da. Uime sin, bha e air a bhroinn ann an trainns cho tric agus cho luath ri fear sam bith. Cha robh alladh a' churaidh fo'n ian do dh'Iain Howard.

Cha robh Dòmhnall Dòmhnallach 'na oifigeach, ach bha e 'na Dhòmhnallach. Chàidh móran iomrall air anns an arm. Cha chromadh a shùil fo shùil an ùghdarrais, agus chan iarradh e fàbhar air neach. Ràinig e Libia 'na shaighdear cumanta ged a bha uiread sgoile aige 's a bha aig fear sam bith san réiseamaid; ach cha robh a dhol as aige a niste. Bha e 'na shuidhe air cùl càir is a chluas ri bocsa frith-theud.

Bha Iain Howard anns an aon chàr is a chluas-san ri bocsa eile. Cha robh iad ach air ùr thighinn do'n bhataraigh anns an robh e.

Bha lasadh de uaill chunnartach ann an Dòmhnall Dòmhnallach.

Cà robh leithid a shinnsre-san anns a' bhlàr? An dà Inbhir Lòchaidh, Allt Eireann, Cill-Saoidh, Raon Ruairidh, Sliabh an t-Siorraim, Sliabh a' Chlamhain, an Eaglais Bhreac! Cà robh leithid nan Dòmhnallach, mur robh taobhan eile a shloinnidh: Leathanaich, Leòdaich, Clann MhicNeacail Sgoirebreac, 'fir mhóra a' Bhràighe', Mathanaich Loch Aillse, Clann MhicRath Chinn t-Sàile . . .! Bha an Gàidheal agus an Lochlannach air am filleadh an Dòmhnall, agus tigh dubh gorm na galla do gach Sasunnach agus gach Gall anns an Ochdamh Arm!

Cha robh cath ann, agus cha robh móran sam bith a' tachairt. Thigeadh is chuirteadh sanas leis a' bhocsa an dràsda 's a rithist. Thigeadh Iarmar gu cùl a' chàir agus chanadh e facal na dhà ri Dòmhnall, agus dh'fhalbhadh e an uair sin; ach cha robh e fada air falbh uair sam bith. Chitheadh Dòmhnall 's a chompanach a-mach air cùl a' chàir, ach chan fhaiceadh iad romhpa, no a-mach air an dà chliathaich. Uime sin cha robh Iarmar 'nam fradharc an còmhnaidh; ach bha fhios aca gun robh e faisg gu leòr airson a h-uile guth a theireadh iad a chluinntinn.

Bha norraidhean cadail a' tighinn air Dòmhnall ged a bha a chluas ris a' bhocsa. Chlisg e as aon norradh le sanas anns a' bhocsa, agus b' fheudar dha iarraidh an sanas a thoirt a rithist. Nuair a thàinig an sanas an dara uair, cha d' rug e air buileach, agus dh' iarr e a thoirt an treas uair. Bha Iarmar a niste 'na sheasamh aig cùl a' chàir.

'Amadain leibidich,' arsa Iarmar. 'Dé 'n donas a tha bhuat? Bheil thu bodhar?'

Thuirt Iarmar facal no a dhà eile, an 'teanga choitchinn' an ochdamh Airm, agus bha Dòmhnall air a thachdadh le tàmailt is le cuthach.

Fhuair Iarmar an sanas agus dh'fhalbh e gu beulaibh a' chàir. Bha an Dòmhnallach mar nach robh e riamh roimhe. Gum bruidhneadh Sasunnach, Gall no Gàidheal fo'n ghréin ris-san mar sud! Agus gun ghuth aige ri fhreagairt! Esan anns an robh fuil Mhic Iain Mhic Sheumais; fuil Iain Ghairbh Mhic Ghille Chaluim; fuil Eachainn Ruaidh nan Cath; fuil Ruairi Bhig Mhic Iain Mhic Ruairi Mhic Mhurchaidh Bhuidhe; fuil 'fir mhóra a' Bhràighe'; fuil . . .! Cha dubhairt Howard guth ris; thuig e gun 'deach an diabhal an gille dubh a' Bhràighe'.

Ann an deich mionaidean thàinig gleadhar luingeas-adhair. Leum Howard a-mach a choimhead, agus ruith e gu beulaibh a' chàir, far an robh an Caiptean Iarmar. An dà mhionaid bha e air ais, ag éigheach, 'Messerschmidtean! Tha 'n Caiptean Iarmar ag iarraidh ort dìon a ghabhail ann an trainns! Sa' mhionaid! Greas ort!'

Cha do ghluais Dòmhnall Dòmhnallach, ach dh'eubh e àird a chlaiginn — gus an cluinneadh Iarmar e 'Messerschmidtean! Can ri Caiptean Iarmar an sparradh . . .!'

Ruith Howard gu trainns, is dh' fhuirich an Dòmhnallach, 's e feadaireachd 's a' mànran ris fhéin, air an fhonn 'The Campbells are coming', mar bu tric a chuala e aig a sheanmhair:

Fir Chloinn Dòmhnaill, leóghainn gharga,
Sìoda 'gan còmhdach, sròl ri 'n garbh chrann;
Oganaich chuimir fhuair urram fir Alba,
Dh'fhàg an crup salach air chumadh na h-earba.

'Saoil,' arsa Dòmhnall ris fhéin, 'am bheil Iarmar air a bhroinn an bonn trainnse, mar a tha Howard agus gach fear eile sa' bhataraigh?' Chàidh sian is sian de pheilearan seachad, glé fhaisg, agus bha toll no a dhà an canabhas a' chàir; ach cha do bhuaileadh Dòmhnall. Cha mhò a bhuaileadh fear sam bith eile. Bha càch uile anns na trainnsean. Saoil an robh Iarmar 'nam measg, air a bhroinn? Cha do chuir Dòmhnall a' cheist sin an uair a dh'fhalbh na h-itealain Ghearmailteach, agus an uair a bha a chuid agus a chliù aige fhéin, an cùl a' chàir, is sogan aige air 'Fir Chloinn Dòmhnaill, leóghainn gharga'.

Thill Howard far an robh e, shuidh e air a bhocsa fhéin, agus cha dubhairt e guth ri Dòmhnall fad chóig mionaidean. An uair sin thàinig an Caiptean Iarmar. Bha sanas eile aige ri thoirt do Dhòmhnall, gus an cuireadh Dòmhnall a-mach e. Cha dubhairt e diog mu na h-itealain Ghearmailteach. Bha mealladh nam bàn òga 'na shùilean bòidheach agus m'a bheul boireann.

An tìr bu mhiann leam

Tha mu cheud gu leth bliadhna o thubhairt Ailean Dall:

Thàinig oirnn a dh'Albainn crois;
Tha daoine bochda nochdte ris,
Gun bhiadh, gun aodach, gun chluain:
Tha'n àirde-tuath air a sgrios.

Chan urrainn do dhuine sam bith a ràdh gu robh Nàdur ro choibhneil ris a' Ghàidhealtachd a thaobh toradh an fhearainn no a thaobh sìde, ach thug làmh an duine fhéin iomadh anacothrom air sluagh na Gàidhealtachd, agus theagamh gum b'e an t-anacothrom air an robh Ailean Dall a' bruidhinn, an t-anacothrom bu mhiosa thàinig riamh. B'e sin fògairt nan daoine air sgàth chaorach, agus fàsachadh nan gleann. Cha deach a' Ghàidhealtachd riamh os cionn sin, agus cha téid mur dèanar, eadhon aig an uair anmoch so, oidhirp na's motha na rinn Gàidheil riamh roimhe.

Feumaidh reusan buarach a chur air a' mhiann agus, a bharrachd air sin, feumaidh am miann e fhéin buil a thoirt a mach anns a' ghnìomh mum bi dad de fheum ann. Uime sin cha ruig sinn a leas caoidh nach 'eil a' Ghàidhealtachd cho torrach am fearann ris an Fhraing no ris an Ukraine, no cho bàidheil an sìde ris a' cheàrn as bàidheile sìde de Africa-mu-dheas; ach cha ruigear a leas a ràdh gu bheil e an aghaidh reusain a bhith miannachadh gu robh a' Ghàidhealtachd air a h-àiteachadh le sluagh cuimseach an àireamh a réir meud na dùthcha agus toradh an fhearainn; sluagh fallain, còir, sona; sluagh Gàidhealach; sluagh a' bruidhinn cànan nan Gàidheal; sluagh le ealain agus rath; sluagh saoibhir anns na buadhan as an urrainn Gàidheal uaill a dhèanamh.

Tha e soirbh gu leòr miann a chur am briathran. 'S e an dòigh air an toirear am miann gu buil ceist eile; agus 's ann mu dheidhinn nan dòighean agus nam meadhonan a dh'éireas a' chòmhstrith. Chan urrainn dhomh-sa leudachadh air beachdan sam bith ach na beachdan ris a bheil mi fhìn ag aontachadh. Seo pàirt dhiubh. Is e mo mhiann-sa gu robh a' Ghàidhealtachd 'na roinn inbhich de Albainn shaoir, sin

Alba fo a riaghladh fhéin, le pàrlamaid dhi fhéin. Tha mi cinnteach gu bheil Alba nas beairtiche a réir àireamh a sluaigh na tha Sasuinn, agus gu bheil Albannaich cho tuigseach air riaghladh 's a tha na Sasunnaich, agus gur i Alba Alba agus Sasuinn Sasuinn, agus gu bheil Alba a cheart cho dligheach air i fhéin a riaghladh 's a tha Sasuinn. Dh'iarrainn Pàrlamaid Albannach de dhaoine cumanta; chan ann de uachdarain fearainn, de luchd an airgid mhóir, no eadhon de fheallsanaich mar a dh'iarr an Greugach ainmeil Plato. Tha na feallsanaich as doimhne a cheart cho buailteach air a bhith calg-dhìreach an aghaidh a chéile 's a tha daoine cumanta; agus, a bharrachd air sin, có thaghadh na feallsanaich? Uime sin tha mi de'n bheachd gu bheil cunntas cheann a cheart cho math ri tomhas a' ghliocais. Tha iomadh seòrsa gliocais ann, agus chan eil còrdadh mu'n deidhinn.

Dh'iarrainn gum feumadh luchd an riaghlaidh cunntas a thoirt gu tric agus gu mionaideach do'n t-sluagh gu léir. Dh'iarrainn nach biodh móran eadar-dhealachaidh eadar bochd agus beairteach anns a' Ghàidhealtachd no an Albainn. Chan e miann airgid a ghin *Cumha na Cloinne* no ionnsaigh nan Gàidheal aig Cùil-lodair no saothair Dhòmhnallaich na Tòiseachd no saothair Chlach na Cùdainn no Mhurchaidh an Fhéilidh. Dh'iarrainn nach biodh aon uachdaran fearainn air a' Ghàidhealtachd. Tha mi tuigsinn gu bheil uachdarain gu tric ag cosg anns a' Ghàidhealtachd beagan de'n airgead a rinn iad mu dheas ach cha ruigeadh Gàidhealtachd cheart a leas am beagan spruidhlich sin. Bu toigh leam fearann na Gàidhealtachd fhaicinn fo thuathanaich bheaga no chroitearan móra, a' pàigheadh màl do'n Stàt, agus sin Stàt a dhèanadh barrachd na's urrainn do Bhòrd an Aiteachais a dhèanamh. Bhiodh daoine mar sin air an dìon leis an Stàt nuair thigeadh tinneas no seann aois orra. An lorg sin, dh'fhaodadh gum biodh e freagarrach gun gluaisteadh cuid bho cheàrnaidhean anns a bheil cus sluaigh gu ceàrnaidhean anns nach 'eil. Dh' fhaodadh, abair, gum biodh cuid de shluagh Leódhais na b'fheàrr an Siorrachd Pheairt, ach dh' fheumadh sin a bhith air a dhèanamh le làn thoil an t-sluaigh a ghluaisteadh. A bharrachd air an fhearann a bhiodh fo thuathanaich bheaga, dh'iarrainn gum biodh an siod agus an seo tuathanas mór aig àireamh chuimseach an co-phàirt, agus gum biodh a roghainn aig a' Ghàidheal a bhith 'na thuathanach beag air a cheann fhéin, no 'na bhall de chompanaidh a dh' oibricheadh tuathanas mór an co-phàirt, mar a thatar ris ann an cuid de rìoghachdan na Roinn-Eòrpa mar thà.

Bhiodh e ceart gu faigheadh tuathanaich na Gàidhealtachd gach comhairle agus gach goireas bho cholaistean obair-fearainn a b' urrainn an Stàt a thoirt, agus gum biodh gach feum a b' urrainn air a chur air clach-aoil na Gàidhealtachd gu bhith a' mathachadh an fhearainn. Tha mi de'n bheachd gu feum a' Ghàidhealtachd a dhol air ais gu togail chruidh air son marbhaidh, agus nach dèan caoraich leotha fhéin an gnothach. Tha an crodh cho math do'n fhearann, agus tha sìde agus fasgadh na Gàidhealtachd cho math air son an geamhrachadh.

Tha fhios gu feum barrachd sluaigh an teachd-an-tìr a thoirt o'n fhearann, agus ma dh'fheumas feadhainn tighinn o na bailtean a dh' ionnsaigh na Gàidhealtachd, tha mi an dòchas gur h-e sliochd nan Gàidheal a thig. Chan urrainn gum bi ceathrar a mach as gach cóignear de shluagh na h-Albann a' fuireach am bailtean móra anns an aimsir ri teachd, oir chan urrainn gum bi marsantachd na h-Albann ri tìrean céine cho mór 's a bha i aon uair. Uime sin, feumar am barrachd feum a dhèanamh de fhearann na h-Albann.

A thuilleadh air obair fearainn, tha mi an dòchas gum bi obraichean eile air an sgapadh air feadh na dùthcha mar tha Riaghladh na h-Eireann a' dèanamh an dràsda; faiceamaid cho ealamh 's a rinn iadsan port itealan móra am feadh 's a bha sinne a' feuchainn ri làn fheum a dhèanamh de Phrestwick. Agus ma tha cumhachd nan uisgeachan air a cur am feum a chum math na dùthcha, faodar sin a dhèanamh ged nach 'eil móran guail air a' Ghàidhealtachd. Dìreach mar a dh'fheumar margadh a' chruidh 's nan caorach a thoirt bho na dròbhairean, feumar margadh an éisg a ghlacas na h-iasgairean a bhith an làmhan feadhainn a bheir barrachd spéis do na h-iasgairean agus do'n t-sluagh gu léir na thatar a' toirt an dràsda. Gu sònraichte, feumar na rathaidean iaruinn agus na bàtaichean smùide a chur fo chumhachd an riaghlaidh gus am bi aig an t-sluagh gu léir facal ciamar a bhios nithean feumail air an craobh-sgaoileadh air feadh na dùthcha; agus feumar iolaichean iasgaich a bhith air an dìon bho thràlairean mar nach eileas a' dèanamh an diugh.

Dé ghabhas dèanamh fhad 's a tha an gnothach an làmhan muinntir nan tràlairean agus an leithid, a nì mar a thogras iad fhéin? Tha cor na Gàidhealtachd a' dol a dhìth cho mór 's nach urrainn do na bàtaichean smùide cumail ris gun chuideachadh bho'n Stàt. Tha muinntir nan trèanachan a' bruidhinn air cuid de na rathaidean iaruinn a dhùnadh a chionn is nach 'eil iad a' pàigheadh dhaibh. Tha muinntir nam bàtaichean agus luchd an rathaid iaruinn an làmhan a chéile, agus an Stàt air an cùl. Nach biodh e riatanach gum biodh riaghladh na h-Albann aca-san aig am biodh tuille tuigse air cor na Gàidhealtachd agus barrachd spéis dhi, agus gum biodh an leithid-san air ceann gnothaichean cho cudthromach?

A thaobh foghluim, dh'iarrainn gu faigheadh gach gille agus

nighean anns a' Ghàidhealtachd am foghlum air a bheil a ghibhtean comasach agus a tha freagarrach dha ge b'e cho bochd 's a tha a phàrantan, agus gum biodh an teagasg so air cùl gach teagaisg eile: gur h-e Alba agus Gàidhealtachd na h-Albann a dhùthaich-san, agus gu bheil e m'a choinneamh-san a dhìcheall a dhèanamh air sgàth na Gàidhealtachd agus na h-Albann agus chan ann air a sgàth fhéin anns na h-Innsean no an Africa no an àite sam bith eile. Dh'iarrainn gu robh a' Ghàidhlig air a meudachadh le faclan ùra o'n Laideann agus o'n Ghreugais air chor 's gum biodh e cho soirbh do fheallsanach labhairt air an nì as diamhaire sa' chruthachadh an Gàidhlig 's a tha e anns a' Bheurla. Bu mhath leam gu robh leth-dusan pàipear naidheachd Gàidhlig 'gan leughadh an dachaidhean nan Gàidheal. B' fheàrr leam gum biodh bàird ann a fhreagradh ar tìm mar a fhreagair an Clàrsair Dall agus MacMhaighstir Alasdair agus Dùghall Bochannan an latha fhéin, agus gu robh sgrìobhadairean rosg ann a sgrìobhadh air ceud dòigh cho ealanta 's a sgrìobhas Dòmhnall MacLaomuinn no Coinneach MacLeòid 'nan dòighean fhéin, agus gu robh luchd-ciùil ùra ag éirigh suas a bhiodh do ar latha-ne mar a bha Pàdruig Mór MacCruimein no an Clàrsair Dall do'n latha fhéin.

Chan 'eil fhios an e doilgheas as fheàrr gu buadhan sluaigh a thoirt am follais no 'n e sonas, ach chan urrainn do neach reusanta doilgheas a ghuidhe do a shluagh ge b'e cho mórail 's a dh'fhàgadh an doilgheas iad. 'S e nàdur an duine sonas a shireadh, agus 's e nàdur mì-fhallain a tha ann, sonas iarraidh troimh'n doilgheas, agus dh'iarrainn nach toireadh eud air son Sailm Dhàibhidh air uimhir de Ghàidheil dìmeas a dhèanamh air òrain Uilleim Rois.

A bheil dòchas ann airson na Gàidhlig?

A chionn gu bheil Alba 'na dùthaich roinnte, gun a riaghaltas fhéin, fo smachd luchd na maoine, biodh an ainm Albannach no coigreach, cha b'urrainn cor na Gàidhlig a bhith ach truagh, air cho libearalach 's a dh'fhaodas réim a bhith an dràsda 's a rithist. Tha a buil dhosheachanta aig eachdraidh nan Gàidheal anns an dà cheud bliadhna on a thòisich claoidh na cainnte, togail na tuatha agus fàsachadh nan gleann. Chan ioghnadh idir gu bheil an t-eu-dòchas trom air spiorad a' Ghàidheil, gu h-àraidh ma tha e 'na bhàrd no 'na sgrìobhadair no 'na fhear oideachais de sheòrsa sam bith. Mar a thuirt am bàrd mór Albannach, MacDhiarmaid:

Feumaidh filidh ar dùthcha
Uallach dàn a dhaoine ghiùlan.

Is dual do'n bhàrd gaol a thoirt do a chànain fhéin mas i cànan a shìnnsre 's i ag cnàmh, eadhon ged a bhitheadh i 'na rud bochd leibideach. Chan eil a' Ghàidhlig 'na cainnt bhochd, ann an ealain co-dhiùbh. Ged nach robh aice ach a h-òrain dho-innse, nach gabh cur ann am briathran eile, bhitheadh i 'na meadhon labhairt air nach cuirear prìs. Uime sin, feumaidh an sgrìobhadair Gàidhealach a bhith 'polaiteach', agus anns an latha anns a bheil sinne beò, 's e teagasg na cànaine prìomh ghnothach a 'pholaiteachd'.

Ri mo linn-sa 's e luchd-teagaisg na Gàidhlig anns na sgoiltean, agus chan e an luchd ealain, a rinn an spàirn as motha ann an togail air an guaillean sgìthe fhéin uallach cor ar cànaine, agus gu h-àraidh iadsan a lean eisimpleir Dhòmhnaill MhicThómais ann an teagasg na Gàidhlig do chloinn aig nach robh i 'na cainnt mhàthaireil.

Cha robh 'Clàs Gàidhlig 1918' gu móran feuma ann an sgoiltean a' bhun-oideachais; ach anns na h-àrd-sgoiltean, fhuair clann aig an robh Gàidhlig cheana an cothrom a leughadh agus a sgrìobhadh ionnsachadh, mar bu trice mura gabhadh iad an Fhraingeis. B'e a' bhuil gu robh teagasg na Gàidhlig air a chumail air cùl dhorsan glaiste anns an iomall shiar, far nach cuireadh e éis air cloinn nam bùirdeasach beaga no meadhonach anns na bailtean móra no beaga no meadhonach. Eadhon anns an Aird-a-tuath fhéin chailleadh leth-cheud bliadhna eadar 1918 agus 1968, oir ged a thòisich Dòmhnall MacThómais agus a bheagan luchd-leanmhuinn ann an Earra-Ghàidheal air an obair mhóir mu 1935, 's e bristeadh-cridhe a bha aca 'nan obair gu 1968. Thòisich Ard-sgoil an Obain air Gàidhlig a theagasg do chloinn aig nach robh eadhon facal dhith aig aois dusan bliadhna, ach ann an cóig bliadhna dh'fheumadh a' chlann sin an t-aon Ard-Phàipear Gàidhlig a ghabhail 's a ghabhadh clann aig an robh Gàidhlig mar cheud chànain. Mhair an staid thruagh nàr sin gu 1968, ach thug 1968 cothrom ùr do luchd-teagaisg agus do phàrantan aig a bheil fìor ùidh ann an cànain an sìnnsre. An diugh tha fada bharrachd ag ionnsachadh Gàidhlig ann an àrd-sgoiltean na h-Aird-a-tuath, ach chan eil ann an seo ach toiseach tòiseachaidh seach mar bu chòir, oir fhathast 's e glé bheag Gàidhlig a thatar a' teagasg ann an sgoiltean na Gàidhealtachd, gun tighinn idir air sgoiltean nam bailtean móra agus na Galldachd. Ma tha iuchair ann a leasaicheas cor na Gàidhlig, 's e foghlum sgoiltean na h-òigridh an iuchair anns a bheil a prìomh dhòchas.

Cha toirear laghannan do ghinias ann an rosg no rann, ach faodar cuideachadh a thoirt dha le goireasan clòtha agus craobh-sgaoilidh. A dh'aindeoin na tha *Gairm* agus Club Leabhar a' dèanamh, chan eil e fhathast soirbh do rosg no rann Gàidhlig clò a ruigheachd gun eadar-theangachadh Beurla 'nan cois. Tha sin glé throm gu h-àraidh air bàrd ma tha barrachd ann an cumadh a bhàrdachd na 'rosg sliseagach' gun bhuaidh air a' chluais. Anns an deich bliadhna fichead mu dheireadh tha bàrdachd thar cuibheis anns a' Ghàidhlig, agus móran de rosg cuideachd a tha beothail annasach — sgeulachdan goirid, aistidhean, dràma, etc. Is tearc fìor bhàrdachd ann an cànain sam bith aig ám sam bith, ach as t-fhoghar-sa chaidh leughadh dhomh air fón Sgitheanach dàn ùr[1] anns a bheil a' ghaoir lireach a mheas Croce agus iomadh sgrùdair eile mar phrìomh chomharradh an nì ris an canar bàrdachd; agus o chionn mìos thuirt sgrùdair ainmeil rium mu leabhar ùr de sgeulachdan goirid[2] (nach fhaca mi fhìn fhathast): 'Ginias, gun aon teagamh'. Is mór am facal 'ginias'.

Cha ghin laghannan na buadhan as àirde, ach faodar a bhith gun dùisg fhathast ann an Albainn shaoir shòisialaich spiorad a shàbhaileas a' Ghàidhlig, air neo gun tig slàinte na Gàidhlig mar bhuil air an spiorad a tha a' strì ri Alba a dhèanamh saor sòisialach.

EARR-NOTAICHEAN

1 *Bliadhna mhór na stoirme* le Caitrìona NicGumaraid.
2 *An Aghaidh Choimheach* le Iain Moireach, Gairm, Glaschu 1973.

Is there a hope for Gaelic?

Since Scotland is a divided country, without its own government, dominated by capitalists, whether their names are Scottish or foreign, the state of Gaelic could not be anything other than wretched, however liberal a regime may be at times. The history of Gaeldom in the two hundred years since the oppression of the language, the clearances and the desolation of the glens began, has its inevitable result. It is no wonder that despair is heavy on the spirit of the Gael, especially if he is a poet, writer or educator of any kind. As the great Scottish poet MacDiarmid has said:

> A Scottish poet maun assume
> The burden o' his people's doom.

It is natural for a poet to love his own language if it is the language of his ancestors and dying, even if it were a poor defective thing. Gaelic is not a poor language, in art at any rate. Though it had only its ineffable songs, which cannot be put in other words, it would still be a priceless medium of expression. Therefore the Gaelic writer must be 'political', and in our day the teaching of the language is the prime business of its 'politics'.

In my lifetime, it has been the school teachers of Gaelic, and not the artists, who have made the greatest effort in lifting on their own weary shoulders the condition of the language, and especially those who followed the example of Donald Thomson teaching Gaelic to children who did not have it as a mother tongue.

The 'Gaelic Clause of 1918' was not of much good in primary schools, but in the secondary schools, children who already had Gaelic got a chance to read and write it, generally if they did not take French. The result was that the teaching of Gaelic was confined behind locked doors to the western extremity, where it would not hinder the children of the petty or middle bourgeoisie in the big or little or middling towns. Even in the Highlands fifty years were lost between 1918 and 1968, for, although Donald Thomson and his few followers in Argyll began their great work about 1935, their work was a heartbreak until 1968. Oban High School began to teach Gaelic to children who had not even a word of it at the age of twelve, but in five years those children had to take the same Higher Gaelic paper as children who had Gaelic as their first language. This sad and shameful state of affairs lasted until 1968, but 1968 gave a new chance to teachers and to parents who have a genuine feeling for the language of their ancestors. Today far more learn Gaelic in the secondary schools of the Highlands, but this is only the beginning of a beginning compared with what ought to be, for even now it is very little Gaelic that is being taught in Highland schools, not to mention the schools of the cities and the Lowlands. If there is a key to improve the state of Gaelic, school education of the young is the key in which its prime hope is.

Laws are not given to genius in prose and verse, but it may be helped by facilities of printing and broadcasting. In spite of what *Gairm* and Club Leabhar are doing, it is not yet easy for Gaelic prose or verse to achieve print without an accompanying English translation. This is very hard especially on a poet if there is more to the form of hs poetry than 'chopped prose' with little impact on the ear. In the last thirty years there has been a more than competent poetry in Gaelic, and much prose that is lively and interesting — short stories, essays, drama, etc. Real poetry is rare in any language at any time, but last Autumn there was read to me on a Skye telephone a new poem[1] in which there is the lyrical cry that Croce and many other critics have considered the first mark of the thing called poetry; and about a month ago a noted critic told me that a new book of short stories[2] (which I myself have not yet seen) was 'genius, without a doubt'. 'Genius' is a big word.

Laws do not beget the highest qualities, but it may be that there will yet awaken in a free socialist Scotland a spirit that will save Gaelic, or that the salvation of Gaelic will come as a result of the spirit that is striving to make Scotland free and socialist.

NOTES

1 *Bliadhna mhór na stoirme* by Catriona Montgomery.
2 *An Aghaidh Choimheach* by John Murray, Gairm, Glasgow 1973.

286

Ceit NicLeòid

Ma théid a' Ghàidhlig bàs caillidh Alba nithean do-labhairt an luach, agus caillidh na Gàidheil cha mhór an uile. Tha an smuain sin 'ga cur an céill cho tric 's gu bheil i air a brìgh a chall agus cha drùidh i oirnn a nis mar bu chòir. Agus, ma thréigeas a' Ghàidhlig, dé bhitheas air fhàgail de'n dùthchas aig ar sliochd? Faodar gu bheil ann, agus gum bi ann, pìobairean gun Ghàidhlig a chluicheas 'Cumha na Cloinne' mo 'Maol Donn' air dhòigh nach tugadh oilbheum do Chloinn Mhic Cruimein no do Chloinn Mhic Aoidh. Their cuid d'an aithne gu faod gum bi — cha ghabhainn-sa orm fhéin barail a thoirt — ach tha fios is cinnt ma dh'fhalbhas a' Ghàidhlig, nach bi neach air an t-saoghal, ge biorach a chluas, a chluinneas 'Oran Néill Uidhir' no 'Cairistìona' no fear sam bith eile de na h-òrain sin a tha 'nan sìor chùis ìoghnaidh do gach cluais a chleachdar riutha. Ged a mhaireas guth Ruari Iain Bhàin no guth Chaluim Mhic Iain air clàir, có gun Ghàidhlig a chluinneas iad? Thig latha anns nach bi neach beò a thuigeas gu h-iomlan an t-eadar-dhealachadh a tha eadar an dòigh anns an do sheinneadh 'Iomair thusa, Choinnich chridhe' le Ceit NicLeòid agus an dòigh anns an seinnear e le 'Hector Hamish MacKay'. Tha feum aig òran air faclan agus tha feum aig faclan air an cànain fhéin; bidh feum aca air faclan an cànain fhéin am beul neach aig a bheil fìor eòlas agus fìor ghaol air a' chànain sin; agus nan cuirteadh a' cheist, có aige an diugh am measg seinneadairean ainmeil nan Gàidheal a tha guth àlainn agus eòlas coimhlionta agus gaol éifeachdach air a' Ghàidhlig, có an t-ainm a leumadh gu gach beul ach ainm Ceit NicLeòid?

Tha iomadh buaidh air seinn Ceit NicLeòid. Mar a nochd mi cheana, tha a h-eòlas air a' Ghàidhlig gun aon mhac-samhuil am measg chàich a fhuair an cliù as àirde anns an t-seinn. Tha a h-eanchainn anabarrach: fhuair i prìomh dhuais na feallsanachd bho Oilthigh Dhun-éideann mu'n ám a fhuair i bonn òir a' Mhòid Mhóir. Tha an t-eòlas ceart aice air ceòl a dùthcha, oir tha Sgìre Nis fada na's saoibhire anns na seann òrain na tha an saoghal a' tuigsinn, agus ma tha nì prìseil ann nach d'fhuair Ceit an Leódhas a dùthchais, fhuair i e bho Chloinn Mhic Iain Bharraidh agus bho thobraichean glana eile an

Uibhist no am Barraidh. Thug nàdur dhith guth soilleir àlainn agus cha do mhill i e le spàirn nan lùth-chleasan 'ciùil' a tha a' mealladh mórain. Tha spéis aice do bheul-aithris a daoine, agus cha do bhreugaicheadh bho sin i le moladh no le di-moladh — agus fhuair i a cuibhrionn de'n dà chuid — agus tha comas aice air rithim nach cuirear an céill ach leis an fhacal 'mìorbhaileach'. Tha an comas sin cho cinnteach an uair a sheinneas i òran mall tiamhaidh 's a tha e anns a' phort-a-beul as mireiniche a ghabhas i: tha gach seòrsa a' tighinn bhuaipe gun strì gun spàirn, mar nach robh seachnadh air, agus is comharradh sin air an ealain as àirde. Their na Sasunnaich 'inevitability' ris a' bhuaidh sin, a' bhuaidh as glòrmhoire a thig gu fear ciùil no fear dàin.

Chan eil Ceit de'n dream a ghabhas orra fhéin leasachadh a dhèanamh air òrain nan Gàidheal. Cha robh i de'n dream sin an uair a fhuair iad urram, agus tha an latha sin seachad. Tha ise, mar gum beadh, de ghnè a' chiùil a chuireas i an céill, agus ma nì i atharrachadh sam bith an òran, tha an t-atharrachadh de fhìor ghnè an òrain. Uime sin, chan eil i uair sam bith a' fiaradh beul-aithris; 's ann a tha i ag cur ris. Tha i fhéin, 'anns a' bheul-aithris'. Chan eil i a' feuchainn ri cumaidhean Sasunnach no Gearmailteach no Eadailteach a chur air ceòl nan Gàidheal agus do bhrìgh sin tha i a' faighinn urraim bho na Sasunnaich, na Gearmailtich agus na h-Eadailtich do'n aithne ceòl.

Is mór an call nach cluinnear i nas trice, oir is mór am feum a tha oirre an dràsda, agus tha a comas cho farsaing 's a tha e anabarrach, agus 's urrainn dhi sòlas as fhiach a thoirt do gach seòrsa. Rachainn fhéin fada g'a h-eisdeachd a' seinn 'A Phiùthrag 's a Phiuthar' no 'Oran Mór MhicLeòid' no 'Fliuch an Oidhche' no 'O 's tu 's gura tu th'air m'aire' no 'Niall Odhar' no 'Calum Sgàire' no 'Làrach do thacaidean' no òran sam bith a thaghadh i á ionmhas ioma-ghuthach ceòl nan Gàidheal.

An t-Ollamh Aonghas
MacMhathain

Chan eil ann glé fhada o chuala mi 'ga ràdh mu sgoilear àraidh: 'Se tha anns an duine 'tycoon'; chan e ollamh foghluim.' Bha am fear a thug a' bhreith ag ciallachadh nach robh am fiosrachadh an 'tycoon' ach uinneag air uinneig de mharsantachd eòlais, agus gu robh e cho trang a' reic a chodach, 'ga cur fa chomhair an t-saoghail mhóir 's nach robh daondachd 'na blàth; gu robh a flùraichean air laomadh gu h-àrd agus gu tioram, agus nach robh fàileadh no mìlse air a siubhal. Chan eil ollamh an Albainn air as lugha dreach an 'tycoon' na Aonghas MacMhathain, agus mar a thubhairt ceannaiche am Port-rìgh ri té a bha ag gearan nach robh a nighean coltach rithe fhéin, cha b'ann bu lugha orm dad e.

Fhuair Aonghas deagh chothrom air a bhith 'na fhìor Ghàidheal, eadhon 'na Ghàidheal air leth. Se Leódhasaich a bha 'na athair 's 'na mhàthair, ach tha fuil Mhurchaidh Bhuidhe Loch Aillse ann cuide ri fuil Dhòmhnaill Chaim Uige. Rugadh e anns na h-Earadh agus fhuair e a' chuid mhór de àrach an Sollas an Uidhist. Fhuair e fhoghlum an Sollas agus an Inbhirnis, agus an Oilthighean Dhùn-Eideann, Bhaile Atha Cliath, agus Bhonn na Gearmailte. Am measg a luchd-teagaisg bha MacBhàtair, Bergin agus Thurneysen agus ficheadan de luchd sgeòil agus òran an Uidhist agus an Leódhas agus anns gach ceàrnaidh de'n Ghàidhealtachd anns an robh e riamh, oir se Aonghas an seòrsa duine air a bheil dà bhuaidh nach tig tric an ceann a chéile: gu bheil an aon ùidh aige am beul-aithris an t-sluaigh agus anns an lamh-sgrìobhainn as sine an Eirinn; agus gur h-e fear do'm fosgail an seanchaidh a bheul, agus chan ann a tha an t-iongnadh, oir, a thuilleadh air a' choibhneas a tha ann — agus gu h-àraidh ris an aois — dh'fhaodadh e an agairt seo a dhèanamh: *nil Gadelicum a me alienum puto*. Tha a' bhuil air, gu bheil eòlas anabarrach aige air cainnt is eachdraidh is beul-aithris gach cinnidh is gach ceàrnaidh anns a' Ghàidhealtachd; ach tha e 'na fhear-eachdraidh cumhachdach air an dòigh as fharsainge cuideachd, agus chan eil a choltas air gun téid e air bhoile le fìon nan Cruithneach, misg nan sgoilearan Gàidhealach.

Tha gibht bheairteach bheothail aig an Ollamh MacMhathain anns na cànainean. Dh'fhaodadh nach eil e ag gabhail air fhéin gu bheil fichead cànain aige, ach tha gu leòr. Chunnaic mi mar a dh'ionnsaich e an Fhraingeis — na fhuair e de eòlas ann an ùine cho goirid, agus chan eil aon teagamh nach eil e nas coimhlionta an Gàidhlig na h-Eireann na tha sgoilear Eireannach sam bith an Gàidhlig na h-Albann, agus uime sin cha robh ann ach mullach an aineolais nan robh Oilthigh Ghlaschu air a dhol gu coigrich a dh'iarraidh fir a lìonadh a' chathair ùr. Dh'fhaodadh nach eil uiread an clò aig Aonghas MacMhathain 's a tha aig cuid, ach cha mheasar sgoilear le a chur a mach an clò. Tha e coltach gu robh doimhne agus géire anns a' bhreannachadh a bha aig an Ollamh MacFhionghuin air litreachas, agus gu robh sin soilleir d'a oileanaich, ach fhad 's as aithne dhòmhsa, cha do nochdadh sin anns na chuir e an clò. Agus, mur do chuir an t-Ollamh MacMhathain a chorran anns gach raon sgrìobhaidh, chuir e as a dheaghaidh arbhar trom ann an raon cho duilich 's a ghabhadh fheuchainn. Chan eil teagamh nach do ghabh e os làimh anns a' chóigeamh leabhar de *Charmina Gadelica* obair cho deuchainneach 's a thigeadh air sgoilear sam bith, agus chan eil teagamh nach eil iomadh annas air a làimh. A thaobh na tha ann de fhìor bhàrdachd — nì glé ainneamh an àite sam bith — agus an sgil leis a bheil i air a deasachadh, tha an cóigeamh leabhar de *Charmina Gadelica* 'na obair foghluim a chuireadh loinn air oilthigh sam bith.

Aig uair mar seo, is Gàidhlig na h-Albann 'na h-éiginn, se nì mór a tha ann gu bheil an cathair Cheilteach Oilthigh Ghlaschu fear air nach toirear bàrr ann am fìor eòlas air cainnt a shìnnsre agus a chomh-aoisean; agus a chionn gu bheil sgoilearan an t-saoghail a' dèanamh toiseach tòiseachaidh air toirt fainear gu bheil luach do-thuigsinn anns na h-òrain Ghàidhlig mar bhàrdachd agus mar cheòl, se nì mór a tha ann gu bheil ann an àrd inbhe an fhoghluim Cheiltich an Albainn fear a fhuair gleusadh cluaise riutha-san an uair a bha e glé òg — fear a thuigeas dé na mìorbhailean bàrdachd a tha an Albainn is 'gun urrainn' sgrìobhte as an déidh — fear a thuigeas gur minic is tréine tuath na aos-dàna — fear d' am b' aithne Donnchadh Clachair agus Calum MacIain cuide ri Thurneysen agus O Rathile.

Tha Aonghas fhéin de'n ghnè ris an canar san Eilean 'duine glan': duine éibhinn còir; duine sònraichte anns gach cuideachd; duine air nach trom sac an fhoghluim; duine nach téid 'na mhaide crìon aig meud a fhiosrachaidh; duine 'soilleir' an iomadh fìrinn, agus 'gu ro shoilleir' ann an cuid; nàdur de 'chosmopolitan' Gàidheil: Uidhist-each de Leódhasach, agus gu math aig a' bhaile anns an Eilean Sgitheanach.

A' Bhaidhearn

Anns a' Mhàrt fhuair mi cothrom a dhol a cheann a deas na Gearmailte air gnothach mu theagasg na Beurla an sgoiltean na Baidhearn (Bavaria). Chàidh sinn ann ceathrar Albannach, thug sinn òraidean do iomadh buidhinn de mhaighstirean agus bana-mhaighstirean sgoile; bhruidhinn gach fear dhinn ri trì no ceithir clasaichean an còrr is fichead sgoil; fhreagair sinn iomadh ceist thuigseach agus iomadh té neònach bho'n òigridh; agus chaith sinn iomadh uair a thìde an còmhradh oidean foghluim de iomadh seòrsa. A' cheud seachdain bha sinn am Muinich, prìomh bhaile na dùthcha. An déidh sin chàidh dithis gu trì bailtean an iar 's a deas air Muinich, agus chàidh an dithis eile gu trì bailtean a tuath agus an ear, Regensburg, Straubing agus Passau. Bha mise air an dàrna dithis, ach mun d' fhàg sinne cuideachd chàidh againn air sgrìob a thoirt a dh' ionnsaigh nam beanntan an oir a deas na dùthcha agus ràinig sinn mullach na té as àirde dhiubh uile.

Chunnaic sinn móran de'n Ghearmailte air an t-slighe. Bha solus an latha againn a' falbh, cha mhór o Hoek na h-Olainde gus an d' ràinig sinn Muinich, ach a chionn gu robh e cho tràth de'n bhliadhna cha robh leathadan casa tìr an Rein fhathast gorm le duilleach nam fìon-lios no geal is dathte le blàthan eile, agus bha an là ciar ceòthach, agus shaoil mi gu robh na bailtean glé ghlas agus bha màbadh a' chogaidh glé fhollaiseach. Nuair a dh' fhàg sinn an Rein agus a chuir sinn seachad Frankfurt agus Aschaffenburg ràinig sinn dùthaich a chòrd rium gu h-anabarrach. B'e sin Unter Franken no Iochdar Franconia, dùthaich le glinn chumhang agus cnuic choillteach, bailtean beaga bòidheach is mullaich dhearga air na tighean, is eaglaisean le stìopaill bhiorach. Ach mar a b'fhaide deas a chàidh sinn, chitheamaid an sud agus an so stìopall air chumadh uinnein, comharradh gu robh sinn a' tarruing dlùth air tìr a' ghnè-togail ris an canar Baroc. Thug mi an aire gu robh na bailtean dùmhail agus gu robh an talamh-àitich a' sìneadh bho na bailtean gun tigh idir air. Tha fìon-liosan anns a' cheàrnaidh so cuideachd, air bruthaichean casa. Tha fhios gu bheil saothair mhór 'nan siubhal.

Tha na srathan a' fàs nas leatha fosgailte gus an ruigear machair na

Baidhearn agus an Donau. Tha a' mhachair a' ruigheachd deas air Muinich ach tha am baile sin faisg air a h-oir dheis oir chithear beanntan nan Alp bhuaithe.

Thugadh comhairle oirnn a dhol gu Garmisch ma bha sinn deònach air deagh shealladh faisg fhaighinn de na beanntan. Ghabh sinn a' chomhairle sin, agus air a' cheud Di-Sathuirne a bha againn saor, ràinig dithis againn fìor mhullach an t-Zugspitze, air là grianach gun neul air adhar. Tha a' bheinn so glé fhaisg air 10,000 troigh os cionn na mara, agus chithear bhuaipe an Gross Glockner, Habicht, Piz Bernina, Piz Palu agus ceudan de bhinneinein eile, deas, an ear-dheas agus an iar-dheas, cuid dhiubh an Astria, cuid anns an t-Suis agus cuid anns an Eadailte. Fada air fàire anns an àird an ear-thuath chithear am Böhmer Wald ann an Seacho-Slobhacia.

Chan eil teagamh nach eil Bràighe na Baidhearn, a' cheàrn a deas so, cho àlainn agus a ni beanntan àrda, coilltean, lochan agus aibhnean tìr sam bith, agus cha ruigear a leas an còrr a ràdh mu obair Nàduir, oir tha móran de obair an duine anns a' Bhaidhearn glé annasach agus pàirt dith glé bhrèagha.

Chan eil e soirbh do Albannach gaol a chridhe a ghabhail air an obair-ghréis bharoc a gheibhear gu saidhbhir ann am mór chuid de eaglaisean na Baidhearn, ach chan urrainn do neach sam bith gun iongnadh a bhith air aig ionmhas a ghnìomhaidh ghil agus òir, agus uidh air n-uidh thig seòrsa de bhàigh an ceann an iongnaidh, gu h-àraidh mas toigh leis muinntir na Baidhearn; agus cha mhór nach canainn-sa, is toigh leis na h-uile iad. Bu toigh leam-sa, có dhiùbh, na chunnaic mi de'n t-sluagh. A dh' aindeoin sin, is fheàrr leam am modh Gotach agus Ròmanasc, agus a bhrìgh sin, chòrd eaglaisean Regensburg rium na b'fheàrr, oir an Regensburg tha iad de'n chuile seòrsa: Romanasc, Gotach, Baroc agus Rococo. Tha fhios nach eil móran bhailtean san Roinn Eòrpa de a mheud — gabhaidh e coimeas ri Obar-Dheadhain an àireamh sluaigh — cho annasach a thaobh togalaichean. Bha fear-teagaisg eachdraidh 'na fhear-iùil againn an Regensburg. Bha e, a réir gach coltais, mion eòlach air gach modh togail anns an Roinn Eòrpa agus chàidh e gu a làn dhìcheall a nochdadh dhuinn gach nì a b'fhiach fhaicinn. Am measg eaglaisean Regensburg tha té ris an can iad Schottenkirche, 'se sin 'eaglais nan Scotach', ach theagamh gu bheil 'Scotach' a' ciallachadh 'Eireannach', oir chuireadh air bonn i mun d'rinn na h-Eòrpaich eadar-dhealachadh eadar Scotaich na h-Eireann is na h-Albann. Tha Regensburg annasach do Ghàidheil an seagh eile. Thatar ag ràdh gur h-e ainm Ceilteach a tha anns an t-sean ainm, Ratisbon, agus gur h-ann mu'n àite so a tha a' cheud iomradh air na Ceiltich anns an Roinn Eòrpa.

Ma tha na maighstirean-sgoile a thachair ruinne coltach ris an t-sluagh eile, 'sa daoine còire uaisle a tha am muinntir na Baidhearn. 'Sann mar sin a fhuair sinne an fheadhainn air na chuir sinn eòlas. Thigeadh iad a chéilidh oirnn anns na tighean-òsda anns an robh sinn, agus dh'fhanadh iad glé anmoch an còmhradh ruinn. Thigeadh fear le càr, agus mur robh càr aige fhéin, gheibheadh e caraid aig an robh agus bheireadh iad sinn gu gach àite a b'fheàrr a b'fhiach fhaicinn. Bha iad saor fosgailte 'nam briathran agus chuala sinn móran a bharrachd bhuapa na bha mi an dùil a chluinneamaid.

Feumar aideachadh gum b'e luchd-teagaisg sgoile a' mhór roinn air an d'fhuair sinn aithne, agus faodaidh e bhith nach eil am beachdan-san an dùthaich sam bith glé choltach ri beachdan an t-sluaigh gu léir; faodaidh gu bheil iad, mar gum b'eadh, 'nan treubh air leth, gun spleadhan luchd an airgid mhóir agus nas farsuinge an inntinn na tha mór roinn an t-sluaigh; agus uime sin dh'fhaodadh nach d'fhuair sinne eòlas sam bith air cor agus spiorad na dùthcha, ach dh'éisd mise le cluais cho geur 's a th'agam ris na thuirt iad agus thug mi mo cheart aire do na rudan nach dubhairt iad, agus dh'fheuch mi ris na dhà a chur ri chéile.

'S iomadh uair a chluinneas sinn Sasannach agus Albannach a' labhairt mar so: 'Chan eil aithreachas sam bith air na Gearmailtich a thaobh a' Chogaidh, ach tha iad duilich nach deach e leotha fhéin.' Chan eil sin fìor a thaobh maighstirean-sgoile na Baidhearn, agus is deacair dhomh a chreidsinn gu bheil e fìor a thaobh mór chuid an t-sluaigh. Chan eil, gu dearbh, déidh mhór aca air na h-Ameireaga-naich, ach tha aobhar àraidh air sin. Nuair a ràinig na h-Ameireaga-naich a' Bhaidhearn tha e coltach nach d'rinn iad eadar-dhealachadh gu leòir eadar na Nàsaich agus càch. Bha sin glé shearbh aig na Gearmailtich aig an robh gràin air Hitler. Bha aon mhaighstir-sgoile glé ghuineach an aghaidh nan Ameireaganaich ach thuirt esan cuideachd: 'Shàbhail iad sinn o rud fada na bu mhiosa.' Chuala sinn aig feadhainn eile gu robh an duine so 'na churaidh an aghaidh nan Nàsach, agus b'e na Ruiseanaich an 'rud fada na bu mhiosa' a bha 'na bheachd. Bha e cho gasda ruinne 's a b'urrainn neach a bhith. Theireadh fear is fear ruinn: 'Cha robh mise riamh 'nam bhall de'n phàirtidh Nàsach' — agus tuigear cho doirbh 's a bha sin do luchd-dreuchd sam bith. Bha e soilleir gu robh còrr agus dà thrian nam maighstirean-sgoile 'nan Caitligich, agus bha iadsan an còmhnaidh a' nochdadh dhuinn mar a sheas an t-Ard-Easbuig Faulhaber an aghaidh Hitler; mar a bha abaid Mhetten 'na phrìosanach an Dachau; agus mar a mharbh réiseamaid SS muinntir eaglais Dom Regensburg.

Thuig mi nach robh móran sam bith deònach air an arm Ghearmailteach a chur air bonn a rithist. 'Tha e ro thràth,' arsa feadhainn. 'Tha cus de'n t-seann seòrsa oifigeach beò fhathast. Tha eagal oirnn gu faigh iadsan smachd air an arm.' Bha argumaidean eile aca a bhios againn fhìn: ge be có gheibh buaidh-làraich, na h-Ameireaganaich no na Ruiseanaich, theid a' Ghearmailte 'na smàl. Cha bhi innte ach blàr cogaidh fo na bomaichean ùra. Tha nàire air iomadh duine còir a tha air taobh Adenauer gu bheil luchd-airgid tìr an Rein agus an Rùr cho déidheil air an arm a chur suas a rithist. Tha an fheadhainn a rinn fortan fo Hitler a' dol a dhèanamh fortan eile le armachadh na Gearmailte.

Cha chuala mi gu robh móran spéis aca do aonachadh na Gearmailte. 'Tha òigridh na roinne an ear caillte. Tha na Comunnaich air an anam a ghlacadh.' Sin barail chumanta.

Tha tàmailt air na Gearmailtich gu bheil a leithid de ghamhlas aig na h-Eòrpaich eile dhaibh, gu h-àraidh aig na Duitsich agus na Lochlannaich. Bha maighstir-sgoile ag innseadh dhomh an tàire a dh'fhuiling e an Lochlann o chionn bliadhna no a dhà. 'Cha chaill na Pòlaich agus na Seacaich an gamhlas dhuinn gu bràth,' arsa fear eile. 'Gabhaidh sin tuigsinn.'

Cha chuala mi iad a' cur gamhlas as leth nan Ruiseanach. Cha chuala mi duine ag ràdh deagh fhacal mu riaghladh na Ruisia ach gun dubhairt aon fhear gu robh uachdarain Ruisia nas comasaiche ann a bhith a' tàladh choigreach na bha na h-Ameireaganaich. Bha iad uile de'n bharail gu robh Ruisia 'na dùthaich bhochd thruagh ach gun robh an sluagh còir, sìmplidh agus cràbhach, ach gu robh iad a' dol nam brùidean le deoch làidir; gu robh iad mìorbhaileach mar shaighdearan, gu robh an cruadal agus an treuntas do-thuigsinn. Bha a h-uile fear ris na thachair mi a bha aois airm eadar 1939 agus 1945 anns a' cogadh, agus 'sann an Ruisia a bha iad uile. Bha fear de'n bharail gum biodh móran de na Ruiseanaich, gu h-àraidh muinntir na h-Ucréin, air taobhadh ris na Gearmailtich mar b'e cho brùideil 's a bha na réiseamaidean SS aig Hitler. Thuirt esan nach d'rinn an t-arm cumanta Gearmailteach rud sam bith nach dèanadh arm eile, ach gu robh na réiseamaidean SS dìreach diabhlaidh. B'e sin beachd duine cho còir tuigseach 's a chunnaic mi sa' Ghearmailt no an dùthaich eile.

Cha chuala mi aon ghuth an aghaidh na Frainge. 'Chan eil dùthaich eile air an t-saoghal,' arsa fear rium, 'anns a bheil an t-saorsa inntinne a mhothaichear anns an Fhraing.'

Cha do chuir mi eòlas air a bheag ach oidean foghluim ach bha fear ag obair anns an tigh-òsda far an robh mi am Muinich a bha 'na phrìosanach anns an dà chogadh mhór. Uime sin chuir e eòlas air móran choigreach. Ars esan rium: 'Na daoine bu choibhneile ri prìosanaich Ghearmailteach — b' iad na h-Albannaich agus na daoine dubha Ameireaganach.' Chuir e a làmhan m'a ghlùinean a nochdadh gum b'e 'gillean an fhéilidh' a bha e a' ciallachadh.

Bha na maighstirean-sgoile gu math fiosrach mu ghnothaichean am Breatainn, ach ma bha iadsan fiosrach bha a' chlann dian le an ceistean. An cuid de na sgoiltean dh'iarradh oirnn labhairt air cuspairean àraidh: sgoiltean na h-Albann; an cluichean; Burns; Wordsworth; bàrdachd ar linn fhéin; Shakespeare. An sgoiltean eile bha againn ri freagairt a thoirt do cheistean de gach seòrsa: dé a' bharail a tha aca am Breatainn air na Gearmailtich; an toigh leis an t-sluagh Churchill; dé tha tighinn eadar Attlee agus Bevan; carson a tha na h-Albannaich diùmbach mu thiotal na Bànrainn; a bheil na h-Albannaich ag iarraidh pàrlamaid dhaibh fhéin; dé an t-eadar-dhealachadh a tha eadar a' Bheurla Shasunnach, a' Bheurla Ghallda agus a' Ghàidhlig; an robh mi fhéin airson imrich a dhèanamh a dh'Ameireaga; có am bàrd Gearmailteach a b'ainmeile am Breatainn; agus mar sin air adhart.

An iomadh sgoil bha agam ri faclan Gàidhlig a ràdh. Am feadhainn dh'iarradh orm dàn Gàidhlig a ràdh agus an sin a chur am Beurla. Ann an aon sgoil rinneadh clàr de mo ghuth ag ràdh 'Ailein Duinn' agus an uair sin 'ga chur am Beurla. 'Nach mìorbhaileach an dàn e,' ars am maighstir-sgoile. Nuair a rachainn a steach do chlas, sheinneadh iad òran Gearmailteach agus òran le Burns. Mar bu trice 'se 'My heart's in ze Highlands' a gheibhinn. Nach mise a bha diùmbach nach robh guth agam fhìn a choisneadh bonn òir a' Mhòid! Mar a bha ann, cha b'urrainn dhomh dad a ràdh ach: 'Tha òrain mhatha aig na Goill ach 'sann aig na Gàidheil a tha na h-òrain!' Tha sgoil Dom Regensburg ainmeil airson ciùil anns an Roinn Eòrpa. Ghabh clas ghillean an sin dhuinn dàn Thómais Reumar le ceòl Gearmailteach ris.

Tha fhios agam nach fhaigh duine eòlas ceart air dùthaich ann an cola-deug agus chan fheuchainn-sa ri fìor chor agus spiorad na Baidhearn a chur an céill. Cha b'urrainn domh a ràdh a bheil barrachd bochdainn anns an dùthaich so na tha an Albainn gus nach eil. Bha an sluagh a chunnaic mi air sràidean Mhuinich pailt cho fallain an coltas 's a tha iad an Dùn-Eideann no an Glascho. 'Sann a theirinn gu robh iad beagan na b'fheàrr an coltas, ach dh'fhaodadh nach fhaca mi a' phàirt as bochda de'n bhaile. Ar leam gu robh barrachd de chomharraidhean bochdainn an Regensburg agus anns na bailtean eile a chunnaic mi na bha am Muinich, ach thuirt na Gearmailtich fhéin gu robh bochdainn gu leòr anns gach baile dhiubh. Chaidh faisg air leth Muinich a leagail le bomaichean. Tha móran togail ùr ann, ach tha iomadh beàrn ann cuideachd agus bithidh a' cheud ghreis.

Some Raasay traditions

I have limited the title because it would be absurd for anyone to claim to carry in his memory more than a very small part of the tradition of any area, and especially absurd for me, three of whose grandparents were born and brought up in Skye and not in Raasay, but our MacLeans have certainly been in Raasay for a long time, seven generations from my own time at least. We are almost, but not quite, certain that our MacLeans came from North Uist, whether directly or via the MacLeod country in Skye we are not sure. The farthest I can go back on my father's side is Calum, son of Calum, son of John, son of Norman, son of John, son of Norman. After that we are not sure. My MacLean great-grandfather John was the only one of his family who did not emigrate either in the 1830s or 1850s. All the children of his uncles, Calum, Neil and Hector, emigrated, except Catherine, a daughter of Calum, married to Donald MacLeod according to Donald MacLeod's great-grandson, the late prominent Raasay man John M MacLeod; but according to Bella MacLeod, the greatest Rassay genealogist of my time, Catherine was a sister of Calum, Norman, Hector and Neil. There are quite a few of Catherine's descendants still in Raasay.

The greatest tradition-bearer I remember was Catherine MacLean, aunt of the very famous piper William MacLean, who was considered by some the greatest of the pupils of Calum MacPherson. She maintained that our MacLeans were the same as hers, and her family were certain that they came from Uist, being descended from an Iain Buidhe Mór, who married a daughter of Mac Gille Chaluim. Catherine (Kate MacLean), who died about 1928 at the age of 85 or thereby, was, according to their genealogy, daughter of William, son of Archibald, son of William, son of Archibald, son of Donald Bàn of Hallaig, son of John, son of Lachlan, son of John, son of Lachlan. I presume that one of the Johns was Iain Buidhe Mór. It is significant that Archibald (Gilleasbuig) was a common name among the MacLeans of Boreray. One would assume that the Calums and Normans were MacLeod names, but Norman did exist among the Uist MacLeans. My MacLean grandfather was a bard and a fine singer, but he died when my father was only eight years of age or so, and I have not heard even a scrap of a song attributed to him. He had the reputation of being an excellent seaman and a good-natured, easy-going, unworldly man with a very good singing voice. My paternal grandmother was Mary Matheson from Braes, but her family had been in Scorr before coming to Braes, and her grandfather and great-grandfather had been millers in Stenscholl in Staffin. She died in 1923, at the age of 84 or 86, when I was not quite 12, and it is difficult for me to say how much of her vast store of song she had learnt in Raasay. She was a very fine singer, which Kate MacLean was not. According to the Dornie MS History of the Mathesons, my grandmother was daughter of John, son of James, son of Dòmhnall Ruadh (who came to Stenscholl from Lochalsh), son of Murchadh Ruadh (who carried the last Fiery Cross through Lochalsh, presumably in 1715 or 1719), son of Ewen of Glas na Muclaich, the son of Murdo, the son of Ruairi Beag, the son of John of Fernaig, the son of Ruairi Mór of Fernaig, the son of Murchadh Buidhe. (The Tiree-Manchester MS makes Ruairi Beag brother, not father, of Murdo of Glas na Muclaich.) What was very remarkable about her was that she had a great number of songs not only from Skye and Raasay but also from Lochalsh and Kintail. She was very much aware of her Lochalsh antecedents and relatives, the descendants of Iain Buidhe, brother of her great-grandfather Donald. She rated her Mathesons as a very superior breed. Among my earliest memories were those of her singing such songs as 'Cumha Iain Ghairbh', 'Luinneag Mhic Leòid', 'Mo shàthghal bochd', 'Na féidh am Bràigh Uige', 'Milis Mórag', 'Ceud soraidh bhuam fhìn', and many others.

My maternal grandfather was a Nicolson on both sides. He was not much of a tradition-bearer, but my maternal grandmother, Isabel MacLeod, was. She, too, was from Braes, but her MacLeods had come from Raasay, and her grandfather, Alasdair MacLeod, was in Torra Mìcheig before it was cleared. He was Alasdair mac Iain mhic Ailein Ruaidh. Bella MacLeod said that Ailean Ruadh's family came from Lewis, but J M MacLeod, whose father was of that family, said they came from Gairloch or Cóigeach. They were buried in the old vault of Mac Gille Chaluim in the churchyard of Clachan in Raasay. My MacLeod grandmother, who died in 1910, was evidently a fine singer and tradition-bearer, especially of songs, although she was a devout Free Presbyterian. My Nicolson grandfather's grandfather, Somhairle na Pìoba, was a piper in the Peninsular War and had to leave the Army because he got very bad frostbite in the fingers during the retreat to Corunna. He is commemorated in a Skye *port á beul* as

'Somhairle na pìoba, an gille grinn a bha 'Holm', and also as 'Somhairle gun chomhairle', presumably because he had been a volunteer. He was Somhairle mac Iain mhic Eóghainn. Eóghainn, or Eóghainn's father, had been put out of his good land near Portree, some said the Bile, for helping in the escape of Prince Charles. My grandfather maintained that his Nicolsons were close relatives of the last Nicolson chief in Sgoirebreac, but not so close as the family of Alasdair Beag Alasdair mhic Armcholla, whose son Alasdair, noted for his physical strength, died not very long ago in Portree.

To revert to Ailean Ruadh, there is, on the east of Raasay, between Kyle Rona and Brochel Castle, a natural jetty called Lamaraig Chloinn Mhic Ailein, but I have not heard that connected with the family of Ailean Ruadh.

I have mentioned so much about my own people to show my advantages and disadvantages as a bearer of Raasay tradition, but I am very much aware that one or two or three people can have only very little of the traditions of a district. That Raasay went completely Free Church in 1843, and 90% Free Presbyterian in 1893, certainly diminished song tradition and also most other really old traditions in the island. But now I realise, when it is too late, that I myself exaggerated the Evangelical suppression of traditions in Raasay, thinking that the Free Church and Free Presbyterian churches had destroyed traditions that had really gone underground. I think now that there existed in Raasay, when I was young, more tradition, especially Clan traditions, than I had suspected.

One of the oldest and best known traditions in Raasay is that of Storbh Mór mac Rìgh Lochlainn. He was killed by Raasay men at a place on the Inver Burn called Beul-àth Stoirbh, and he is buried between two big trees in front of the old house of Brae, near Glam. (Brae in Raasay is known from the story of Captain Malcolm MacLeod, famous in the '45.) Storbh's sister devastated Raasay with fire in revenge for her brother's death. The last occupant of the old house of Brae was Eachunn Iain Eachuinn mhic Dhòmhnaill mhic Uilleim. Sometime in the 1920s Eachunn made a haystack, or was alleged to have made a haystack, over the grave of Storbh. Kate MacLean was outraged and vented her wrath in notable words: 'Eachunn 'ain Eachuinn mhic Dhòmhnaill mhic Uilleim a dhol a dhèanamh cruaich air uaigh Mac Rìgh Lochlainn.'

There is, however, an older legend located in Rona, obviously a variant of the Deirdre story, but the princes buried are not Irish but Greek. The flagstone is called Leac Chlann Gréige. Were they the children of a Byzantine emperor? At any rate, two or three brothers and a princess are said to be under Leac Chlann Gréige.

Raasay tradition is unanimous that the immediate predecessor of the first MacLeod chief, Gille Calum, was Iain Mór MacSuain, and that he was a great warrior and a good man. Most traditions say that it was he who built Brochel Castle. I heard, about 1924, a strange and rather ridiculous tradition about his death. He had taken as a foster-son Gille Calum, a younger son of MacLeod of Lewis. MacSwan was childless himself and became devoted to his foster-son, who, he decided, ought to marry a daughter of MacLeod of Dunvegan. So they both set out for Dunvegan, but as MacSwan was bending down to drink at a well on Guala Dhruim Muigh, a few miles from Portree, Gille Calum put his dagger through his back. The reason for the murder was not that Gille Calum wanted to be chief of Raasay but that MacSwan's face was so formidably ugly that he would frighten the Dunvegan girl. I heard this tradition from John Gillies, Iain Raghnaill mhic Eóghainn, who was then in his eighties.

As I said, most Raasay traditions ascribe the building of Brochel Castle to John MacSwan, but several attribute it to the MacLeod chiefs. The most detailed one I heard was from the same John Gillies about the same time as I heard that about the death of John MacSwan. The chief character in this tradition was a MacLean refugee who had become the right-hand man of Mac Gille Chaluim. MacLean's audacity and resourcefulness had resulted in the acquisition of a great crock of gold but was also provoking a threatened invasion of Raasay, and the crock of gold was enabling Mac Gille Chaluim to pay for the building of a specially strong fort. It is interesting and significant that the circumstances that led to MacLean's becoming a refugee from somewhere unspecified was much the same as a Mull story about the castration of a follower of MacLaine of Loch Buie and the kidnapping of a son of that chief, but I have forgotten most of the story.

I have since found in a note-book of my uncle, Alexander Nicolson, a very different tradition of unspecified source, but a much less detailed one. It has nothing about any henchman of Mac Gille Chaluim or any name other than Mac Gille Chaluim's own and the MacKenzies, who are threatening the invasion. There is no mention of a crock of gold. Incidentally, I did hear, from the same John Gillies, an account of a MacKenzie invasion foiled by the wonderful archery of a Fionnlagh Dubh nan Saighead, obviously a transposition of the name of the legendary archer among the Kintail MacRaes, also called Fionnlagh Dubh nam Fiadh.

To leave the MacLeod chiefs for a time, probably the greatest name in heroic tradition in Raasay is Faobairne MacCuidhein. Most of the Skye MacCuidheins took the name MacDonald, which was very rare, but did exist, in pre-Clearance Raasay. I have recently found out that Faobairne MacCuidhein's name also exists in legends in Minginish in Skye. All I heard of him, mostly from Kate MacLean, was that at a very early age he astounded his neighbours by carrying a stirk, with its four legs tied together, suspended on a pole that he held over his shoulders; that he was slightingly referred to as Ailean Riabhach, whereupon his mother, Nic Othail or Nic Codhail, interposed: 'Chan e m'Ailean Riabhach ach m'Ailean Sgiamhach.' The story of his death was well known. He pursued a band of raiders who had beached their boat on Faoilinn Aoighre, the Raised Beach of Eyre, at the south of Raasay. He seized the boat by the bows just when the raiders had managed to get it floating, but they killed him with arrows and got off. When Nic Othail heard that he was dead, she went up to 'Mullach an Eilein', presumably the high ground south and south-west of Dun Can, and said:

> Mura b'e mo cheann
> dhèanainn eubha theann ghoirt:
> a sgoilteadh gach uile thìr
> 's ann arm fhìn a thàinig an lochd.

(Were it not for my head/I would utter a high-pitched sore cry/that would split every land:/it is on me the hurt has come.)

She uttered the cry, which was heard in Applecross (over eight miles away) and split, not every land, but her own skull. Until about 1930 some big bones were kept in a niche in the old ruined church of Clachan (Kilmaluag) in Raasay. They had been shown to Johnson and Boswell in 1773 and were supposed to be some of the bones of Faobairne MacCuidhein.

Among other legendary men of Raasay was the Gobha Mór, the Big Smith, whose daughter was destroyed by a water-horse in Loch na Mnatha, the second in size of the two biggish lochs near Dun Can. The Big Smith built a kind of cavern at the north-east end of the loch. He then roasted a sheep to entice with its smell the water-horse, which ate and slept until the Smith transfixed him with a red-hot coulter. Whether a water-horse could be killed or not is not clear but, at any rate, he could be hurt and discouraged from further abductions. The Gobha Mór is not given a name, but I know a Raasay MacKenzie genealogy which goes back for eleven generations and ends with an unnamed Gobha Mór. The cairn just on the east side of the north end of Loch na Mnatha is still called Obair a' Ghobha Mhóir, 'The Work of the Big Smith'.

There is another Big Smith in Raasay traditions. Among those who testified before the Napier Commission in 1883, there were three MacLeod brothers in Arnish: Charles, Alasdair and Roderick. They were old men in 1883. Their ancestor, some four or five generations before 1883, was not really a MacLeod but a MacBeath from Applecross. The story is that a MacGille Chaluim went to Applecross with a team of Raasay men for athletic competitions with the men of Applecross. On the way one of the Raasay men fell sick or had some disabling accident. MacGille Chaluim had no reserves, but a Mac-Beath from Applecross agreed to stand in. He did so well and incurred so much Raasay approbation and Applecross odium that MacGille Chaluim persuaded him to come to live in Raasay and gave him the very good land of Peighinn a' Ghobhainn. Some of his male descendants were in Arnish in 1883. It was Charles who referred to Raasay's having been called 'The Island of the Big Men' (Eilean nam Fear Móra), an allusion to the great aggravation of poverty caused by the Clearances and the consequent crowding of the people who remained in Raasay on the poor land north of Brochel Castle, of which Arnish is part.

It is said that there are five MacLeod families in Raasay who are not connected as far as is known on the male MacLeod side. Some years ago, I asked the late Ewen MacLeod, Eóghainn Thorcuill Chaluim mhic Tharmaid, then in his nineties, of which of the five families he was. His reply was: 'Chan ann a mhuinntir Ratharsair a bha sinne idir; 's ann a thàinig sinne a Leódhas o Thorcull Dubh a chaidh a chrochadh.' ('It is not of the people of Raasay we were at all. We came from Lewis, from Torquil Dubh, who was hanged.')

As far as I could gather, he did not realise the significance of what he said, namely that he could be the man whom most Lewis MacLeods would regard as the rightful chief of all the MacLeods. One of Torcull Dubh's sons was a Norman. Ewen's eldest son, Torquil, now lives in the house in which I was born. I remember Torcull Chaluim mhic Tharmaid, a very handsome man.

On the north-east coast of Raasay, not far from Lamaraig Chloinn Mhic Ailein, there are two conical rocks, each about 20 feet high, one standing immediately above high-water mark and one just below. The story was that Iain Garbh and his foster-brother Mac Muire Bàine were one day knocking limpets off rocks on the Applecross shore. (Iain Garbh's mother was a daughter of Mackenzie of Applecross.) The two wagered as to who could throw his limpet-hammer over to

Raasay. Of course, Iain Garbh had the longer throw, but only just. Nobody seems to have heard any other name for Mac Muire Bàine. His mother is always 'Muire' not 'Màiri'.

Traditional versions of the death of Iain Garbh were numerous. The first I remember hearing was more than usually fantastic. On his way to conquer Lewis, he called on MacDonald at Duntulm. When they were at dinner, their dogs fought under the table, and, of course, Iain Garbh's dogs won the fight. MacDonald was so vexed and jealous that he bribed Iain Garbh's wet-nurse, a witch, to drown him. She got to help her some of the great perennial witches of Gaelic tradition, Gormshuil Mhór Mhoghaidh, Bean an Lagain, An Doideag Mhuileach, Cas a' Mhogain Riabhaich from Ardnamurchan, and one from Tiree whose name I have forgotten, much the same company as the Doideag had before convened to sink the Spanish Armada. The witches alighted on gunwale, yards, or similar. Iain Garbh made a cut at the nearest of them, missed and split the galley from the gunwale to keel. His nurse, repenting, made the famous lament, ''S mi 'nam shuidh' air an fhaoilinn'. There are a few versions of this great song, but this is how my grandmother, Mary Matheson, and my aunt, Peggie MacLean, had it. The third and fourth lines of each quatrain are the first and second of the succeeding quatrain, and so on.

'S mi 'nam shuidh' air an fhaoilinn
'S mi gun fhaoilte gun fhuran,
Cha tog mi fonn aotrom
O dhi-h-aoine mo dhunaidh.

   Hì leò
   Hìl ó ro hó
   Hìl ó ro bha hó
   Hìl ó ho robhan hìl leò.

On a chailleadh am bàta
Is a bhàthadh an curaidh.

Siod na fir a bha làidir
Ged a shàraich a' mhuir iad.

Gille Calum a b' òige
'S Iain mór, mo sgeul duilich.

Ann an clachan gun tràghadh
Tha mo ghràdh-sa air uirigh.

Thu gun bhann air do léinidh
'S i gun fheum air a cumadh.

Thu gun shìod' air do chluasaig
Air lic uaine na tuinne
or
Air leacan fuaraidh na tuinne.

Tha do chlaidheamh 'na dhùblan
'S e fo dhrùdhadh nan uinneag.

Có 's urrainn a ghiùlan
No rùisgeas e tuilleadh?

Tha do mhìol-choin air iallaibh
'S iad gun triall thun a' mhunaidh.

Tha do choinnl' air an smùradh
'S tu gun dùil ri bhith tilleadh.

Our family did not have Mary MacLeod's Lament for Iain Garbh,
nor the one beginning 'Och nan och 's mi fo léireadh', nor the one
beginning 'Moch 'sa' mhaduinn Di-Dòmhnaich', which is printed in
MacLean Sinclair's *Clarsach na Coille*, but they had a version of that
one made famous by the singing of Mr James C M Campbell of Dornie
and London. James Campbell's version begins 'Sgeula nach binn
leam'. This is how my Aunt Peggie's version went:

'S mi 'nam shuidh' air an tulaich
'S mi ri feitheamh na fàire,
Leis an luasgan th' air m' aigne
Chan eil an cadal 'na thàmh dhomh.

> 'S na hé ho
> 'S na hì rirì
> 'S na hì u bhì
> 'S gun thu thighinn fallain i ó.

Fhir mhóir o Shìol Torcuill,
'S e do chorp a bha làidir,
'N am bhith caitheamh a' chuspair
Cha b'e uchdag a' ghàrlaoich.

Tha na staimh dhut 'nan lainnir
Ann an clachan gun tràghadh:
T'fhaotainn marbh air a' charraig
Mar ri Calum do bhràthair
or
Mar ri Mac Muire Bàine.

Tha a' ghàir-thonn 'gad luasgadh
Is 'gad bhualadh ri stalla,
'S tha do ghàirdean gun tuairmse
Ge bu chruaidh' e na 'n darach.

303

My father's older brother Alasdair, who died in 1964, at the age of about 90, began the song:

Seall a mach an e 'n là e
'S mi ri feitheamh na fàire

just as it begins in Gleannach's *Songs of Loch Ness-side*, but the rest of my uncle's version was like Peggie's.

We had a few versions of the circumstances of Iain Garbh's death, and the tradition that one of his sisters made a lament every Friday for a whole year after his death.

John Nicholson's *History of the Nicolsons* says that Margaret, a sister of Iain Garbh, married Calum Nicolson, son and heir of Donald Nicolson, the then chief of the Nicolsons. My grandmother and Aunt Peggie had a big version of a song which could be the celebration of such a marriage. As far as I know, the tune has been found nowhere else, nor any words older than those I used to hear in the 1920s, except a very few lines that John MacInnes of the School of Scottish Studies got in the 1950s. My Aunt Peggie had more of it than my grandmother had, including all the lines from 'Doilleir dorch' to the end.

Ceud soraidh bhuam fhìn gu m' eòlas
Gu Sgoirebreac am bi chòisir

   ù hoireann ó hì rí oho
   ù hoireann ó hí riri rì u
   ì hoireann ó hì rì oho

Gu talla farsaing Chlann Dòmhnaill
Gu taigh mór an ùrlair chòmhnaird

Far am faighte fìon ri òl ann
A cupan donna bheòil bhòidhich

Miosairean 's truinnsearan feòdair
'S amar bruithidh an eòrna

Deoch cho làidir 's thig o'n Olaind.

'S b' aithne dhomh fhìn beus bu dual dut
'S beus dhe d' bheus bhith suirghe ghruagach

'S ag cur nan geall, 's ann leat bu bhuadhar.

'S gheibhte siod an taigh an uasail
Bhith 'g òl fìon á pìosan fuara

'N taigh mór farsaing 's ùrlar sguabte,
Ruighleadh ubhal sìos is suas air.

'S gheibhte siod an taigh mo leannain
Muc 'ga sgrìobadh 's mart 'ga feannadh

'S coinnleir òir air bhòrdaibh geala.

Doilleir dorch' air oidhche reòta
Chàidh do bhàt thar Rubha Rònaidh

Dol troimh na caoil a null a Bhròchaill
Dh'amharc air maighdean an òr fhuilt

'S fhuair thu chéile 's cha b'i 'n òinid,
Cha b'i 'n amaid (*or* ainnis), cha b'i 'n òinnseach,

Nighean fir á Caisteal Bhròchaill,
A Ratharsair mhóir nan Leòdach,

Tìr nan gaisgeach air an òrlaich,
Iain mór is Iain Og dhiubh

A Shìol Torcuill thig á Leódhas.

'Talla farsaing Chlann Dòmhnaill' probably ought to be 'Talla farsaing Clann Dhòmhnaill', i.e. 'the children of Donald (Nicolson)', not 'Clan Donald'. An interesting point historically is that Rev. Donald MacKinnon has deduced from other sources that Iain Garbh had a brother Iain as well as brothers Calum and Alasdair. He was delighted to have his finding apparently confirmed by this song. My brother John and I had long been puzzled over the line 'Tìr nan gaisgeach air an òirlich' (as we took it to be), which seemed to mean 'land of heroes to the inch', until John noticed in Dwelly *òrlach*, a variant of *àrlach*, a variant of *àrach*, 'a battle-field'. Among our Raasay traditions about the death of Iain Garbh was that the storm was so great that waves rose as high as the Coolins, and the boulders of Mol Stamhain were hurled far above the shore cliffs and deposited on dry land.

Of course, my grandmother and Aunt Peggie had many songs and stories not at all connected, as far as they knew, with Raasay. For example, Peggie had a great version of 'Coisich a rùin', with no mention of John Campbell of Harris, and a song addressed to a daughter of MacKinnon of Strath, which I have never heard elsewhere, much as I have tried, except that Mrs Kate MacDonald of Gearraidh-Sheilidh in South Uist had snatches of words somewhat like its words, and a tune slightly like it. Of course, this could be a Raasay song; for, among other reasons, there were a surprising number of MacKinnons in pre-Clearance Raasay. I give it as I heard it in 1936 from Peggie. The refrain, with its very long second line, to be sung without a break, is repeated after every line of the song.

Ceud furan 's ceud fàilte
  ì hóireann ó roho
  ì hoireann ì u o ì hóireann ó roho
Bhuamsa, Mhàiri, gus t'fhaicinn
Gu bean a' chùil fhàinnich
Is nam blàth shùilean maiseach
Gura math a thig gùn dhut
Air tigh'nn ùr as an fhasan
'S gura math a thig bréid dhut
Latha féille 'sa' chlachan.
Nighean oighre Shrath Shuardail
Dh'am bu dual a bhith beairteach,
Gura minig a bhà sinn
Muigh air àirigh le martaibh,
Ann an lagan beag riabhach,
Mharbhte fiadh is laogh breac ann
'S coileach dubh air bhàrr géige
Greis mun éireadh an dealta.

Among the many fragments of song that Peggie remembered in her last years was one that I never heard elsewhere. It had a refrain, 'Chuisil ó, chuisil éile' and a line ''g éisdeachd ri rod a' chladaich'. I don't think the word *rod* for 'surf' is used in many places except Raasay and Braes. She had a very good verse of 'Moch Di-luain ghabh i 'n cuan', with the lines:

Chuir i h-aghaidh deas air Ile
'S a cùl ri tìr Mhic Ghille Chaluim

where Kenneth MacLeod from Eigg had — naturally — ''S a cùl ri tìr Mhic Mhic Ailein'. My Nicolson grandfather confirmed that he had heard 'ri tìr Mhic Ghille Chaluim' in Braes in the same context.

Kate MacLean (Catrìona Uilleim), being very consciously a Mac-Lean, had a great deal about Lachlainn Mór Dhubhaird, but it was my Aunt Peggie who had the most intriguing thing about Lachlainn Mór. She had an octave to the tune of 'Mo rùn geal òg', ending with the refrain 'Mo Lachlainn Mór'. The verse was very obviously the same as a verse, beginning 'Cà facas air thalamh', from the well-known elegy by Eachunn Bacach on Eachunn Ruadh, who was killed at Inverkeithing in 1651. It may be that the verse is an echo of an older song about Lachlainn Mór who was killed in Islay in the 1590s.

Bella MacLeod maintained that Pòsadh Piuthar Iain Bhàin was a Raasay song, and that the home-coming was to Screapadal in Raasay. Of course, the claiming of songs by districts is very common. For example, my Matheson grandmother said that 'Milis Mórag' was a Staffin song. She had a striking version of one verse of it that I have not heard or seen elsewhere.

Droch bhàs dh'an Fhrangach
Nach tug e 'n ceann dhiot
Mun d' leig a nall thu
Chur anntlachd oirnn.

She never sang 'Gur milis Mórag', just 'Milis Mórag'. Her chorus was:

Milis Mórag,
Laghach Mórag,
Milis Mórag,
Horó am bò.

One forenoon in 1936 my Aunt Peggie announced that she had remembered three songs that she had forgotten for many years. One of them was the song to the daughter of the 'heir of Strath Swordale'; another was a fragment without any proper names or clues to locality.

Seo a' bhliadhna dh'fhàg mi dubhach
    huiribhi huiribhi hi o roho
Chaill mi mo bhràthair is mo phiuthar
    hi ibh o hì air faral il lò
Chaill mi mo bhràthair is mo phiuthar
    huiribhi etc.
Chan e sin a tha mi cumha
    hi ibh etc.
Ach òigeir òg an òr fhuilt bhuidhe
Bhith 'n ciste chaoil ri taobh a' bhalla,
Saoir 'ga dùnadh 's ùird 'ga barradh.

The third was her version of 'Coisich a rùin:

Coisich a rùin hu il ho ró
Lùb nan geallamh o hì o bhó
'S minig a bhà hu il ho ró
Mi fo t' earradh och óireann ó
'S minig a bhà hu il ho ró
Mi fo t' earradh o hì o bhó
Do làmh fo 'm cheann hu il ho ró
'S an téile tharam och óireann ó

'S mi fo chirb
Do bhreacain bhallaich,
'N lagan uaigneach
Chluain a' bharraich,
Sìoban nam beann
Sìor chur tharainn,
Uisge fìor-ghlan
Fuar-ghlan fallain,
An cois an fhéidh
As àirde langan.

'S mise bhean bhochd
A th' air mo bhuaireadh,
Ma thug Clann Nèill
Druim a' chuain orr',
Luchd nan rò seòl
'S nan long luatha,
'S nam brataichean
Dearg is uaine,
'S nan claidheamhnan
Geura cruadhach,
Nach laigh smal orr'
Anns na truaillibh.

'S mise bhean bhochd
A th' air mo sgaradh,
Mur h-e Leódhas
Mhór ur cala,
Mas e 's bobhstair
Dhuibh a' ghaineamh,
Mas e 'n t-slaodach
'S aodach tarruing,
Mas e na ròin
Ur luchd faire,
Ur coinnlean àrd
Na reultan geala,
'S ur ceòl fìdhle
Gaoir na mara.

I have referred to Bella MacLeod as the great genealogist of Raasay in my time. She was called Bealag an Achaidh, from the Achadh near Kyle Rona. She was a sister of the late Rev. James MacLeod, Free Presbyterian minister latterly in Greenock. They were of a noted family of pipers, of whom the best-known was Dòmhnall mac Sheumais. It was said that he could compose words and tune, and play the tune, all simultaneously. My brother John has a paper, in Vol.

XLI of the *Transactions*, on the Raasay traditions about the MacKay pipers.

He got them chiefly from William MacLean, Kilcreggan, the pupil of Calum MacPherson. Calum MacPherson was actually born in Raasay. His father and mother had some relationship to the MacLeod tacksman of Suidhisnis (anglicé Suisnish). This MacLeod was called 'Ain mac Sheoc. 'Ain mac Sheoc had a shop as well as the tack of Suisnish. He emigrated to Australia. The rock below Suisnish House is called Sgeir Dhubh 'Ain mhic Sheoc.

Among my Aunt Peggie's many songs were two quatrains of a love song that some woman made for her MacLean great-grandfather. It is to the glorious tune used later as a tune of a Kintail song by the Tàillear Crùbach of Glen Elchaig, whose surname was MacCulloch. The song for my great-great-grandfather is as follows:

A Tharmaid 'Ain mhic Tharmaid
'S e t' sheanchas a leòn mi,
Bhith cuimhneachadh do shùgraidh
Gun dùil ri do phòsadh.

A Tharmaid a' Chaolais,
Nan gorm shùilean bòidheach,
Cha d' aithnich thusa raoir mi
Seach maighdeannan Osgaig.

This Norman was remembered, for example, by Patrick Bàn Nicolson, who died about 1890, as one of the very biggest men in Raasay, and his brothers, Calum, Hector and Neil, were all called 'Mór'. His sister (or niece), Catherine, who married Donald MacLeod, Dòmhnall mac Uilleim, had sons noted for their size and strength. Norman and his son John married very small women, thereby reducing the size of the Raasay MacLeans.

In the early 1920s, and before that, many of the boys of Osgaig and Clachan used to meet in the house of Caitrìona Uilleim (Kate MacLean), who lived alone. She was not a singer, but had most kinds of folk-lore, especially Clan traditions and Heroic Tales. Her favourite Heroic Tale was that of Conall mac Rìgh Cruachan, of which she had 'runs' not in Campbell's *West Highland Tales*. Years later, in the 1930s, I wrote down from my memory the 'runs' I could remember, but I have lost the papers on which I wrote them. About 1948 my brother Calum got the same runs from my Aunt Peggie, but there were quite a few differences in the words. This is how I remember some of them. I think the following was the first 'run', and this is how I remember it.

> Latha dhomh air Sliabh an Leirg an Eirinn
> Mar bha 'n deamhain an tràth an latha sin
> 'S ann dhomhsa b'aobhar feirg.
> Cheangail sinn ar mìol-choin air iallaibh caola gorm
> 'S ar coin bheaga bhaotharra
> Gu daingeann daoidhri dorch.

Later there came:

> Cois a' bhile robhair mi,
> Lean mi gu beul bòchain,
> 'S fhuair mi anns a' chala sin
> an curach taobh-gheal òraidh.
> Fhuair mi lorg na féile mhnatha
> Ann an cois na mara fuaire
> 'S lean mi 's cha bu shona dhomh
> Gu dorus beul na h-uamha.

In the cave Conall finds a lady seeming to try to push a young child into a fire. He asks her: 'Dé fàth do bhòcanais ris an òigear tha gun chéill?' It comes out that she has been ordered to roast him for the home-coming of the giant. She says:

> Fhir mhóir mhaisich fhìnealta
> Fhir mhóir fhìnealta mhaisich
> Cuir thusa 'n t-òg ri teine dhomhsa
> Lorg t' inbhe 's do ghaisge.

He makes a plan to save the child and lies down himself on the top of a heap of corpses to be devoured. He hears the giant coming:

> Fochann agus feuralachd
> chuala mi dol trìd a' chéile,
> 'S far na thàrla dhomh bhith 'n uair sin
> Bu sheachd feàrr dhomh bhith as eugmhais.

He does not get off without losing 'staoig dhe m' asnaidhean asam air fad mo dhrama'.

The last 'run' I remember is when Conall is down in a deep pit, crevasse or mine, filling creels of gold, which the giant pulls up with a rope. He is not doing his work properly and the giant sends down his own son, with the Claidheamh Geal Soluis, to deal with him. Conall kills the giant's son, takes the sword, hides in the creel and sends up a signal to the unsuspecting giant to pull up the creel.

Or fodham 's òr tharam,
'S rinn mi m'fhalach air màs (*or* tòn) cliabhain.
Thug mi liom an Claidheamh Geal Soluis,
Taom bu shona chinnich riamh dhomh.
Leis an tartar a bha 'na chluasan
'S mèud a ruathair dh'a mhac,
Thug mi tarruing air an làimh chlì
'S na cóig cinn gun sgath mi dheth.

In Volume XXXIX-XL of the *Transactions*, my brother Calum printed some of the songs he got from our uncle, Angus Nicolson, but nearly all those songs were really from Braes, and most of them came from Mary MacIntosh, Mairi 'Ain mhic Chaluim of Achnahaid in Braes, who died in 1917. Our uncle Angus did live in Raasay from 1940 to 1957, but his songs all came from Braes, except those he learned in different parts of the mainland, such as Ardgour, Glen Euchar and Glen Lyon.

In Volume XLI of the *Transactions* my brother John, in his paper on Am Pìobaire Dall, gave some of the traditions of the Raasay MacKay pipers, all of which he got from William MacLean of Kilcreggan, to whom I have already referred.

I have to conclude with the words of a song common to our people in Braes and in Raasay, but it was from my aunt, Flora MacLean, that I got the rocking refrain, which none of the rest seemed to have.

Tha mo shealgair 'na shìneadh
      'na shìneadh
      'na shìneadh
Tha mo shealgair 'na shìneadh
'S e 'san fhrìth gun tigh'nn dachaidh.

  Hì an ó an ò í an
  Hì an ó an ò í an
  Hì an ó an ò í an
  Hó an ì an ho ró an

Tha mo shealgair gun éirigh
      gun éirigh
      gun éirigh
Tha mo shealgair gun éirigh
'S tha na féidh air an leacainn.

Tha na féidh am Bràigh Uige
    'm Bràigh Uige
    'm Bràigh Uige
Tha na féidh am Bràigh Uige
'S e mo dhiùbhail mar thachair.

Tha mo chrodh air na lóintean
    na lóintean
    na lóintean
Tha mo chrodh air na lóintean
'S na laoigh òga 'nan casaibh.

Iad gun togail ri aonaich
    ri aonaich
    ri aonaich
Iad gun togail ri aonaich
Fireach fraoich agus ghlacaibh.

Gura fuar Lag na h-àirigh
    na h-àirigh
    na h-àirigh
Gura fuar Lag na h-àirigh
'S tha mo ghràdh fo no leacaibh.

The late Mrs MacLaren, from Waternish and Edinburgh, gave me one verse, which I have not heard elsewhere.

Tha mo chrodh am Beinn Eata
    'm Beinn Eata
    'm Beinn Eata
Tha mo chrodh am Beinn Eata
'S mo ghille beag aca.

I wonder if Beinn Eata should read Beinn Eadra, which would rhyme with 'beag'.